Workers and Working Classes
in the Middle East

SUNY Series in
the Social and Economic History of the Middle East

Donald Quataert, Editor

Workers and Working Classes in the Middle East

Struggles, Histories, Historiographies

Edited by

Zachary Lockman

STATE UNIVERSITY OF NEW YORK PRESS

Cover Photograph: Istanbul flannel factory, c. 1891.

Production by Ruth Fisher
Marketing by Bernadette LaManna

Published by
State University of New York Press, Albany

For information, address the State University of New York Press,
State University Plaza, Albany, NY 12246

Library of Congress Cataloging-in-Publication Data

Workers and working classes in the Middle East : struggles, histories,
    historiographies / edited by Zachary Lockman.
        p.   cm. — (SUNY series in the social and economic history of
    the Middle East)
        Includes index.
        ISBN 0-7914-1665-8 (acid-free). — ISBN 0-7914-1666-6 (pbk. : acid
    -free)
        1. Working class—Middle East—History—19th century. 2. Labor
    movement—Middle East—History—19th century. 3. Working class-
    -Middle East—Historiography. I. Lockman, Zachary. II. Series.
    HD8656.W67   1994
    305.5'62'0956—dc20   92-42701
                                                                          CIP

For Melinda

—ZL

Contents

Acknowledgments

The workshop at which all but one of the essays in this volume were originally presented as papers was sponsored and funded by Harvard University's Center for Middle Eastern Studies. I would like to thank Roy Mottahedeh, who was then serving as director, for generously extending to me the center's financial and logistical support. My thanks, too, to the center's staff, for their assistance in organizing the workshop.

I must also thank the Shelby Cullom Davis Center for Historical Studies, Department of History, Princeton University, and particularly its director, Natalie Zemon Davis. A year's Visiting Fellowship at the Davis Center during 1991–92 provided not only a stimulating intellectual environment but also enough time away from teaching to prepare this manuscript for publication and write the introduction.

On behalf of all the contributors to this volume, I would also like to thank the three anonymous individuals who reviewed the manuscript for the State University of New York Press and provided helpful comments and criticisms. They should not be blamed if we did not always choose to accept their advice.

Zachary Lockman

Zachary Lockman

Introduction

Not so very long ago the historical literature on workers, working classes, and labor movements in the modern Middle East was distinguished mainly by its sparsity. A number of Soviet scholars had, it is true, addressed these subjects; but the scholarly value of much of their work was diminished by the necessity of conforming to Stalinist dogma and the Soviet foreign policy of the day, and little of even the best Soviet research was translated into either Middle Eastern or Western languages.

Historians outside the Soviet bloc were in general not much interested in Middle Eastern workers and labor movements. In the Arab countries, Turkey, and Iran, historians were for a lengthy period preoccupied with other issues, notably European encroachment and domination, the emergence of their countries as nation-states and ongoing struggles for independence, and they did not produce much work of the kind that would later be characterized as "social history." In the United States, and to a lesser extent Western Europe, modernization theory long reigned as the dominant paradigm in historical (as well as sociological) writing on the Middle East in the late nineteenth and twentieth centuries. This approach depicted intra- and interelite conflict as the primary motor of social change and therefore displayed little interest in the circumstances, perceptions and activities of subaltern groups. The result was a dearth of scholarship on working-class formation in the Middle East, the emergence and evolution of labor movements, and various forms of worker identity and action within and outside the workplace.

This neglect of workers and their history by both Western and Middle Eastern historians, rooted in the perception that workers did not constitute a distinguishable social group, had not played (and were in the future unlikely to play) any significant role in political or economic life, and therefore did not merit much attention, may not, perhaps, seem all that surprising. After all, for most of this century and in all the countries of the Middle East, wage workers employed in large enterprises have constituted only a minority of the urban working population and an even smaller proportion of the population as a whole, whose great majority has until recently consisted of peasants. Moreover, labor unions and workers' movements in the Middle East seemed to play a less significant and autonomous role in their countries' political and economic life than some of their counterparts in Western Europe or even the United States. It was, therefore, relatively easy for historians to avoid paying serious attention to workers and labor history without feeling that they were neglecting something important.

However, this neglect may also have been a product of the conviction—widely shared among historians—that it was inappropriate or even counterproductive to apply class analysis to the modern Middle East. As a framework for identity and action (whether individual or collective) in the Middle East, class was traditionally seen as very much subordinate to religion, ethnicity, tribal affiliation, village solidarity, regional origin, and so forth. A certain "Middle Eastern exceptionalism," a product of the lingering (and interacting) influence of both modernization theory and certain strands of Orientalism, was at work here. Historians of the Middle East tended to take it for granted that whatever its utility for understanding other regions, class was at best irrelevant and at worst distorting when used as a category of analysis for Middle Eastern societies past or present, and this assumption also helped stifle the development of Middle Eastern working-class history.[1]

In sharp contrast to the preceding period, the last three decades or so have witnessed the publication of a substantial body of research on Middle Eastern labor history. Several factors have contributed to this development, though to varying degrees and in different ways in each country of the region. For one, industrial development (often state-sponsored) enlarged the size and social weight of the working class, leading indigenous and foreign observers to take greater note of it and spurring a new interest in its origins and evolution. In addition, in the 1960s intellectuals in the Middle East were influenced to an unprecedented degree by Marxist (and, more broadly, socialist) ideas, prompting reconsideration of the ways in which their countries' histories had traditionally been written and a new interest in the working class.

Contemporary political debates within the left—for example, the challenge that various "New Left" groups in Iran posed to the Tudeh party—also prompted new writing on working class history. In Turkey, the establishment of parliamentary democracy after the 1960 coup made possible the emergence of a legal Left that sought through historical research and writing to construct for itself a usable past, based in part on the struggles of Turkish workers. In that same period, regimes in several Arab countries were espousing "Arab socialism" or Ba'thism as their official ideology, which helped open the way for historians to begin the process of retrieving the histories of subaltern social groups, including workers, and incorporating them into reworked historical narratives. These new narratives moved away from the narrowly conceived political and diplomatic history emphasizing the actions and personalities of rulers and statesmen that an earlier generation of historians had produced. Instead, they portrayed "the people" (one component of which was the working class) as the prime subject and object of national(ist) history. The upshot of these and other factors was publication by historians in the Middle East of important work on workers' history that, whatever its limitations in retrospect, nonetheless opened up the field and laid the groundwork for further research.

The turn in the 1960s of a younger generation of historians in Britain, the United States, and (in somewhat different ways) Western Europe to "social history"—a phenomenon that was of course connected with the radical upsurge of that decade—also ultimately led to special attention to the history of Middle Eastern workers. One of social history's main thrusts was the recovery, through the practice of "history from below," of the stories of groups that had been largely left out of the conventional narratives: workers, women, the poor, members of minority groups, colonial subjects, and so forth. Several of the younger historians who began research on Middle Eastern workers' history in the later 1970s (myself included) were originally inspired by the example of E. P. Thompson's classic *The Making of the English Working Class*, first published in 1963, which emphasized the self-activity of English workers as shaped by their own culture and experience.

The accumulation of a substantial literature on the history of labor movements and working classes in various countries of the Middle East prompted the convening of the workshop at which all but one of the chapters that make up this volume were originally presented as papers. It seemed like a good idea to bring together some of the scholars who had been doing research in the field of Middle Eastern working-class history—mostly from the United States, since unfortunately not enough funding was available to bring many scholars from the Middle East or Europe—to take a comprehensive look at the work that had been done so far and explore some of the theoretical issues that bear on this field. The workshop, sponsored by Harvard University's Center for Middle Eastern Studies, was entitled Middle East Labor and Working Class History: Concepts and Approaches, and it was held in April 1990.

Among the questions we hoped would be addressed in the papers presented at the workshop and in the ensuing discussions were the following:

- How did indigenous workers, labor activists and political leaders, indigenous and foreign scholars, colonial officials, and others implicitly or explicitly conceptualize and define the working class and the labor movement?

- How did these conceptualizations reflect and structure different processes of class formation, labor organization, and individual and collective action?

- How did these conceptualizations implicitly or explicitly involve issues of gender, relationships with other social groups (artisans, peasants, etc.), and the roles workers have played (or have been seen as playing) in broader national histories?

- How did the formation of working classes and labor movements in Middle Eastern countries subject to European political or economic influence or domination resemble or differ from obstensibly analogous processes elsewhere in the region, in the "Third World" and beyond?

- To what extent are concepts and categories drawn from Western European, African, Asian, or other contexts appropriate and useful for understanding working classes and labor movements in the Middle East?

- How useful are cultural, structural and other modes of interpretation in Middle Eastern workers' history?

Our broader goals in organizing this workshop were to facilitate comparisons across national boundaries in the region and to help Middle Eastern labor and working-class history (and Middle Eastern history in general) escape its relative isolation from methodological and theoretical debates in the broader field of historical study. We were especially eager to foster discussion of how current debates on the question of representation and the utility of discourse analysis might bear on our research and writing on Middle Eastern workers' history.

As is usually the case at such events, there was not enough time for all the issues that surfaced to be fully discussed. But I think it is fair to say that the participants came away feeling that the workshop had been valuable and that the dialogue begun at Harvard should be continued elsewhere. In the interim, participants revised their papers for publication in this volume, and one additional contribution (that of Kristin Koptiuch) was solicited.[2] I believe that these essays will be seen to stand on their own, but also to interact in interesting ways. By way of introduction, I would like to discuss some of the broader issues raised by the study of workers, working classes, and labor movements in the Middle East and consider how these essays address them.

I will begin with two questions that are implicitly posed by the very title of this volume. First, does it make sense to take the Middle East as our unit of analysis? Second, have "workers" in Middle Eastern countries actually constituted a distinct social group with a history of its own that can legitimately be taken as an object of inquiry?

The first question might be posed more clearly by asking what artisans and workers in Egypt, Iraq, Iran, Turkey, and Ottoman Damascus and Istanbul—the locales covered in this volume—actually had in common with each other, other than the facts that most of them were nominally Muslims and that the places in which they lived and worked have in the last century come to be categorized as parts of the "Middle East"? By structuring the field in this way, are we not doing violence to the lived experience of the objects of our research, the workers and labor activists in their various locales? Should we not instead confine ourselves to those smaller political or cultural units that would seem to possess some more direct or obvious relevance or meaning for those whose histories we are trying to write?

This has not, at least until recently, seemed a problem to some historians, who have simply assumed that the Middle East, including Iran, Turkey, and the Arab lands of the *Mashriq* (and sometimes even North Africa as well), possesses such a high degree of cultural unity that in all of the countries that compose this vast geographic region working-class formation and worker activism (among many other things) were significantly shaped by the same set of cultural patterns, often subsumed under the rubric of "Islam". This is of course a central premise of much of Orientalist discourse, but it surfaces in scholarly studies operating from within modernization theory as well.

By way of example we might consider *Social Forces in the Middle East,* edited by Sydney Nettleton Fisher and published in 1955.[3] This volume consists of chapters on various social groups ("The Nomads," "The Villager," "The Bazaar Merchant," "The Entrepreneur Class," and so forth), originally presented as papers at a 1952 conference on The Near East: Social Dynamics and the Cultural Setting sponsored by the Social Science Research Council and held at Princeton University. Although E. A. Speiser's effort to provide the volume with a theoretical framework explicitly rejects the idea that the Near East is a viable "fundamental unit" and instead argues that the region is composed of many distinct "ethnemes," the other contributors seem to have taken no notice. The chapter on "The Industrial Worker," for example, simply abstracts workers in Egypt, Syria, Lebanon, Iran, and Saudi Arabia into "'the worker' in the Middle East," makes some very broad generalizations and has little to say about history. That the Middle East constitutes a plausible unit of analysis is assumed rather than argued.

Alternatively, one might seek to ground the coherence of the region in the ways in which the histories of the working classes and labor movements in each of the various components of the Middle East were in the modern period influenced (if in different ways and to varying extents) by many of the same (largely exogenous) processes and forces. Among the most important of these processes was the integration of the region into the capitalist world economy, a development that in the nineteenth century directly affected the Istanbul guild members and Anatolian miners and railwaymen whose activism Donald Quataert explores, the Damascus weavers of whom Sherry Vatter writes, and the Egyptian artisans I discuss.

Throughout the twentieth century as well, indeed up to the present moment, working-class formation, identity, and activism in Iran, Turkey, and the Arab states has in large measure been shaped by the complex and changing ways in which those countries' economies have been articulated with the world economy: witness for example the profound effects on Egypt's economy and society (and thus on the character of social conflict, including worker activism) of the massive migration of Egyptian workers to the oil-producing countries of the Persian Gulf in the 1970s and 1980s.[4] One might also point to the ways in which the historical development of the entire region, and the character and orientation of its workers' movements, have been profoundly affected by the threat or reality of European (and later American) hegemony.

The essays in this volume on Egypt, Iraq, Iran, and Turkey certainly incorporate into their analyses the ways in which workers' struggles were often bound up with broader national struggles against foreign influence or control.

I would suggest, however, that such attempts to portray Middle Eastern workers' history as a legitimate field by virtue of the region's common culture, or of the similar historical processes to which its various parts have been subjected, are bound to be unsatisfying. The region's cultural diversity will not allow for much more than superficial generalizations of little help for concrete historical analysis. Nor will an abstract and ahistorical "Islam" provide much of a common basis: the diversity of practices and discourses understood by Muslims as "Islamic" is striking, and in any event those practices and discourses can never be detached from local contexts, which vary widely across space and time.

As for treating the region as a single entity by virtue of the common transformations that its components underwent over the past two centuries, we might note that working-class formation and labor movements in Africa, Latin America, and Asia (not to mention Europe and North America) were also profoundly influenced by changing relationships among the various components of an increasingly integrated world economy, and much of the rest of the world outside Western Europe and North America was, like the Middle East, subject to foreign political or economic influence or control. Why, then, should we compare Egypt and Iran, rather than Egypt and Nigeria or Iran and China?

We may therefore have to take a different tack and simply acknowledge that the Middle East as it has come to be defined is an entity of relatively recent invention with no internally or externally generated essence that endows it with coherence. (The same is of course true of Africa, Latin America, and Europe, though the power/knowledge matrix within which each of these geographic entities was constituted differed significantly.) Whatever its origins, the Middle East today exists as an entity with substantial effectivity in the world, reproduced through contemporary geopolitical discourse and practice. It is a legitimate entity because it has meaning for many people, within the region itself and outside of it, however that meaning was originally produced. And for better or worse, Middle Eastern studies has been institutionalized as a distinct academic field, and within it modern Middle Eastern history.

Prevailing disciplinary and institutional structures and rules may sometimes constrain us to operate within the framework of these fields. This is, I think, acceptable so long as we remember that these are historically constructed rather than natural entities and remain vigilant to the dangers of slipping into essentialism. From this perspective, then, Middle Eastern working-class history has as much claim to be a distinct and legitimate field as African, Latin American, or for that matter European working-class history—on all of which there is an extensive literature. At the same time, we will want to make every effort to transcend disciplinary boundaries and see what can be learned from comparisons between working classes and workers' movements in Middle Eastern countries and those in countries outside the region. The essays in this volume by the two discussants at the Harvard workshop, Edmund Burke, III, and Dipesh Chakrabarty, are very helpful in this respect, because they explore how some of the theoretical and historiographical issues raised at the workshop and in this volume relate to recent trends among historians of working classes in Europe, the United States, and South Asia and more generally to current debates within the humanities and social sciences.[5]

This brings us to the second question I raised earlier: can we speak of "worker" as a significant form of identity and "the working class" as a coherent historical agent, or as coherent object of historical study, in Middle Eastern countries? As I noted earlier, classical Orientalism and modernization theory generally suggested (whether implicitly or explicitly) that the answer to this question was "no," whereas the conventional paradigm of Middle Eastern labor history left the question unasked, taking it for granted that the answer was an unequivocal and self-evident "yes." That paradigm, largely informed by an economistic and positivist version of Marxism, began from the premise that, in each of the Middle Eastern countries, capitalist development brought into being a new category of wage workers and that by virtue of their social location those workers would over time tend to acquire greater class consciousness, to act more like a coherent working class pursuing its own specific interests. From this perspective, the working class was deemed to exist as an entity defined by its objective position within the structure of capitalist society, and its members' consciousness was seen as having been determined primarily by their experience of (and struggle against) subordination, exploitation, and oppression in the workplace.

In recent years, developments within the Middle East as well as new intellectual trends in a variety of fields have led many of us to question this paradigm and seek other ways of approaching Middle Eastern workers' history. Many of the essays in this volume manifest a sense that much of the literature has dealt with workers and working classes in an essentialist and reductionist manner. For example, some implicitly or explicitly question the portrayal of the working class as a homogeneous entity whose members all share the same perceptions, outlooks, and aspirations by virtue of their common social location. There is also a widespread (though by no means universal) rejection of the privileged status that much of the literature has traditionally accorded to one (relatively small) segment of the working class—industrial workers employed in large factories—who have been defined a priori as the core and natural vanguard of the working class and workers' movement.

Several of the essays also criticize what they see as the pronounced teleological character of much writing on workers and labor movements. Workers and working classes have, they suggest, been made to play a set role within a narrative of historical process whereby capitalist development produces a growing and ever more conscious working class, which is ultimately destined to achieve the overthrow of capitalism and the establishment of a postcapitalist social order. This teleology has imparted to a good part of the literature on Middle Eastern workers the same "peculiar property" that Margaret Somers has identified as characteristic of studies of European working-class formation:

> Rather than seeking to explain the *presence* of radically varying dispositions and practices, they have concentrated disproportionately on explaining the *absence* of an expected outcome, namely the emergence of a revolutionary class consciousness among the Western working class....Why is it that the standard problem to be explained in class analysis is how to explain not what is or has been empirically present, but rather the failure of people to behave correctly according to a [Marxian] theoretical prediction?

Studies of class formation, Somers adds, are "rooted in an *epistemology of absence.*"[6]

The contributors to this volume have responded to the problem in different ways. The essays by Sherry Vatter and Donald Quataert, which seek to situate workers and workers' struggles in their cultural and political contexts, might be read as proposing something of a Thompsonian "culturalist" alternative to the conventional paradigm's excessively "structural" focus. Assef Bayat advocates a similar agenda in his critique of the historiography of Iranian workers, emphasizing the importance of consciousness and culture while insisting that objective class position not be lost sight of. In the same vein, Marsha Posusney's detailed study argues for the usefulness of the "moral economy" paradigm in explaining Egyptian workers' behavior while stressing the importance of both ideological and structural factors. Feroz Ahmad's essay investigates the growth of class consciousness in the Turkish working class and activists' struggle to build an independent and militant labor movement, from the collapse of the Ottoman Empire at the end of World War I through the 1980s.

Ellis Goldberg's essay takes a somewhat different tack by proposing a way of understanding why labor movement organization and class consciousness vary so dramatically over time and space. Rejecting both the conventional Marxian political economy and Durkheimian political culture approaches, Goldberg suggests that Egyptian workers' behavior can best be understood through the prism of one variant of "rational choice" theory. His essay turns the conventional wisdom upside down by arguing that it was workers rather than employers who in the 1930s and 1940s were seeking to make the large textile factories at Mahalla al-Kubra in Egypt more productive and "rational." In fact, he suggests, these employers used labor so inefficiently that owners of small weaving shops seem paragons of capitalist efficiency by comparison.

In an effort to push the the break with essentialism and teleologies even further, a few of the essays in this volume draw on poststructuralist theory. Though poststructuralism has been understood and used in many different ways, in general this approach can be said to insist that language is constitutive rather than reflective of what we habitually characterize as "external reality" and to take a particular interest in the ways in which the social production of meaning is inextricably bound up with systems of power. With respect to workers, this suggests a focus on workers' discursive as well as material practices, and on the representations through which "worker" as subject position, working classes as historical subjects and objects, and narratives of labor and national history have been constructed.

Thus Kristin Koptiuch analyzes the conditions under which, within a specific historical conjuncture, the artisan (and petty commodity production generally) came to play certain roles within both Western and Egyptian discourses on the Egyptian economy and society. My own essay explores representations of workers and the working class in late nineteenth and early twentieth century Egypt and various narratives of labor history; and Joel Beinin analyzes the premises, contexts, and consequences of the debate within the contemporary Egyptian Left over the meaning of the popular protests that swept Egypt in January 1977 and, more generally, of Egyptian workers' history. In his investigation of the formation of the Iraqi working class and of the ways in which various political forces have represented its history, Eric Davis draws on the work of the Italian Marxist activist and thinker Antonio Gramsci, whose effort to develop what might be characterized as a nonessentialist and nonteleological Marxism has certain affinities with the poststructuralist project.[7]

Clearly, the contributors to this volume are not all of one mind as to how the history of workers in the Middle East should be approached. I see this multiplicity of viewpoints as a strength rather than a weakness, because it may help provoke the kind of vigorous debates about theory and method of which this field is very much in need. However, despite the very real differences among us, elucidated by the discussions at the workshop itself, I think it can be said that all the essays in this volume are in a sense revisionist, because whether through explicit theoretical contention or through pathbreaking empirical work they contribute to the ongoing effort to critique and rethink the premises of Middle Eastern working-class history.

One such premise, addressed in several essays, is the sharp dichotomization of artisan and worker. The Middle Eastern artisan is conventionally depicted in the literature as a relic of the past, essentially "traditional," static, and unchanging, bound by the narrow horizons of the small workshop, the family, the allegedly moribund guild, and the urban neighborhood. As a social stratum the *artisanat* would seem to have no future: it is doomed by capitalist development, mechanization, the development of new patterns of consumption and new marketing systems, and so forth. By contrast, the worker is generally portrayed as quintessentially "modern," as a person (normatively male) who is freed of all the old constraints (including property) and is now a member of a new and growing social class employed in large mechanized enterprises wherein he (*sic*) and his fellow workers are exposed to new influences and may acquire that flexible and adaptive personality which modernization theory posits as the hallmark of the modern individual or (alternatively) that proletarian class consciousness which certain variants of Marxism have imputed to the working class.

In this volume this dichotomization is problematized in several ways. Sherry Vatter presents a case in which "premodern" crafts workers in Damascus seem to be engaging in a "modern" form of struggle and criticizes the privileging of industrial workers, whereas my essay argues against the imputation to workers in large enterprises of a purely "modern" subjectivity. After all, it is clear that both "artisans" and "workers" in Middle Eastern countries often lived in the same neighborhoods, partook of a common culture, and engaged in similar activities, and for long periods it would seem that neither they themselves, nor the society in which they lived, distinguished clearly (or at all) between "artisans" (or "craftsmen") and "workers" in the modern sense.

Donald Quataert addresses a related point by showing the continuities between Ottoman guilds and unions, highlighting the need to refrain from essentializing what has been seen as the quintessential form of "premodern" artisanal organization, the guild, by treating it as a unitary and unchanging thing. Guilds clearly varied in form, content, and meaning not only over space but over time; they were not necessarily static and tradition-bound, nor were they internally unconflicted. The guild form seems to have disappeared in many Middle Eastern countries during a certain period, but in some cases the new unions that arose among workers—some of them actually crafts workers or even petty proprietors whose trades had not much earlier still been organized in guilds—may have taken on (at least initially) some of the same meanings, as well as some of the same functions, as the defunct guilds.[8]

Kristin Koptiuch usefully extends this discussion by noting that although capitalist industrialization did lead to the demise of some crafts industries, it also gave birth to new ones, while yet others survived by finding new roles in a changing economic system. Those employed in small workshops continue to this day to play a very important role in urban economic and social life in the Middle East; indeed, Koptiuch argues, the petty commodity production sector in effect subsidizes the wages of workers in larger, more mechanized, and heavily capitalized enterprises by providing cheap goods and services, and it also contributes to the ideological reproduction of capitalist hegemony.

Clearly, then, it will no longer suffice to use uncritically the categories produced by census officials and treat those classified as having been employed in "large" enterprises, which may have had as few as ten or a dozen employees, as "workers" subject to some abstract logic of the capitalist workplace, while ignoring or dismissing those employed in small workplaces as irrelevant precapitalist vestiges, all without much concrete investigation into the labor processes and relations of authority that actually prevailed in those workplaces, large or small. Such investigation may well show significant differences between the large factory and the small workshop, but it may also show important similarities.[9]

Problematizing the artisan/worker and guild/union dichotomies so widespread in the literature opens the way to reconsideration of another important issue, raised most explicitly by Sherry Vatter but implicit in some of the other essays as well. Historians, Vatter argues, cannot remain only "within the factory gates." That is, they cannot assume (as has often been the case) that workers' consciousness is formed solely or even mainly within the workplace. She insists—and I believe most if not all of the other contributors would agree—that to make sense of the lives of working people one must locate them in their broader cultural, social, and political contexts. After all, workers (like all of us) are deeply embedded in many overlapping social matrices and enact many different cultural roles, all of which help shape consciousness and behavior within as well as outside the workplace. This reality makes it problematic to impute a specific consciousness to workers, or explain their actions, solely or mainly in terms of their relationship to the means of production, though that is certainly one important factor.

This cultural embeddedness has an impact on the practice of working-class history in many ways. For example, throughout this century many (if not most) members of the urban work force in the Middle East (and throughout the Third World) have been recent migrants from the countryside who have often retained significant connections with their home villages and reproduced some of the discourses and practices of peasant life in their new urban environments and even within their new places of work. They therefore cannot be reduced to "instant proletarians," suddenly possessed of a "pure" working-class consciousness (whatever that might be) the minute they enter the factory gates. From another angle, new means of mass communication—the print media, radio, television, the audiotape player, and the video cassette recorder— have exposed all segments of society to a commodified popular culture, affecting identities and dispositions both within and outside the workplace in complex ways. And even at the level of individual workers' life trajectories, many people who for some period of their lives are factory workers have also—serially or even simultaneously—engaged in petty trade or craft work or some other occupation.

It is also obvious that workers (and therefore the processes of working-class formation and the forms and content of labor activism) have never been insulated from local and national politics. On the contrary, workers and workers' movements in the Middle East have been deeply involved in, and profoundly influenced by, political struggles in which nonworker conationals have also participated, whether those struggles were directed against foreign domination (Egypt, Iraq), a despotic and unjust regime (Iraq, Iran), antilabor economic policies (Egypt), or for democracy and workers' rights (Turkey). In the Middle East as elsewhere, workers' consciousness, movements, and struggles have been inextricably bound up with these larger political, social, and cultural contexts and cannot be understood apart from them.

This is a point brought home once again by the Iranian revolution of 1978–79, which whatever one thinks of the regime that it brought to power surely ranks as one of the great popular uprisings of this century. As Assef Bayat's essay shows, the new Islamic-populist discourse that emerged during the revolutionary conjuncture both articulated and constrained Iranian workers' grievances and sense of identity, while the revolution and the establishment of the Islamic regime have greatly affected worker activism and organization. Chakrabarty develops this point theoretically by criticizing the tendency to oppose "religion" (or "ethnicity") to class- or interest-based solidarities. In a closely related argument he also questions historians' treatment of the state as external to society and argues that class formation is inextricably bound up with state formation.

Yet another aspect of this same problem unfortunately receives little or no attention in this volume. This is the question of gender. In this regard, these essays for the most part share the bias of labor history as a whole: "workers" are assumed to be male, and the working class, its struggles, and its history are essentially about men. Yet we know that from the very beginnings of industrialization in the Middle East, in small workshops as well as in large enterprises, women have been a significant proportion of the work force. Even if women workers have generally played a relatively minor role in organized manifestations of collective action by workers—though further research may compel us to discard that assumption—historians cannot simply ignore the presence of women in the workplace. Nor can we ignore the ways in which male and female workers' consciousness was profoundly (and differentially) shaped by the discourses of gender that pervaded these (and all other) societies, and the practices in which those discourses inhered. The task of recovering and interpreting the lives and struggles of workers in the Middle East also requires exploration of how gender relations shaped, and were shaped by, class and other social relations (including religion, ethnic or national identity, and so forth) in specific and concrete ways. This vitally important project of bringing gender into Middle Eastern workers' history has only just begun.[10]

This volume's insufficient attention to gender notwithstanding, the contributors do seem to agree that historians must range widely outside the factory gates, starting from the premise that the category "worker" overlaps, intersects, and interacts with many other social categories; that workers' identities are as multidimensional and contingent as everyone else's; and therefore that workers' consciousness or behavior is the product of many determinations. This is not to say that what goes on within the workplace is unimportant; it is, however, to insist that it cannot be uncritically posited as the sole or even primary factor in shaping consciousness and behavior. Joel Beinin sums up one of the key thrusts of this volume when he argues that historians must treat Middle Eastern working classes as heterogeneous ensembles of many different groups shaped by a wide variety of influences and possessing differing perspectives and interests. This in turn suggests that we need to pay greater attention to differences, complexities, and discontinuities, seeing working-class identity as always complex and contingent and working-class action as always overdetermined.

These essays also seem to be in agreement that our narratives of Middle Eastern workers' history cannot and should not be forced to conform to some perceived norm derived from a certain narrative of European workers' history—especially because (as both Terry Burke and Dipesh Chakrabarty point out) that narrative, and the metanarrative of modernity that underpins it, are themselves facing powerful challenges. This means respect for the historical specificity of each and every working-class and labor movement and the abandonment of all teleologies, whether derived from a bankrupt modernization theory or from a positivist version of Marxism. Aristide Zolberg has usefully characterized "exceptionalism" with regard to national variations in both the structure of capitalism and the forms of working-class consciousness, organization, and action as a "false problematic," and we might profitably apply this insight to the study of Middle Eastern workers. "Capitalism became flesh in a variety of forms," Zolberg notes,

> and each of these disparate incarnations functioned as a distinctive experiential matrix for the workers it called into life. Given the multifarious character of industrial capitalism, it stands to reason that the working class emerged concomitantly as an array of disparate groups subjected to different conditions and hence inclined to respond in different ways. Since differentiation was a key aspect of the process that governed the formation of the western working class, variety was a constitutive element of its eventual character.[11]

This formulation might be improved upon, I think, by emphasizing two further points. First, class formation is not something that "happens" once and for all to produce a working class with a fixed character. It is rather an open-ended, ongoing process, as classes are constantly remolded by changing economic, political, and cultural forces. Second, variations among workers *within* a single country may be as significant as variations *among* different countries. For example, local circumstances may make workers at one enterprise or in one industry or area more militant, organized or politicized, or active in different ways than those employed elsewhere. Moreover, although class solidarity may provide a basis for common action at the local level—in the neighborhood, at a single workplace or within a specific city or region—it is usually more difficult to achieve and transform into effective action at the national level. With these provisos in mind, we can certainly agree with Zolberg that to the question "How many exceptionalisms?" the appropriate response is "As many as there are cases under consideration."[12]

It is also worth noting that many of these essays exhibit a heightened concern with language and representation. In Donald Quataert's discussion of the language of protest used by Ottoman workers, in Feroz Ahmad's discussion of the changing terms used in Turkey for "worker" and "class" and his presentation of the slogans Turkish workers carried on their banners during the spring 1989 strike wave, in Assef Bayat's analysis of the changing terminology by which "worker" has been denoted in Iran, and elsewhere in this volume as well, we can see a new kind of attention to the complex systems of meaning, manifested in language, through which people understand and define themselves, their society, and the world. This attention to discourse, to representation, is not a substitute for investigation of the ways in which identity and action are powerfully shaped by the process of capital accumulation and the specific environments in which people live and work; it is complementary to it or better yet an inseparable part of the same project of inquiry.

As several of these essays make clear, the writing of history also inevitably poses the problem of representation. The deployment of different categories, paradigms, periodizations, and narrative strategies will yield different stories about the past, each of which will in turn have different consequences for the present. Moreover, in the Middle East as elsewhere, the past is an important political battleground, as Eric Davis demonstrates in his discussion of the Iraqi Ba'thist regime's rather crude efforts to promote a version of Iraqi working-class history that erases the historic role the Iraqi Communist party played in building the Iraqi labor movement and magnifies the Ba'th party's own rather modest contribution. But beyond the question of blatant manipulation and distortion, representation remains an epistemological issue which historians must confront.

The critique of essentialist and teleological representations of the working class implicit or explicit in many of these essays evinces a recognition that we must try to be aware of the premises and consequences inherent in our own choice of categories and narrative strategies. Yet however much we try to make those categories and narratives complicated, contingent, and provisional, we must in the end still relate some relatively coherent story about the past, keeping in mind that it is to a large extent through the stories we tell about and to ourselves and others that much of human social life is represented and grasped. Moreover, however important it is to problematize and deconstruct categories to further historical understanding, we must remember that in specific conjunctures people (ourselves included) often do define themselves in terms of some essence (for example, as workers, Egyptians, Muslims, women, African-Americans, Americans, citizens demanding their constitutional rights, people endowed with human rights, etc.) and act collectively as relatively coherent historical subjects. These categories are "real" because at times people act as if they are real: they (we) live through these identities, see them as manifesting a sense of self and community as well as a set of interests, and sometimes even die for them. Nor can we afford to simply jettison experience and agency, whether individual or collective: these categories can and should be subjected to critical theoretical scrutiny, but they nonetheless remain the frameworks within which people usually understand their own sense of grievance and self-interest, as well as their beliefs, decisions, actions, and histories.

In other words, there may be an inevitable tension between our commitment to an antiessentialist epistemological stance and the deconstruction of stable categories and identities, on the one hand, and on the other, our commitment to retrieving, reconstructing, and making coherent the stories of actual working people and their struggles, fashioned into a narrative of working-class history. But perhaps we can try to see that tension not as debilitating but creative. In an admittedly "against the grain" reading of the work of the *Subaltern Studies* "school" of historians of India, Gayatri Spivak has identified what she terms a "*strategic* use of positivist essentialism in a scrupulously visible political interest."[13] In the writing of Middle Eastern working-class history as in other fields, there may be no alternative to a similar strategy. At the very least, though, this imposes on us a responsibility to be aware of and explicit about the assumptions and methods that underpin our choices and to recognize that, as several of these essays demonstrate, the writing of history must go hand in hand with historiographical critique and theoretical contention.

With all this in mind, I would suggest that to the question of whether Middle Eastern working classes constitute coherent historical subjects and legitimate objects of inquiry we can respond with a properly nuanced and contingent "yes." It is true that labor history has too often essentialized the working class and cast workers in a starring role in a historical drama written by others. Yet as the essays in this volume and a fairly extensive literature demonstrate, it is also true that over the past century workers in Middle Eastern countries have struggled to defend their interests and achieve their goals; they have at times seen themselves as members of a distinct working class and acted on that basis. The literature also shows that collective action by workers— "spontaneous" resistance, organized protests, strikes, the formation of labor movements, tacit or formal accomodations with employers and the state, etc.—has had a significant impact on the political and economic life of several Middle Eastern countries.

The fact that the "languages" through which workers expressed their identity and articulated their grievances were not always purely "proletarian" in the classical Marxist sense but were inflected by many discourses (nationalism, religion, craft, local origin, etc.) only strengthens the argument that one can in fact speak of class in this context; for precisely the same is true even of those working classes in the most developed capitalist countries that are usually held up as the norm. Class, and the working class as an historical agent, is there to be found in modern Middle Eastern history. Worker resistance and activism in many forms have been facts that employers and governments have had to take into account; we should expect no less of historians.

It has lately been suggested that the growth of Islamist movements in various parts of the Middle East in recent decades once again "proves" the irrelevance of class as a category of social analysis in this region: instead, a dehistoricized and abstract "Islam" is taken to be the sole authentic component of consciousness in the Middle East. I must confess that this approach makes no sense to me. I noted earlier that several of the contributors to this volume insisted that Middle Eastern workers and workers' movements must be studied in their cultural context, which of course includes Islamic discourses and practices. It seems to me that the converse holds as well: although Islamist movements must not be reduced to their class dimension, they cannot be understood unless one takes that dimension into account and situates them in the context of the social, economic, cultural, and political changes that the countries of the region have undergone over the past few decades.

That the working class remains a significant social agent is evidenced by the struggles of Egyptian workers Marsha Posusney and Joel Beinin document and by Assef Bayat's analysis of the role Iranian workers played in the struggle to overthrow the Shah,[14] as well as by recent reports of worker protest from various places in the Middle East and North Africa. Mired in a profound economic and social crisis, and under unrelenting pressure to restructure their economies in accordance with the prescriptions of the International Monetary Fund, regimes across the region have hesitated and equivocated for fear of popular reaction, and perhaps especially of worker reaction. However the current crisis unfolds, members of the urban working class broadly defined are likely to continue to have a role to play, whether as workers under their own banner or as a component of other groupings that will nonetheless be infused with the energy of working-class grievances and demands.

To insist that the working class (conceived in this nonessentialist manner) may remain an actor on the stage of history may seem ironic, perhaps even perverse, in light of the recent collapse of the regimes in eastern and central Europe that claimed to rule on behalf of the working class. At a time when many people seem to take it for granted that all human relationships should be subordinated to the logic of the market, it may seem equally strange to be devoting a volume to Middle Eastern working-class history and insisting on the continuing utility not only of class analysis but of some of Marx's (and Marxism's) insights into the workings of capitalism, insights which are to be understood not as dogma but as contributions to critical social thought.

I can say in response only that I (and, I would venture to say, most if not all of the other contributors to this volume) do not believe that history has come to an end just yet. Capitalism has certainly shown itself to be more dynamic, flexible, productive, and protean than most of its nineteenth century critics could have imagined. Yet as we approach the twenty-first century, we also have continuing evidence of capitalism's profoundly contradictory character, manifested most brutally in the economic and ecological devastation afflicting much of the Third World but visible also in the extreme disparities of wealth and power and the grave social crisis increasingly evident even in the most economically and militarily powerful capitalist country of them all.

Class remains a salient dimension of social life everywhere, and not least in the Middle East, whose peoples continue to struggle to overcome the traumas of underdevelopment, tyranny, national and social oppression, patriarchy, and war. Class analysis as a way of understanding these societies therefore also remains salient, obligating us to pay close attention to the grievances and struggles of working people in the Middle East and continue our efforts to retrieve and understand their past.

Notes

I would like to thank Joel Beinin, Melinda Fine, and Robert Vitalis for their helpful comments on drafts of this Introduction.

1. See Joel Beinin, "Class and Politics in Middle Eastern Societies," *Comparative studies in Society and History* 28, no. 3 (July 1986): 552–557.

2. At the workshop Salim Nasr presented an extremely interesting and valuable paper that reflected on the character and evolution of the Lebanese labor movement, before but especially during the civil war that tore that country apart beginning in 1975, and discussed the efforts of trade unionists to build a broad-based coalition of the forces of "civil society" that could effectively oppose the "war system" and those

who benefitted from it. Unfortunately, he was unable to revise his paper in time for inclusion in this volume. The paucity of solid research on Lebanese trade unionism remains a serious lacuna in the literature, and I very much hope that Salim Nasr's essay will be published sometime soon.

3. Ithaca, N.Y.: Cornell University Press.

4. The volume edited by Edmund Burke, III, *Global Crises and Social Movements: Artisans, Peasants, Populists, and the World Economy* (Boulder, Col.: Westview Press, 1988), is an important effort to locate specific social movements in their global context.

5. A useful model for comparative work is *Working-Class Formation: Nineteenth-Century Patterns in Western Europe and the United States*, ed. Ira Katznelson and Aristide Zolberg (Princeton, N.J.: Princeton University Press, 1986), which includes two or three essays apiece on France, the United States, and Germany, with attention to the case of Britain as well, framed by two theoretical-comparative essays written by the editors. But see also Margaret Ramsay Somers, "Workers of the World, Compare!" *Contemporary Sociology* 18, no. 3 (May 1989): 325–329, for a critical review of Katznelson and Zolberg.

6. Somers, ibid., p. 325; emphases in the original.

7. Readers may find Dipesh Chakrabarty's recent study *Rethinking Working-Class History: Bengal 1890–1940* (Princeton, N.J.: Princeton University Press, 1989) useful and provocative, especially Chapter 7.

8. On this question see also Ellis Goldberg, *Tinker, Tailor, and Textile Worker: Class and Politics in Egypt, 1930–1952* (Berkeley: University of California Press, 1986).

9. In this connection see the essays collected in *The Historical Meanings of Work*, ed. Patrick Joyce (Cambridge: Cambridge University Press, 1987).

10. A number of recent works touch on this topic and provide useful bibliographies; see, inter alia, Judith Tucker, *Women in Nineteenth-Century Egypt* (Cambridge: Cambridge University Press, 1985); Nadia Hijab, *Womanpower: The Arab Debate on Women at Work* (Cambridge: Cambridge University Press, 1988); and Deniz Kandiyoti, ed., *Women, Islam and the State* (Philadelphia: Temple University Press, 1991). Linda J. Nicholson's *Gender and History: The Limits of Social Theory in the Age of the Family* (New York: Columbia University Press, 1986) provides an insightful theoretical framework through which to approach this question. On both gender and labor history, see also Joan Wallach Scott, *Gender and the Politics of History* (New York: Columbia University Press, 1988).

11. Katznelson and Zolberg, *Working-Class Formation*, p. 433.

12. Ibid., p. 455.

13. "Subaltern Studies: Deconstructing Historiography," in Ranajit Guha and Gayatri Chakravorty Spivak, eds., *Selected Subaltern Studies* (New York: Oxford University Press, 1988), p. 13, emphasis in the original. In this connection see also Denise Riley, *"Am I That Name?" Feminism and the Category of "Women" in History* (Minneapolis: University of Minnesota Press, 1988).

14. See Assef Bayat, *Workers and Revolution in Iran: A Third World Experience of Workers' Control* (London: Zed Books, 1987).

Sherry Vatter

1

Militant Journeymen in Nineteenth-Century Damascus: Implications for the Middle Eastern Labor History Agenda

To date the literature in the field of Middle Eastern labor studies deals almost exclusively with workplace organizations, consciousness and political activities of unionized industrial wage workers employed in large factories and the modern transportation sector. It makes short shrift of the experience of waged workers employed outside the factory setting, in small workshops and homes.[1]

The lopsided distribution of research is informed by assumptions, rooted in Marxist theory, about each group's role in history.[2] Labor historians have identified large-scale capitalist enterprise as the crucible necessary for the rise of a revolutionary class-conscious proletariat who will spearhead the inevitable transition from capitalism to socialism. In contrast, there is the expectation that workers employed in small workshops and homes will contribute little, if anything, to this revolution because such environments are viewed as obstructing workers' ability to engage in sustained class-conscious political activity that might render them effective historical actors.

It is my contention that neglect of Middle Eastern workers employed in small workshops is unwarranted. They can and have engaged in the type of collective labor struggle that distinguishes the proletariat from other subaltern groups and justifies labor history's status as an independent field of study. Thus they constitute a legitimate subject for labor historians. This paper makes the case for including this segment of the working class within the parameters of Middle Eastern labor studies by examining a concrete instance of labor activism by waged nonfactory workers: the strikes mounted by journeymen weavers employed in Damascus's artisanal sector between 1870 and 1914.[3]

The assertion that artisans engage in modern forms of labor struggle finds little support in the literature. Gabriel Baer was in good company when he observed that "organization along class lines within the guild and of a class struggle between guild strata and ranks was absent."[4] Scholars have assumed that the artisanal structure prevented journeymen from viewing themselves as a group with interests distinct from and antagonistic to those of the masters.[5] Presumably, journeymen were inclined to view masters as friends and beneficiaries rather than adversaries, because masters were not merely employers but coworkers who worked at their side. They taught journeymen their trade and were role models who embodied hopes of promotion to the rank of master and setting up a business of one's own.

A journeyman had good reason to remain on good terms with a master even if disaffected with him. The acquisition of an independent shop was a prerequisite for promotion to the rank of master. Because the number of commercial spaces designated for the practice of each craft was limited, presumably a journeyman needed the goodwill and support of one or more masters if he hoped to prevail over other contenders when such a space became available.[6]

The existence of a craft corporation or "guild" to which both journeyman and master belonged reinforced the positive bonds between them by giving substance to the notion of a shared professional identity and common interests. Masters in leadership positions in guilds visibly served journeymen's interests by striving to maintain high levels of employment and a decent standard of living for all members and settling disputes among members. The rhetoric of craft solidarity and rituals also bolstered harmony, as, for example, in initiation ceremonies, which presented unequal positions as sequential stages in a career imbued with potentially divisive issues with nondivisive meanings. If, in spite of these checks, large numbers of journeymen became dissatisfied with their masters, the fragmentation of the work force into small productive units rendered collective action against them difficult.

The Damascus weaving industry in the late Ottoman period exhibits the features believed to ensure harmony between different strata of craftsmen. In the 1870s, 6,000 to 7,000 handloom weavers were employed in this provincial Ottoman capital, of whom 4,000 to 5,000 were journeymen, the remainder master craftsmen and apprentices.[7] Masters, journeymen, and apprentices worked side by side, weaving silk-cotton combinations known as *alaja* or durable cottons such as *dima* and *mabrum*.[8] Production took place in small workshops scattered throughout the city, with three or four weavers working in each.[9] Membership in a craft corporation of weavers was open to masters and journeymen alike.

Nevertheless, there was little harmony between journeymen and master weavers in late Ottoman Damascus. By the 1870s, the city's journeymen weavers were regularly mounting strikes against the masters who employed them. Though such strikes probably predated the 1870s, only in this decade did they occur with enough frequency to occasion comment. Writing in 1879, the British consul in Damascus noted that "strikes are common in Damascus in this particular branch of industry."[10] Though journeymen did not always meet with success, they continued to agitate for better conditions though World War I.[11]

These protests were collective, disciplined actions, not "spontaneous" expressions of mob sentiment. The strike of early 1879 exemplifies their character.[12] On that occasion, more than 3,000 of the city's 4,000 to 5,000 journeymen weavers struck to protest a cut in piecework wages, from 16 to 13 piasters. To ensure that all journeymen honored the strike, militants threatened potential strike breakers and cut threads mounted on looms to keep them from working. After a work stoppage of four weeks, the masters reinstated the old pay rates and journeymen returned to work.

How did a group of ostensibly premodern craft workers come to engage in a recognizably modern form of labor struggle that is associated with industrial wage workers employed in the advanced capitalist sector?

Part of the answer is that the structure of artisanal production was less egalitarian and more conducive to antagonism than is usually acknowledged. The journeyman weaver in nineteenth century Damascus was a propertyless wage worker, the master was an employer who profited at his expense. The master craftsman owned or rented the workshop in which both worked, hired journeymen on a piecework basis, provided them with workspace and cotton or silk for weaving, and rented them the looms on which they worked.[13]

Master weavers were not independent producers, but subcontractors. A local textile merchant determined what would be woven, engaged a master weaver to arrange for the weaving of the fabric, provided him the material to be woven, and paid him on completion of the work. The master in turn retained a portion of the subcontrator's fee for himself and passed the remainder on to journeymen who wove the fabric.[14] This transaction highlighted the exploitative nature of the master-journeyman relationship.

In theory, a journeyman could escape this unequal and exploitative relationship by setting up his own shop. By the mid-nineteenth century, however, his prospects of doing so were poor. As a wage worker who owned neither workplace, nor materials, nor the tools of production, he was unlikely to accumulate sufficient capital to purchase his own loom, much less rent or buy the workshop he needed to set up in business on his own.

Scholars have paid little attention to conflicts of interest between different strata of artisans in part because they have based their picture of the artisanal economy on the ideology and structure of the craft corporation, an institution that embodied the concept of craft harmony, rather than upon concrete relations of production.

Yet even the craft corporation provided a basis for journeyman-master conflict, for it was not a democratic institution. A small group of masters—the elite of the weaving community—together with a "guild" shaykh monopolized power within it and exercised control over the journeyman's life in ways not always agreeable. Masters decided if and when a journeyman would attain the rank of master, and thus determined his chances for self-employment.[15] It is unlikely that masters were able to transcend their interests as employers when called upon to settle disputes between journeymen and masters.

The Damascus weavers' militant labor activism cannot be explained by structurally defined conflicts of interest alone. Though the artisanal structure remained constant from the late eighteenth through the early twentieth centuries, strikes became regular only after 1870. Local responses to novel economic conditions also played a part.

In the late eighteenth and early nineteenth centuries markets for Damascene and other Ottoman textiles expanded, aided by the withdrawal of French competition after the French Revolution and by the expansion of rural demand for textiles. Spurred by hopes of profit, janisarries, merchants, and other nonweavers opened weaving workshops throughout the region.[16] This industrial expansion proved to be a liability for Damascus's weavers. Historically, corporate leaders had managed to keep wages relatively high and minimize unemployment by limiting the number of workshops and weavers. The masters' state-recognized monopoly over the operation of weaving shops in Damascus facilitated this task. The proliferation of weaving establishments operated by nonweavers, beyond the control of the craft elite, eroded corporate leaders' ability to insulate weavers from market forces. The result was higher levels of unemployment during economic downturns and probably a gradual lowering of real wages.[17]

The employment problem worsened during the 1830s and 1840s. Thousands of Damascene weavers lost their jobs when relatively inexpensive Western European textiles flooded Ottoman markets and made substantial gains at the expense of Damascene fabrics.[18] The number of looms in use in the city fell, from 5,000–6,000 during the 1830s to under 2,000 throughout the 1840s, leaving in doubt the survival of the Damascus textile industry.[19] Guild masters proved unable to prevent the industrial decline or to secure the jobs that remained for themselves and their employees.

An incident in 1842 illustrates the masters' ineffectiveness in this novel economic environment. Citing their exclusive right to operate weaving shops in the city, the masters asked the local authorities to close a weaving workshop operated by a merchant, Mr. Mishaka. Despite the weight of corporate authority and "traditional" rights on their side, Mishaka successfully defied the order with the backing of the British consul.[20]

Weavers were not the only Damascene artisans unable to assert their exclusive right to jobs. Warpers attempted, also unsuccessfully, to eliminate unauthorized competitors.[21] In 1847 the largely Muslim practitioners asked the acting governor to prevent the most conspicuous interlopers, a handful of Christians who had worked as warpers for only twelve years, from exercising their craft or teaching it to their children. While the acting governor supported their request, the governor reversed his decision and ruled in favor of the newcomers.

The masters' failure to secure the closure of "illegal" shops cannot be attributed solely to foreign intervention. Ottoman authorities did little to help guild members secure the few jobs still available. Whether they believed that competition favored economic growth or whether they felt that runaway shops had become too numerous and too much a part of the economic fabric to be done away with, local Ottoman officials attempts to uphold corporate monopolies were less than wholehearted.[22]

By the 1850s Damascus's commercial textile sector began to rally. The number of looms inched up, from under 2,000 in 1848 to 3,500 in 1859 and close to 7,000 in 1879, leveling off at about 5,000 by the end of the century, until World War I.[23] The expanding rural demand for textiles in the wake of the grain boom of the 1850s and the cotton boom of the 1860s played a part in the revival. So did the development of new fabrics that appealed to changing consumer tastes, a growing appreciation among consumers that local fabrics might cost slightly more than imports but were of better quality, and Ottoman fiscal policies that encouraged local industry.[24]

Merchants' abilty to lower the real price of Damascene fabrics also contributed to the recovery. From the mid-1830s to 1862, the market price of a piece of the lowest quality *alaja* remained at 80 piasters though the cost of living more than doubled.[25] Merchants kept the price of Damascene fabrics steady by freezing wages. Piecework rates for weaving *alaja* in 1836 were 8 to 10 piasters. By 1850 they had fallen sightly, to 6 to 10 plasters, where they remained until the late 1860s.[26] Journeymen's wages, higher than those of most Damascene artisans and affording them a comfortable standard of living in the 1830s, were on a par with those of day laborers by the early 1870s.[27]

The fall in real wages meant that a journeyman was less likely than ever to accumulate the capital needed to purchase the right to operate a weaving workshop and looms or to rent a workshop. Journeymen's hopes of self-employment were dimmed even more after the middle of the nineteenth century by the spread of large merchant-owned and operated handicraft factories that functioned alongside the smaller artisan-run workshops. The Nissans, Asfars, Sarkis, Arouanis, and other merchant families established large workshops in which they hired a single well-paid master weaver to supervise a large number of journeymen.[28] The increase in the ratio of journeymen to masters that allowed capitalists to benefit from economies of scale transformed journeymen into factory workers.

As the journeyman's hopes for the future receded, so did the basis of his identification with the master and a reason for not antagonizing him. The guild leadership's inability to ensure full employment or good wages eliminated another reason for the journeyman to respect and defer to masters' wishes. By the 1870s, the guild hierarchy had virtually no say in determining the economic conditions under which artisans labored. Merchants set employment and wage rates in response to the dictates of the global economy.

If conditions during the economic crisis undermined the bonds between journeymen and master weavers, the masters' selfish pursuit of their own interests turned the journeymen against them. The craft elite laid the grounds for journeyman-master conflict. In mid-century, the Ottoman state used the guild leadership to impose new taxes on and raise military conscripts from the weaving community. Apparently masters used their authority to place a disproportionate part of these burdens on journeymen.[29] It was the masters' actions in their capacity as employers, however, that pushed journeymen to confront masters openly.

Once the survival of the industry seemed assured, merchants increased the market price of Damascene fabrics. The price for the cheapest grade of *alaja* rose from 90 to 95 piasters in 1862, and to 90 piasters in 1879.[30] These increases allowed merchants, masters, and journeymen to recoup some of the losses they had sustained since the 1830s. Higher prices translated into bigger profits for merchants, higher subcontracting fees for masters, and higher piecework wages for journeymen weavers. Piecework rates for weaving *alaja* rose from 6 to 10 piasters in the early 1860s to 12 to 15 piasters by 1869 and to 16 piasters by 1878.[31]

Journeymen remained dissatisfied with the wage increases for several reasons. First, the raises came nowhere near restoring their standard of living to what it had been prior to the crisis. Second, ordinary weavers who had sacrificed much, and without complaint, in order to secure the industry's survival, resented that the benefits of recovery were going disproportionately to others. The lion's share went to the textile merchants, who were making healthy profits "of not under 30 percent" by 1872.[32] The masters' gains were modest by comparison. Most managed only to ensure the survival of their small businesses.

Based on these facts alone, one might expect journeymen to turn against the merchants. Instead, they went on strike against the masters. The journeymen targeted the latter for two reasons. First, the masters' modest gains were more obviously made at the journeymen's expense. Masters recouped their losses in the only way open to them, by increasing their portion of the subcontracting fees received from the merchant. They might wait until merchants raised the subcontracting rate, which allowed them to simultaneously improve their position and that of the journeymen, or they might, as in 1879, improve their position by lowering the journeymen's wages.

Second, the journeymen expected better treatment from masters than from merchants. On the occasion of the 1879 strike, for example, these weaver-activists justified their actions by pointing to the masters' flagrant violation of their obligation to protect the journeymen's interests as well as their own. The strikers maintained that they would have accepted a wage cut had it been instituted to lower fabric prices—a move that might make Damascene fabrics more competitive and translate into more work for them. They did not accept the reduction because the masters lowered wages to serve their own narrow economic interests and "still sold silk at the old prices."[33]

This instance of modern labor struggle within the confines of the artisanal sector was a consequence of the responses by different classes and strata of Syrians to the challenges and opportunities presented by the modern capitalist economy in the nineteenth century. Artisanal structures were subjected to the logic of capitalist relations, undermining ties between different strata of artisans, exacerbating old tensions, and revaluing the social significance of a long-standing artisanal structure.

Although Damascus's journeymen weavers engaged in disciplined strikes, they do not meet all the Marxist criteria for class-conscious workers. Most significant, the journeymen's militancy did not signal the absence of communal artisanal identity, but was spurred on by the perception that masters had an obligation as fellow weavers to look out for their interests. Journeymen legitimized their behavior in terms of a "moral economy" framework rather than class struggle.

Can the Damascene journeymen legitimately qualify as workers without exhibiting a fully developed Marxist class consciousness? I answer in the affirmative, although much about these workers is still unknown, including their names, leaders, mode of organization, and how they viewed their relationship to waged workers in other occupations, other sectors of the economy, or in other parts of the empire. First, what we do know indicates that by the late nineteenth century Damascene weavers had acquired a degree of class consciousness. Consciousness of themselves as a class of wage workers coexisted and competed with the journeymen's corporate identity. Forty years of disciplined strikes supports this contention. So do signs that journeymen were disengaging themselves from the craft corporation. By the 1870s many skilled journeymen trained within the corporate system, working in workshops run by masters, and in principle subject to decisions taken by the guild leadership, were not formally entered on the corporate rolls as journey-men.[34] Though they did not participate in an organized movement or openly defy the corporate leadership, presumably these journeymen no longer viewed the guild as serving their interests, at least not enough to justify the cost of membership.

Another argument in favor of viewing Damascus's nineteenth century journeymen weavers as workers is that Middle Eastern industrial workers in the advanced capitalist sector have not been excluded from this category for the lack of a fully articulated Marxist class consciousness. In the past 100 years, though many Middle Eastern industrial workers have joined unions and participated in strikes, few have engaged in the type of revolutionary working-class politics that Marx deemed a precondition of socialism. Typically, workers have subsumed their class identity to that of nation or faith and thus have tended to view harmony rather than conflict as the natural and desirable state of interclass relations.[35] Class consciousness has not proved to be an all-or-nothing attribute.

The overlap between theoretically distinct categories of the working class, artisans and modern industrial workers, is not limited to their consciousness. In the late nineteenth and early twentieth centuries many skilled factory workers were recruited from and hardly differed from artisans. Though they worked in large workshops or factories, artisanal hierarchies and relationships frequently remained intact.[36] If Damascus's militant journeymen qualify as workers, do artisans merit recognition as a distinct category of workers? Are the Damascene weavers strikes representative of a broader social phenomenon or are they unique? I maintain that they are not unique. Until recently, most scholars have viewed artisans as unlikely to engage in labor struggles.[37] The few examples of strikes by artisans in the scholarly literature on Middle Eastern artisans or labor seem to support this belief. The scarcity of concrete information about the work-related political activity of artisans seems more a function of scholars' failure to look for such behavior, rather than its absence. A few concrete examples of artisans engaging in labor struggles supports this contention.

Tensions between journeymen and masters and labor activism by journeymen was fairly widespread in late nineteenth century Damascus. In his description of Damascene craft corporations in the last third of the nineteenth century, Iliya Qudsi took conflict between masters and journeymen to be the norm throughout the artisanal sector. He situated the *shawish*, the guild shaykh's messenger, thus:

> As far as I could gather, the shawish is closer to the artisans than to the other members of the guild, and considers himself to be one of them, to such an extent that when the artisans demand higher pay from the masters it is he who goes around urging them to insist on the granting of their demands.[38]

Labor struggles by Damascene artisans did not end with the fall of the Ottoman Empire. In 1919, artisans faced with high food prices went on strike for higher wages.[39]

Artisans outside Damascus responded to the pressures of the capitalist economy in a like fashion. Recent scholarship on Middle Eastern labor in the late Ottoman period indicates that tailors, cobblers, bakers, and porters, not just miners, railway, workers, and others in the advanced capitalist sector, formed unions and struck. Although not recognized as such, most of the former are better described as artisans than as "modern" workers. Typically they worked in small dispersed workshops, for a skilled craft worker who had trained them.[40]

Donald Quataert's study of Anatolian carpet workers in the late Ottoman period reminds us that wage-earning artisans frustrated with employers and capitalists did not necessarily engage in sustained, disciplined forms of labor struggle. These Anatolian hand-workers engaged in "Luddite"-like attacks on the foreign-owned factories and machines that threatened them with redundancy.[41]

Conflict between different strata of Middle Eastern artisans was not limited to the late Ottoman period. In seventeenth century Bursa, journeymen satin cloth makers routinely struck against their masters over lowered wages.[42] In this instance, the discrepancy between the image and realities of artisanal relationships was greater than in late Ottoman Damascus. Journeymen and masters formed distinct, antagonistic social groups. Master velvet weavers had assumed the role of capitalist employers; they employed skilled craftsmen in workshops that housed as many as fifty looms.[43] The craft corporation did little to generate harmony among craftsmen because only masters belonged to it.[44] The institution functioned as an employers' association and a vehicle of state administration.[45]

I do not mean to suggest that the conditions and significance of labor activism in seventeenth century Bursa and nineteenth century Damascus were identical. Though both periods were characterized by market growth, conflicts in the former are explained by increased domestic production rather than the reverse.[46] More important, by the nineteenth century, labor struggles had acquired a different and potentially greater social significance because they occurred in the context of a global, industrial capitalist economy.

Nor should one assume that the two periods are linked in a linear fashion. If stratification and conflict increased during the sixteenth century in the Ottoman heartlands, the trend may have subsequently been reversed.[47] We still know too little about the lives and day-to-day work relationships of workers in this sector, or about the specific contests in which they functioned, to construct a narrative of artisanal protest during the Ottoman period.[48] Yet there is no doubt that some Middle East artisans participated in labor struggles and possessed a degree of class consciousness before the region's confrontation with the industrial capitalist economy or that many artisans became more militant and class conscious as a result of this confrontation.

I would like to take this sequence a step further, and suggest a link between the class awareness of activist artisans and the labor struggles of "modern" railway and factory workers in the late Ottoman period. This suggestion cannot be dismissed as an exercise in nationalist apologetics, an attempt to deny the external origins of "modern" social forms, even if available literature gives the impression that Middle Eastern labor activists have derived little, if anything, positive from their own society. Ignorance about Middle Eastern vocabularies and traditions of protest that predate the advent of industrial capitalist structures has inclined scholars to look outside the Middle East for the roots of labor activism. The industrial capitalist structures deemed necessary for progressive social change and the models for labor activism appear to be European imports.[49]

The historiographical disjuncture between the experience of modern industrial labor and that of waged artisans is conceptually flawed. Inherited vocabularies of meaning and models of action shape peoples' understanding of what constitutes reasonable and even possible responses to new conditions. Individuals borrow, but selectively, choosing what appears appropriate and useful in terms of existing social arrangements. Any novel behavior, "modern" or otherwise, is necessarily rooted in the actor's past, even while it registers external pressures for change.

We might well ask to what extent early twentieth century Egyptian labor strikes documented by Zachary Lockman were rooted in artisanal modes of action.[50] It would be foolhardy to deny that Egyptian tram workers learned lessons from European workers, but it would be equally foolhardy to fail to acknowledge that these workers had an activist tradition of their own to evoke. This argument is all the more persuasive because many skilled factory workers had been recruited from the artisanal sector.

Persons employed in the artisanal sector and traditionally incorporated trades are historically significant not merely by virtue of their impact on workers in the advanced capitalist sector, but in their own right. Contrary to the prediction that they would disappear when confronted with the modern capitalist economy, these so-called traditional workers constituted the majority of Middle Eastern workers until well after after World War I.[51] On numerical grounds alone they must be recognized as a section of the labor movement, with its own concerns and role in determining labor's place Middle Eastern society.

Even if the current lack of information about the indigenous political influences on Middle Eastern factory workers before World War I does not permit us to specify how "traditional" workers contributed to the emergence of "modern" industrial labor movements, or their impact on the evolution of Middle Eastern societies, artisanal experience in other societies during the nineteenth century demonstrates that such input was a real possibility.

Sean Wilentz's study of journeymen in New York City from the late eighteenth through the mid-nineteenth centuries shows that waged artisans employed outside the advanced capitalist sector could unionize and engage in culturally and politically significant mass movements, in spite of working in small groups in dispersed locations.[52] Wilentz concludes: "It is to craft workers and their employees that we must look in order to understand the most dramatic changes in class relationships in early nineteenth century New York."[53] Jean Quataert's study of rural, female outworkers who organized around health care issues in late nineteenth-century Germany demonstrates that political consciousness and organization can occur outside the urban-based workshop.[54]

Does nineteenth century artisanal activism have any significance for the understanding of Middle Eastern labor in the late twentieth century? I suggest that it does. Though artisans have largely disappeared in the Middle East, workers employed in small workshops and at home have not. Contrary to Marx's expectations, this segment of the working class has not been absorbed into the advanced capitalist sector, but constitute the majority of the region's workers both in quantitative and productive terms and show no sign of disappearing.[55] This fact renders their experience relevant, if not critical, to our understanding of the consciousness and behavior of the universally acknowledged subject of labor history: the modern industrial proletariat.

The narrow focus on workers in the advanced capitalist sector divorces them from the broader social context in which they function. The workers in the factory setting rather than the working class as a whole becomes the object of study. Middle Eastern workers employed in modern factories, mines, and railroads remain a minority and thus by necessity are enmeshed in and subject to the influence of social worlds whose values and social forms originate outside the modern capitalist setting.

Waged workers employed in small shops and homes deserve the attention of labor historians for another reason. Given their persistence in a society well integrated into the global capitalist economy, presumably the dynamics and course of social change will diverge from Marxist expectations.[56] We would expect such workers to play a larger role in social evolution, whether for good or for ill, than Marx assumed.[57]

Labor historians recognize that the structural changes that inform Marx's neglect of nonfactory workers have not been realized in most Middle Eastern societies and that "modern" industrial workers have not performed as expected. Most scholars, however, still focus on unionized workers employed in the advanced capitalist sector and their interactions with state and nationalist leadership.[58]

The argument that labor historians should widen their research horizons to include waged workers employed in small shops and homes is not to deny the privileged political position of "modern" industrial labor, but rather to acknowledge that the impact of capital is felt beyond the factory gates. If the study of the labor history of the Middle East is to shed light on what Middle Eastern workers have done and what they might achieve in the future, the discussion of the relationship between politics and culture must be informed by the concrete realities of Middle Eastern society as well as theoretical expectations about the future. To fully appreciate the specificity of that context, Middle East labor historians cannot remain within the factory gates.

Notes

1. See, for example, Ra'uf Abbas, *Al-Haraka al'-ummaliyya fi misr, 1899–1967* (Paris, 1974); Kamal Mazhar Ahmad, *al-Tabaqa al-'amila al-'Iraqiya: Al-Takawwun wa-bidayat al-taharruk* (Baghdad, 1981); Joel Beinin and Zachary Lockman, *Workers on the Nile: Nationalism, Communism, Islam and the Egyptian Working Class* (Princeton, 1987); Ellis Goldberg, *Tinker,*

Tailor, and Textile Worker: Class and Politics in Egypt, 1930–1952 (Berkeley, 1986); Abdallah Hanna, *Al-Haraka al'ummaliya fi Suriya wa-Lubnan* (Damascus 1973); Amin 'Izz al-Din, *Ta'rikh al'-tabaqa al'-amila al-misriyya*, 3 vols. (Cairo, 1967–1971); Elisabeth Longuenesse, "Industrialisation et sa Signification Sociale", in *La Syrie d'Aujourd'hui*, ed. A. Raymond (Paris, 1980), pp. 327–358; Elizabeth Longuenesse, "La Classe ouvrière dans les pays arabes: la Syrie," *La Pensée* 20 (1978): 120–132. Most studies of Middle Eastern industrial workers outside the factory setting appear under the rubric of women's rather than labor studies. See, for example, Gunseli Burek, *Women Carpet Weavers in Rural Turkey: Patterns of Employment, Earnings and Status*, Women, Work and Development Series, no. 15 (Geneva, 1987); Mine E. Çinar, *Labor Market Opportunities for Home Working Women In Istanbul, Turkey*, von Grunebaum Center for Near Eastern Studies, Working Paper no. 2 (Los Angeles, 1992). For a study of male waged labor employed outside the modern industrial setting, see Ellis Goldberg, "Artisans and Craftsmen in Nineteenth Century Egypt: A Premature Announcement of Their Deaths" (unpublished paper, 1988).

 2. Karl Marx and Frederiek Engels, *The Communist Manifesto* (New York, 1930), pp. 25–54.

 3. This argument could be made for waged workers employed in small workshops, shops, and homes, whether or not they are industrial workers.

 4. Gabriel Baer, "Ottoman Guilds: A Reassessment," in *The Social and Economic History of Turkey (1071–1920)*, ed. O. Okyar and H. Inalcik (Ankara, 1980), p. 99.

 5. For example, Gabriel Baer, *Egyptian Guilds in Modern Times* (Jerusalem, 1964); Dominique Chevallier, "Un exemple de résistance technique de l'artisanat syrien aux XIXe et XX siecles: Les tissus ikates d'Alep et de Damas," *Syria* 30 (1962): 300–324; Bakr ad-Din al-Siba'i, *Adwa' 'Ala ar-Rasmal al-'ajnabi fi Suriyya: 1850–1958* (Damascus, 1958), p. 284. The definitive late nineteenth century description of Damascus's artisanal structure is Iliya Qudsi, "Notice sur les Corporations de Damas," *Actes du XIeme Congrès des Orientalistes*, part 2 (Leiden, 1885), pp. 7–34. For a contemporary overview, see Abdul-Karim Rafeq, "Craft Organizations, Work Ethics, and the Strains of Change in Ottoman Syria," *Journal of the American Oriental Society* 111 (1991): 495–511. These assumptions are not unique to Middle Eastern studies. See Sean Wilentz, *Chants Democratic: New York City and the Rise of the American Working Class* (New York, 1982), pp. 7–8.

 6. The right to weave in a particular workshop was restricted to specified commercial spaces. The purchase of *gedik* (the equipment in the workshop) and *khilu* (the right to use the shop) of a workshop were deemed a prerequisite for setting up a weaving establishment. Both were attached to a specific space and were bought and sold independent of the building of the workshop and land on which it stood. Rafeq, "Craft Organizations," pp. 503–504; André Raymond, *Artisans et Commercants au Caire au XIIIIe Siecle* (Damascus, 1973–74), pp. 271, 550, 583.

 7. The commercial weaving of luxury textiles was a male preserve in late Ottoman Damascus. For numbers of looms, see Gilbert to Waddington (no. 5), 24 April 1879, AF CCC 5 Damascus. For the calculation of the number of weavers from this figure, Sherry Vatter, "A City Divided: A Socioeconomic Study of Damascus, Syria 1840–1870," (UCLA Ph.D. diss., in progress).

8. *Alaja* were luxury fabrics, on which the city's long-standing reputation as a textile manufacturing center rested. For the central importance of silk-cotton combinations in the eighteenth century, see M. P. S. Girard, "Memoire sur l'agriculture, l'industrie et le commerce," *Déscription de l'Égypte*, 24 vols. (Paris, 1821–29), vol. 17, pp. 290–310. For their importance in the nineteeth century, see John Bowring, *Report on the Commercial Statistics of Syria* (London, 1840; reprinted New York, 1973), p. 20; Dominique Chevallier, "Un exemple de résistance," Muhammad Sa'id al-Qasimi, *Oamus al-Sina-'at al-Shamiyya*, 2 vols., ed. Zafir al-Qasimi (Paris, 1960), vol. 1, pp. 39–40. *Dima* and *mabrum* emerged as mainstays of Damascus's textile industry after 1860. For evidence of their importance after 1860, see Gilbert to Waddington (Damascus, no. 5), 24 April 1879, AE CCC 5 Damascus.

9. De Ségur to Ministre des Affaires Étrangères, 18 April 1849, AE CCC 3 Damascus. Textile workshops could have as few as one and as many as eleven looms in nineteenth century Damascus. Rafeq, "Craft Organization," p. 504.

10. "Report by Vice-Council Jago on the Trade and Commerce of Damascus for the Year 1879," PRO FO 37 (1978–1879), vol. 70, part II, Damascus, pp. 614–616.

11. In 1902 they failed to win higher wages. Mohammad Sa'id Kalla, "The Role of Foreign Trade in the Economic Development of Syria; 1831–1914" (The American University, Ph.D. diss., 1969), p. 232, n. 121; Weakley, "Report on the Conditions and Prospects of British Trade in Syria," vol. 87 (Great Britian, *Accounts and Papers*).

12. This account is based on "Report by Vice-Council Jago. . .1879." For a more extended discussion of the context for this incident, see Sherry Vatter, "Journeymen Textile Weavers Lives in Nineteenth Century Damascus: A Collective Biography," in *Struggle and Survival in the Modern Middle East*, ed. E. Burke, III (Berkeley, 1993).

13. Nineteenth-century journeymen usually rented looms from masters on an annual basis. De Ségur to Ministre des Affaires Étrangères, 20 Jan. 1850, AE CCC 3 Damascus.

14. For master-merchant relationships see De Ségur to Ministre des Affaires Étrangères, 18 April 1849, AE CCC 3, Damascus; and Rick J. Joseph, "The Material Origins of the Lebanese Conflict of 1860" (Oxford University, Magdalen College, B. of Lett. thesis, 1977), pp. 25–26. For merchant capitalists involved in textile production see Bowring, *Report*, p. 94.

15. Masters settled disputes between members, distributed state imposed taxes among their members, as well as protected artisans' livelihoods. Abdul-Karem Rafeq, "The Law Court Registers of Damascus with Special Reference to Craft Corporations During the First Half of the Eighteenth Century," in *Les Arabes par leurs Archives (XVIe#XXe siècles)*, ed. J. Berque and D. Chevallier (Paris, 1976), pp. 53–55.

16. For the expansion of local textile production beyond guild boundaries, see Paul Saba'a, "The Development and Decline of the Lebanese Silk Industry" (Oxford University, Balliol College, B. of Lett. thesis, 1977); Butrus Labaki, *Introducion á l'histoire économique du Liban, soie et commerce entérieur en fin du période Ottoman (1840–1914)* (Beirut, 1984).

For evidence of nonproducers' direct involvement in textile production in Damascus, see De Ségur to Ministre des Affaires Étrangères, 18 April 1849, AE CCC 3 Damascus.

17. The restructuring of artisanal production was not unique to Damascus, see Jean-Claude David, "Alep, degradation et tentatives actuelles de readaptation des structures urbaines traditionnelles," *Bulletin d'Etudes Orientales* 28 (1975): 19–50.

18. The annual average value of European imports into the Southern Syrian provinces of the Ottoman Empire in the 1763–1767 period was 953,400 francs. François Charles-Roux, *Les échelles de Syrie et de Palestine au XVIIIe siecle* (Paris, 1928), p. 82. Imports declined between the French Revolution and the 1910s and then increased once more. By 1841 they reached 14,852,825 francs. Charles Boislecomte, *La mission du baron de Boislecomte, L'Égypte et la Syrie en 1833*, ed. George Douin (Cairo, 1927), pp. 255, 256; Joseph, "The Material Origins," pp. 37, 39, 43, 44, 50.

19. Bowring's figure of 4400 looms for the mid-1830s is for silk and cotton production. Bowring, *Report*, p. 20. Poujade to Guizot (52), 10 Sept. 1845, AE CCC 4 Beirut; De Ségur to Ministre des Affaires Étrangere, 20 Jan. 1850, AE CCC 3 Damascus.

20. Wood to Canning (Damascus copy no. 45), Damascus 12 July 1842, encl. No. 1 in Wood to Aberdeen, Damascus (no. 55), 13 July 1842, FO 78/499.

21. "Requête des ouvriers oudisseurs catholiques to Monsieur le Consul de France," 16 Oct. 1946, encl. in Tippel to Guizot (no. 35), 29 December 1846, AE CCC 2 Damascus.

22. Local officials were following the lead of Ottoman policy makers in Istanbul. Engin Deniz Akrali, "The Uses of Law Among Istanbul Artisans and Tradesmen: The Story of Gedik and Implements, Mastership, Shop Usufruct and Monopoly, 1750–1850" (unpublished paper). By the 1880s the lack of guild membership was no longer considered a valid reason for closing a shop. Qudsi, "Notice sur les Corporations," note p. 16.

23. De Ségur to Ministre des Affaires Étrangères, 20 Jan. 1850, AE CCC 3, Damascus; "Report on the Trade of Damascus," encl. in Brant to Bulwer (no. 21), 12 June 1859, encl. in Brant to Malmesbury, (Damascus, Con. no. 9) 18 June 1959, PRO, FO 78/1450 (1859); Gilbert to Waddington (no. 5), 24 April 1879, AÉ CCC 5 Damascus. The upward climb was interspersed with lows. All production came to a standstill after the Damascus riots in the summer of 1860, but had returned to over 3,000 looms by 1862.

24. Merchants and masters cooperated to develop new fabrics, see Nu'man ibn 'Abduh al-Qasatli, *Kitab al-rawda al-ghana' fi Dimashq al-fayha* (Beirut, 1879), p. 123. In 1874 the Ottoman state repealed internal duties on raw materials and domestic manufactures passing within Ottoman territories. "Report on the Trade and Commercie of Beyrouth with a Note on the Agriculture of Central and Northern Syuria for the Year 1874," Beirut, Dec. 1874 (*Accounts and Papers* 34) Trade Reports, part 2, 368.

25. For prices of *alaja*, see Bowring, *Report*, p. 20; Lecquard to Thouvenel (6), 21 Aug. 1862, AE CCC 4 Damascus; Outrey to Comte Walenski (Comm. 9), 21 Oct. 1856, AE CCC4 Damascus. For the fall in the standard of living, compare Bowring,

Report, pp. 49, 50, with "Further Reports from Her Majesty's Diplomatic and Consular Agents Abroad Respecting the Condition of the Industrial Classes and the Purchase Power of Money in Foreign Countries, 1872," Acting Consul Jago to Earl Granville (Damascus), 20 Dec. 1871 (*Accounts and Papers* 27), vol. 62, p. 394; and "Report by Vice Consul Jago on the Trade, Commerce, and Agriculture of the Vilayet of Syria During the Year 1875," Beirut, Dec. 31, 1875 (*Accounts and Papers* 33), Trade Reports, part 4, vol. 75, p. 1015.

26. Bowing, *Report*, 20; De Ségur to Ministre des Affaires Étrangères, 20 Jan. 1850, AE CCC 3, Damascus.

27. Compare with Bowring, *Report*, 29.

28. Georges Nissan, interview, Damascus (31 Aug. 1977); Shafiq Imam, interview, Damascus (29 Aug. 1977).

29. In the Ottoman period the state lent credibility to the idea of unity between different strata of weavers by assigning the guild leaders the job of representing weavers interests in the broader society. Moshe Ma'oz, *Ottoman Reform in Syria and Palestine, 1840–1861): The Impact of the Tanzimat of Politics and Society* (Oxford, 1968).

30. Lecquard to Thouvenel (no. 6), 21 Aug. 1862, AE CCC 4, Damascus; Gilbert to Waddington (no. 5), 24 April 1879, AE CCC 5, Damascus.

31. "Report by Vice-Council Jago. . .1879"; Roustan to le Prince del la Tour d'Auvergne (no. 14), Oct. 20, 1869, AE CCC 4, Damascus.

32. "Report by Consul Skene on the Trade, Navigation, Agriculture, Manufactures, and Public Works of Northern Syria for the Year 1873," Aleppo, 31 Dec. 1872, in May 1872 "Reports from Her Majesty's Consuls on the Manufacture, Commerce &c. of Their Consular Districts," (*Accounts and Papers* 26), vol. 64, p. 571.

33. "Report by Vice-Council Jago. . .1879."

34. Qudsi, "Notice sur les Corporations," note p. 16.

35. Beinin and Lockman, *Workers on the Nile*; Goldberg, *Tinker, Tailor, and Textile Worker*; Longuenesse, "Industrialization et sa signification", _____, "Etat et syndicalisme en Syrie: discours et practiques," *Sou'al* 8 (1989): 97–130; and Feroz Ahmad's chapter in this volume.

36. See references in the preceding note.

37. Hanna expresses the majority position when he notes the decline of popular movements in Damascus after 1860 due to repression and economic decline. Abdullah Hanna, *Harakat al-'amma al-Dimashqiyya* (Beirut, 1985), pp. 279–283. Karl Marx, *The Communist Manifesto*.

38. Qudsi, "Notice sur les Corporations," p. 15.

39. *Al-'Asima* (16 June 1919), pp. 1–2. The full text of this article was translated from Arabic and provided to me by James L. Gelvin.

40. For a detailed chronology of labor movement in the Asian provinces of the Ottoman Empire, see Yavuz Selim Karakisla, "The Development and Characteristics of the Turkish Industrial Working Class. 1839–1923" (paper presented at the Institute for Social Research, Amsterdam, March 1992). This paper is scheduled to appear in *The Development and Characteristics of the Turkish Working Class, 1850–1950*, ed. Donald Quataert, scheduled for publication in 1993.

41. Donald Quataert, "Machine Breaking and the Changing Carpet Industry of Western Anatolia, 1860–1908," *Journal of Social History* 3 (1986): 473–489.

42. Gerber indicates that journeymen justified their strikes under the rubric of custom. Haim Gerber, "Guilds in Seventeenth Century Anatolian Bursa," *Asian and African Studies* 11 (1976): 68, 82.

43. Halil Inalcik, *The Ottoman Emnire: The Classical Age, 1300–1600* (New York, 1973), p. 157.

44. Membership was contingent on payment of taxes and thus restricted to master craftsmen. Gerber, "Guilds," pp. 62–63.

45. Baer, "Ottoman Guilds," p. 96.

46. Inalcik, *The Ottoman Empire*, p. 158.

47. Relationships between artisans during the Ottoman period appear to have lacked uniformity between locations at any point in time and over time. See Baer, "Ottoman Guilds."

48. Recent studies that specified artisanal relationships in specific contexts include Akarli, "The Uses of Law Among Istanbul Artisans and Tradesmen" and Haim Gerber, *Economy and Society in an Ottoman City: Bursa 1600–1700* (Jerusalem, forthcoming).

49. Beinin and Lockman, *Workers on the Nile*, p. 56.

50. Ibid., pp. 56–57.

51. Hanna expresses the majority position when he notes the decline of popular movements in Damascus after 1860 due to repression and economic decline. Abdullah Hanna, *Harakat al-'amma al-Dimashqiyya* (Beirut, 1985), pp. 279–283. So does Marx: Karl Marx, *The Communist Manifesto*. For evidence of the resiliance and viability of this sector during and after the region's encorporation into the world capitalist economy, see Goldberg, "Artisans and Craftsmen in Nineteenth Century Egypt" and Vatter, "A City Divided."

52. Sean Wilentz, *Chants Democratic: New York City and the Rise of the American Working Class* (New York, 1982). See also Eric Hobsbawm and Joan Scott, "Political Shoemakers," *Past and Present*, 89 (1989); and Paul F. Johnson, *A Shopkeeper's Millennium: Society and Revivals in Rochester, New York, 1815–1837* (New York, 1978).

53. Wilentz, ibid., p. 11.

54. Jean H. Quataert, "Workers' Reaction to Social Insurance: The Case of Homeworkers in Saxon Oberlausitz in the Late Nineteenth Century," *Internationale Wissenschaftliche Korrespondenz zur Geschichte der deutschen Arbeiterbewegung* 20 (1984): 17–35.

55. For Marx and Engels's expectations, see Marx and Engels, *Communist Manifesto.* This section of the working class remains a numerically significant social category in other dependent economies. In Mexico City, for example, such workers are on the rise as industrial capitalists attempt to reduce costs. Lourdes Beneria and Martha Roldan, *The Crossroads of Class and Gender: Industrial Homework, Subcontracting, and Household Dynamics in Mexico City* (Chicago, 1987).

56. For a rejection of the notion of a single historical trajectory and the specificity of newly industrializing societies, see Frank Perlin, "Proto-Industrialization and Pre-Colonial South Asia," *Past and Present* 98 (1983): 30–95; Charles F. Sabel, "Changing Models of Economic Efficiency and Their Implications for Industrialization in the Third World," in *Development, Democracy and the Art of Trespassing: Essays in Honor of Albert O. Hirschman,* ed. A. Foxley et. al. (Notre Dame, 1986), pp. 27–55. For evidence of the importance of outwork and small scale production in advanced capitalist societies, see Suzanne Berger and Michael J. Piore, *Dualism and Discontinuity in Industrial Societies* (Cambridge, 1980).

57. The notion that members of an organized class-conscious group necessarily hold the key to the future or will determine its shape belies the complexity of the historical process and has been criticized by "new" social historians. See Perry Anderson, "Agency," in *Arguments Within English Marxism* (London, 1980), pp. 16–58; and Pierre Bourdieu, *Outline of a Theory of Praxis,* trans. R. Nice (Cambridge, 1977); Eric Hobsbawm, *Workers: World of Labor* (New York, 1984); Perry Anderson, *Arguments Within English Marxism* (London, 1980); Jean Quataert, "An Approach To Modern Labor," *Comparative Studies in Society and History* 28 (1986): 191–216. The "new" social history approach and the debate over its usefulness has remained largely unacknowledged in the self-defined field of Middle East labor studies in spite of such studies as Borek's of contemporary Turkish women weavers employed in rural handicraft factories and Çinar's of women employed as outworkers and in retail shops in present-day Istanbul. Dellafar's study of unwaged rural Iranian women weaving for the market raises question about the relationship of the "expanded working class to non-waged workers." See Arlene Dellafar, "The Underestimation of Women's Economic Activity in Subsistence Economies," *Nimeye Digar* 5 (1987).

58. See references in note 1 of this chapter.

Donald Quataert

2

Ottoman Workers and the State, 1826–1914

During most of Ottoman history, the state dominated the Ottoman working classes in an unequal relationship that limited workers' options and the methods they could employ to achieve their ends. At certain points, however, the Ottoman working classes were more successful in obtaining their demands, or at least they had a greater potential for doing so. Wars enhanced their negotiating powers as the state relied on the guilds for logistical support. Similarly, when central authority weakened, guilds played a more important role in organizing and maintaining political life and social stability. The autonomy of workers and guilds seems to have reached a certain peak, for example, during the eighteenth and early nineteenth centuries, when unsuccessful wars raged and the central state was especially feeble. In these years, urban guilds, workers, and janissaries presented a common cause, employing uprisings and demonstrations, intimidating or toppling governments.[1] But when the janissary corps was eliminated in 1826 and state power mounted, the potential for these kinds of workers' actions became sharply curtailed. Thereafter, workers' methods to obtain sought-after goals generally were less direct; but they were not always necessarily unsuccessful.

This chapter examines Ottoman urban workers between c. 1826 and 1914. It gives disproportionate attention to the period immediately following the Young Turk Revolution of 1908 because, at this time, state power weakened briefly, a lacuna that permitted unprecedented public, visible action by the workers. The history of the Ottoman urban working class during the nineteenth century is not at all clear, even in its main lines. For example, the craft guilds sharply declined in economic importance but the significance of this development for the workers is not yet understood. During this century, urban workers, who numbered c. 250,000 in manufacturing alone, did not constitute a self-consciously organized group. These workers probably did not collectively share a sense of group consciousness.[2] But they formed a working class nonetheless: they earned their living from their labor, were identifiable to outsiders as a separate group, and as we will see, possessed and defended their own interests against encroachments from outside.

A primary goal is to illuminate the ways in which these workers presented themselves when negotiating with their employers and the Ottoman state. Before proceeding further, several caveats are in order. This study is confined primarily to workers who were both urban and organized. Thus, the rural workers are excluded, not merely those in agriculture but also the many who engaged in part- and full-time manufacturing in the countryside. These most likely numbered in the many hundreds of thousands. In addition, I have neglected those urban workers who formed neither guilds nor unions. Once again, this is a serious omission: this group was very large indeed; still worse, nonguild urban labor probably grew in importance during the nineteenth century. Also, this study stresses the actions of workers in the Ottoman capital of Istanbul (just as accounts of French workers sometimes are heavily weighted toward Paris).[3] Such omissions and emphases were hard to avoid and evolved from the sources employed here. Most of the documents presently available are government generated, from the upper echelons of the imperial administration, and concerned with the politically sensitive capital city. On matters relating to labor, these documents treat—nearly exclusively in the materials that I have consulted during my fifteen year interest in the Ottoman work force—guild organizations. Workers' groups outside the guilds are represented rarely and usually become visible only when posing some kind of security threat to the government.[4]

Unions and syndicates, for their part, have been almost totally invisible in the government documents that I have consulted; they seem to have fallen outside standard official channels of communication. The emphasis on Istanbul also derives from its role as the publishing as well as the political capital of the empire. In the brief free press era after 1908, workers organizations became visible, usually in the form of unionlike bodies, concentrated in the capital, and used local printers to publish their pamphlets, brochures, and manifestos. This capital-city bias could become less pronounced if the field of Ottoman labor history continues to mature and utilize local archival and published sources in the Ottoman provinces.[5]

Overall, we will see that workers fought a class war on two levels between 1826 and 1914. The first was on the level of language, using the language of the state and its elites to achieve goals and win victories and to protect themselves from being crushed by a state that always was more powerful. The second was on the level of direct action, violence in the workplace, a path that briefly had seemed likely to succeed between July and September 1908.

Workers Before 1908

Petitions presented to the government are the major source utilized here for understanding guild workers in the nineteenth century. The content of these petitions reveals much about how guildsmen—nineteenth century Ottoman guilds were overwhelmingly and probably exclusively male—represented their interests before government officials. Overall, the workers revealed in these documents range from proud and independent artisans to humble and demoralized suppliants. Many times the guilds appealed to tradition for protection from changes that would ruin the property of poor subjects of the empire. Commonly, the petitioners asked the state for help on the ground that their guild had worked in the craft for a long time. But, sometimes, the guildsmen requested the overthrow of tradition for their benefit, at another group's cost.

Many guilds' petitions are quite matter of fact in approaching the state for action, pointing to existing regulations and requesting official enforcement of their rights, self-assuredly and confidently using the language of the state to obtain their objectives. For example, when confronted with rising demand for their products during the early 1860s, the tinners' guild responded by expanding the number of their shops. Normally, a certificate (*gedik*) was required to have a shop, and their number was fixed by a joint guild-government decision. In 1864, however, the guild petitioned that shops in a certain (the sixth) district of the capital be allowed to operate legally without a certificate. A year later, the shops were operating, but outside the law, because the government had failed to act. So, the guild again petitioned, stating that, to protect the certified shop owners from injustice, shops without certificates should pay double the fee that certified shops paid. This would be fair, the guild concluded, to certificate holders and the arrangement would bring the treasury some revenue as well.[6] The behavior of the tinners guild, incidentally, hardly suggests an ossified corporate structure that rigidly limited production: in an expanding market, the guild was quite happy to improvise a way to get around the problem posed by the fixed number of certificates. This successful petition is *not* the appeal to existing rights that commonly appears in guild correspondence with the state. Rather, it, and many other petitions like it, requests a break, a deviation from standard practice. Therefore, this is additional evidence that the guilds were dynamic and evolving rather than stagnant and unchanging institutions.

On other occasions, the petitioners were less assured; they appealed not to rights but for merciful intervention by a paternalist state. In 1866, to take one example, the historically powerful and important Istanbul tanners' guild sought exemption from certain customs fees, imposed on hides that it imported from Egypt and America and levied again when the treated hides were reshipped to other Ottoman areas. Such practices, the guild said, were unjust (not illegal), would drive the members from their livelihoods, and should be repealed. Mixing appeals for mercy with those of state self-interest, the guild noted that favorable action would save an industry that supported many persons and provided revenue for the imperial treasury.[7] In other cases, guildsmen altogether abandoned appeals to mutual interest and simply threw themselves on the mercy of the state. In 1865, the pipestem makers' guild wrote to Istanbul municipal authorities, saying that it had fallen on hard times and the number of workshops had decreased from 180 to 30. Most guild members were old and poor and could not pay the dues that legally were owed. In its response, noting the age of the workers, the government forgave payment of the taxes.[8] During the 1840s, a long dispute split the ranks of Istanbul silk cloth makers and dyers as some sought to maintain and others wanted to remove existing restrictive practices. The petitioners requesting continuation of monopolies stressed the importance of tradition and the need to prevent the masters, journeymen, apprentices, and their families from going hungry.[9]

A rare case concerning nonguild workers recorded persons from the district of Nevşehir in central Anatolia who regularly labored in Istanbul. Most worked in the laundry business but several other occupations, such as boatmen, were included as well. In 1845, these persons banded together and collectively petitioned the state for exemption from a new income tax (*temettü vergisi*), pointing to the poor agriculture of their home districts. We are in poverty, they said, our families are poor, miserable, and perplexed.[10] Thus, they appealed for mercy, not justice. These Nevşehir migratory workers of different occupations mobilized on the basis of their common district of origin. In all of the guild examples, however, the workers mobilized on the basis of common occupation—as weavers of particular kinds of silk cloth, or as tanners or pipestem makers.

Here, it seems appropriate to raise the issue of the relationship between worker identification by occupation and that by religion-ethnicity and under what conditions the latter overrode the former. This is a favorite theme in Ottoman and Middle East history, the role of religion and ethnicity as destructive elements in the process of working-class formation. Many scholars, including the present author, correctly have pointed to the rise of intercommunal violence that started becoming prominent in the 1860s. There is no doubt that the practices of foreign merchants and the hiring policies of foreign corporations strongly influenced ethnic-religious relations. These firms routinely hired foreigners for the top jobs, foreigners and Ottoman Christians for the middle positions, and Muslims for the lower ranks.[11] In such circumstances, divisions among workers not surprisingly often assumed ethnic and religious overtones.

But many guilds' petitions are in the name of a specific mixed Muslim and non-Muslim guild (*esnaf—islâm ve reayya fukara kullarī* or the *islamiyan ve zimmiyan fukara* or the *islâm ve reayya lonca*). Guilds commonly had mixed membership, and multireligious guilds were an ordinary and commonplace part of the nineteenth century economic scenery in Ottoman cities. In 1838, for example, fully 50 percent of some sixty-eight enumerated Istanbul guilds, possessing 28,000 workers, contained both Muslim and non-Muslim workers.[12] As a corollary, workers of different religions who labored together also mobilized to obtain redress of grievances.[13]

There are, however, many instances in which members of multireligious guilds temporarily left this ecumenical shelter to mobilize on religious lines. Let me offer three examples, the first an 1860 petition from an Istanbul grocers' guild. The petition, concerning changing coal prices, came from a normally religiously mixed group and contained over 100 signatures. Every signature or seal was from a non-Muslim.[14] Second, in 1846, the Greek patriarch and the Christian merchants in the city of Aleppo mobilized to request reduced taxes on various textiles so that local industry could better compete with foreign goods. The petitioners cast themselves as representatives of the people (*abali*) of

Aleppo and sought aid to protect workers' families and children and to provide funds for the public treasury.[15] Third, twenty years later, in 1866, the Aleppo textile industry sent another petition, this one containing thirty-nine seals (*mühürs*). In this case, however, the petitioners were all Muslims (except for one European) and there were no signatories from the non-Muslim community. Like their Christian predecessors in 1846, the petitioners spoke on behalf of a larger constituency, in this case the Muslims of Aleppo, and requested a reduction in customs duties.[16] At this point in the research, we do not know if such petitions by religious group are a nineteenth century innovation or part of a long-standing pattern. But, in these examples, we clearly are in the presence of porous boundaries between identification by religion and occupation, where primacy changes according to the particular circumstance.

Many, likely most, of the unions that came into existence after 1908 were multiethnic and multireligious. An important example is the Salonica tobacco workers' union, which had two branches in Salonica, one at Gevgeli, and one at Kukus with a total membership of 3,200. Of the members, 63 were Jewish and Greeks, Muslims, and Bulgarians formed the balance; among them, apparently, there were no visible ethnic tensions.[17] There is another interesting example, of two ethnically homogenous unions merging to form a single, heterogenous organization. Originally, one union for Muslim commercial employees had been founded in the Muslim section of Istanbul and a second one in the Christian section. Each had met separately, and both had elected assemblies. After perhaps a month, they united, with a new set of regulations, and to explain the new situation, a meeting was planned for Muslim employees only, in the Muslim quarter.[18]

It might be that we have been overstating the case for communal violence by too uncritically adopting the view of the European consuls and other Western observers who saw Turkish-Armenian or Muslim-Christian hostility behind every olive tree. We need to recall the instances of intercommunal economic cooperation, such as those just seen. We also must remember that when European contemporaries saw religious fanaticism, there often actually was mobilization and self-interested actions by workers. To explore this problem, let me offer an extended example from the early 1860s, when the British consul at Bursa in western Anatolia reported the destruction of an Armenian-owned silk factory in this famed silk production center. The town had just experienced a boom in silk factory building, followed by a sharp short-term

downswing in the business cycle. A "numerous mob. . . met in the Grand
Mosque, excited by some fanatics among the ulema, softas or sheikhs,
and after some pourparlers with the authorities who requested them
to disperse," marched to the mill, pulled it down, and "next set fire to
the mass of leveled ruins." Throughout the report, the British consul
continuously referred to Muslim fanaticism, stirred up by construction
of the mill over a former Muslim cemetery, as the cause of the violence.
Muslim sensibilities about cemeteries explicitly were offered as the
explanation and the actors are identified by religious categories. But in
the final lines of the report, the consul accidentally offers a different
view of the affair. *All* (my stress) the silk mills of Bursa, he says, would
be imperiled if decisive measures were not taken by the authorities. It
was not the presence of the cemetery but of a downswing bringing low
wages and unemployment that impelled a riot.[19] Therefore the actors
here were not fanatics but workers who used the political language of
Islam to defend their economic interests.

Workers After 1908

The Young Turk Revolution of 1908 has a double significance for
the Ottoman labor historian. First, the ensuing freedom of the press
affords details on workers' processions, petitions, and perspectives that
simply are not found in the official documents presently available for
the pre-1908 era. For a time, the newspapers published announcements
of workers' organizational meetings as well as demonstrations and protests.
These accounts are welcome but they do reflect the interests of
newspaper editors that were, it can be assumed, different from those
of the workers. Newspapers offering a perspective closer to that of
workers did not appear until several years later.[20] By then, antistrike
legislation had been passed, and the atmosphere was very different from
the heady days of the autumn of 1908, when a new era really seemed
to be at hand. This brings us to the second significance of July 1908.
Ottoman (and foreign) workers had taken the revolutionary slogan at
its word and assumed that "liberty" included the right to organize and
to strike. Therefore, in the months following the July 1908 coup, scores
of unions and syndicates appeared, and many struck. By one count,
there were 104 strikes in 1908 alone.[21] By early twentieth century Middle
East standards, this figure is impressive, particularly when you consider

that the strikes began only in late July, after the Revolution had been achieved.[22] Primarily propelled by demands for higher wages,[23] these strikes sometimes were quite violent and literally terrified the regime.

Ottoman worker unrest had been building for some time. An 1889 law had expressly forbidden the formation of workers' associations, meaning Western-style unions and syndicates, anywhere in the empire. Passage of the law demonstrates government unease with such new and unfamiliar forms of labor organization that were emerging in the late nineteenth century era of direct foreign investment. Thus blocked, some workers formed mutual aid societies, for example, coal miners at Eregli on the Black Sea coast, workers for the Istanbul ferryboat company (Şirketi Hayriye), as well as workers at the state-run Feshane and Hereke textile factories. Similarly, workers and employees of the vast Anatolian Railway Company established a mutual aid society in 1895. In July 1907, they pressed for wage increases. The late December 1907 formation of a pension fund for company officials, which excluded daily wage workers, suggests growing agitation as well as divisions within the work force.[24]

When Ottoman workers struck in the months following the July revolution, they usually obtained a good part of the demanded wage increases. In confronting the companies, the workers often sought the mediation of members of the revolutionary Committee of Union and Progress and of various government officials. Two unionists, Ali Riza Tevfik Bey and Selim Sirri Bey, were quite busy in this period, serving as mediators between many different groups of workers and company managements.[25] As a French-language paper approvingly noted: "The workers have confidence in this friend of the people [Ali Riza Tevfik Bey]."[26] The role of these mediators deserves to be stressed here. All were comparatively well educated and from different social strata than the average Ottoman workers. But they publicly concurred in the workers' belief that wages *had been* too low and ought to be increased, a sentiment shared by the spokesman of the French Chamber of Commerce in Istanbul and dominant elements of the government. At this point, let me put forward two explanations as to why workers and elites agreed that wages were too low. In the first (for reasons discussed in the conclusion later), state representatives, the foreign merchant community, and the workers possessed a common understanding of what was fair and just. In the second explanation, the state and its agents are seen as seeking to impede workers' mobilization with a series of timely concessions designed to placate the bulk of the workers and isolate those pushing for radical change.[27]

Ottoman Workers in 1908: Images from Above

The Istanbul press greeted the 1908 strikes with responses that ranged from paternalist disapproval to panic and hysteria, growing from a conviction that they were witnessing days of anarchy and the impending collapse of organized society. The Ottoman-language paper *Sabah*, in mid-August 1908, complained that workers were insufficiently organized and seemed unable to appoint delegates to negotiate with managers and owners. Because there were no representatives, negotiations were impossible. The editors continued the lecture, opining that the ability to compete internationally was tied to the cheapness of wages and availability of capital. Because the Ottoman Empire lacked capital, local entrepreneurs paid higher interest rates than in Europe. High tariffs further raised costs. If, *Sabah* concluded, strikes increased workers' wages, there would be little difference between Ottoman and Western wages, and it would be impossible for Ottoman industry to compete.[28]

In late August, the owner-editor of the French-language *Stamboul* cautioned the workers against overzealousness in the new age of liberty. "Now is the time for everyone to work together in this grand endeavor; this is not the time to substitute class struggles for racial or religious wars. The workers know that the new regime favors them. But they shouldn't chase chimeras. It would be dangerous—it would be impossible—to destroy the social hierarchy."[29]

By September, as the strike wave continued to mount, some of the foreign-language press in the capital began referring to an "Ottoman proletariat" that had the right to strike but not the right to prevent others from working.[30] In mid-month, when workers of several railway companies struck, they seem to have stirred up memories among some foreign-language journalists of the Reign of Terror, or the July Days of 1848, or perhaps of the Paris Commune. "It had to happen. Anarchy from below had to succeed anarchy from above. We have a workers question. . . . For twenty-four hours, we have been menaced by a class war."[31]

The published memoirs of an Ottoman official afford another view from above. Mehmet Ali Ayni Bey was the chief administrative officer of a district in which important mines were located. At end of August 1908, Mehmet Ali Ayni writes, he was ordered to the mines to restore order. The mine workers had menaced the foreign engineers and left work, demanding that the company director increase wages. Mehmet

Ali Ayni arrived in the area and was met on the road by several thousand workers, led by a Kurd named Mevlud. Learning of his journey, the workers had rented a house for this state official and even had decorated its rooms with furniture, rugs, and flowers! He met with the mine officials who accepted his recommendation to increase wages. Then Mehmet Ali Ayni met with Mevlud and the other ringleaders, and as they had coffee and tea together, he spoke of freedom, justice and equality. Mevlud and his friends agreed to return to work the next day.[32]

Can we believe this account, which was published in 1945, deep in the republican era of modern Turkey when labor and labor organizations were under very tight state control? Probably yes, although Mehmet Ali Ayni himself was a part of the republican Turkish elite that repressed workers. It is also likely that his memoirs record how he wished his readers to remember worker-state relations. Nonetheless, his account of workers' dependence on government officials for assistance fits very well with the contemporary newspaper accounts we have seen of Young Turk mediation efforts and with many guild petitions to the state.

Thus, there seem to be two distinct views from above. For some members of the foreign press in Istanbul, Ottoman workers had emerging class interests distinct from and threatening to the ruling strata. But for some in the Ottoman press and among the Young Turks, the view from above insisted that the state and the workers were cooperating to maintain equity and harmony.

The Voices and Self-Representations of Ottoman Workers in 1908

There certainly was no lack of worker violence in the postrevolutionary days. In a strike on the Aydin railway, there were open clashes between the military and workers and, in one exchange, a worker was killed and several wounded.[33] In strikes at the Eregli coal mines, workers destroyed several locomotives that hauled the coal, and somewhat later, striking miners wounded a foreign strike breaker.[34]

But if some used violence, other workers presented themselves quite differently. On July 27, 1908, for example, a large procession was held in which some workers participated. The procession overall was led by two orchestras that alternately played the Hamidiye, the anthem of Sultan Abdul Hamid II. In the parade were cadets of the Naval School and students of the Admiralty Practical School; but there also were workers

from the Arsenal and from the tobacco monopoly factory. Together, the groups, numbering some 5,000 persons—students and workers alike and all carrying Ottoman flags—marched to the Sublime Porte and the Ministry of War. Included were female workers from the tobacco factory, who participated in this demonstration at a distance, following the parade in carriages. In response to the procession, the sultan sent his thanks.[35]

There are photographs of striking railroad workers that show Ottoman labor in a similarly conciliatory light. As they halted a train near Aleppo, the strikers, for the camera, pointedly displayed the Ottoman flag, thus assuring all of their patriotism and commitment to the new constitutional regime.[36] About a month before this event, pharmacists had met in Istanbul to form the Ottoman Pharmaceutical Union. At their meeting, they first pledged allegiance to the Constitution. A band, provided by the Ministry of Marine(!), then opened with the Hamidiye March and, for good measure, played the hymn of liberty. Having established their patriotism beyond question, they opened the meeting and formed the new society.[37] In a like manner, during August 1908, some 2,000 workers and officials at the fez factory took oaths of loyalty in the presence of a member of the Committee of Union and Progress.[38] The nascent union of the Anatolian Railway workers and employees spoke loyally and reassuringly of the Ottoman nation (*millet-i osmaniye*). But, in the same breath, it informed the government of its intent to organize the union not only in the big cities of Istanbul, Bursa, and Salonica, but everywhere in the empire. (This is the only reference found so far that shows workers aiming at empirewide rather than geographically circumscribed organizations.) The implied threat of such an organization seems clear enough.[39] Railway workers' actions certainly provoked quick responses from the capital and the state. The government passed its first antistrike legislation immediately after the great Anatolian Railway strike of 14–16 September 1908.

Two comparatively extensive documents give intimate self-portraits of Ottoman workers during the fall of 1908. The first is a pamphlet published by the union of workers and employees of the Anatolian and Baghdad Railway Companies. The pamphlet was written in French and published in the European quarter of Istanbul. The second is a 1911 book indicting the administration of the Anatolian and Baghdad Railway Companies, written by A. Gabriel, former president of the union of company workers and employees.[40]

The published union pamphlet records a long list of demands put forward by the employees and workers of the Anatolian and Baghdad

Railway Companies; these included recognition of their union, wage and salary increases, bonuses, protection for sick workers, and double pay for night work.[41] But the focus of attention, at least that of the union leaders, shifted, beginning with a 17 August 1908 petition of 450 signatures[42] and continuing at a 22 August 1908 meeting in a theater near the Haydar Pasha station at the head of the line. Putting aside their other demands, the leader insisted on the immediate dismissal of the company director, Edouard Huguenin. A subsequent and third general meeting of the new union was held due to the "increasingly aggressive and intransigent attitude" of Huguenin, and sought member support to demand his removal. The leaders spoke of "deplorable, despotic, tyrannical, humiliating and arbitrary conduct," a nineteen-year-long reign of terror and tyranny. They first had appealed to the company as early as July 1907, because of the increasing cost of living, and had asked for consideration. But Huguenin, they said, "has never deigned to listen to the cries of famine and has always remained deaf to all our prayers."

Because their earlier appeal had "struck against a heart of bronze," the personnel had formed the union. Their goal was "not of disturbing work, order and discipline, but of appealing for justice and requesting an end to our suffering..." The provisional union committee that had been formed, they said, had managed to prevent a strike until now but workers' "suffering has reached the limits of its endurance." Therefore, the leadership put aside the other grievances and sent telegrams to the grand vizier, the Unionists, and the German ambassador, as well as to the Deutsche Bank administration in Berlin, demanding the dismissal of Huguenin as the sole means of obtaining calm.

In response, a government representative stated that the Ottoman Constitution guaranteed the right of liberty, on the sole condition that it not encroach on the rights of others. It was legal to protest and demand improvements, he said, but the union had no right to ask for a change of director. That was the business of the company and the Ottoman government. And, he closed, be patient, the company has promised favorable action on the wages issue.

The union provisional committee responded with its own barrage of legalese: as a legal body, it said, it had the right to demand that the company board of directors fire Huguenin. If it did not, the union would call a extraordinary meeting of the shareholders to demand the dismissal both of Huguenin and the Council of Administration.

> The government must know that it is with great patriotic sentiment that we appreciate well how a railroad is an indispensable tool for the country,

especially in the present conditions. . . . The government must also know that we consider as sacred the property of all capitalists, Ottoman or non-Ottoman, it can be assured that not one atom of this property will be lost.

Before striking, the union leaders promised, they would explore every single legal avenue.

For these reasons, we did not take any action against the law, good breeding, or public security and tranquillity at the moment when M. Huguenin took his post. . . . Huguenin effendi enjoys individual liberty as we all do. . . . Huguenin effendi has added a last act to all his infamous deeds. He has styled our association and the personnel who comprise it revolutionaries and anarchists. He has told the government that the Haydar Pasha station is being transformed into a river of blood.[43]

Thus, the pamphlet shows the workers adroitly protecting themselves through a very careful use of accepted vocabulary regarding patriotism, capitalism, security, and appeals for equity. On the one hand, they clearly informed the government that *they* knew how easily the railroad could be shut down and that its operations were at their mercy. On the other hand, having made their point, the workers quickly moved to reduce the chances of military repression by offering assurances of their loyalty and moderation.

The book by A. Gabriel is a remarkable document, the only one of its kind that I have found. Published in 1911, it was part of a more widespread attack then taking place against foreign corporations, their autonomy within the Ottoman economy, and their infringements on Ottoman sovereignty.[44]

When he wrote the book, Gabriel was "ex-medecin du chemin de fer ottoman d'Anatolie" and former "president de l'Association fraternelle du personnel de ce chemin de fer." He had been president for more than two years (and may well have authored the 1908 union pamphlet cited previously) and had been a physician for the railroad for sixteen years. The company, he said, had tried both intimidation and cooptation to keep him silent about unconstitutional abuses; when these failed, they fired him. He published the book with three stated goals: first, to bring about state intervention against the company directors; second, to prove to the general public and the commercial sector that the company was protecting its own interests at public cost; and finally, to reveal to the Berlin administration of the railroad and the

German government itself that the Istanbul-based board was besmirching Germany's reputation.[45] Thus, in addition to seeking to bring domestic pressure on the Istanbul administration of the railroad, he also was attempting to embarrass the Berlin government into forcing corporate changes more favorable to workers, such as those that social democracy (in its compromise with Bismarck) had provided to German labor.

In the book, company director Huguenin stands out as evil incarnate, a man who had failed to live up to the responsibilities of his office. For Gabriel, company directors as a class were not the enemy, but directors as individuals were. Thus, the first Anatolian Railway Company director, Kuhlmann, had been bad. (Kuhlmann has some notoriety in Ottoman labor history for stating that Ottoman workers did not require high wages because they could get along on a few morsels of bread and some dried olives.) His successors Zander and Helferrich were good men but had failed to see that under their administrations Huguenin, who was hired in 1890, all the while had been amassing power from his lower ranking position. To bring down this tyrant, Gabriel collected a dossier that showed "one of the most cruel, inhuman, arbitrary" regimes imaginable.[46]

In the book, Gabriel keeps blaming personal avarice or greed, never stating that it was the nature of the company and of capitalism to seek profits and keep wages down. Take, for example, his exposition of an 1899 company decision to pay an hourly rather than daily wage and to obtain the hourly rate by dividing the daily wage by eleven. He attributes this to the personal qualities of Huguenin just as he blames the individual cruelty of a particular German section head for the practice of docking a worker a full hour's pay for being two minutes late.[47] In print, Huguenin was this physician's heart of darkness. He is outraged that Huguenin and other directors gave free rail passes to their close friends and family and that the director had special trains for his own use and that his of family, not to mention the special pastry shops for high-ranking officials. While this is going on, he points out, the company offhandedly dismissed a twenty-year employee with a large family, because the man had sent union correspondence over the rails without paying the necessary fee.[48] For years, Gabriel asserts, Huguenin amassed power, hiring and promoting fellow Swiss, carefully grooming and protecting the forward progress of each one. He claimed that 90 percent of all top company functionaries were countrymen of the director. Huguenin hired his own father-in-law as a section head and tripled his salary in sixteen years. Corruption was everywhere; one section head hired by Huguenin was a deserter from German military service. Almost all section heads were corrupt or incompetent or both.

The wage scales were similarly unjust. Swiss railway workers were paid more than workers on the Anatolian line and worse, the former were paid monthly while the latter received hourly wages.[49] "In Switzerland, the state gives to the great, to the directors, enough according to their social station and to live in comfort, but it never forgets the weak (*les petits*)."[50] That is, those in power have an obligation to those under them; in Switzerland but not the Ottoman Empire elites remembered this obligation.

To bring about Ottoman state intervention, Gabriel gives many examples to prove that the company was cheating the government. He displays patriotic anger when revealing the details of how the company repeatedly and illegally changed regulations to enhance profits at state expense.[51] (In these arguments, we can hear clear echoes of the guilds' assertions that measures beneficial to them also would provide increased revenues for the treasury.)[52] Gabriel urged the state to greater vigilance in overseeing fulfillment of the concession agreements and stated that the Ministry of Public Works had been totally inept in policing the company.[53]

A resident and subject of a state encrusted by overlegislation and government control, Gabriel insisted on legality. He emphasized the legal obligations of the company and the right of the state to enforce the agreed-upon provisions. He leaves the impression that hiring so many foreigners was reprehensible mainly because it was illegal. Here, he appears as particularly skilled in engaging in the discourse of the official Ottoman world. In his arguments, the labor organization's right to exist did not rest on any a priori ground but rather because it satisfied the state's definitional requirements. Thus, he did not challenge passage of the antistrike law, but instead helped the union to reorganize itself and obtain legal recognition as an association.[54]

Conclusion

On one level, Gabriel's obsession with Huguenin illustrates the tendency among workers and Ottoman society in general to hold those in power personally accountable. Thus, the janissaries had demonstrated before the sultan or government ministers for redress of injustices, demanding the head or the resignation of individuals seen as responsible. Other examples illustrate this point. Hungry bread rioters in Sivas, in

June 1908, sought to lynch the mayor and, when he escaped, they torched his home.[55] In 1903, mutinous troops angry over unpaid salaries beat up the Army commander whom they held responsible.[56] Ottoman workers demanded fairness from their supervisors and held them responsible when affairs went awry. Hence the demands for Huguenin's dismissal and, similarly, for example, the successful efforts of striking Istanbul tramway workers, in 1908, to obtain higher wages as well as the dismissal of the company director.[57]

Thus, there are strong elements of continuity in the ways that workers in guilds during the nineteenth century and those in unions after 1908 represented their interests before the state. The railway union's "prayers" for relief from "suffering" are the pleas of the "poor" and "old" pipestem makers and other guild workers whom life had "utterly destroyed" and who appealed to the authorities for aid. We see similar behavior in a letter that a group of Armenian silk workers sent, in 1910, to an Ottoman socialist newspaper, İştirak. The letter described their working conditions in terms that mixed working-class consciousness with appeals for mercy. Written in Armenian and translated into Ottoman, the letter purported to represent 5,000 female workers in the silk mills at Bursa, in western Anatolia. It began with the now-familiar wails of woe. "We are poor unfortunate women totally separated from the attentions of humanity and have fallen into poverty. . . . No one pities us in our condition. We find pity in no one's heart." They next presented a long list of grievances including poor pay, no rest periods, sexual abuse, physical abuse, terrible working conditions, and very long working hours. The letter then shifts gears, moves away from appeals for pity, and concludes with a demand for justice that recalls guilds' self-confident approaches to state authorities. "Thus, all of us, Turk, Greek, Armenian and Jewish workers want an end to such conditions, we want an end to the practice of night work, this is our right."[58]

Over the course of the nineteenth century, Ottoman workers were confronting a very powerful state with a mounting record of success against domestic challenges to its authority. The state had eliminated the janissary protectors of the urban workers, it had coopted much of the ulema religious classes, curbed the power of local notables, and crushed most of the tribes; hence the nineteenth century guilds' circumspection in approaching the state and the careful manner in which they presented entreaties. Sometimes they spoke to the state's economic self-interest and often they blended appeals based on the government's sense of justice with those based on pity and mercy. The Young Turk Revolution seemed to workers (and many others) to be a chance to redress the internal balance of forces in favor of those outside the state structure. The achievement of economic goals and even of corporate autonomy and power via the unions seemed to be within grasp. Many workers in the immediate postrevolutionary period continued to use the old successful methods of representing their interests by using the language of the state; hence the patriotic speeches and demonstrations. But some other workers during the July–September days of 1908 went further. The powerful railroad workers sprinkled protestations of loyalty and moderation among guarded warnings of their ability to disrupt. And some workers, believing that state repression would be withheld in the new age, turned to force and militantly confronted the government in pitched battles. But they were mistaken; gunboats, battalions and antistrike laws crushed these strikers, curbed their paths of action, and reasserted the domination of the state.

Gabriel's fascinating book was written after this repression, which made clear the dangers of directly confronting the state. He is struggling to use language to protect what he can of labor's interests. He does this by seeking to divide the foes of the Ottoman working class. In attacking Huguenin personally and inviting his dismissal by the Istanbul board, the Berlin administration, and the German government, he is attempting to divide foreign capital against itself. In demonstrating company violations of the concession, he is seeking to separate the interests of the Ottoman government and foreign capital and set one against the other. And, in this struggle, he offers Ottoman labor as an ally.

Notes

1. See, for example, Robert W. Olson, "The Esnaf and the Patrona Halil Rebellion of 1730: A Realignment in Ottoman Politics?" *Journal of the Economic and Social History of the Orient* 17 (1974): 329–344; and his "Jews, Janissaries, Esnaf and the Revolt of 1740 in Istanbul: Social Upheaval and Political Realignment in the Ottoman Empire," *Journal of the Economic and Social History of the Orient* 20 (1977): 185–207.

2. Paul Dumont, "À propos de la 'class ouvrière' ottomane à la veille de la revolution jeune turque," *Turcica* (1977). Also see the valuable Mete Tunçay, *Türkiye'de sol akīmlar 1908–1925*, 2d ed. (Ankara, 1967).

3. William Sewell, *Work and Revolution in France* (Cambridge, 1980).

4. But there are many classifications in the Başbakanlĭk Arşivi (Prime Ministry Archives), hereafter BBA, that have not been exploited systematically. These include Babī Âlī Evrak Odasī, Dahiliye, and Zaptiye classifications, that cover the periods, c. 1890–1914. All subsequent archival references are from the Prime Ministry Archives.

5. The kadi court records (*şeriye sicilleri*) hold much promise for breaking this bias. For a fuller treatment of the sources for Ottoman labor history, see my "Labor and Working Class History during the Late Ottoman Period, c. 1800–1914," Turkish Studies Association *Bulletin* (September 1991): 357–369.

6. BAA I MV 24162 with many enclosures from 1282/1865.

7. BBA I MV 25171, 12 ca 1283/1866.

8. BBA I MV 24072, 5 ra 1282/1865.

9. BBA I MV 505, 8 L 1257/1841.

10. BBA I MV 1289, 25 Ş 1261/1845.

11. Donald Quataert, "Employment Policies of the Ottoman Public Debt Administration, 1881–1909," in *Wiener Zeitscrift für die Kunde des Morgenlandes* 76 (1986): 233–237.

12. An 1887 enumeration listed 287 guilds in the Istanbul area, listing the names and taxes due from the usta's, Kalfa's, and cirak's in each one. BBA, I MM 4031, 12 cr 1304/March 1887.

13. Ebuzziya Tevfik, *Yeni Osmanlīlar Tarihi*, vol. 3 (Istanbul, 1974), pp. 495–501, for details of an 1873 cross-religious labor action.

14. BBA I MV 19045, 17 XI 1276/1860.

15. BBA Cev Ikt 2024, 11 L 1262/1846.

16. BBA I MV 25281, 22 ca 1283/1866.

17. Stefan Velikov, "Sur le mouvement ouvrier et socialiste en Turquie après la Révolution Jeune-Turque de 1908," *Études Balkaniques* 1 (1964): 29–48.

18. *Ikdam*, 2 September 1908.

19. Great Britain, Foreign Office 195, reports of Consul Sandison from Bursa.

20. See Tunçay, *Türkiye'de sol akĭmlar* for details.

21. Şehmus Güzel, "Faire la greve en Turquie," in A. Gökalp, ed., *La Turquie en Transition* (Paris, 1986), p. 219.

22. When the strikes erupted, the Ottoman-language press routinely referred to them as *tatil-i eşgal* and sometimes the French *greve*. Neither term appears in the standard Ottoman lexicography, published by Redhouse in 1890 and reprinted in 1926, which defines only the word *tatil*. The relevant definitions offered therein are "1. A making or letting be temporarily unemployed. 2. A making or letting work or duty be temporarily suspended; hence, a vacation" (p. 563).

23. Elsewhere, I have noted the economic crisis and rising food prices preceding the July revolution and the objective of most strikers to obtain higher wages in compensation. Donald Quataert, "The Economic Climate of the 'Young Turk Revolution' in 1908," *Journal of Modern History* (1979): D1147ff.

24. Oya Sencer, *Türkiye'de işçi sınıfı* (Istanbul, 1969), p. 160; Anatolian Railway Company Annual Report for 1907.

25. For details on their lives see, Selim Sirri (Tarcan), "Hâtıralarım" in *Canlı Tarihler*, vol. 4 (Istanbul, 1946) and Münise Basıkoğlu, "Babam Riza Tevfik," *Tarih ve Toplum*, No. 57-63. My thanks to Y. S. Karakışla for these references.

26. *Stamboul*, cover story by Regis Delbeuf, 15 August 1908.

27. See Donald Quataert, *Social Disintegration and Popular Resistance in the Ottoman Empire, 1882-1908* (New York, 1983) for a fuller discussion.

28. *Sabah*, 18 Recep 1326/15 August 1908, signed by Aşıkizade Halīt Ziya.

29. *Stamboul*, 29 August 1908, signed by Regis Delbeuf.

30. *La Revue commerciale du Levant*, editorial of September 1900, "Les erreurs du proletariat ottoman," pp. 408–411. The stress is mine. This journal was the organ of the French Chamber of Commerce in Istanbul.

31. *Stamboul*, 15 September 1908.

32. Mehmet Ali Ayni, *Canlı Tarihler*, vol. 2 (Istanbul, 1945), pp. 59-61. The agreement then broke down because of a foul-up within the Committee of Union and Progress. Also, see Sencer, *Türkiye'de işçi sınıfı*, p. 194.

33. Ibid., pp. 192–193, dates of 1 and 5 October 1908.

34. Quataert, *Social Disintegration*, pp. 64–65 and 75, for details on Kurdish workers assaults on foreign workers.

35. *Stamboul*, 28 July 1908.

36. *L' Illustration*, Samedi, 17 October 1908.

37. *Stamboul*, 22 August 1908.

38. *Ikdam*, various issues. This group seems to have formed when the "imprimeurs" of Istanbul met in the hail of the Societé St. Blaise at Pera. Formation of syndicate of "typographes" and "lythographes d'imprimerie" of Istanbul also included a 200 member meeting in the hall of the Societa Operaia Italiana.
The president of the Ottoman Typesetters Association (*Mürettebin Osmaniye Cemiyeti*) at about this time filed a public notice that typesetters wishing to change jobs first had to obtain association permission.

39. *Ikdam*, 5 September 1908.

40. *Compte-Rendu de la 3mé Assemblée Generale du 27 Août 1908* of the Union des Employees du chemin de fer Ott. d'Anatolie (Constantinople, Galata, 1908). A. Gabriel,

Les dessous de l'administration des chemins de fer Ottoman d'Anatolie et de Baghdad (Constantinople, 1911). There is an Ottoman Turkish version of the latter that I have not had the opportunity to consult.

41. Also see Gabriel, ibid., pp. 183–188.

42. Ibid., pp. 159–162, is the source for the petition. Otherwise, see the union pamphlet cited in note 41.

43. In closing, the leadership thanked to the newspapers *Yeni Gazetta, la Patris, la Turquie, and Nea Ephimeris* for their support. Also the *Manzume-i Efkâr* for first bringing their grievances to the public. Signed by the committee of the union at Haydarpasha 31 August 1908.

44. Gabriel quotes 1910 statements made in the Ottoman Parliament as well as in the *Jeune Turc* newspaper that support his efforts and those of the railway union, by then called an association in conformity with the antilabor legislation of 1909.

45. Gabriel, *Les dessous,* pp. ii–v.

46. Ibid., p. 151.

47. Ibid., pp. 110, 114.

48. Ibid., pp. 32–37 151. Elsewhere, Gabriel lets it slip that the worker in question was the vice-president of the association-union, Yashar Mehmet Effendi, most probably a Muslim. Gabriel describes him as a twenty-year *chef de train,* fired without cause when he sent a union letter without paying for it. Ibid., p. 168.

49. Ibid., pp. 134–137.

50. Ibid., p. 137.

51. Ibid., pp. 65–68, 74.

52. Ibid., pp. 96, 146.

53. Ibid., p. 175.

54. Ibid., pp. 168–169. In 1910, the Council of State (*Şurayī Devlet*) formally recognized the employee-worker group as an association but Huguenin, according to Gabriel, falsely was accusing the association's leadership of running a syndicate. This matter, Gabriel said, was before a court of appeal, and he was confident there would be a favorable judgement.

55. *Atatürk Ansiklopedesi,* vol. 1 (Istanbul, 1973), pp. 404–405.

56. Ibid., vol. 1, p. 397.

57. *Tanin* 14, 1 Ağustos 1324/14 August 1908, 3.

58. *İştirak* 2, 20 Şubat 1325/5 March 1910.

Kristin Koptiuch

3

Other Workers: A Critical Reading of Representations of Egyptian Petty Commodity Production at the Turn of the Twentieth Century

At the turn of the twentieth century, representations of petty commodity production figured prominently in the political discourses of colonialism and nationalism in Egypt. Yet retrospective historical narratives of the formation of Egypt's working class during that period accord scant importance to these forms of production and to artisans' contributions to the politics of class and nation in Egypt. In this chapter, I draw both on revisionist Marxist theories of the articulation of modes of production/reproduction across a global division of labor and on feminist reappraisals of women's "unproductive" domestic labor under capitalism to critique the classical Marxist privileging of modern industrial wage workers as the chief historical agents of insurgent resistance to colonialist and capitalist exploitation. Such privileging, I argue, is a discursive "way of seeing" that underwrites the predominant scholarship on the social history of "the" Egyptian working class and is not contingent on the (admittedly sparse) availability of historical source materials about other kinds of laborers and other cultural consciousnesses. I draw on feminist deconstructive and postcolonial criticism to address questions of representation and power that undergird such exclusionary strategies of power-knowledge production. Attending to the contesting ways in which Egypt's artisanry is "figured" in turn-of-the-century discourses alerts us to both the critical importance of petty commodity production and the performative power of discourse.

My interest in this chapter is less in a retrieval of a more authentic, truer history of petty commodity production that can be disentangled from an historical collusion between orientalist scholarship and colonialist technologies than in displaying its implications for the present context of Egypt's newly defined place in transnational political economy and culture. The reinscription of artisanry as "informal sector" in discourses of state and international development since the 1970s alerts us to problematics similar to those encountered in the earlier moment in Egypt's history explored here.

Problematizing Persistence

My own ethnographic fieldwork, undertaken in 1980 in Cairo and Qina, Egypt, focused on the pottery industry, a craft that long preceded Egypt's integration into the capitalist world market and continues to enjoy a viable, though reduced, market for its utilitarian water jars and other assorted pots. Pottery is a prime artifact of the past, our sole text for many extinct cultures. It may be one of the first items to approach commodity status in prehistory, and one of the first artisanal specializations to develop following sedentarization and agricultural production. Its status at one time was certainly anything but petty. But, in the scope of a broader argument,[1] pottery must be set in the context of the wide range of small-scale, labor-intensive enterprises that provide the bulk of the subsistence consumer goods and employment for most of Egypt's urban population. Other examples of the quotidian commodities with which I am concerned here include clothing, shoes, food, furniture, metal products, repairs, housing construction, and transportation. Although some of these trades have an ancient and still vital history, many of these enterprises were established relatively recently, some making use of recycled modern industrial products as raw materials (e.g., Gamaliyya aluminum products[2]), and others are articulated more or less directly with the transnational capitalist economy. A few local manufacturers even produced imitations of the imported European-brand goods coveted by many Egyptians because of their novelty status prior to the era of Open Door economic liberalization.[3] Yet whether ancient or wholly novel, most of these enterprises assume a stubbornly persistent, sweatshop-style, petty commodity form of production that typically involves work relations, familial idioms, and cultural practices that evoke images of premodern times.

As the contemporary configuration of Egypt's political economy attests, it has by now become well established that petty commodity production—in its peasant or craft forms—did not disappear in the course of capitalist development in world regions under Europe's imperial umbrella, regions that came to be known as the *Third World*. Recent studies of petty commodity production, particularly in Third World urban centers, have shown that petty service, craft, and small-scale entrepreneurial activities have tended to persist and even proliferate rather than disappear. This history calls into question Marx's nineteenth century evolutionist equation for capital as defined by generalized commodity production and wage relations and challenges dominant strands of Marxism that envisaged capitalist development as a linear, rational systems process reprising Europe's path.[4] In its history of expansion, capitalist relations of production have not always and everywhere required the destruction or elimination of preceding modes of production, especially the social relations of exploitation that characterized these modes of production. To the contrary, at historic conjunctures of major transformation, capitalist regimes of accumulation often retained and reinforced these same relations of exploitation, in part because new, world-changing regimes profited from the provisioning of goods and laborers from earlier forms of production. "Modes of production" theorists have argued that the preservation of artisanal manufacturing or peasant agricultural relations, where labor was often unwaged (e.g., "family" labor), made possible the reproduction of cheap labor power utilized by nearby capitalist-intensive enterprises (and beyond, as European industry later benefited from Third World migrant labor). These conditions in turn sustained a global restructuring of regimes of capital accumulation, among whose effects was the "unequal development" of Third World regions as compared to the West.[5]

Clearly then, any notion of "preservation" of petty commodity productive forms must be qualified, for in their encounter with modern monopoly capitalism, traditional forms were "preserved" in a rather precise way: preserved through their subsumption to the exigencies of capital accumulation and deprived of autonomous means of social reproduction.[6] In effect, they were *paradoxically preserved* through destruction. In other words, in their articulation with capitalism, originary forms of petty commodity production became something other, a change perceptible less in their intrinsic *form* and organization than in the historical effects of their new *relation* to national and global divisions of labor and capital. At the same time, colonial or indigenous capitalism too was profoundly transformed by its sometimes violent articulation with and exploitative subsumption of other productive forms. Modern capitalism was restructured by the exigencies of its own conditions of reproduction, which thereafter would include the social and productive forms it incorporated and harbored via paradoxical preservation.

Feminist research on the role of domestic labor, gender, and housework under capitalist conditions contributed to this discussion by rethinking the so-called unproductive status attributed to domestic labor in dominant narratives of political economy. Gendered perspectives on the transnational division of labor suggest that the *reproduction* of the material and social conditions and relations of production is as crucial to capital accumulation as is the production of commodities that more self-evidently fuels the GNP.[7] Like housewives, workers in petty commodity enterprises exist in a relation of superexploitation to capital, a relation that remains invisible to a perspective that divides and privileges production over reproduction. Though second-string to industrial workers, petty commodity producers provide cheap goods and services that satisfy both their own (and their families') consumption requirements and also those of workers in highly capitalized industry and other salaried employment (such as government bureaucracy). In effect, the petty commodity or "informal" sector subsidizes the wages of workers in the "formal" sector, thereby enabling its industries to pay lower wages and retain a higher percentage of relative surplus value produced by their workers. This subsidy permits a higher rate of capital accumulation, which characteristically does not accrue to petty commodity enterprises, because of their indirect exploitation by capital, but rather to capitalist industrial and financial concerns. Whereas surplus value is appropriated directly through the wage from laborers in capitalist industry, the exploitation of workers involved in reproductive activities is in a sense once removed, for it is through the same wage paid to the industrial worker that capitalists indirectly appropriate the surplus produced by domestic laborers in the "social factory."[8] Much like housewives, whose specific, socially necessary (but unwaged) labor supplements the family wage by contributing to the reproduction of the labor power of household members who are past, present, or future wage workers, the labor of petty commodity producers produces value indirectly.

Because of this internal relation, the importance of petty commodity production is not altogether unambiguously aligned with capital: its critical role in reproducing regimes of capital accumulation means that petty commodity production is imbricated within the complex texture of a social formation to an extent that makes it at once indispensable and potentially disruptive: "The continuance of such forms of production simultaneously favors the reproduction and expansion of the capitalist mode of production and presents it with severe problems."[9] Thus the very specific manner of capitalism's incorporation of petty commodity producers means that, although the workshop floor may not present itself as a self-evident site of struggle to these "other" workers, they should not be too hastily written off as altogether acquiescent.

Notably, strikes and other explicitly labor-related struggles historically have been absent in petty commodity enterprises. It may well be that their constituents are encumbered by culturally defined and reinforced sets of responsibilities, attitudes, beliefs, and social institutions that deter the emergence of a free-labor proletarian consciousness that might be potentially disruptive to capitalist hegemony. But these do not preclude other sites of struggle, other subaltern consciousnesses. The construction of artisan-cum-workers' subjectivities lends a distinctive heterogeneity to the dynamics of subaltern struggles that have doggedly accompanied the historical process of the unequal development of capitalism and its manifestation as colonialism, nationalism, and imperialism in the Third World. For in addition to the control over labor power and the production and accumulation of surplus value, the continued reproduction of capitalist hegemony depends on a certain degree of consent on the part of the subaltern classes—consent to labor under conditions rational (to capital) for the production of that surplus, consent to live under conditions that the workers consider at least minimally habitable.[10] This depends, preferably, on a certain kind of subjectivity for whom that consent need not be secured by coercion, but disappears into the natural fabric of everyday existence. If old forms of production and social life did not submit gracefully to their own demise, how do we track figures of subaltern resistance against the grain of dominant discourses whose chief "epistemic violence" has been their repression from, or discounting in, historical narrative?

The concrete forms of petty commodity production extant in Egypt today, as at the turn of this century, and the social relations and cultural practices of craft workers and their families are effects of the historical process of paradoxical preservation explained previously. Because this history, for Egypt and other social formations like it, is a discontinuous one, clustered around moments of rupture and transformation in national and global fields of political economy and culture, its telling requires a different kind of narrative than that offered by Eurocentric dependency theory or universalizing, world-systems master narratives. Sensitivity to the repressions (of class, gender, race, nation) that are virtually prerequisite so that such linear narratives achieve their rhetorical coherence and persuasiveness (sometimes simply legitimated by "insufficient data") requires a more partial, less totalizing story, one that must be able to track the various ways petty commodity production was historically inserted into particular social formations that experienced capitalist development. Among the questions tobe considered are these: what are the relations that over time have tended to dissolve or preserve (or in very recent times, even simulate) the distinctions between petty commodity and capitalist forms of production? How do intensified, petty commodity productive forms function as an active structuring principle of the particular configuration of modern (and now postmodern) capitalism in the Third World? To what extent is this structuring principle an effect of the cultural practices and subjective identities of subaltern class fractions?

By holding competing representations of petty commodity production constantly in relation to structures of power and interest in play at the specific historical conjunctures during which they appear, we can attempt to reassess the disparaged political significance of this productive form and its constituents.

A Turning Point

The period from the 1880s to the 1920s was one of profound global structural transformation that witnessed European imperialist expansion and the international consolidation of the capitalist world market system. The shift from mercantile to monopoly capitalism established new conditions for the process of accumulation and capital's expanded reproduction in the periphery. New articulations had to be worked out with productive forms already existing in those regions. These changes provided fertile ground for the formation of revised class structures, incorporating emergent, antagonistic class fractions and shaped by shifting alliances. Reformist nationalisms and independence movements frequently became the venue for negotiating conflicting interests and constituencies within new colonial and class political discourses.

In this general context, Egypt's integration into a global economy accelerated as it formally became in 1882 a colonial appendage supplying cotton to Britain's textile mills and a market for its manufactures.[11] Not surprisingly, capital-intensive industrial development was adamantly discouraged by the colonial administration through unfavorable trade and tariff regulations (e.g., import duties on raw materials and fuel and excise duties on locally produced goods). But although certainly some indigenous crafts were destroyed by the nineteenth century forces of dissolution (centralization and monopoly by the state under Muhammad 'Ali, competition from European industrial goods. and reorganization of the economy for export agriculture after imperial capitulations treaties), other crafts that utilized local raw materials and catered to the subsistence requirements of the local population were by no means eliminated (e.g., construction, textiles, dying, metals, woodworking, tanning, shoes, flour milling, soaps, oils, jewelry, animal-drawn transport, pottery). Near the turn of the century, petty commodity production began to proliferate in response to new conditions: the internal migration of peasants, "freed" from their lands during the consolidation of large private estates linked to cotton export, swelled the urban population of towns like Cairo and expanded commodity and labor markets.[12] Because waged jobs in the few modern industries (e.g., cigarette rolling, textiles, sugar refining) and infrastructure developments (irrigation, transport) that were established in Egypt about this same time were insufficient in number to provide a livelihood for these displaced peasants, the majority of the urban work force was employed in the ateliers of artisans and small traders.

Although many of the same classic artisanal (and peasant) forms of petty commodity production persisted after Egypt's advanced integration into the world economy (same basic production processes and continued artisanal possession of the means of production, though often with dependence on merchants), the economic environment in which they were carried out was transformed into one of intense competition—both among themselves and with newly emergent capitalized industries forced by shifts in the world economy to produce for the domestic market rather than for export—with no or minimal regulation on job entry or production of domestic goods.[13] The low value of labor power and consequent cheap cost of commodities made those petty commodity forms that did survive all the more important to the social reproduction of all economic life in Egypt. Thereafter, modern capital accumulation would be contingent on this effective subsidy of the social costs of labor power by urban petty commodity producers, peasants, and domestic laborers (including women's home labor[14]). This meant that the surplus value produced by these "unwaged" workers could be appropriated indirectly through the reduced wage paid to workers in highly capitalized industries (many of whom were European immigrants seeking respite after the 1907 financial crash and recession).

This new and nearly invisible division of an emergent Egyptian working class into waged and unwaged workers perhaps in itself marks this moment in the process of class formation as distinctively "modern." This restructuring virtually became the condition of possibility for modern capital in Egypt and would continue to daunt labor organizers and the trade union movement until today.

Reciprocally, the new structural conditions of the colonial capitalist economy effectively became the conditions of possibility for petty commodity producers; they were now able to realize the conditions of their own reproduction only as sellers of labor power or commodities and as markets for colonial production. Both commodity and expanded reproduction circuits were complete for Egypt's peripheral capitalist economy only by virtue of its integration into the colonial system. Because labor was not fully commodified due to continued possession of means of production by peasants and craftsmen, capitalists in Egypt had to compete with petty commodity producers for labor and markets. Thus the subsumption of petty commodity forms by colonial capital was less a matter of imposition of the exigencies of an unstoppable imperialism than it was a consequence of the necessity of incorporating other thriving forms of production already extant in the economy to achieve effective hegemony.

The preservation of petty commodity forms within the new dominant mode of production was not simply a matter of functional integration. Rather, it can best be seen as the result of widespread struggle and resistance to the reconstitution of Egypt's political economy by colonial forces of capitalist integration (trade and marketing regulations, new production processes, indebtedness to and control by foreign interests), which entailed the often violent transformation and reformation of traditional ways of life. At the turn of the twentieth century Egyptian artisans revolted against the remaining guild structure, which anyway by this time had ceased to protect them and had become a form of labor contracting that only facilitated their exploitation. The popular classes were attracted to the nationalist movement as well. Thousands of skilled artisans whose trades were threatened by Egypt's transformation joined the short-lived Manual Trades Workers' Union, organized by leaders of the bourgeois Nationalist party just prior to World War I in a bid to broaden their political base.[15]

Dissatisfied with the price of cotton on the world market after the crash of 1907 and the halt this put to a period of speculative investment in rural land and urban property, an emergent segment of the large-scale landowning bourgeoisie aligned itself temporarily with agents of foreign capital other than British (e.g., French, Belgian, or Greek). Commodity shortages incurred from the disruption of foreign trade during World War I also drove home to this group the desirability of local industries to offset imports. This class fraction sought its interests in the global turn toward modernity and finance capitalism by pressuring the colonial government to open conditions for industrial investment. They established in 1920 the first Egyptian national bank (Bank Misr) to finance such ventures and escape the strictures imposed by foreign capital. Although ultimately they were not strong enough to sustain this effort for long, the bank served for the Egyptian bourgeoisie, in Eric Davis's view, as a central rallying feature of a social movement allied with nationalism and independence.[16]

At a time when agriculture reigned as the preeminent concern of the British colonial administration, it is perhaps not so curious that representatives of these aspiring indigenous industrialists seized on Egypt's long handicraft tradition (as if unbroken by Muhammad 'Ali's attempt in the early nineteenth century to restructure the crafts and channel profits to the state[17]) as a vivid, even populist image on which to hinge the rhetorical persuasiveness of their counterimperial discourse.

Figuring Egypt's Artisanry

In contrast to British reports that would as soon consign the crafts to an irreparable oblivion, writings by a loose alliance of national and foreign bourgeoisie called attention to the still vital but neglected "traditional industries." They lamented the rudimentary skills and poor conditions under which noble, laboring artisans and their families worked and lived and attributed this deplorable situation to state neglect or abuse. It is worthwhile to characterize some of the concerns of a few examples of this early twentieth century literature.

Perhaps the best known of these sources is Germain Martin's *Les Bazars du Caire et les Petits Métiers Arabes*, published in 1910, for it has informed scholarship on the Middle East by contemporary authors, such as Gabriel Baer, André Raymond, Charles Issawi, and Samir Radwan.

This remarkable work combines a history of Egyptian guilds, based on sketchy information derived less from the Egyptian case than from Martin's knowledge of European guilds (about which he had previously written a thick two-volume work), with a sort of ethnographic study of the existing crafts of the time. Based on a six-month stay in Egypt, the latter includes data from Martin's interviews with artisans. Martin points out that, because there were very few large, modern industries in Egypt at that time, traditional petty industry predominated. These he describes as carried out in accordance with archaic technology and occupying the majority of the urban population. Martin constructs for his readers a continuous narrative of artisanal traditions dating at least from the early nineteenth century French expedition:

> The present is pregnant with the past; to convince ourselves of this, it suffices to consider the engravings annexed to the description of Egypt published by the savants of the French mission. Whoever sees these engravings and places them, in mind's eye, beside the image of a present-day atelier, arrives at a superimposition of which all the traits agree. For a hundred years, there have not been any modifications in technique nor in the overall look of the crafts of Cairo. The influences that explain their existence, their formation, are far off![18]

On the one hand, Martin attributes this persistence to the singular tenacity of tradition in Egypt, which reasserted itself despite the attempted reorganization of the crafts in the early nineteenth century, and somewhat less heroically, to the retention of the spirit of routine, to the sluggishness of hot countries, to the absence of a will to control nature, and further tropes that typify conventions of Orientalist othering.[19]

But Martin offers additional reasons that deserve more serious consideration

> 1. He notes the persistent habits of indigenous buyers who continued to bring raw materials to the artisans to be worked with care into products preferred over European-made ones, and to the native enjoyment of the palaver of the marketplace, where time seems of little importance either for the artisan or his client.[20] One must reconsider, of course, whether such "preference" may be so glibly attributed to habit or to budgetary limitations. Also, the remark on the native sense of time seems more aptly to illuminate Martin's own conceptions: such laxity did not conform well with the protestant ethic of a European.

2. Martin remarks that the lack of available alternative employment meant that, although production was slow, at least the meager earnings permitted the thousands of individuals engaged in petty crafts to live.[21]

3. He notes a consonance between the cheapness of labor and the artisan's minimal needs, suggesting that the impoverished conditions of the workers in petty industry was held in check by the same unfavorable tariff regulations that inhibited the development of large-scale industry in Egypt at that time, as agriculture was already saturated with labor. In other words, if the artisans were to raise the price of their products to increase their own remuneration, this would only facilitate the competitive pricing of foreign manufactures and promote further destruction of Egypt's petty industries.[22] This represents, it seems, a not-so-off-handed attack against Britain's restrictive regulation of the development of industry in Egypt in order to concentrate on cultivating the cotton required by English textile factories in Lancashire (Martin more explicitly implicates Britain in a couple of instances[23]).

Martin offers many more insights into the problem of petty commodity production that I will touch on here but briefly. He describes the sweatshoplike working conditions of the artisans: long hours, deplorably unhealthy conditions, the tedious attention required, and the numerous young children employed in dank workshops.[24] He cites the necessity for many women and children to obtain waged employment to supplement the income of their households.[25] He records the catharsis sought through drugs and religion, an observation that seems to affirm the presumed dichotomy between the modern industrial working class and the premodern artisan. He argues that relations between workers and employers in petty industry precluded any notion of opposing class interests, since both lived an equally sordid existence and were equally indebted to supplier merchants.[26] This calm, even if not altogether rosy, picture seemed especially ideal to Martin in light of the rash of disruptive strikes since 1904, organized by labor unions in the few existing large industries (cigarette rollers, tramway company workers, tailors, metallurgists, and even law clerks), which he enumerates at length.[27] In fact, Martin concludes his study by remarking that the traditional organization of labor in petty industries justly could be called an *age d'ôr*, the ironic sense of which is poignantly illuminated by this qualifier: "Yet this gold is made of the good fortune that bestows calmness and resignation more than riches."[28]

For the future, Martin foresaw a further drawing back of those petty industries whose products were in competition with European manufactures.[29] But he urged that serious effort be made to attempt to improve the kind of crafts producing commodities that did *not* face direct competition from Europe, in particular, "traditional" objects that would sell on the tourist market. He urged wealthy Egyptians to patronize local artisans to facilitate a "renaissance of Arab arts" in Cairo, instead of buying "foreign furniture of dubious taste."[30] A more specific procedure for rehabilitating the crafts Martin neglected to spell out.

In another vein, René Maunier, in a 1912 article published in *L'Égypte Contemporaine*, discusses the contemporary organization of the apprenticeship system in Egyptian petty industries and suggests possible reforms.[31] Maunier likens the decline witnessed by Egypt's petty industries to a parallel movement in the case of Europe, due to the superior technology and market competition of large industries. He adds to this reasons specific to Egypt, among them the "traditionalism" of the workers, the "weak development of the spirit of savings" that inhibited the availability of capital for investment, the prestige of Europe's industrial products in the eyes of the Egyptian consumer, and most especially the decadence of the apprenticeship system.

Restoring the apprenticeship system, he argues, would contribute toward a revival of the existing local industries (e.g., the metal, pottery, and textile industries) and give rise to a multiplicity of industries that Egypt lacked, this being desirable so that Egypt not remain dependent on cotton production alone (a common theme of essays of this sort from the period). Furthermore, apprenticeship would help solve the problems of unemployment, increased "vagabondage," and juvenile delinquency, the increase of which he attributes to the decline of the guild system and the resultant lack of juridical regulation of the trades. In Maunier's view, the decadence of the apprenticeship system could also be attributed to the "lack of foresight" and the poverty of parents who would rather their children earn money immediately than undergo a prolonged, unpaid apprenticeship. Maunier concludes, on the basis of the lessons learned from Europe's experience with this problem, by making an explicit call for strong state intervention and initiative in subsidizing private efforts and for the state organization of institutions of technical education, as well as legislative regulation that would make apprenticeship obligatory in petty industry.

Whereas from Martin we learned of the persistence of petty industry as far as its prevalence at that time in occupying the majority of the Egyptian nonagricultural workers, Maunier laments the degenerate state of such industries and offers a directive toward their improvement: active state intervention into what he considered to be the core of the artisanal system of production, apprenticeship. By attributing their poor condition to deficient administrative regulation of the technical formation necessary to overcome the "endemic limitations" of the "traditional rationality" of the artisans, Maunier offered a double slant on the problems petty industry represented:

1. In reprimanding the state for its negligence of petty industry, he indirectly implicates the unfavorable industrial policy of the British colonial government.

2. By indicating that the route to rehabilitation is through intervention and control of apprenticeship, the artisan's socialization process, he implies that the production process of petty industries had become too autonomous and remained frustratingly outside the sphere of rationality of capitalist development, which Maunier presumes is the desirable path for Egypt to follow.

Thus, through officially legitimate manipulation of the organization and labor power of petty commodity industries, a channel might be opened for feasible entrepreneurial investment, a channel that, as it turned out, certain elements of the society were eager to flood.

Francois Bourgeois, in his 1916 *L'Égypte Contemporaine* article on the ceramic industry in Egypt, like Maunier places the onus of responsibility for the backward state of Egyptian industry on (1) the absence of protective encouragement offered to indigenous aspiring capitalists to provide the capital necessary to create large-scale industries and (2) the mentality and character of the Egyptian workers, which inhibited the availability of a reliable labor force with a "willingness to put out continuous work effort."[32] Bourgeois argues that of all Egyptian industries, ceramics (especially common and building pottery) presented the most favorable characteristics for development and expansion, including the local availability of raw materials, a ready market for the products within Egypt itself, and protection from foreign imports by the high cost of pottery transport from abroad, guaranteeing a competitive advantage to indigenously made pottery.

But capital must be provided to establish the large-scale ceramic industry Bourgeois envisions, so he calls for the formation of credit associations of indigenous capitalists—this would be feasible only in a supportive atmosphere capable of quelling misgivings held by wealthy Egyptians as to the risks involved. By inference, the British administration was indicted for failing to encourage such an atmosphere.

To Bourgeois, an effective system of education must be created to train workers above all in a new attitude toward work:

> The Oriental has but one objective: to avoid effort. He reduces his needs to the minimum, works just to earn enough to satisfy these, then lives a contemplative life until necessity obliges him to take up his labor again.
>
> Industrial people par excellence have precisely the opposite conception of life.[33]

We can interpret Bourgeois's dismay at the "irrational" views of Egyptian workers in petty industry as his regret that the artisans were able to maintain a frustrating degree of autonomy from Egypt's emergent capitalist economy; they worked for their own subsistence, not for other's profit. Their "rationality" should be characterized less as "deficient" than decidedly different in its objectives, a difference resistant to easy incorporation. At the same time, this capacity for autonomy presented an attractive model to indigenous investors, who were effectively blocked by state policy from initiating export-oriented industries.

Traditional Crafts in the Modern Market

This cluster of monographs and essays can be supplemented with others from the period.[35] The cluster is particularly striking in that it is rare to find contemporaneous writings (especially in European languages) dealing with the topic of petty commodity production either before this period or after the late 1920s. Prior to this time the topic was virtually ignored (with notable exceptions in the early nineteenth century by the French savants and during the restructuring of Egypt's economy under Muhammad 'Ali), when colonial and indigenous capitalists were content with Egypt's agricultural development as their discursive threshing ground.[36] Later, most interest focused on the development of modern, highly capitalized industry, which found a more welcome climate after the expiration in 1930 of unfavorable commercial tariffs and a shift to protectionist state policies designed to develop local industries for import substitution.[36] It is therefore appropriate to investigate why writers at this particular point in time were concerned to analyze and publicly report on the state of Egypt's artisanal industries.

Furthermore, there is a remarkable contrast in the discursive narratives of Egypt's artisanry put forward by these early twentieth century writers and post-World War II studies of this same period of Egypt's modern history. To take the prime example, Gabriel Baer's widely respected discussion of Egyptian guilds[37] documents their disappearance by the end of the nineteenth century (with a few exceptions). Historian Baer's work is very much entangled in the debate among modern Orientalists over the status of guilds in the Middle East. The evidence he marshals derives from administrative archives of the state, interpreted in a literal, empiricist manner. His preoccupation with organizational structure and administrative and fiscal functions of the guilds comfortably allows him to bring his historical narrative to a close at the time of the disappearance of all formal guildlike institutions, and Baer is at pains to push this gradual demise into the twentieth century. Implicit in Baer's argument is a linear history of a degenerative process whose golden age is posited in a distant, medieval past that far outpaced the capabilities of twentieth century Arab artisans, much as did the European manufacturing and commercial systems that superseded them.

Unlike Baer, authors such as Martin, Maunier, and Bourgeois give a clear impression that many of the petty industries that gave rise to the by then disaggregated guilds were still extant well into the twentieth century, even if they did persist in a state of neglect. Their descriptions also stand in vivid counterpoint to British representations of the state of Egypt's artisanal dissolution, as exemplified in Lord Cromer's Report on how well his colonial administration was faring in 1905:

> Quarters that were formerly hives of busy workmen—spinning, weaving, braiding, tassel making, dyeing, tent-making, embroidering, slipper making, gold and silver working, spice crushing, copper beating, water skin making, saddle making, sieve making, wooden-bolt making, lock making etc. have shrunk to attenuated proportions or have been entirely obliterated. Cafes and small stores retailing European wares are now to be found where productive workshops formerly existed.[38]

To Cromer, this state of affairs was only to be expected, given the evident superiority of European manufactures. Cromer heralded, in a self-congratulatory way, the benefits of modern progress brought to Egypt under British colonial tutelage. Yet the persistence of many such industries a few years later during the time of Martin and even today, attests to their changing but continued pertinence, with certain mutations, despite the atrophy of the guild structure. The problematic posed by the early twentieth century writers, then, suggests that Baer's rigid, empiricist focus on the "facts" of the guild as institution effectively precluded his tackling what is the more cogent problem: whether one could still speak of "guilds" in twentieth century Egypt, many forms of petty commodity production nevertheless existed. An investigation into artisans' relationship to merchants, Egypt's cotton economy, and the interests of foreign capital would have been well deserved. In a sense, Baer's exclusion of such considerations makes his historical narrative complicit with the trope of empire motivating Cromer's self-interested description.[39]

To gain a new perspective on how Egypt's traditional industries became the object of renewed interest and concern in the cosmopolitan public discourse of the early twentieth century writers, we must refract their representations against the social and political text in which they were inscribed. This reengages us with the themes raised earlier. The historical context of shifts in Egypt's positioning in the world market and the impact of interimperial rivalry and shifts in Egypt's class structure and cultural formation, all combined to place industrial development on the agenda.

The year 1910, when Martin's book was published, followed a disastrous year for Egypt's cotton production. A bad crop caused by insect damage (and possibly poor drainage), coupled with constraints on American cotton production (and its requirement for U.S. mills), resulted in a "cornering" of the market and high prices for British textile manufacturers. Lancashire trade associations pushed inquiries into improved cotton production in Egypt and India, and its possible extension into the Sudan (the Gezira scheme was hatched). In Egypt, an administrative effect of this pressure was a massive organizational campaign directed at the fellahin. Peasants were fined and prosecuted for not obeying governmental instructions on reporting boll worms, and corvées of hundreds of thousands of children were drafted to pick infected cotton leaves.[40] Given that the objective of the colonial government was to protect Britain's access to Egyptian cotton, a sense of panic about decreasing crop yields is clearly palpable here. Little wonder Britain's technocrats in Egypt had no time for crafts.

Due to recession, war, and depression, the control over the world market by European capital was weakened. At the same time, the Egyptian bourgeoisie began to coalesce its solidarity into a nationalist movement by which they sought to rid themselves of British control in order to shift their own economic basis in accordance with the general world market trend. But to carry on with their own plans, both foreign and indigenous capitalists had to contend with a growing array of serious difficulties posed by Egypt's working class of peasants, artisans, and industrial laborers. Expanding population began to present a problem, leading to the growth of urban slums, increased unemployment and juvenile delinquency, and in the rural areas, to sharply increased rents that augmented the indebtedness of the peasants to usurious money lenders. Labor strikes plagued the existing large industries (a Labor Disputes Conciliation Board was established in 1919 after the war "as the need arose"[51]). Such problems can be seen as the outcome of the contradictions ensuing from the spread of capitalist relations of production. Any venture toward industrial development on the part of the Egyptian bourgeoisie required close attention to these "social ills" as well as to the policies of the British occupation; any viable solution to the constricted predicament faced by indigenous capitalist expansion would depend on some sort of resolution to the worsening predicament confronted by indigenous labor.

In 1916 a Commission on Commerce and Industry was set up in Egypt by the British government, prompted perhaps as much by pressure exerted by the indigenous bourgeoisie as by a shift in the nature of British capitalism from commodity to finance capital. The recommendations of this commission charged with the task of surveying Egypt's manufacturing capacity again called for the improvement of petty industry (as well as large-scale industry), almost as a necessary evil that would inevitably remain. The commission's report[42] emphasizes that the fate of Egyptian industry was virtually paralyzed by undeserved indifference and neglect due to the entrenched belief held even by the "enlightened class" and the governmental authorities that Egypt could not depend for the solution of its economic ills on any resources other than agricultural products. Lack of encouragement and control, the commission argues, had reduced Egyptian artisanry to decline in the face of competition from European manufactures. As a result of this inertia, "defects" had been acquired by the formerly talented Egyptian handicraftsmen, such as minimal effort, poor workmanship, and "lack of taste." In the opinion of the commission, "Here then are the two ills that have to be corrected, first of all, in order to have a renaissance of Egyptian industry: the indifference of the people and of the public authorities, and the defects in the character and education of the Egyptian worker."[43]

Significantly, the commission set out to dispel the prejudices that favored agriculture as both the mainspring of British colonial policy and the lifeblood of the large-landowner bourgeoisie. It attempted to prove that for Egypt, "industrial expansion constitutes an immediate necessity."[44] In the process, the commission indirectly lambasts the occupation government's industrial policy that left petty industry—in all its neglected, inefficient state—as possibly the only recourse for the expansion of indigenous capital. It urges a radical change in the state's industrial policy and calls for technical education to reconstitute the defective artisan into a proper laboring subject fit for modern industry.

It seems to me, then, that the early twentieth century studies of petty industry must be seen in this context of the continuing struggle between the interests of foreign and indigenous capital for control of the surplus value that Egypt's economy could produce. In fact, the interimperial rivalry between Britain and France is relevant as well. The 1904 Entente Cordiale agreement between the two powers secured British rule in Egypt in exchange for a laissez-faire policy towards the French in Morocco. Such broad geopolitical exchanges created the internal parameters within which the proceding discourse on Egyptian artisans was situated.

It is of interest to note, then, that the authors of this literature have French surnames, although whether they are French citizens or locals of foreign extraction in Egypt I have not been able to ascertain. But if the obituary notice I located for Germain Martin should turn out to be even remotely indicative of the identities of the other authors, significant light would be shed on the interimperial rivalry as it was discursively played out on an Egyptian battle ground in the periphery of the world market:

> Paris, October 6, 1943—Germain Martin, Finance or Budget Minister in several pre-war governments, died today in his Paris residence at the age of 76.
>
> The brother of Louis Martin, late director of the Pasteur Institute, Germain Martin was a graduate and later a professor in L'École des Chartes. He was elected a deputy in 1928 and served in Poincaré's second

Cabinet as Minister of Postal Service and afterwards in the Briand Cabinet in the same office.

M. Martin was a member of the French delegation to the League of Nations in Geneva and at several international conferences. He was a member of the Academy of Moral and Political Sciences and the author of a number of works on financial subiects.[45]

Also, at the time he wrote *Les Bazaars du Caire* in 1910, already well into his career at the age of 38, Martin held a post as professor of political economy in the faculty of law at Dijon, France. He had been sent to Egypt by the French directorship of higher education of the Ministry of Education, at the request of the Khedival Society of Political Economy, Statistics, and Legislation. Affiliated for six months with the Egyptian University, his charge was to assist in the organization of the Khedival Society and to establish a journal that would treat questions of interest to the society, a task he seems to have accomplished.[46] His qualifications, then, root him firmly within the intellectual and institutional province of the official French mainstream, both of the academy and of the state.[47]

Certainly the general tenor of Martin's book is on the one hand representative of the priorities of the Occident, as opposed to those of the Orient he studied, and we have seen earlier how the characteristics of his work locate his discourse squarely within the framework of Orientalism.[48] In view of Martin's posting to Egypt as an emissary of France, it seems legitimate to consider the perspective he brings to his study of Egyptian artisans as representative of French interests in particular. His sympathetic view of the Egyptian artisans and his hostile attitude toward the policies of the British occupation government must be construed as two sides of the same coin, a coin minted in the crucible of the desires for the expansion of French hegemony and the ills French capitalism faced at home. That is to say, the monograph by Martin (and, because they share a general perspective, those other authors we have discussed) represents not only the interests of the West vis-à-vis the Orient, but also of France vis-à-vis Great Britain.

I suggest, then, that this literature calling for a renovation of the artisanry discursively constructs a temporary ad hoc class alliance between the indigenous bourgeoisie and representatives of French capital, both of whom were engaged in a struggle with Britain for control over Egypt's capabilities for the production of surplus value. Britain pursued its own best advantage in cotton production, employing its political hegemony to achieve effective domination of Egypt's agricultural domain. The Egyptian landowning bourgeoisie throughout the nineteenth century had profited from this relatively secure agricultural venture as well. Subsequent changes in the importance of cotton on the world market, in combination with the changes within the class itself, upset their alliance with British imperialism, however, leading a faction of the bourgeoisie to seek more profitable alternatives in which to invest the capital they had accumulated. They contested the colonial government's strict tariff regulations that effectively prohibited the viability of any indigenous mass production of commodities for export, and indeed curtailed their domestic market as well. The French and Belgians too, Britain's industrial rivals at the center of the world economy, were closed out of the Egyptian market, apart from their efforts in sugar refineries and transport systems, and hence they could afford to extend a hand into the periphery to the struggling Egyptian bourgeoisie despite the anticolonial sentiment that pervaded the emerging nationalist movement.

The result of these maneuverings is demonstrated in the literature we have considered, where the interests of the aspiring Egyptian and French capitalists coalesce. First, we found in evidence an underhanded though pointed attack against the industrial policy of the British colonial government, whose bureaucratic constrictions were dubbed by one author "cette nouvelle Bastille."[49] Second, I suggest that this literature can be fruitfully perceived as an exploration of the possibilities offered by the only likely avenue for capital investment then in evidence: production of petty commodities for a primarily internal market, with possible future prospects for export. This helps to explain the rather sudden concern about "traditional" forms of artisanal production which, as I have argued, far from being dissolved by Egypt's integration into the capitalist world market at this historical conjuncture, had become an integral part of it. After 1930, once Britain loosened Egypt's industrial policy as a result of changes in its own less preeminent role in relation to global capitalism and permitted indigenous industrial ventures with support of foreign capital, petty commodity production ceased to be an issue of intense interest to the Egyptian bourgeoisie and their European allies. Tellingly, after this time representations of artisans seem to have dropped out of the historical record virtually entirely (save some postcolonial socialist-realist genuflection to crafts as legacy of Egypt's glorious industrial heritage), or were subordinated to other figures, until they recurred in the 1970s when a frenzy of information retrieval about the newly discovered "informal sector" brought petty commodity production back to the top of the charts.[50]

The plea to rehabilitate Egypt's traditional handicrafts issued by Martin, Bourgeois, Maunier, the Commission on Commerce and Industry, and other early twentieth century writers, also implicitly recognized the importance of petty commodity production in social reproduction at a critical point of local and global transformation (providing cheap commodities and services, absorbing unemployment, keeping overall wages low, blocking full proletarianization). Although the authors I have discussed tend to conceptualize the relationship between traditional artisanal forms and "modern" forms of production as one of separate—even if unequal—adjacency, the evidence they invoke, regardless of their motivation for doing so, in effect indicates a more internal, constitutive sort of relation. Their concern about poor working conditions, laxity of the apprenticeship system, the lack of credit and capital, the "irrational" economic decisions of the craftsmen, and the comparative stability of workplace relations among artisanal fractions of the emergent working class highlights the potentially disruptive situation that could have been caused by a total suppression of petty commodity production and denial of artisanal subjectivity, once again calling attention to the subversive power of laborers in the disparaged "domestic" economy. Indeed, the figure of the traditional artisan and its rejuvenation was deployed as metaphor in the discourse of the bourgeois nationalist class struggle. It could thus play a part in the construction of the national-popular and serve as a rallying call to articulate "the people" (another new sign conjoining artisans and peasants, as well as proletarians) into the emergent bourgeois nationalist political discourse.[51] Such an internal relation marks a potential site of resistance to exploitation and domination that remains all but invisible to a perspective obsessed with production. Due to their technocratic preoccupation with modern production methods as the route to development, post-World War II modernization theories predefined as unproductive and dismissed out of hand those primitive, petty commodity forms paradoxically persisting in modern Third World cities like Cairo. Leftist writings on the proletarian working class at the time also shared this perspective. Ultimately, however, the "true product" of the petty commodity sector is not only goods and services plain and simple, but also the reproduction of lives, labor power, and conditions for social relations of production. Egypt's modern capitalist political economy was obliged to accommodate itself to this petty commodity sector now harbored, as it were, within the breast of the beast. Perhaps not unexpectedly, the relations of social reproduction established at the turn of the century again became problematic in Egypt's liberalized economy and culture since the 1970s, when the sutures that consolidated the nation's unstable hegemony were rent asunder by national and global struggles, and once again Egyptian petty commodity production became contested terrain.

Conclusions

The turn of the twentieth century marked a turning point in economic and class relations within Egypt, in the emergent consciousness of its people caught between class and nation, as well as in its advanced integration into the transforming, crisis-ridden, global capitalist system poised at the moment of modernity. Inscribed in the interimperial and national class struggles that took as one of their terrains the most adequate representation of Egypt's artisanry is the historical shift in its relation from dissolution to that rather paradoxical preservation proposed earlier. *Paradoxical preservation* is essentially the subsumption of a new, *modern* form of petty commodity production (that nonetheless retains the persistent image of tradition) to colonial capital by virtue of this new form's inability to realize its own reproduction except insofar as that reproduction was tied to the expanded reproduction circuits of peripheral capitalism. In terms of a *discourse of exploitation*, the incorporation of petty commodity production was a fundamental condition for the emergence and ongoing reproduction of unequal exchange relations that channeled accumulation away from Egypt's peripheral capitalist economy. This incorporation, whose disruptions of precapitalist relations were not met without struggle, also went a long way toward staving off a more cantankerous proletariat by adding a divisively heterogeneous character to Egypt's working classes. In terms of a *discourse of domination*, this weighty, unorganized fraction of Egypt's working population nonetheless must be acknowledged to wield a significant political potential. Precisely the unclear political affiliation of artisans and craftsmen historically made them a crucial terrain of struggle in national class politics, as antagonistic interest groups of hegemonic and subaltern classes sought at particular conjunctures to articulate these workers' social identities into one or another class ideological discourse.

So although "traditional" forms of artisanal and agricultural production formerly held an important productive role in their own right and even competed with some success against foreign capital, by the early twentieth century they already had come to stand in a distinctly different relation to the dominant mode of material and cultural production. They also had come to stand in a different relation to the ways working people lived with and defined their relation to each other, to other classes, and to their conditions of life. Thus the relations between different forms of production and between the classes of which they were composed not only emerged historically in the struggle between these forces, but became itself the terrain of that struggle.

To deconstruct the persistent opposition between proletarian and artisanal labor (or between formal and informal sectors), it is not enough merely to *reverse* the privilege accorded the proletariat in studies of "the" working class, by pointing to the integral importance of petty commodity production to the social reproduction of regimes of capital accumulation in the Third World. To this reversal must be added a *displacement* that pushes our inquiry beyond the problematic, dichotomous categorization proletarian/artisan that so often impedes understanding the relation between the two. Comparative historical counterpoint, and attention to the poetics of discourses on political economy, provide a lever to effect such a displacement. In the case of representations of Egypt's petty commodity production, the figurative shift from artisanry (turn of the century) to informal sector (1970s onward) in discursive fields of colonialism, nationalism, or developmentalism alerts us to a historical *dis*-continuity belied by the continuing resemblance of productive forms in a political-economic field. Each moment of discontinuity marks the historical shift in the relationship between atavistic forms of production and labor relations constituting the artisanry and informal sector and the restructured political economy of the nation and *its* place in the broader transnational field. As Alejandro Portes has argued, "the articulation of different modes of production, reflected in the formal/informal division, is ultimately a *political* process dependent on control of the state"[52] and, need we add, on imperial intervention. Certainly the internal relation between formal/informal economy was established historically, and the specific character of that articulation is inflected by the history of the state in relation to class struggles. Rereading the inscriptions of power in the eminently political contest over the most adequate representation of petty commodity production in early twentieth century Egypt discloses "tradition" (and its various permutations: backwardness, underdevelopment, informal sector) to be less an accurate description than a trope of incorporation punctuating modernist, masculinist, and orientalist discourses of knowledge.

Among these discourses must be included the master narrative of Egyptian labor history. The omission of, or negativity toward, petty commodity production in this narrative nonetheless has had certain positive functions as a technology of power. First, petty commodity production constitutes an empty place, a blank spot, which enables and structures the positive consistency of the labor history narrative and the assured class positionality and identity of the subjects it privileges (proletarian labor and identity).[53] Second, discounting the subjective agency of artisanal culture effectively denies the coevalness of its workers, as if their purported location in an atavistic mode of production acts as a barrier to their participation in ongoing social struggles in the present.[54] Third, the dominant labor history narrative is decidedly masculinist in that it privileges (male) "productive" labor over (female) "unproductive" domestic activity and explosive, deliberate, virile forms of struggle (strikes, organized political parties) over "feminine" subtler forms of resistance embedded in the practices of everyday life.[55] In each of these three problematic areas, the masterful narrative of Egyptian labor history continues the protocols of orientalist alterity and mimics early twentieth century imperialist discourse. Its claims to the status of critical, radical, counterdiscourse has supplied the labor history narrative with an armory of alibis that continue to permit historians and economists to treat as inconsequential the fact that most Egyptian working men, women, and children do not fit the classical proletarian description. But this heterogeneity is precisely the point: the figuration of class fractions in the form of precapitalist, patriarchal, petty-bourgeois bourgeois precedents assists in consolidating the preconditions for the transnational reterritorialization of labor and capital.

In contrast, I have tried to suggest that petty commodity productive forms and "traditional" subaltern subjectivities were not preexistent or external to, but rather both constitutive of and constituted in, the terrain of struggle for hegemony over Egypt's economic, political, and cultural life at the moment of modernity. Petty commodity production is, in a sense, a "traumatic limit"[56] that (like other forms of domestic labor) prevents the final totalization of the social-ideological field of Egyptian history within a master narrative of class or modes of production.

Something is clearly indeterminate or undecidable about petty commodity production as object and petty commodity producers as subjects. In the literature I have discussed, we get a clear sense that the sometimes antagonistic representations of Egyptian petty commodity production refer to *something more* than a positive reality of productive relations and coherent identities. I am most interested in tracking this "something more," this other kind of surplus value, a surplus of meaning that exceeds straightforward referentiality and is liable to appropriation, as when each version of representation staked out a privileged figure on the undecidable ground of Egypt's political economy. The representations function as signifiers in a sliding and contradictory chain of discourses that had their own specific history, conditions of possibility, relations of production, and discursive strategies. Names like *artisanat* and *informal sector* attest to the cultural imagination, to a certain fantasy, to interests of power and desire invested in a form of production and their constant reconstitution through specific exclusions, conventions, and material and discursive practices. If such figures emerge most forcefully in the "authoritative" discourse of the agents and ideologues of competing and contradictory international and state interests, it is because, even where subaltern voices are silent, excluded, repressed, or complexly encoded, dominant discourse always registers that which its constituents perceive as a threat to their political-economic hegemony. But just as we must rethink dominant narratives, so too we must be prepared to read against the grain of artisans' everyday life experiences and the words that petty commodity producers "speak for themselves," allegorically discovering yet other sorts of stories embedded in representations by or about subaltern subjects.[57] Petty commodity production's heterogeneous composition undermines attributions of shopfloor subject positions or unified identity assigned to "the" working class, and these "different" kinds of worker remind us not only of the existence of multiple forms of domination and exploitation, but also of the necessity to combat these complexly interconnected forms of oppression by making more coherent multiple sites of resistance.

Notes

1. This chapter is part of a larger work developing a poetics of Egyptian political economy. The study is based on a year of ethnographic fieldwork conducted in Egypt

in 1980, among potters and other petty commodity producers and their families, and on historical research into Egyptian artisanry since the nineteenth century; see Koptiuch, "A Poetics of Petty Commodity Production: Traditional Egyptian Craftsmen in the Postmodern Market" (unpublished Ph.D. dissertation, University of Texas at Austin, 1989). For their support of this work I wish to thank the Social Science Research Council-American Council of Learned Societies, the American Research Center in Egypt, and the University of Texas at Austin. For critical assistance on this chapter my thanks to Robert Fernea, Peter Gran, Zachary Lockman, and Martina Rieker.

2. Georg Stauth, "Gamaliyya: Informal Economy and Social Life in a Popular Quarter of Cairo" (paper presented at an SSRC workshop, The Informal Sector in the Middle East, Tutzing, Germany, 1986).

3. John Waterbury, *The Egypt of Nasser and Sadat: The Political Economy of Two Regimes* (Princeton, N.J.: Princeton University Press, 1983), p. 178.

4. Research on "industrialization before industrialization" disputes the assumption that a clean transition to capitalism uniformly characterized even all regions of Europe. See Peter Kriedte, Hans Medick, and Jurgen Schlubohm, *Industrialization Before Industrialization: Rural Industry in the Genesis of Capitalism*, trans. Beate Schempp (Cambridge: Cambridge University Press, 1981; original German publication 1977). For recent perspectives on petty commodity production, see Hamza Alavi, "The Structure of Peripheral Capitalism," in *Introduction to the Sociology of "Developing" Societies*, ed. Hamza Alavi and Teodor Shanin (New York: Monthly Review Press, 1982), pp. 172–191; Jonathan Barker and Gavin Smith, eds., "Special Issue: Rethinking Petty Commodity Production," *Labour, Capital and Society* 19 (April 1986); Philippe Hugon, ed., "Secteur informel et petite production marchande dans les villes du tiérs monde," special issue of *Tiérs Monde* 21, no. 82 (1980); and Carol A. Smith, "Forms of Production in Practice: Fresh Approaches to Simple Commodity Production," *Journal of Peasant Studies* 11, no. 4 (1984): 201–221. For other reasons, under the sign of the newly discovered "informal sector," developmentalist studies of petty commodity production also evince awareness of the same critique of linear models of progress and "stages" of development, but turn it toward more efficient consolidation of transnational capitalism. The temporal metaphor of post-World War II modernization theory has given way to a spatial metaphor that envisions "complementary" formal and informal socioeconomic sectors harmoniously coexisting within a single national economy. On Egypt's informal sector, see Mahmoud Abdel-Fadil, "Informal Sector Employment in Egypt," *Cairo Papers in Social Science* 6, no. 2 (1983): 55–89; Suzanne Berger, "Problems and Prospects of Egyptian Small-Scale Industry," Draft Report (Cairo: USAID, 1978); World Bank, *Arab Republic of Egypt: Survey of Small Scale Industry* (Washington, D.C.: World Bank 1977). For critiques, see Koptiuch, "Informal Sectorization of Egyptian Petty Commodity Production," in *Anthropology, Industry, and Labor: Studies of the New Industrialization in the Late Twentieth Century*, ed. Frances Rothstein and Michael Blim (New York: Bergin and Garvey, 1992), pp. 149–160; Maria Mies, *Patriarchy and Accumulation on a World Scale: Women in the International Division of Labour* (London: Zed Books, 1986); Alejandro Portes, "The Informal Sector: Definition, Controversy, and Relation to National Development," *Review* 7, no. 1 (1983): 151–174.

5. Theorized, among others, by Samir Amin, *Accumulation on a World Scale*, vols. 1 and 2 (New York: Monthly Review Press, 1974); *Unequal Development* (New York: Monthly Review Press, 1976); Claude Meillassoux, *Maidens, Meal and Money. Capitalism and the Domestic Community* (Cambridge: Cambridge University Press, 1981, original French publication 1975); Pierre-Philippe Rey, *Les Aliances de Classes* (Paris: Francois Maspero, 1973). Alain Lipietz puts their theses into a critical, complex, historically contingent perspective in *Mirages and Miracles: The Crises of Global Fordism* (London: Verso, 1987).

6. Jacques Chevalier "There Is Nothing Simple About Simple Commodity Production," *Journal of Peasant Studies* 10, no. 4 (1983): 153–186; Meillassoux, *Maidens, Meal and Money*, p. 97.

7. See for example Mariarosa Dalla Costa and Selma James, *The Power of Women and the Subversion of the Community* (Bristol: Falling Wall Press, 1972); Annette Kuhn and Ann Marie Wolpe, eds., *Feminism and Materialism: Women and Modes of Production* (London: Routledge and Kegan Paul, 1978); Mies, *Patriarchy and Accumulation*.

8. On the subsumption of petty commodity production to capitalism, see Chevalier, "There Is Nothing Simple About Simple Commodity Production." On "unwaged" labor and the "social factory," see Harry Cleaver, *Reading* Capital *Politically* (Austin: University of Texas Press, 1979).

9. Olivier LeBrun and Chris Gerry, "Petty Producers and Capitalism," *Review of African Political Economy* 3 (May–October 1975): 32.

10. Richard Johnson, "Three Problematics: Elements of a Theory of Working Class Culture," in *Working-Class Culture, Studies in History and Theory*, ed., John Clarke, Charles Chrichter, and Richard Johnson (London: Routledge and Kegan Paul, 1979), pp. 201–237. This notion of consent is, of course, derived from Antonio Gramsci, *Selections from the Prison Notebooks*, ed. and trans., Quintin Hoare and Geoffrey Nowell Smith (New York: International Publishers, 1971).

11. For general discussions of the development of capitalism in Egypt during this period, see Joel Beinin and Zachary Lockman, *Workers on the Nile: Nationalism, Communism, Islam, and the Egyptian Working Class, 1882–1954* (Princeton, N.J.: Princeton University Press, 1987), Eric Davis, *Challenging Colonialism: Bank Misr and Egyptian Industrialization, 1920–1941* (Princeton, N.J.: Princeton University Press, 1983), Roger Owen, *The Middle East and the World Economy, 1800–1914* (London: Methuen, 1981), Alan Richards, *Egypt's Agricultural Development, 1800–1980: Technical and Social Change* (Boulder, Colo.: Westview Press, 1982).

12. It should not be a foregone conclusion but a matter for historical study— and political perspective—to determine whether this migration should be regarded as a result of capitalist manipulation of peasant workers or as a form of peasants' resistance and refusal to accept the terms offered by a recomposing capitalist class.

13. Roger Owen, "The Study of Middle Eastern Industrial History: Notes on the Relationship Between Factories and Small-Scale Manufacturing with Special References to Lebanese Silk and Egyptian Sugar, 1900-1930," *International Journal of Middle East Studies* 16, no. 4 (1984): 475–487.

14. Mona Hammam, "Capitalist Development, Family Division of Labor, and Migration in the Middle East," in *Women's Work: Development and the Division of Labor by Gender*, ed, Eleanor Leacock, Helen I. Safa, et al. (South Hadley, Mass.: Bergin and Garvey, 1986), pp. 158–173.

15. Joel Beinin, "Formation of the Egyptian Working Class," *MERIP Reports* 94 (February 1981): 14–23; Beinin and Lockman, *Workers on the Nile*; Amin 'Izz al-Din, *Tarikh al-tabaqa al-'amila al-misriyya munthu nash'atiba hatta thawrat 1919* [The History of the Egyptian Working Class from its Establishment Until the 1919 Revolution] (Cairo: Dar al-Katib al-'Arabi, 1967), pp. 123–131.

16. Davis, *Challenging Colonialism*.

17. Afaf Lutfi al-Sayyid Marsot, *Egypt in the Reign of Muhammad Ali* (London: Cambridge University Press, 1984).

18. Germain Martin, *Les Bazars du Caire et les Petits Métiers Arabes* (Cairo: Université Egyptienne, 1910), p. 8. My translation.

19. Ibid., pp. 48–50.

20. Ibid., pp. 79, 87.

21. Ibid., pp. 87–88.

22. Ibid., pp. 66, 88.

23. Ibid., pp. 49, 88.

24. Ibid., p. 61.

25. Ibid., pp. 41, 83.

26. Ibid., p. 84.

27. Ibid., pp. 85–86. See also Jean Vallet, *Contribution à l'Étude de la Condition des Ouvriers de la Grande Industrie au Caire* (Valence: Imprimerie Valentinoise 1911), which focuses on these large industries; and Beinin and Lockman, *Workers on the Nile*.

28. Martin, *Bazars du Caire*, p. 94.

29. Ibid., p. 87.

30. Ibid., p. 88.

31. René Maunier, "L'Apprentissage dans la Petite Industrie en Égypte, l'Oganisation Actuelle, les Reformes Possibles," *L'Égypte Contemporaine* 3 (1912): 341–369.

32. Francois Bourgeois, "L'Industrie Ceramique en Égypte," *L'Égypte Contemporaine* 7 (1916): 467–484.

33. Ibid., pp. 480–481.

34. Among others, Pierre Arminjon, *La Situation Économique et Financière de L'Égypte* (Paris: Librairie Generale de droit et de jurisprudence, 1911), pp. 173–191; I. G. Levi, "L'Industrie et L'Avenir Économique de L'Égypte," *L'Égypte Contemporaine* 18, no. 100 (1927):

359-382; A. G. Politis, *L'Hellenisme et L'Égypte Moderne*, vol. 2 (Paris: Felix Alcan, 1930); *Rapport de la Commission du Commerce et de L'Industrie*, reprinted in *The Economic History of the Middle East 1800-1914*, ed. Charles Issawi (Chicago: University of Chicago Press, 1922), pp. 452-460; S. Sornaga, *L'Industrie en Égypte* (Cairo: Imprimerie M. Roditi, 1916).

35. An untapped resource for information about artisans, who of course continued to exist during this time, may lie in the folklore of the period. See, for example, Yacoub Artin Pacha, comp., *Contes Populaires racontés au Caire (de 1870 à 1886)* (Cairo: Librarie Centrale, 1903). In view of the publication date of Artin's compilation, however, even these popular narratives could be considered amid the corpus of works from the early twentieth century period.

36. See A. E. Crouchley, *The Economic Development of Modern Egypt* (London: Longmans, Green and Co, 1938), André Fournet, "Artisanat Égyptien: sa contribution à la formation de la doctrine artisanale," *L'Égypte Contemporaine* 32 (1941): 849-1000, A. A. I. El-Gritly, "The Structure of Modern Industry in Egypt," *L'Égypte Contemporaine* 241-242 (November-December 1948): 363-582; G. H. Selous, *Report on Economic and Commercial Conditions in Egypt* (London: His Majesty's Stationary Office, 1937). During World War II, the Middle East Supply Center frantically worked throughout the Middle East to consolidate and restore traditional artisanal industries for the local production of commodities badly needed for domestic and military use. Great Britain, Foreign Office (Archives in the Public Record Office, London), FO 922.

37. Gabriel Baer, *Egyptian Guilds in Modern Times* (Jerusalem: The Israeli Oriental Society, 1964).

38. Great Britain, "Report by H.M. Agent and Consul General on the Finances, Administration, and Condition of Egypt and the Sudan" (1905), *House of Commons Sessional Papers*, vol. 137 (1906): 572.

39. Historian Roger Owen has made a consistent attempt to absolve Cromer of the accusations by other European and Egyptian contemporaries that his colonial administration was not on principle opposed to opening the way to industrial development in Egypt. I am tempted to read his interpret this controversy as scarcely short of an apology for empire. See Owen, "Lord Cromer and the Development of Egyptian Industry 1883-1907," *Middle East Studies* 2, no. 4 (1966): 282-301; "The Attitudes of British Officials to the Development of the Egyptian Economy, 1882-1922," in *Studies in the Economic History of the Middle East*, ed. M. A. Cook (London: Oxford University Press, 1970), pp. 485-500; and *Middle East and the World Economy*.

40. Great Britain, Foreign Office, FO 368.

41. Owen, "The Attitudes of British Officials," p. 498.

42. Egyptian Government, *Taqrir lajnat al-tijara wa'l-sina'a, 1918* [Report of the Committee on Commerce and Industry] (Cairo: al-Amiriya Press, 1925).

43. *Rapport de la Commission du Commerce et de L'Industrie*, p. 454.

44. Ibid., p. 459.

45. *New York Times*, October 7, 1943, p. 29.

46. *L'Égypte Contemporaine* 1 (1910): 17. The inaugural volume of this journal was edited and introduced by Martin and published for the Khedival Society in 1910 by the printing office of the L'Institut Français d'Archaéologie Orientale. This first issue contains several articles on Egypt's artisanal manufactures.

47. Martin aptly seems to exemplify the sort of French intellectual Paul Rabinow associates more generally with this same moment of French modernism. His "techno-cosmopolitanism" attempted to balance contemporary technology with historical and natural elements (the latter would seem to include the artisans themselves, represented as timeless elements of nature) to fashion Egypt's petty industry as an appropriate object of regulation and control. *Fench Modern: Norms and Forms of the Social Environment* (Cambridge, Mass.: MIT Press, 1989).

48. Edward Said, *Orientalism* (New York: Pantheon Books, 1978).

49. Sornaga, *L'Industrie en Égypte*, p. 14.

50. I discuss this recent history in Koptiuch, "Informal Sectorization."

51. See Stuart Hall, "Notes on Deconstructing 'the Popular,'" in *People's History and Socialist Theory*, ed., Raphael Samuel (London: Routledge and Kegan Paul, 1981), pp. 227–239; Ernesto Laclau, *Politics and Ideology in Marxist Theory* (London: New Left Books, 1977); Zachary Lockman, " 'Worker' and 'Working Class' in Pre-1914 Egypt: A Rereading," the next chapter in this volume.

52. Alejandro Portes, "The Informal Sector: Definition, Controversy, and Relation to National Development," *Review* 7, no. 1 (1983): 168.

53. Because the dominant narrative of "the" Egyptian working class tends to be antiheroic, we might ask just who these subjects are. My theoretical argument here is inspired by Slavoj Zizek, *The Sublime Object of Ideology* (London and New York: Verso, 1989).

54. Johannes Fabian, *Time and the Other: How Anthropology Makes Its Object* (New York: Columbia University Press, 1983).

55. See Michel DeCerteau, *The Practice of Everyday Life* (Berkeley: University of California Press, 1984); Rosalind O'Hanlon, "Recovering the Subject: Subaltern Studies and Histories of Resistance in Colonial South Asia," *Modern Asian Studies* 22, no. 1 (1988): 189–224. The political sophistication evident in the "subaltern studies" project by South Asian scholars has not (yet?) surfaced to my knowledge in Middle East studies. See Ranajit Guha and Gayatri Chakravorty Spivak, eds., *Selected Subaltern Studies* (Oxford: Oxford University Press, 1988).

56. Zizek, *The Sublime Object of Ideology*.

57. A full treatment of these complexities must be postponed, but key theoretical resources can be found in Luce Irigaray, "Interview," in *French Philosophers in Conversation*, ed. Raul Mortley (London: Routledge, 1987), pp. 62–78; O'Hanlon, "Recovering the Subject"; Gayatri Chakravorty Spivak, "Can the Subaltern Speak?" in *Marxism and the Interpretation of Culture* (Urbana: University of Illinois Press, 1988), pp. 271–313.

Zachary Lockman

4

"Worker" and "Working Class" in pre-1914 Egypt: A Rereading

Over the last quarter of a century, the scholarly literature on Egyptian working-class history has expanded enormously. From virtual nonexistence in the early 1960s it has burgeoned to include several book-length studies by Egyptian as well as foreign scholars, a number of unpublished doctoral dissertations, and numerous articles. As a result, we have reconstructed a coherent and fairly comprehensive chronology of major strikes and the formation of labor unions and can make some tentative statements about patterns and trends; we have considerable "background" information about wages, working conditions, employment in various occupations, commodity prices, economic conditions, and so forth; we have some knowledge (though far from enough) about conditions, relations and dynamics within certain workplaces and unions; we know a lot about the relations among certain groups of workers, certain unions and union federations, and various political movements, including nationalists (especially the Wafd), communists, and Islamists (notably the Muslim Brothers); and, last but not least, we can meaningfully discuss (and even debate) the attitudes and policies of various Egyptian regimes toward workers and labor organizations.[1]

Having contributed to this literature, I have absolutely no desire to downplay the great value of what has been achieved so far or to belittle the toil and trouble it took. However, in the interest of advancing the field of Egyptian working-class history, and of Egyptian social and cultural history more broadly, I would like in this chapter to focus on some of the problems and lacunae that I believe characterize much of that literature. These include an "objectivist" conception of class; an understanding of working-class formation as fundamentally a structural and economic process, thereby obviating exploration of the cultural aspects of the process of class formation; and a tendency to depict the working class in a rather essentialist and teleological manner.

I will begin by critically discussing some of the theoretical premises of traditional labor history, which has been largely informed by an economistic and positivist variant of Marxism, on which the Egyptian literature has drawn as well. These premises have to a large extent underpinned the dominant paradigm of working-class formation and development and helped produce (in Egypt but also much more generally) a historical narrative of labor history that I believe needs to be reexamined.

As an alternative, I will be proposing that we try to think about "worker" and "working class" as categories that are certainly profoundly shaped by a certain set of material practices (i.e., capitalist production relations, of a certain kind and scale), but whose coherence and social effectivity nonetheless cannot be directly derived either from workers' structural position or from their "experience," often taken as an unproblematic alternative to a crude economic determinism. Instead, within a specific socioeconomic matrix these categories are produced in and through discourse—through systems of meaning expressed in language and other signifying practices, material and otherwise.[2] Because they are historically and socially constructed, not only economically but also culturally, neither the working class as a perceived social actor nor workers' subjectivity—the various ways in which those we label workers feel, think, and make sense of themselves and their relation to the world—can be assumed to be singular or unified or coherent or fixed in meaning, or guaranteed by any teleology or historical master narrative, especially one derived from some dubious reading of a purportedly coherent, singular, and relevant "Western European experience."

After this theoretical excursus, I will discuss some of the problematic assumptions, categorizations, and periodizations that underpin conventional readings of late nineteenth and early twentieth century Egyptian working-class history. The resulting narrative has, I argue, tended to impute to those it characterizes as workers a certain form of class consciousness and to the working class a certain essential character and historical trajectory. What I propose here as a rereading will be less a substantive new version of this history than a critique of some of the old ways of telling this story. Nonetheless, I hope that it will at least point to new and more productive ways of conceptualizing the history of the Egyptian working class, ways that may help remedy at least some of the deficiencies of past work (including my own) and point to new directions for future research.

Working-Class Formation in Egyptian Historiography

Most interpretations of working-class formation in Egypt (as well as most other places) have portrayed it as the more or less direct and automatic product of capitalist development and the oppression and exploitation to which it subjected workers. By way of example I would cite the two most substantial studies by Egyptian historians: Amin 'Izz al-Din's *Ta'rikh al-tabaqa al-'amila al-misriyya mundhu nash'atiha hatta thawrat 1919* (Cairo, 1967) and Ra'uf 'Abbas's *al-Haraka al-'ummaliyya fi misr, 1899–1952* (Cairo, 1967). For both of these historians, an Egyptian working class emerged between 1882 and 1914 as a certain form of capitalist development created large-scale enterprises in which significant numbers of wage workers were employed. In this view, Egyptian workers responded to their experience of exploitation, oppression, and abuse in these new workplaces with collective action (including strikes and organization), thereby manifesting that they were beginning to think and act in "class" ways.

In partial contrast, Ellis Goldberg's *Tinker, Tailor, and Textile Worker: Class and Politics in Egypt, 1930–1952* (Berkeley, Calif., 1986) includes an admirable and important discussion of how (all?) Egyptian workers of the 1930s understood what it meant to be a worker. But because it focuses on the link between workers' experience in specific workplaces and the organizational forms and strategies they adopted, *Tinker, Tailor, and Textile Worker* is not significantly concerned with the cultural construction of the categories of "worker" and "working class," nor with the broader social contexts within which they were imbedded. Class, class consciousness, and class struggle are already present at the start, although for Goldberg their contents are neither predetermined nor uniform across time and space but the product of experience and conflict.

The introductory chapter of *Workers on the Nile: Nationalism, Communism, Islam, and the Egyptian Working Class, 1882–1954* (Princeton, N.J., 1987), by Joel Beinin and myself, lays out a theoretical perspective (derived in part from a formulation of Adam Pzreworski) that rejects the notion that "relation to the means of production uniquely determines whether a given group of people will emerge as a class conscious of its own interests and acting in the economic and political spheres to further those interests." Instead, it argues, "classes are formed in the course of social and political conflicts in which multiple historical actors seek to organize a given group of people as members of a particular class, as citizens of a nation, as adherents of a religious group, or around some other pole of identity."[3] It seems to me now, however, that the promise of this basically sound theoretical perspective is inconsistently fulfilled in the book itself, where the very paradigm criticized in the introduction sometimes resurfaces.

Class and Class Consciousness

That paradigm is premised (usually implicitly) on a view of class as an entity that exists "out there" in the "real world," prior to meaning and separate from the ways in which it can be thought and talked about in language. That is, it is rooted in the belief that class, defined in terms of relationship to the means of production, income level, or any other "objective" criterion one chooses, is *pregiven* in external reality and that objectively determined class location gives rise to a specific consciousness. Underpinning this assumption is a theory of knowledge that makes a more or less unambiguous dichotomy between that which actually exists in the real world (in this case, a social class), on the one hand, and its (admittedly sometimes distorted or refracted) reflection in consciousness, on the other.

This dichotomy manifests itself in Marx's well-known distinction between "class-in-itself" (the working class as an objective social category brought into existence and continually reproduced by the process of capital accumulation) and "class-for-itself" (the situation that prevails when those objectively defined as members of the working class have come, as a result of their experiences, to perceive that they do in fact belong to a distinct class in conflict with other classes, and they unite in pursuit of their common interests as workers). According to one influential reading of Marx, the failure of workers to promptly grasp the singular meaning of their objective structural situation and their common class interest, and beyond that to struggle to overthrow capitalism and replace it with a system that objectively corresponds to their needs, is explained by "false consciousness." Reification, manifested in the capitalist production process as commodity fetishism, mystifies reality and hinders conscious access to the way the system actually operates by representing exploitative social relations among individuals and classes as equal exchange relations among things, among commodities in the market. Reality *represents itself* as other than it really is and thereby interferes (at least for a time) with the ability of workers to grasp the truth of their individual and class situation and its systemic causes and to acquire thereby the consciousness and strategy required for radically altering the structure of society.

The concept of reification is certainly valuable, for it reminds us that the social order is an effect of the ensemble of human social practices, rather than the product of divine decree or extrahistorical "objective" laws of nature or of economics. The false consciousness model that classical Marxist theory derives from it is arguable, however. Empirically, it is clear that those whom historians, socialist and communist activists, and so on, define as workers, that is, as members of the working class by objective criteria, have in many (perhaps most) times and places not actually behaved as the preceeding schema predicts that they should. The historical record in both advanced and underdeveloped capitalist countries suggests that an approach that, from the fact of their employment in large industrial and transport enterprises, deduces that workers display (or will eventually overcome false consciousness and come to display) a certain form of class consciousness and a propensity toward certain specified forms of collective action, will not get us very far.[4]

Efforts have been made to overcome the problems raised by the rigid distinction found in some readings of Marx between class-in-itself/class-for-itself (or, to put it differently, between class as thing, as objective entity, and class consciousness, as subjective perception and meaning) by appealing to "experience" as the missing link. E. P. Thompson has supplied the classic formulation of this position, which he sees as an alternative to structuralist variants of Marxism that have tended to stress the objective "thingness" of class, ignore or reject culture and eliminate human agency:

> I do not see class as a "structure," or even as a "category," but as something which in fact happens (and can be shown to have happened) in human relationships. . . . And class happens when some men, as a result of common experiences (inherited or shared), feel and articulate the identity of their interests as between themselves, and as against other men whose interests are different from (and usually opposed to) theirs. The class experience is largely determined by the productive relations in which men are born—or enter involuntarily. Class-consciousness is the way in which those experiences are handled in cultural terms: embodied in traditions, value-systems, ideas, and institutional forms.[5]

In its prioritization of culture and its insistence on the need to investigate the perceptions, attitudes, and actions of actors in concrete historical situations, Thompson's formulation is without question a great advance over the propensity of structuralist and positivist approaches to deduce class from objective relation to the means of production and then to deduce consciousness and behavior, actual or putative. It does not fully resolve the problem, however, because it can still be read— whether or not this is Thompson's intention—as depicting the sphere of "experience" as distinct from or prior to "culture" itself. That is, it seems to be saying that certain objective circumstances produce in the consciousness of those on whom they impinge certain experiences, which are then "handled" or processed culturally to produce certain meanings.

To the extent that this way of putting things does not insist that all experience is *already* cultural, in other words that there is no pure, direct experience that is not *already* representation, hence socially determined, we are still, epistemologically speaking, within the realm of empiricism, if at its outermost margins. As Gareth Stedman Jones has usefully put it, "consciousness cannot be related to experience except through the interposition of a particular language which organizes the understanding of experience, and it is important to stress that more than one language is capable of articulating the same set of experiences."[6]

It is certainly true that in many places capitalist development has brought into being a category of people employed in relatively large, mechanized, and highly capitalized enterprises, employing substantial numbers of wage earners. Nor should the reality or importance of resistance by workers be denied or downplayed: over the past century and a half, workers across the globe have resisted what they have perceived as unjust or arbitrary domination, oppression, and exploitation; and they have often done so by engaging in very similar forms of collective action (strikes, trade unions, political activism). Yet we know too that those we label workers respond to circumstances in a wide variety of ways, not necessarily collectively or as workers. Moreover, we cannot assume that resistance (itself a by no means unambiguous term) results simply from workers' experience of domination and exploitation translated directly and uniformly into identification as workers and class action nor that it is always informed by some abstract, "rational" (in the capitalist-economistic sense of that term), classical "proletarian" form of subjectivity, as much of the literature seems to do.[7]

Can we, for example, take it for granted that an Egyptian worker who at the turn of the century went on strike or joined a trade union understood or meant precisely the same things by those actions as a worker somewhere else or in Egypt during another period? Or that there was uniformity either *among* all Egyptian workers at any given time or even *within* the consciousness of single individual, whose understanding of himself or herself and the world was not necessarily unified and unfragmented but may have been the product of different (and sometimes conflicting) identities and outlooks interacting in complex ways, with results that are not entirely predictable? Working-class identity *may* be one component, one subject position, within the subjectivity of those we label workers, but it is unlikely to be the only or necessarily the most important one.

This is not to say that the social conditions of existence of language are arbitrary or that there is no link whatsoever between what are conventionally dichotomized as "social being" and "social consciousness." Rather, instead of starting from the premise that "class" *produces* "class consciousness," we might challenge that very dichotomy by taking seriously Joan Scott's argument that "class and class consciousness are the same thing—they are political articulations that provide an analysis of, a coherent pattern to impose upon, the events and activities of daily life. Although the rhetoric of class appeals to the objective 'experience' of workers, in fact such experience only exists through its conceptual organization."[8] So to the extent that what is commonly called class consciousness does in fact emerge among workers, it can be understood not so much as either reflective of objective class position or the product of unmediated immediate experience, but as *constructed* in and through political and ideological struggles—which are always discursive struggles, struggles about meaning. In this sense, "workers" and a "working class" as forms of identity, perceived social categories, and historical actors can be seen as products, effects, not only of certain material practices but also of a discourse that, by providing categories of worker and class identity, gives people a language with which to make sense (or rather, to make one of several possible kinds of sense) of their experience and to interpret the world and their own place and possibilities within it.

Egypt Before Class

In the senses in which they are used today, the terms ʿamil (plural ʿummal) and al-tabaqa al-ʿamila—usually translated as "worker" and "working class," respectively—are relatively recent arrivals on the Egyptian scene.

Only within the last hundred years did they begin to acquire their present meanings as designations for a specific form of individual social identity and for a specific category of people composed of these individuals and said to possess a collective agency. This process involved not only shifts in the socially accepted meanings of these specific words, but also the emergence and spread of a new constellation of conceptualizations of individual identity, the social order, the state and the nation. For many (though by no means all) Egyptians, *worker*, *working class*, and (more generally) *class* came thereby to be meaningful categories of social identity and action, with significant political, economic, and cultural implications and consequences.

To gauge the significance of these interacting shifts whereby some Egyptians (as well as some foreign observers) came to believe that Egyptian society contained a category of people called workers who collectively constituted a "working class," it may be useful to go back and look at an earlier period, the late eighteenth and nineteenth centuries. There were of course at that time, as always, various distinct—sometimes competing, sometimes overlapping—discourses of social identity. For our purposes what is important is the prevalence of a system of categorization that classified the great bulk of the Arabic-speaking urban male population in terms of affiliation to a specific craft or trade (*hirfa* or *san'a*), rather than as members of a class that incorporated all wage workers across occupational lines.

The organizational framework within which all those engaged in a particular handicraft, commercial, and service trade were organized was generally referred to as a *ta'ifa* (plural *tawa'if*). In the historiographical literature, *ta'ifa* has sometimes (and all too easily) been assimilated to the medieval European guild, even though the Arabic term in Egypt also was used to denote groups constituted along ethnic/religious and other lines and did not necessarily convey the same meanings associated with its English or French counterparts. In any event, the *ta'ifa* encompassed not only those who owned tools, some working capital, a stock of raw materials or finished products, a workplace or other property, and were deemed "masters" within the trade, but also those who owned no means of production and lived by selling their labor power, the journeymen and apprentices. In both cases occupational identity was generally specified by the participial form commonly used in Arabic to denote trades: *nahhasin, sabbaghin, jabbasin, sarrajin, dabbaghin, hajjarin, saqqa'in,* and so forth, although other forms were also used.

Possession of knowledge about, or skills in, a specific trade was the defining characteristic of occupational affiliation, rather than possession of property.

It is true that, in his pathbreaking study of artisans and merchants in late eighteenth-century Cairo, André Raymond speaks of a distinct "proletariat," a class that would appear to cut across occupational lines. His discussion relies heavily on Chabrol's essay in the *Description de l'Égypte*, which uses the term *ouvriers* with reference to the poorest domestic servants, stableboys, donkey drivers, watercarriers, and day laborers. To this "proletariat" Raymond himself adds itinerant street peddlars whose income kept them at the margins of subsistence.[9] *Ouvrier* is, however, Chabrol's term rather than an indigenous category of identity, and in Raymond's usage membership in the "proletariat" seems to be essentially a matter of income. It is evident from Raymond's discussion that the standard participial form was used to denote most if not all of the trades engaged in by the members of Raymond's putative "proletariat."

There probably did exist in late eighteenth and early nineteenth century Cairo a stratum of more or less unskilled, propertyless workers who took whatever short-term jobs were available and were not identified with any specific craft. Their specific and unique *structural* position notwithstanding, however, the members of this stratum do not seem to have been regarded as a distinct social category; rather they tended, by virtue of their extreme poverty, to be subsumed within the broader categories of the "poor," the "needy," the "wretched," the "rabble." The term *ajir* (plural *ujara'*), suggesting someone who is hired for a wage (*ajr*), was in use, but it referred to a journeyman who was paid a wage by a master within the framework of the *ta'ifa*. Most of those who performed low-status menial tasks, such as watercarriers and garbage collectors, were categorized by their trade, were referred to by occupational names, and were perceived as constituting a *ta'ifa* rather than as adhering on an individual basis to an undifferentiated proletariat.

There may well have been conflicts among apprentices, journeymen, and masters over piece rates or wages and working conditions, for example, or over advancement within the *ta'ifa*. But it seems that despite the existence of clear hierarchies of status, income, and power both within each trade (among masters, journeymen, and apprentices, or between the wealthiest merchants dealing in a particular commodity and their smaller competitors) and among the trades (for example, goldsmiths versus tanners, those who traded in luxury items versus street vendors, men's *tawa'if* versus women's *tawa'if*), the dominant discourse conceptualized most (if not quite all) individuals as part of some occupational group.[10] This categorization encompassed even certain occupations that today would be generally considered on the margins or outside the boundaries of "society" proper, such as prostitutes and pickpockets.[11]

Despite the profound social, economic, and political changes that Egypt underwent in the course of the nineteenth century, occupational identity displayed a high degree of persistence. Some occupational categories contracted or even disappeared under pressure from new competition (often machine-made imports), changing consumption patterns and shifts in market networks. Other trades were transformed to a greater or lesser degree as they struggled to adapt to new conditions, whereas some entirely new occupations emerged, making use of both old and new skills and technologies. Toward the end of the nineteenth century, as their functions were eliminated, taken over by a burgeoning state apparatus, or reallocated, the *tawa'if* gradually disappeared, at least as organized and recognized entities. Yet through that period, indeed into the twentieth century, the discourse of occupational identity still remained powerful.

As in earlier periods, this survival can be traced in linguistic usage. Occupational designations continued to be standard in both official and general public discourse. When for example Muhammad 'Ali began in the 1820s to forcibly recruit members of the urban *artisanat* for his new industrial enterprises, official orders did not make reference to any generic category of "workers," but only to specific occupational categories or to apprentices. Even orders and reports dealing with the labor force within the state-run factories, arsenals, shipyards, and construction sites, some segment of which was tending or operating machines, usually employed either the old craft names, or the more generic *sanayi'i*, which in *ta'ifa* vocabulary meant a journeyman. Only occasionally were such broader terms as *shaghghala, fa'ala*, or *'ummal* used, and then apparently in the general sense of "employees" or "work force."[12] With the contraction and ultimately the dismantling of Muhammad 'Ali's industrialization project in the later 1830s and 1840s, the thousands who had willingly or otherwise found employment in state enterprises seem to have reintegrated themselves back into the *artisanat* with relative ease.

Little seems to have changed in the course of the following generation. 'Ali Mubarak's monumental compilation of data on Egypt and the Egyptians, published in the late 1880s but for the most part written a decade earlier, still employs the old nomenclature for the urban crafts. When Mubarak uses the terms *shaghghala* and *mushtaghilin*, it is with the sense of all those who are engaged in a particular craft or trade.[13] These craftsmen, even when employed for a wage, are not conceived of as "workers" by virtue of their structural position, nor is there any hint that "working class" is as yet a socially meaningful category.

Peasants and Corvée Labor

It is possible, of course, that we are looking in the wrong place. Wage workers engaged in urban crafts, indeed all those engaged in urban crafts and trades, after all constituted only a small proportion of Egypt's population in the nineteenth century. The vast majority consisted of peasants, fallahin, substantial numbers of whom were, for longer or shorter periods in the course of the century, recruited for *corvée* labor.[14] From early on in Muhammad 'Ali's reign, peasants had been drafted on an increasingly large scale, not just to repair and maintain the existing system of earthworks and canals that sustained basin irrigation in the vicinity of their home villages—this was nothing new—but to implement the pasha's ambitious plans to extend perennial irrigation by building a new system of canals, dams, and levees. Labor was also required for port development and then, from the 1850s, on an unprecedented scale for two huge new projects: railway development and the Suez Canal.

For at least the first three decades of railway development, the great bulk of the labor used for construction work—preparing roadbeds, laying track, building bridges, and so on—was secured by *corvée*. The Suez Canal, the concession for which was granted by 'Abbas's successor Sa'id in 1854, involved an even more massive use of *corvée* labor: several hundred thousand peasants had been coerced into contributing their labor before the canal was completed in 1869. The Egyptian National Archives (*Dar al-Watha'iq*) in Cairo has preserved considerable material on the recruitment, transport, treatment, and provisioning of peasants conscripted for railway work; and one may presume that the system for Suez Canal labor was not dissimilar. The central government set quota for *corvée* labor for entire governorates, and these were then broken down into district and finally village quota, at which level the village *'umda* or shaykh would round up and send off the unlucky conscripts.

Dispatches from railway officials to provincial governors demanding that the latter fill their quota of laborers were frequent and insistent. For example, a dispatch dated 29 Muharram 1271/22 October 1854 calls on the governors of Gharbiyya and Minufiyya, in the Delta, to send the workers required for construction on the Cairo-Suez line without delay. Another dispatch, dated 4 Shawwal 1272/8 June 1856, demands 1,000 over and above the 2,000 already asked for. Some of the dispatches provide evidence of the hardships and dangers these conscripts faced: for esample, a telegram of 2 Dhu al-Qada 1277/12 May 1861 asks about a pension or allowance (*ma'ash*) for one Muhammad Hayla, whose left leg had been amputated after an accident at work.[15]

These texts allow us to get some sense of how the Egyptian state regarded those conscripted for work on its large-scale projects. Although this work force consisted overwhelmingly of peasants, the term by which these laborers were generally referred to—in the official dispatches concerning the railroad, but probably elsewhere as well—was not fallahin but *anfar* (the plural of *nafar*). Even in the singular, *nafar* can signify not only an individual, a person, a single man (especially for numerative purposes), but also a group or band of persons. It thus lends itself to usages that refer to one or more individuals *arranged* in some way, *organized* in accordance with some coherent and visible pattern; hence, its suitability for military usage, to mean both an individual soldier, especially one of low rank, and a troop of soldiers, a military unit.

The official bureaucratic discourse of the Egyptian state in the middle of the nineteenth century drew on this sense in referring to the thousands, indeed tens and (cumulatively) hundreds of thousands, of peasants it mobilized by force and compelled to perform hard labor, for meager renumeration, under conditions that were often brutal, subject to a significant risk of death or injury from exhaustion, disease, maltreatment, or accident. In the vocabulary of the state and from its standpoint, they were not—at least for the duration of their service— quite fallahin any longer. They were rather conceived of as unindividualized, interchangeable objects of a new machinery of power, who could be ordered up by telegram in large batches from remote provinces, mobilized, and made to work in semimilitary fashion to effect the huge projects the state deemed necessary or desireable.

In reality, of course, this machinery was never as efficient as the state would have wished. Apart from shortages of capital and management problems, the peasants' capacity for resistance also had to be reckoned with. Peasants collectively and individually manifested their refusal to accept the oppressive circumstances in which they found themselves in many ways, including evasion of *corvée* or escape from it, low productivity, "shirking," pilfering, and even open revolt.[16]

Although the experience of *corvée* labor in its mid-nineteenth century form may well have had some impact on the consciousness of those peasants unfortunate enough to have been swept up into it, there is no reason to believe that they ever came to accept the state's categorization of them as *anfar*. If anything, the experience is likely to have strengthened peasants' sense of the state as an oppressive, alien, and sometimes even lethal institution and their inclination to see their own communities as sources of solidarity and bases for resistance.[17] There is therefore no evidence of class consciousness among those peasants subjected to *corvée* labor, despite the fact of their (admittedly coerced) employment for (admittedly meager) wages in large concentrations.

Peasants as Workers: The Coalheavers of Port Said Reconsidered

In the 1880s the use of *corvée* was officially abandoned by the state. There had long been opposition to it in Egypt and in Europe on humanitarian grounds. More important, the spread of perennial irrigation had in many parts of Egypt reduced or eliminated the dead season during which peasant labor could be recruited for work outside of agriculture; and Egyptian large landowners (among them the Khedive and high state officials) were now reluctant to be deprived of their labor force for significant portions of the year. In addition, the desire of Egypt's new British masters to reduce expenditures dictated a scaling-down of the grand, sometimes grandiose, schemes of Muhammad 'Ali and his successors.

Anfar continued to be mobilized for large-scale infrastructural projects, including further railway development and the extension of perennial irrigation into the Sa'id through the construction of new canals and of a dam at Aswan. But they could now be recruited not by physical coercion through the bureaucratic and repressive mechanisms of the state—at least not openly—but rather through the less obviously coercive mechanism of the market, which just as effectively kept wages low and working conditions inhuman. An increasingly large stratum of landless peasants available for work at low wages had begun to appear in the last third of the nineteenth century, a product of changes in agrarian relations (exacerbated by rapid population growth) that had led to the large-scale dispossession of the peasantry. Labor contractors were therefore able to supply the state and private employers with the necessary *anfar*, for the most part peasants no longer able to subsist on the income from their tiny landholdings or lacking any holdings at all.

Even those peasants employed for wages on a relatively steady and long-term basis in large-scale enterprises outside of agriculture do not in this period seem to have regarded themselves, or to have been regarded by others, as workers or members of a distinct and coherent working class. To explore this further, and to address the more general question of the construction of narratives of Egyptian labor history, I would like to juxtapose two interpretations of the April 1882 strike by several thousand coalheavers in Port Said, at the Mediterranean end of the Suez Canal, and of its aftermath.[18]

These coalheavers were largely peasants from the Sa'id, employed by English coaling companies via labor contractors referred to as *shaykhs* and paid by piece rate. Their strike for a higher rate, which coincided with (and was facilitated by) a deepening political crisis that would culminate a few months later in the British occupation of Egypt, received the attention of the Egyptian government and press and foreign observers. The strikers were able to effectively stop coaling operations on the canal, prompting their employers to threaten to import strike breakers from Malta. The Egyptian government, then in the hands of a nationalist civilian-military coalition led by Colonel Ahmad 'Urabi, intervened on the strikers' behalf; and the coalheavers were able to extract a higher piece rate from the coaling companies. A few months later, however, the British occupation allowed the employers to regain the upper hand and drive the piece rate back down.

It is not implausible to read this strike as illustrative of "early labor activism," as I did in an earlier work.[19] It does seem to have been Egypt's first large-scale strike in modern times, and after a hiatus of almost two decades the strike would in fact become an increasingly common form of social action. More specifically, one can certainly find in the coalheavers' strike elements that would also appear in later actions by peasants employed in wage labor outside agriculture. The Port Said coalheavers can thus be understood as wage workers subject to an essentially capitalist system of labor contracting, hence comprehensible within a narrative of modern labor activism.

At the same time, however, it is important to keep in mind that this representation and the narrative strategy that accompanies it implicitly assume substantive continuity between this incident of 1882 and the strikes that erupted in the first decade of the twentieth century. Both are read as positing a fixed common subject ("workers") engaging in more or less the same action, "labor activism." This approach may divert attention from discontinuities and complexities in the narrative, among other things by neglecting the actual subjectivities of the coalheavers themselves, the way they understood their own identity (or identities) and the meaning (or meanings) of their actions, and the conditions under which those meanings were produced and reproduced or altered.

To illustrate this point, we may compare my account of the Port Said coalheavers with another, rather different discussion of this same group. For Gabriel Baer[20] the coalheavers in 1882 were not wage workers subject to capitalism but rather members of a guild, implicitly understood as an essentially precapitalist institution. This representation is justified mainly by Baer's definition of a guild as "a group of town people engaged in the same occupation and headed by a shaykh."[21] For Baer the Port Said coalheavers were, however, different from other guild members in one key respect. As he tells it, although almost all Egyptian guilds gradually and undramatically faded out of existence at the end of the nineteenth century, masters, journeymen, and apprentices all together, the coalheavers and a few other guilds instead split into two classes, pitting shaykhs turned exploitative labor contractors against guild members turned exploited contracted wage workers. And within this small set of cases, it was only among the coalheavers that a class struggle developed.

Baer does not see this class struggle manifesting itself in the 1882 strike, which is mentioned in passing but never discussed. At that point, the workers and shaykhs were still apparently harmoniously united within the framework of their guild. Over the following decade or so, however, "the development of shaykhs into contractors. . . resulted in a social cleavage inside the guild. " The exploited coalheavers submitted a petition in 1896 to Lord Cromer, the de facto ruler of Egypt, setting forth their grievances about ill-treatment and exploitation by the shaykhs, which for Baer "clearly reflect[s] the new economic and social relations" that had torn apart the coalheavers' guild.[22] In this reading, then, the 1882 strike is not a harbinger of labor activism to come, within the context of Egypt's growing integration into the world capitalist system; it is rather a relatively insignificant event, one that did make the coalheavers "notorious among foreign residents" but was at bottom only a manifestation of the general decline of the guild system. The focus of attention shifts instead to the 1896 petition, depicted as signifying the supercession of the decayed guild system by class conflict.

In my view Baer's definition of guild is too rigid (and too positivist) to be very useful. It lumps together artisans in long-established trades in old urban centers like Cairo, for whom there is historical evidence of corporate identity manifested in (and reproduced by) a variety of practices, and groups like the Port Said coalheavers who were, as we have seen, Sa'idi peasants recruited by labor contractors for low-skill employment at a new occupation in a town that had not existed two decades previously. Baer simply and unproblematically defines both groups as guilds, and the term *shaykh* is assumed to carry the same meaning in both cases.[23]

At the same time, it now seems to me that both my own earlier account and that of Gabriel Baer share the same problem: they seek to determine the meaning, the "truth" of this incident in terms of the coalheavers' objective structural position—for examples their employment for wages in the framework of an emergent capitalism in Egypt or (alternatively) their putative membership in a guild. Both these ways of posing the problem implicitly assume that fixed meanings corresponding to or reflecting an objective reality can be assigned to entities or categories (such as "worker," "working class" or "guild") and that the object of the history we write is a unified, rational subject whose identity, and the meaning of whose agency, remains stable and coherent across time and space.

We might instead start from an examination of the social construction of meaning, by investigating how (for example) the coalheavers, within a specific structural context, made sense of themselves, their actions and the world, not in terms of an assumed singular and "authentic" consciousness but rather as subjectivities constituted by competing (and sometimes contradictory) discourses. At the same time, it will be necessary to look at the discourses through which the meaning of the identity and action of the coalheavers, and of Egyptian wage workers more generally, was constituted for other social agents in Egypt at this time.

This is, admittedly, a rather difficult agenda to implement. In this period the great majority of Egyptians who worked for wages were illiterate, leaving behind few sources that might facilitate such an analysis, and the literate segments of society were for the most part not particularly interested in recording the thoughts or sentiments of the lower orders. Despite the paucity of information, though, it can be said with some degree of certainty that for the coalheavers themselves, the 1882 strike did not signal the emergence of a new self-identification as workers that replaced other, older identities as peasants or Sa'idis; nor does there seem to have been any significant shift in the course of the following decade and a half. Similarly, for Egyptian and foreign contemporaries, the 1882 strike did not signal the emergence on the social scene of a coherent and active working class. It was grasped as basically a local affair, one in which national politics may have played some part—it is likely that the coalheavers were emboldened to act by the fact that a sympathetic nationalist government was in power in Cairo—but not as a portent of things to come.

So although it may for certain purposes be appropriate to group together the actions of the Port Said coalheavers in 1882 with, for example, those of the Cairo cigarette rollers in 1899 and the Cairo tramwaymen in 1908 under the common rubric of "labor activism," by virtue of the participants' similar relationship to the means of production and use of the strike, it should also be kept in mind that this classification and the narrative it generates—or Baer's alternative, for that matter—can be problematic if taken as reality itself, as what "actually" happened, rather than as a representation that brings into play specific assumptions and consequences.

The Meanings of "Early Labor Activism"

In the years after 1882 other strikes took place in Egypt. In 1894, for example, Muhammad Farid—later the leader of the Nationalist party—recorded in his diary a report of a strike (broken by government repression) for higher wages by "wheat transport workers" in Port Said.[24] In what might be called the official *company history* of the Suez Canal, published in 1901, J. Charles-Roux tells of a strike that began in August 1896: some 190 European workers operating dredges and *bateaux-porteurs* at Port Said stopped work for two months to demand a guarantee of ten months' work a year. This strike failed and its leaders were deported to their countries of origin, but the Suez Canal Company's chief engineer was soon thereafter assassinated outside his home in nearby Isma'iliyya, presumably in revenge for the suppression of the strike.[25] A few months before the cigarette rollers' strike, workers at the Khedival Steamship Company had gone on strike against a wage cut.[26] There were probably other strikes, too, that simply went unreported or unrecorded.

Historians of Egyptian labor have tended to choose the Cairo cigarette rollers' strike of December 1899–February 1900 as the "real" starting point for their narratives, thereby either ignoring earlier strikes or implicitly regarding them as outside the framework of their story, as isolated events of little significance. This is the case with both 'Izz al-Din and 'Abbas; it is also at least partially the case with *Workers on the Nile*, which as we have seen does deal with the 1882 strike but nonetheless argues that the 1899 strike marks the beginning of "substantial and sustained labor activism culminating in the formation of trade unions."[27]

The cigarette rollers' strike did in fact display features that set it apart from previous instances of collective action by workers. It involved several thousand skilled workers from many different workplaces, some of them quite large, who went on strike simultaneously and remained out for two months, suggesting a strong sense of solidarity and a capacity for effective organization. The strikers were also quite successful in their efforts to confront employers' attempts to deploy strike breakers. The fact that the strike occurred not in the Suez Canal area but in the very heart of the capital brought it to the immediate attention of the government, the press, and the public. As a result much more information is available about this strike than about any of its predecessors. Even many contemporary observers saw it as the first of its kind. And the fact that subsequent years would witness other strikes with similar features, along with the first attempts by workers to establish trade unions, also made the choice of the cigarette rollers' action as a starting point plausible.

It may nonetheless be useful to discuss two interrelated aspects of this depiction and the narrative that flows from it. First, what are we actually talking about when we deploy terms like "labor activism" and "union" with reference to the pre-First World War period in Egypt? Second, how were these phenomena constituted as objects of knowledge, by contemporaries as well as by historians, and what are the implications for Egyptian labor history of constituting them in different ways?

When we talk of labor activism and trade unions in this period we are, I believe, usually grouping together under a common rubric what may in fact be several different things, and we thereby also make some assumptions about what those things are. The Cairo cigarette rollers' strike of 1899–1900 may serve as one example. The incident can be, and usually has been, depicted as essentially a conflict between capital and labor, between the capitalist proprietors of large cigarette factories and the proletarians employed in them; as such it serves as a suitable jumping-off point for a history of the class struggle waged by Egyptian workers, a first manifestation of something that would gradually become behavior characteristic of all Egyptian workers.

But it is worth keeping in mind that this representation implicitly relegates to secondary status another dimension of this incident. The great majority of the cigarette rollers who struck in 1899–1900 were Greeks who had come to Egypt relatively recently, as were most of their employers. The strike was thus not just about "the working class in Egypt," with the strikers depicted as proletarians simply doing what supposedly comes naturally to proletarians. It was also very much a struggle within the Greek community in Egypt, possessing on that account complex dimensions of meaning that the standard accounts too easily ignore. It is, for instance, probably significant—this has not yet been adequately explored—that the short-lived craft association of cigarette rollers that emerged from the strike was headed not by a worker but by a physician prominent in the Greek community. The way this story is usually told is thus not necessarily wrong, but it should not be taken as exhaustive of this incident's possible meanings.

A look at some of the incidents of labor activism and organization in the early years of the century may help make this point more clearly. Apart from the Cairo cigarette rollers—who were the elite of their industry, the most highly-skilled and best paid among the cigarette workers, and who would strike again in 1903—several other groups of relatively skilled wage workers employed in large capitalist enterprises went on strike, organized unions, or did both. These included the Alexandria tramway workers, who struck briefly in 1900; Italian construction workers at the Aswan dam; workers at Egypt's only mechanized textile mill, also in Alexandria; and the cigarette rollers of Alexandria. But craft workers employed in small workshops also went on strike or formed unions: for example, printers at an Italian-language newspaper; tailors in Alexandria; barbers' apprentices; coachmen; office employees; and lawyers' clerks. Most (though not all) of those involved in both of these categories were foreigners. By contrast, a third category consisted essentially of Egyptians, unskilled workers like the coalheavers who in September 1900 went on strike at the port of Alexandria against a wage cut and for shorter hours.

We are dealing, then, with a diverse set of phenomena and must be cautious about attributing to them a single unitary meaning. It is certainly true that, in the first decade of the century, strikes and the formation of various kinds of labor organizations became a feature of the Egyptian scene. We cannot, however, assume that each of these phenomena meant the same things to those actually involved in them. Some of the new organizations consisted of both wage workers and small proprietors in "traditional" trades: the coachmen, for example, who organized mainly to secure for the trade as a whole higher fares, lower fines, and an end to the extortion of *baqshish* by the police.[28] The coachmen's action could thus plausibly be read not as an instance of "modern" labor activism, but as an instance of the kinds of things that the "premodern" guilds used to do. The Alexandria tailors were concerned not so much with wages as with maintaining a piece rate that would ensure them a reasonable income.[29] By contrast, the Alexandria coalheavers seem to have been—like their counterparts at Port Said two decades earlier—peasants recruited by labor contractors for heavy manual labor and cannot be incorporated into a narrative of labor activism without some qualification.

The Uses of Niqaba

Perhaps the best example, for the purposes of this discussion, is provided by the Manual Trades Workers' Union, or MTWU (*Niqabat 'Ummal al-Sana'i' al -Yadawiyya*), founded in 1909 under the auspices of the Nationalist party. It is, I think, significant that its organizers chose the Arabic noun *niqaba* to denote this organization, rather that *jam'iyya*— usually translated as "association" or "league"—by which the labor organizations established up to that point had referred to themselves (insofar, that is, as they were not made up of foreigners who knew little or no Arabic) and were referred to by observers and the Arabic-language press. *Niqaba* would gradually become the standard term for a union, but it was, as far as I can tell, first used with reference to the MTWU.

This term had earlier possessed strong guild connotations. In the seventeenth century, the *naqib* of the guild served as a sort of master-of-ceremonies, appointed by the guild's shaykh to administer various rituals for the induction and promotion of guild members. This position, and the term used to denote it in its guild-related meaning, seems to have disappeared by the nineteenth century, although *naqib* continued to be used with reference to the head or chief—perhaps most literally, the syndic—of other corporate groups: for example, the *naqib al-ashraf*, the syndic of the corporation of descendants of the Prophet in a particular city. In the eighteenth and nineteenth centuries—at least as far as one can judge from contemporary dictionaries—the term *niqaba* normally referred to the post held by the *naqib*, that is, the "syndicship" of some group.[30] Its usage to denote the group itself seems to date from around the turn of the century. *Niqaba* would soon thereafter be used to denote not only labor unions but also—much like its best equivalent, the French *syndicat*—other occupational groups, including "agriculturalists" (i.e., large landowners), lawyers, journalists, and engineers.

We do not know exactly why the workers and Nationalist party activists who participated in the formation of the MTWU, and of the Cairo tramway workers' union two months later, decided to use *niqaba* to denote these organizations. It may have been an effort to claim authenticity and legitimacy for the new labor unions by implicitly assimilating them to the old *tawa'if*, at a time when Cairo craftsmen bearing the tools and symbols of their trades still paraded past the governorate each year.[31] Using *niqaba* also differentiated these organizations from the craft unions recently formed by foreign workers. In any event, the choice may tell us something about the discursive framework within which its sponsors and members conceived of the organization.

The MTWU: Guild or Union

Contemporary sources seem to have conceptualized the MTWU's membership as divided naturally along craft lines. In their understanding the MTWU was composed not so much of generic "workers," classic proletarians abstracted from craft and portrayed in stark opposition to capital large and small, nor even as propertyless wage workers, but rather as members of specific trades in which they were deeply rooted, loosely grouped together under the rubric of the "manual trades." And, in fact, the organization encompassed not only craftsmen employed for wages in small workshops but also self-employed artisans and probably even small proprietors and employers in a variety of trades.[32]

From its inception, a significant proportion of the MTWU's membership consisted of wage workers—metal workers, mechanics, stokers, and others—employed at the Egyptian State Railways workshops (*al-'Anabir*) in Bulaq, which with 2,400 workers was one of the country's very largest concentration of wage workers. Within the framework of the MTWU, however, these railway workers—classic proletarians by the usual definitions—were conceptually mapped not by place of employment, nor even as generic "railway workers," but rather by craft, alongside masons, weavers, barbers, carpenters, painters, and so forth, with no indication that where or under what conditions they worked was deemed significant. These 'Anabir workers engaged in a brief but violent strike in October 1910, an incident that bears many of the features associated with modern labor activism; yet the MTWU members among them seem to have retained a strong sense of craft identity, a sense perhaps reproduced by the fact that much of the work in the railway shops was in fact carried out by work teams led by skilled workers and paid by the job.

One can therefore define the MTWU simply as a "labor union," and its activities simply as "labor activism," only at the risk of losing other dimensions of meaning that could be attributed to it. It may be just as plausible to see it as a sort of confederation of *tawa'if*, an organization constructed within an older discourse of occupational identity. This latter reading is supported by various pieces of evidence, in addition to the categorization of the membership by craft and the apparent weakness of any conception of "workers" entirely distinct from craft. For example, the MTWU's statutes required that new "active members"—that is, workers rather than middle-class supporters, who could be "contributing" or "honorary" members, depending on the extent of their financial support—have at least two years of work experience in a specific trade. In 1910 the MTWU leadership appointed a special committee to organize "for each of the affiliated trades a competition for 'masterpieces'," which would seem to suggest the persistence of an ethos of craft pride.[33]

In addition, much of the MTWU's membership seems to have perceived its key problem as not so much inadequate wages, long hours or miserable working conditions as the threat of foreign competition. This makes a great deal of sense if the MTWU is conceptualized as an organization of the indigenous urban *menu peuple* whose livelihood was in danger as a result of European competition, in the form both of European craftsmen who had migrated to Egypt and European machine-made imports. A passage in Muhammad Farid's address to the Nationalist party's 1910 congress, while emphasizing his party's interest in the education, moral and social uplift, and (not least) political mobilization of urban indigenous craftsmen, suggests that the threat to their livelihood was prominent among the concerns of the latter. "There is no way," Farid told his audience,

> to establish the blessed [union] movement in Egypt, so that the craftsman and the farmer [*al-sani' w'al-muzari'*] might be safe from poverty and destitution when they are old or sick, except by opening more night schools in the cities and villages, to teach them their rights and obligations and to make them understand the importance of unions and cooperative societies. Our blessed party has already begun to implement this idea by establishing four schools for craftsmen, in the districts of al-Khalifa, Bulaq, Shubra and al-'Abbasiyya, each of which has 120 students of various trades. We find the carpenter next to the shoemaker and the stonecutter next to the cook, all of them yearning for education and working hard to attain it, so that some of the students learn to read and write in less than six months. This movement has spread to many of the country's cities and villages, by virtue of the sincere activists of the Nationalist party and others. The champions of the workers have not been satisfied with this: in al-Khalifa they established a society for oratory [*jam'iyya l'il-khitaba*] that holds its meetings every Thursday night, at which the teachers deliver addresses, and [also] the workers themselves, with almost perfect style. I attended one of these sessions with some of my colleagues and heard two of the members speak; they were both shoemakers, and their address concerned the need to protect industry from the competition of foreigners.[34]

I am not trying to argue here that the MTWU was "really" an essentially premodern guildlike formation disguised as a modern labor union; but neither should one take for granted its character as a "modern" labor union. It is a mistake to try to force the MTWU into either of these conceptual boxes constituted by the discourses of our own day. Instead, we need to try to look at the conditions under which this specific conception of who was a worker and what workers should be doing—a conception that allowed the MTWU to encompass both shoemakers fearful of foreign competition and railway workers demanding higher wages, shorter hours, and better working conditions from their employer, an agency of the Egyptian state—was constructed and reproduced. At the same time, we need to keep in mind that this conception did not exist in isolation; it coexisted and interacted with other discourses of identity, in society at large and in the subjectivities of workers themselves.[35]

There were thus other ways in which people could be organized as workers: for example, the short-lived Cairo tramway workers' union formed in 1909, though set up with Nationalist party support around a core of activist Egyptian conductors and drivers, was in principle open to all the company's employees regardless of job or nationality. The tramwaymen engaged in two major strikes, in October 1908 and again in July–August 1911. There is also the somewhat different example of the Cairo cigarette workers' union, established in 1908. It was open to all cigarette workers regardless of nationality, skill level, or location; but it seems to have been dominated by, and intended primarily to defend the interests of, the largely Greek rollers, who by that time were facing the threat of mechanization—the employers' response to their earlier militancy as well as to intensified competition in the cigarette industry worldwide. And, of course, there were other social and political forces in Egypt espousing other forms of social identity within which "worker" had no significant meaning: for example, discourses of religious, ethnic, or local identity of various kinds, all seeking to promote specific forms of identity and social agency.

Who and What Are the "Workers"?

Even as we explore the specific meanings attached to "worker" and "union" in this period, however, it is worth keeping in mind that despite the strikes that had taken place and the unions that had been formed, not a few well-informed contemporary observers did not perceive the emergence of a new working class or even of a distinct new social category of urban wage workers. One could understand this as a "failure" on those observers' part to grasp observable reality, to recognize that an Egyptian working class really was emerging. But it might be more productive to consider it not as a question of truth or falsity but as one of competing representations of society, rooted in differing premises and conducing to different consequences.

By way of example, let us take a book published in Paris in 1901: *Situation économique et sociale du fellah égyptienne*, by Joseph F. Nahas (Yusuf al-Nahhas), an Egyptian lawyer. For Nahas Egypt is an essentially agricultural land, and likely to remain so; hence the importance of studying the economic and social situation of the "fellahs" and of seeking ways to ameliorate their condition. For Nahas, however, the term *fallah* applies not only to the agricultural population, the peasants in the villages, "but also to the artisans and the lowly [*bas peuple*] in the cities, and. . .equally to Muslims and Copts." He continues:

> It must be said, however, that the lowly people of the big cities do not much like this appelation and that the Beduins, who for some time have blended with the inhabitants of the countryside and shared their life, reject it as insulting and vile. But from our standpoint there are no significant differences between the lower class in the cities and the inhabitants of the countryside, between the pure fellahs and the Beduins, the negroes [*nègres*] or the half-breeds [*métis*] who have mixed with them. All live on little, work a lot and are early risers and robust; they all have the same primitive simplicity, the same serenity of spirit and imperturbable fatalism; the greatest misfortunes and the most crying injustices find them resigned and docile. Living in the cities does not impart to them the ideas of civilization and of refinement; happy with their frugal life, they pass indifferently and without envy by the beautiful things which modern luxury flaunts before their eyes.[36]

Nahas is by no means unaware that there are "fellahs" working for wages outside of agriculture, and he is at pains to refute Europeans who argue that big industry could never succeed in Egypt, among other reasons because of the Egyptian worker's alleged lack of aptitude for industrial work. As evidence Nahas cites the Egyptian worker's "marvelous" capacity for emulation, his endurance and his strength; this would soon make him a serious competitor for the European worker.[37] Yet he gives no hint that, for the Egypt of his own time, any distinction can plausibly be made between peasants and workers. On the contrary, he repeatedly insists that the Egyptian "fellahs" (broadly defined) are completely unlike European workers. "They likewise do not know the malaise from which the workers of Europe suffer, and they are not tormented by needs which are every day more numerous, rendering their wages insufficient and pushing them toward strikes and revolution," he writes.[38] Precisely because Egyptians are so fatalistic and docile, Nahas argues, the government must look after their interests:

> In the first place our working classes, and this applies equally to workers in the cities and the countryside, are too ignorant to take charge of

defending their cause by themselves. The habit of suffering without complaint, acquired over long centuries, has diminished (if not completely eliminated) among them the spirit of protest that one encounters with the European worker. Finally, professional associations as well as combinations and strikes by means of which workers protest are unknown in Egypt, because the need for them is felt above all in industrial countries with advanced civilizations.

In a footnote to this passage Nahas discusses the 1899 cigarette rollers' strike in Cairo, only to dismiss it as "without importance": it involved privileged foreign workers whose action received no public or press support, and in any case "the natives of the country do not seem well-inclined to [strikes]."[39]

Nahas's use of *fellah* is not entirely coherent. It functions as both a social category and an ethnic category, encompassing the indigenous lower classes of town and country but neither the indigenous middle and upper classes nor (apparently) members of the "Turco-Circassian" elite. It is clear, however, that not only does Nahas not differentiate between workers in large enterprises and craftsmen in small workplaces, he also sees both these groups as essentially identical in character to the peasantry. This seems to have been a not uncommon view in this period, among both foreigners and members of the educated Egyptian middle and upper classes. To illustrate this further, let us look at one of the most substantial studies of Egypt in this period, Pierre Arminjon's *La Situation économique et financière de l'Égypte*, published in Paris in 1911.

Arminjon, a professor at the Khedival School of Law, devotes an entire section of his 700-odd page survey to "Les industries nationales—les cultures industrielles," yielding a portrait of Egypt—and a definition of the *fellah*—rather different from those found in Nahas. "If Egypt used to appear to the more superficial observer as an essentially agricultural land in which the fellahs form the great mass of the population, it is not the case that industry holds an insignificant place there." In fact, he argues, some 1 million persons in Egypt subsist from industrial work, a figure that includes family members.

The vast majority of these are in the handicrafts sector, in which, Arminjon insists, time has virtually stood still. "The nature and the objects of this work have hardly changed as long as Egypt has existed. Divided among small workshops, the workers apply traditional processes while making use of instruments already handled by their ancestors since time immemorial." On the other hand, Arminjon notes that even if Egyptian artisans' methods of production have not changed, their "moral conditions" and the juridical system within which they operate have, and he goes on to discuss the disappearance of the guilds and the problems that foreign competition has caused in many trades. He also discusses the industries in which more heavily capitalized enterprises employing several hundreds of workers apiece exist, devoting whole chapters to the industrial sectors based on cotton and sugar. Arminjon argues that, although the development of cotton spinning mills and other large enterprises is not impossible, it would make more sense for the state to aid and encourage artisanal production, especially in trades producing commodities not subject to competition from cheaper foreign imports. He suggests that artisans and small manufacturers help themselves by forming *syndicats* to secure mutual credit, buy raw materials more cheaply, and market their goods more effectively; and he also stresses the importance of developing a system of apprenticeship.

Nowhere in this tome does Arminjon distinguish between artisans or crafts workers in small enterprises, on the one hand, and workers in the large enterprises whom he discusses at some length. In addition, though he does not follow Nahas in including the urban as well as the rural lower classes under the rubric of "fellahs," he does attribute the same essential character traits to both groups.

> Vigor, activity, endurance, sobriety, an alert and lively intelligence— these are the natural gifts and innate qualities of the fellah and the Egyptian worker; improvidence, thoughtlessness, lack of perseverance, disorder, superstitious credulity, routine apathy—these are the faults, in a certain measure no doubt fixed by heredity, which if one may perhaps at least be permitted to conjecture were inflicted on him as much by geographic milieu as by a defective political and sociar regime.
>
> The vitality of this race is quite remarkable; it reveals itself at a single glance in the robust, nervous, agile bodies of workers in the *atelier* and in the fields. . . .
>
> The urban worker is naturally at least as thoughtless as the peasant. In the opinion of the industrialists whom I questioned on this point, this defect would be a serious obstacle to the formation of native work teams capable of tending machines without being themselves under the supervision of Europeans. "The native worker," they state, "succeeds in carrying out his work well, he is very resistant to fatigue, but he has no notion of time nor any sense of responsibility." It must be added that the lively, easy and extensive intelligence of the Egyptian is equalled

neither by his good sense nor by his judgment, nor by his firmness of character, probably because these qualities depend much less on nature than on education.[40]

Jean Vallet Discovers the Egyptian Working Class

Not all contemporary observers saw the same working class emerging in Egypt. There is, for example, Jean Vallet, whose *Contribution á l'étude de la condition des ouvriers de la grande industrie au Caire* was also published in 1911. Vallet shares, in fact he quotes as authoritative, Arminjon's evaluation of the virtues and defects of the Egyptian worker and goes on to add that the faults which Arminjon enumerates "in many cases destroy the [good] qualities of the Egyptian worker."

> Modern industry is not conducted exclusively by physical force. It tends more and more to reduce the role of the worker to one of surveillance. Stationed next to his machine and keeping it in view, he must maintain it in good condition, keep it supplied, repair it if it suffers an accident or stoppage. The natural apathy of the Egyptians predispose them poorly to this kind of work. Once their machine is operating, they light up a cigarette or take a siesta without paying attention to anything else.[41]

But although its members display the same character traits, Vallet's working class is not quite that of Arminjon or of the nationalists. For Vallet this new object of knowledge is not all workers, including craftsmen and artisans, but rather the workers in "big industry," represented as a distinct and unique social group. Vallet in effect portrays himself as the "discoverer" of this new social group. "The Egyptian fellah," he writes, "has tempted several monographists. The artisan in small local industry has been obligingly described. But the worker in big industry has not been the object of any special study." Vallet provides several reasons for this neglect, among them the fact that "for many people no big industry exists in Egypt." But, he argues,

> This opinion can arise only from an imprecise estimation of the constituent elements of industry in general and of big industry in particular. Obviously, Egypt does not presently exploit important mines or quarries. No metalurgical industry exists there. But if one can call "industry" all the operations that conduct to the production and

circulation of wealth, and "big industry" those operations that employ substantial capital and a numerous and divided personnel, big industry is represented in Egypt.[42]

In sharp contrast to other contemporary observers, Vallet insists that workers in big industry can and must be sharply differentiated from artisans and crafts workers in small workshops.

> In fact, despite the identity of race, religion, and language, there is neither contact nor rapprochement between the artisans in petty industry and the workers in manufacturing or factories. In the "souks" of Cairo, the latter are treated like pariahs. Too many differences separate them. The proximity of their workshops to their lodgings intimately mix family life with production for the artisans in the petty crafts. And the corporate remnants that are preserved link the workshops of a single trade and, to a certain extent, the different trades with each other. The conditions of work and wages change completely when one goes from small to large industry. A joiner belonging to the first category earns a daily wage that ranges from 10 to 15 piastres, while that of a joiner in the large construction enterprises reaches from 15 to 25 piastres.
>
> The Egyptian workers in large industry thus constitute a class that is quite distinct, separated from the bosses by race, religion, interests, and habits, separated from the artisans by their mode of existence and conditions of work, hostile to the former, suspect to the latter, deracinated as it were and divided by competition.[43]

Vallet's *Contribution* is a detailed and invaluable study of wage workers in large enterprises. He insists that the state must take this "new class" seriously by promptly enacting labor and social legislation that will ameliorate the terrible conditions these workers endure. For the moment this class is still relatively quiescent and timid; but the strikes and unions that Egypt has witnessed in the previous decade suggest to Vallet that, "if the critical period drags on, who knows of what destructive energy such a mass of workers is capable?" To convey his sense of the dangers that failure to reform and regulate may bring, Vallet concludes by evoking fears of the masses' uncontrolled agency widespread among both European and Egyptian bourgeois observers. "The triple hostility of race, of class, and of religion risks giving every social struggle that may take place in Egypt an extraordinarily violent character: collectivism combined with the 'holy war.'"[44]

Despite the value of Vallet's study, it must be said that his insistence on the sharp dichotomy between workers in large and small enterprises makes little sense. It is, I would argue, rooted less in contemporary realities than in his eagerness to show that Egypt was already well-advanced along the "European path" of capitalist development, leading inexorably toward large-scale proletarianization and growing social differentiation within the urban working population. More than a decade would pass before one can first begin to discern, among some segments of the Egyptian working class and some of the intellectuals and political activists involved with it, a more or less clear differentiation between workers in large and small enterprises, a definition of workers as proletarians, which Vallet claims was already well-established in 1911. In a longer time frame, Vallet's sense of "working class" would come to be the dominant one. Even then, however, it can be argued that several different discourses about the composition of the Egyptian working class and the consciousness and mode of organization appropriate to it, continued to coexist and sometimes to conflict.

Nationalists, Workers, and Class

All this having been said, by the outbreak of World War I there were quite a few Egyptians—workers as well as nonworkers—for whom 'amil and 'ummal had come to have something close to their current sense.[45] I have elsewhere explored at some length the key role that, I argue, members of the Egyptian nationalist movement (drawn largely from the educated middle classes) played in the discursive construction of an Egyptian working class.[46] After 1906 nationalist leaders and activists began for the first time to grasp manifestations of discontent among urban workers, and their apparent capacity for collective action and for organization, not in terms of "disorder" and an imported social "sickness," but as manifestations of the potential of a new constituency whose agency might (if properly defined and guided) serve the national project. Egyptian workers had been petitioning and striking and organizing for some years, without the nationalists having paid much explicit or positive attention; but now these actions acquired new meanings and were quite quickly reinscribed in the discourse of Egyptian nationalism.

The nationalists saw the human race as naturally divided into nations, of which Egypt was certainly one. Yet they had also assimilated a new conception of society as composed of a mass of atomized individuals. In this new discursive field *tabaqa* ("class"), and specifically *tabaqat al-'ummal* or *al-tabaqa al-'amila*, came to operate as a sort of middle term, providing a largely functional category that grouped together individuals labeled workers, regardless of craft affiliation or skills and permitted their mobilization in the service of (the bourgeois nationalists' vision of) the national cause. It is in the context of this discourse that we can understand the conception of "the workers" embodied in the MTWU. All those who worked with their hands were defined as "workers," regardless of their actual relation to the means of production, thereby encompassing most of the urban *menu peuple*.

This conceptual breadth (or, if one prefers, vagueness) was not really a disadvantage: it allowed the construction of a new category of political actors, workers deemed to constitute in their collectivity a working class that encompassed most of the urban population and that could be represented as possessing a distinct consciousness of itself as a class that was at the same time entirely harmonious with the larger "imagined community" of which it was a segment—the nation.[47] A large section of the urban population was thus classified as "workers" and situated within a European-derived narrative of working-class identity and action so as to facilitate their political mobilization and their simultaneous recasting in an image that the bourgeois nationalists found desireable.[48]

This is not to suggest that Egyptian workers were passive recipients of a new identity crafted by their social superiors. On the contrary, workers (however they are to be defined) actively possessed their own identity(ies) and agency, and they "made themselves" at least as much as they were "made." However, we do not yet know a great deal about this very crucial dimension of the process of working-class formation in Egypt. In part our ignorance is attributable to the paucity of sources that might shed light on the lives, perceptions, and visions of these impoverished and largely illiterate workers. But the problem goes deeper: as I have suggested here, by depicting them as standard, off-the-shelf "proletarians" and subsuming their multiple, ambiguous, and unfinished stories within an all too coherent narrative of proletarianization and growing class consciousness, historians have often lost sight of the specificities of these workers' lives, identities, and practices.

A great deal more research will therefore be necessary before we have a better understanding of how these coalheavers, cigarette rollers, tramway conductors, blacksmiths, barbers, shoemakers, and railway workers of eight or nine decades ago saw themselves and their world. Despite all that has been written, we still know much too little about how, for example, the MTWU's members made (the same or different) sense of that organization, what content they gave to the concept of "worker" by which that organization's leaders designated them, and the ways in which that category and organization did or did not resonate with other forms of identity, other systems of meaning.

The same is true of workers in large enterprises, whose outlook (and the meaning of whose actions) we often assume to be obvious and unproblematic. For example, we know that the 'Anabir workers' strike of October 1910 was initially general, encompassing most or all of the Muslim, Coptic, Greek, Italian and other workers employed there. But when police and soldiers arrived to break the strike, only the Muslim workers remained to confront them; the non-Muslims apparently fled. A second example: in 1911, when the Arabic newspapers published what turned out to be a inaccurate report that Ottoman Turkish forces had retaken Tripoli from the Italian invaders, crowds ("mobs," from the perspective of the British police official who related the story) quickly formed in the poor neighborhoods of Alexandria, especially near the docks where large numbers of dockworkers and coalheavers lived, disorder spread through the "workmen's districts," and thousands of Egyptians began to surge toward the center of the city and its European quarters, where they clashed with the police and Greek residents.[49] Surely episodes such as these should cause us to rethink the content of popular consciousness, by (among other things) taking Islam (and religious belief generally) seriously, instead of implicitly or explicitly shunting it aside as inherently irrelevant or marginal, especially when counterposed to true "proletarian" consciousness, presumed to be essentially secular and "rational."[50]

To be most useful, then, future research will need to be guided by theoretical perspectives different from those that have hitherto largely dominated the field of labor history. Among other things, instead of using "experience" as a way of directly linking objective circumstances with specific forms of worker consciousness, we will need to look at the discursive field within which there were available to workers several different (though interacting) ways of comprehending (or perhaps more precisely, structuring) their circumstances, their experiences, and themselves. Among these may have been some that posited class (in whatever exact sense) as a meaningful category, but also others that did not, including craft identities, gender identities and relations, kinship ties, loyalties to neighborhood, and what might be called popular-Islamic conceptions of justice and equity.[51]

Us and Them

Through a critical discussion of early Egyptian labor history, I have argued that the dominant narrative has generally assumed that its chief object, Egyptian workers, were "just like us"—members of the species *homo economicus*, sharing the same economic rationality, essentially secular, proletarians in the good old-fashioned nineteenth century sense. By way of conclusion, I would like to say a little more about the question of "us and them."

On the one hand, as I have suggested here, it is not clear that "they," those Egyptian workers of the pre-World War I era, were in fact "just like us," in terms of the material and discursive practices of which their lives were made up. But, it might be objected, is not the assumption that "they" are not "like us" the very premise of certain important variants of Orientalist discourse? Does not suggesting that Islam (even if conceived of in a nonessentialist way) is not just a form whose "real" content is something else (social discontent, nationalism, etc.), that it has to be taken seriously as a discourse that helps construct subjectivity, bolster the kind of argument advanced, for example, by Nadav Safran, who (in *Egypt in Search of Political Community*) depicts the Egyptian masses of this period as motivated by an irrational Islamic xenophobia that provides the real content of nationalism, beneath its Western-rational veneer?

I do not think so, because the real problem with such approaches is, first, that they start from the ontological premise that "they" are not "like us" in certain very specific ways, instead of investigating concrete similarities and differences on their own terrain; and, second, that they also "know"—a priori—how and why this ontological difference exists, attributing it largely to different civilizational "essences" or to different locations on the road to modernity.[52]

Essentialist Orientalisms and modernization theory (as well as economistic and positivistic Marxisms) are also defective—and this brings us to the second problem with the assumption that these Egyptians were "just like us"—because they assume that "we" are "just like us." That is, they assume that unlike those people over there, "our" societies are essentially rational and secular, untouched by the "defects" characteristic of "traditional" societies, and that (unlike the less developed peoples who are ruled by irrational superstitions, ignorance, fear of the unknown) we ourselves possess coherent, unified, rational, and sovereign subjectivities. This assumption will not get us very far if we want to understand the ways in which people in our own "Western" societies make sense of themselves and the world and act in it. This is true "even" of those workers and working classes in the advanced capitalist countries who have sometimes been depicted as (potentially) the most class conscious, the most economistically rational, the most purely "proletarian" in outlook; they too, it turns out, are (just like us) deeply embedded in and shaped by "culture," and their consciousness and their agency will be comprehensible only if seen as overdetermined within a dense, complex, and frequently internally contradictory discursive matrix. Their class identity may well be important in any serious analysis, but it should not be unduly privileged, much less taken as exhaustive of social meaning.

I have tried in this chapter to provide a critique that at the same time points toward theoretical bases for a nonessentialist and nonteleological rereading of the history of the Egyptian working class, one that treats "class" (along with "nation" and all the other categories we have been using) not as things or essences pregiven in reality, but rather as constructs, as effects of historically specific material and discursive practices. To do this right, we as historians will have to confront how our objects of knowledge have been constructed and why they were constructed in these ways; for example, the origins and consequences of definitions of the working class that largely exclude women. We will also have to avoid assuming singularity and fixity of meaning and be sensitive to the consequences of our definitions and narrative strategies, to how the stories we tell and declare to be "history" get put together and how the past might be read differently. Admittedly, all this promises to complicate our lives by forcing us to grapple with new dimensions of complexity. But what is the alternative, if we want to better understand the past, engage with the present, and (not least) imagine a future we will want to inhabit?

Notes

My thanks to Tim Mitchell and Val Moghadam, and of course to the workshop participants, for their helpful comments on earlier drafts of this chapter, which is part of an ongoing research project on popular culture and social change in Cairo,

1882–1919. Some of my arguments here are developed more fully in "Imagining the Working Class: Culture, Nationalism and Class Formation in Egypt, 1899–1914," *Poetics Today* vol. 15 (1994).

    1. I cannot here supply a complete bibliography; interested readers might begin by consulting the bibliographies of the works cited here, as well uncited articles by the scholars I mention.

    2. In *Colonising Egypt* (Cambridge, 1988) and elsewhere, Timothy Mitchell has argued that the very distinction between "material" and "discursive" practices is an effect of the separation of the "material" from the "conceptual" that is a hallmark of modern Western thought. Although I am sympathetic to his argument and agree that the conventional dichotomy between the "ideal" and the "material" should be questioned, the distinction is nonetheless often analytically useful, if not indispensible. For a perspective on this question, which emphasizes the materiality of language, see Raymond Williams, *Marxism and Literature* (Oxford, 1977), especially chapter 2.

    3. See pp. 4–5.

    4. As Stuart Hall has put it rather nicely, the theory of false consciousness implicitly assumes that "vast numbers of ordinary people, mentally equipped in much the same way as you or I, can simply be thoroughly and systematically duped into misrecognizing entirely where their real interests lie. Even less acceptable is the proposition that, whereas 'they'—the masses—are the dupes of history, 'we'—the privileged—are somehow without a trace of illusion and can see, transitively, right through into the truth, the essence, of a situation. Yet it is a fact that, though there are people willing enough to deploy the false consciousness explanation to account for the illusory behavior of others, there are very few who are ever willing to own up that *they* are themselves living in false consciousness! It seems to be (like corruption by pornography) a state always reserved for others." In *Marxism and the Interpretation of Culture*, ed. Cary Nelson and Lawrence Grossberg (London, 1988), p. 44.

    5. *The Making of the English Working Class* (New York, 1964), pp. 9–10. For a later and more detailed formulation, see "Eighteenth-Century English Society: Class Struggle Without Class?" *Social History* 3, no. 2 (May 1978): 146–150; and also Thompson's *The Poverty of Theory* (London, 1978).

    6. *Languages of Class: Studies in English Working-Class History* (Cambridge, 1983), p. 101. See however Joan Wallach Scott's useful critique of Stedman Jones in *Gender and the Politics of History* (New York, 1988); and also Assef Bayat's chapter in this volume. On the question of experience, see also Joan Wallach Scott, "The Evidence of Experience," *Critical Inquiry* 17, no. 4 (Summer 1991): 773–797. The extent to which this discussion draws on the work of Stedman Jones and Joan Scott, among others, will be obvious. I must also thank Kristin Koptiuch, from whom I have learned a great deal; see her contribution to this volume, and "A Poetics of Petty Commodity Production: Traditional Egyptian Craftsmen in the Postmodern Market" (Ph.D. dissertation, University of Texas at Austin, 1989).

    7. The assertion in *Workers on the Nile* that workers' "impulse to respond collectively derives from their own grievances as well as from the very structure and logic of the industrial experience itself" (p. 80) might be read in this way.

8. *Gender and the Politics of History*, p. 56.

9. André Raymond, *Artisans et Commerçants au Caire au XVIIIe Siècle* (Damascus, 1974), vol. 2, pp. 383–387.

10. It is important to keep in mind, however, that (at least according to Gabriel Baer) the *tawa'if* generally seem to have been segregated by sex: men and women engaged in the same occupations had separate organizations, and many trades were exclusively male (and a few exclusively female). The *tawa'if* also seem to have been religiously and ethnically homogeneous. See Gabriel Baer, *Egyptian Guilds in Modern Times* (Jerusalem, 1964), pp. 27–33.

11. Ibid., pp. 166–176.

12. See 'Ali al-Jiritli, *Ta'rikh al-sina'a fi misr fi nisf al-awwal min al-qarn al-tasi' 'ashara* (Cairo, 1952), Chapter 5.

13. For instance, "'adad al-shaghghala bi-tilka al-hiraf w'al-sana'i'", or "'adad tawa'if sana'i' al-mahrusa w'al-mushtaghilin fiha"; see 'Ali Mubarak, *al-Khitat al-tawfiqiyya al-jadida li-misr al-qahira* (Cairo, 1969) vol. 1, pp. 247–248. See also "'Ali Mubarak's *Khitat* as a Source for the History of Modern Egypt," in Gabriel Baer, *Studies in the Social History of Modern Egypt* (Chicago, 1969), pp. 230–246.

14. This is of course in addition to the relatively very large numbers of peasants drafted into Muhammad 'Ali's army in the 1820s and 1830s, and in smaller numbers thereafter.

15. These records can be found in the *Dar al-Watha'iq* among the materials classified under Mahfuzat Majlis al-Wuzara', Nizarat al-Ashghal, Maslahat al-Sikka al-Hadid, "Mawdu'at Mutanawwa'a," cartons marked "28 February 1910–November 1923" and "2 January 1882–22 December 1918".

16. For a survey of instances of revolt among the Egyptian peasantry see Baer, *Social History*, Chapter 6.

17. This is not to suggest, however, that the peasant community was ever an idyllic, internally cohesive, and solidaristic entity, untouched by conflict. The nineteenth century witnessed growing social differentiation among the peasants and the rise of a new class of indigenous large landowners allied with, and often in control of, the machinery of state at the local and (subject to British tutelage after 1882) national levels. It is also not safe to assume a unified, unchanging, "authentic" *fallah* consciousness, as "moral economy" models of peasant consciousness and behavior sometimes do. On Egyptian peasants in the nineteenth century, see Nathan Brown, *Peasant Politics in Modern Egypt: The Struggle against the State* (New Haven, Conn., 1990).

18. Sources for this incident are to be found in Wolff to Malet, Port Said, May 25, 1880, Egypt no. 3 (1880), C. 2606, p. 11, in House of Commons, *Accounts and Papers 1880*, vol. 75; Public Record Office, FO 141/160 (April–May 1882), FO 141/165 (October–November 1882), FO 141/332 (May 1896), and FO 633/8 (Cromer Papers, May 1896);

and *al-Ahram*, April–May 1882, quoted in Sulayman al-Nukhayli, *al-Haraka al-ʿummaliyya fi misr wa-mawqif al-sihafa waʾl-sulutat al-misriyya minha min sanat 1882 hatta sanat 1952* (Cairo, 1967).

19. *Workers on the Nile*, pp. 23, 27–31, 48.

20. In *Egyptian Guilds*, passim.

21. Ibid., p. 18.

22. Ibid., pp. 99–100; see also p. 136.

23. In his forthcoming book on the social and cultural origins of the ʿUrabi revolt, Juan Cole defends Baer's depiction of the Port Said coalheavers. I think that Cole's argument is an important contribution, but believe that there is still more to be said about this issue.

24. ʿAbbas, *al-Haraka*, pp. 49–50.

25. *LʾIsthme et le Canal de Suez* (Paris, 1901), vol. 2, pp. 258–260.

26. See al-Nukhayli, *al-Haraka*, pp. 16–17.

27. See pp. 48ff.

28. Jean Vallet, *Contribution à lʾétude de la condition des ouvriers de la grande industrie au Caire* (Valence, 1911), pp. 143–144.

29. See Germain Martin, *Les Bazars du Caire et les petits metiers arabes* (Cairo/Paris, 1910), p. 86.

30. It should be noted, however, that after a discussion of *niqaba* in the sense of "syndicship," Dozy does give *syndicat* as a secondary meaning, though he provides no illustrative quotations or examples of usage.

31. Martin, *Les Bazars*, p. 8.

32. For example, see Vallet, *Contribution*, and Malika ʿAryan, *Markaz misr al-iqtisadi* (Cairo, 1923), p. 88. The MTWU had 979 members in 1909, 2,365 a year later, and 3,139 in 1911.

33. Vallet, ibid., pp. 155, 158.

34. Quoted in ʿAbd al-Rahman al-Rafiʿi, *Muhammad Farid: ramz al-ikhlas waʾl-tadhiyya* (Cairo, 1948), pp. 150–151.

35. In *Workers on the Nile* it was argued that the apparently unproblematic inclusion in the MTWU of both artisans and wage workers in large enterprises "reflected the continuing predominance of craft industry over modern mechanized industry, hence the low level of social differentiation between the new working class, whose members were employed in large-scale enterprises, and the traditional *artisanat*" (p. 69). As the preceding discussion will have suggested, I now think this issue might be better

approached somewhat differently. That the small-scale handicraft industries employed (and in subsequent decades would continue to employ) many more workers than large-scale, highly capitalized, mechanized industry is undoubtedly true. But I am not sure that the degree of "social differentiation" can be directly inferred from this fact, at least not for all purposes. This formulation posits, or assumes, a certain pattern of development, easily transformed into a teleology, whereby the growth of employment in large-scale enterprise—a specific "social being"—leads directly and inexorably to a specific "social consciousness." The predominance of craft industry might more usefully be seen as one of several *conditions of possibility* of the low level of social differentiation, but not as its direct or sole *cause.*

36. Nahas, *Situation,* pp. 68–69.

37. Ibid., pp. 38–39.

38. Ibid., p. 68.

39. Ibid., pp. 92–93.

40. Arminjon, *Situation,* pp. 152, 155.

41. Page 9.

42. Vallet, *Contribution,* pp. ix–xi.

43. Ibid., p. 150.

44. Ibid., p. 200–201.

45. It was around this time that *'ummal* definitively replaced older forms such as *'amala* to become the standard plural for *'amil,* denoting a category of people detached from any specific craft identity who performed physical labor for wages. As Abdellah Hammoudi has pointed out to me, this shift can be seen as parallel to the contemporaneous transition in the plural form most widely used for *talib* ("student"), from the older *talaba* (which had connotations of membership in a corporate body) to the more abstract *tullab.*

46. See Zachary Lockman, "Imagining the Working Class: Culture, Nationalism and Class Formation in Egypt, 1899–1914," *Poetics Today* vol. 15 (1994).

47. This is of course Benedict Anderson's term; see *Imagined Communities: Reflections on the Origin and Spread of Nationalism* (London, 1991). My argument here could perhaps be boiled down to the statement that, like the nation, the working class is very much an "imagined community" and needs to be studied as such.

48. It can, I think, be argued that throughout the pre-1952 period, such class consciousness as (some) Egyptian workers displayed was very closely bound up with, indeed operated largely within the discursive field of, the national project: to a considerable extent the language of class for Egyptian workers *was* the language of nationalism. This was, one might argue, true even of the Egyptian communists of the 1940s and early 1950s, who saw themselves as the most vigorous and forceful proponents

of authentic and appropriate working-class identity, perspective, and sociopolitical mission. Even their vision of the working class was largely constructed within a broader discourse of "national liberation" whose central object was Egypt.

49. Thomas Russell, *Egyptian Service, 1902–1946* (London, 1949), p. 146.

50. See on this question Ranajit Guha, "The Prose of Counter-Insurgency," especially sections XIII–XIV, in Ranajit Guha and Gayatri Chakravorty Spivak, eds., *Selected Subaltern Studies* (New York, 1988). This discussion also draws on arguments advanced by Dipesh Chakrabarty, *Rethinking Working-Class History: Bengal, 1890–1940* (Princeton, N.J.: 1989) and by Patrick Joyce, *Visions of the People: Industrial England and the Question of Class, 1848–1914* (Cambridge, 1991).

51. I explore some of these questions more extensively in "Imagining the Working Class," cited earlier.

52. I am not proposing that our project should be the retrieval of a presumed singularly "authentic" consciousness of Egyptian workers; that would amount to sneaking essentialism back in by the back door. For an important discussion of this question see Rosalind O'Hanlon, "Recovering the Subject: *Subaltern Studies* and Histories of Resistance in Colonial South Asia," *Modern Asian Studies* 22, no. 1 (1988): 189–224.

Ellis Goldberg

5

Worker's Voice and Labor Productivity in Egypt

Students of labor movements have usually been interested in explaining institutional variations in the labor movement or variations in the class consciousness of workers, whereas students of industrial organization and labor economics usually focus their attention on variations in productivity. These two research agendas are rarely studied together although they appear to have a certain congruence. The perceptions workers have of the context within which they labor and the institutional framework through which they are tied to capitalists should have something to do with their willingness to increase economic productivity.

It might be worth looking at the problem of why workers do what they do in terms of the worker-owner relation within productive enterprises as well as through historical sociology, macroeconomics, or political culture. It is within firms that the antagonisms between worker and owner develop as well as whatever compromises and cooperative endeavors they ultimately undertake.

Looking at the relations between workers and owners in this way sends us in a different direction than the Marxist, Weberian, Durkheimian, or Foucauldian approaches that students of Middle East labor movements have favored to the present.[1] It is doubtful that we understand firms very much better today than when Ronald Coase first suggested we try to explain why they exist at all in 1937.[2] That firms do exist was puzzling to Coase because in neoclassical economics the price mechanism alone ought to provide an efficient way to adjust demand to supply and production to consumption.[3] Coase's elegant argument is summed up by saying that the operation of a market costs something and that, for forming an organization and allowing some authority (an "entrepreneur") to direct the resources, certain marketing costs are saved. If any given entrepreneur does not or cannot so organize his firm he is replaced by other firms that do or by an open market.[4]

What does this have to do with labor and laborers? For Coase the primary test of his analysis was that firms were most likely to exist to save transaction costs in regard to labor markets where entrepreneurs and workers bargained over their relationship. Analytically in such cases the employer-employee relationship is that of master and servant in which one party defines exactly the tasks of the other and monitors to assure completion. The master-servant relationship may be distinguished analytically from a very different kind of relation: that of principal and agent. The former employs the hierarchical organization of the firm whereas the latter employs the coordination of the market.[5]

The hierarchical command relationship requires a variety of monitoring costs. It is therefore easy to imagine that entrepreneurs guess wrong in two kinds of ways when they allocate labor to various tasks in the firm. They may guess incorrectly about whether the tasks they wish performed can be cheaply monitored—perhaps significant discretion in the performance remains to the person performing them. They may also guess incorrectly about the allocation of workers to different tasks—incorrectly assigning too many or too few workers to parts of the production process.

The easiest tasks to monitor are those that involve simple repetition. The most difficult (and hence most expensive) are those complex tasks in which the worker must use her own judgment. Tasks in which the worker must use her own judgment in the best interests of the owner are principal-agent tasks in which one person must make a decision to enhance the welfare of another.

In real firms, it will not be very easy to draw the line between tasks appropriate for master-servant relations and those embodying agent-principal relations. Real firms will typically contain both elements. All that we can say with certainty would be that to the extent (1) the market for what the firm produces is large and (2) the products can be standardized, there would be a tendency for much of the worker-owner relation to be "pure" whereas when markets are small or for highly differentiated products owners would require workers to be much more like agents. Even within the historical life of a firm, however, the product cycle itself might take the firm from one end of the spectrum to the other.

Thus in real firms there will always be a tension within the worker-owner relationship between the strictly hierarchical command relation and the market relationship of agent to principal. The most important conclusion to be drawn, however, is that what we typically think of as a smoothly running modern, capitalist firm or its opposite—the Third World factory with its recalcitrant workers and low productivity—are not really dichotomous realities to be taken whole.[6] They are instances, taken at a historical moment, of a more general variation: are the costs of organizing production by creating a firm less than the costs of organizing it by creating and maintaining a market? Concretely, are owners substituting control costs for bargained prices?[7]

It could be said that this distinction between ways of organizing work (master-servant on the one hand and agent-principal on the other) represents an especially late capitalist European theory that would have little application to either the behavior or the perceptions of Egyptians in 1930s. However, such a dichotomous view of economic cooperation parallels features of Islamic law.

That Islamic law distinguishes between the servant relationship and the agent relationship is well established. Sarakhsi's discussion of agency (*wakalah*) begins not only by defining it as a handing over of authority but includes the idea that one does so in settings in which (for example) the principal has insufficient knowledge to make a wise decision or is too overburdened to properly assess information he does have.[8] Servants are simply an extension of their masters and as such have no independent existence.[9] Medieval Islamic lawyers need not have had an analysis identical to that of Coase for contemporary Egyptians to be able to capture intuitively through concepts drawn from Islamic law a sense of the difference between contracting partners and servants. Not only economic gain but dignity and social standing distinguish the two.

The relationship of the agent-principal problem to productivity is clear enough. Owners want workers to work as hard as possible to make owners rich and believe they can accomplish this efficiently by using quasi-coercive rather than bargaining techniques. They want workers to act as agents without having a share in the productivity gains so realized. In such a setting workers are unlikely freely (in both the economic and moral senses of the term) to do what is in the principal's interest.[10] Workers do generally have valuable knowledge about the work process that they therefore do not share.

Given the argument so far I think I can be fairly successful not only in showing that the decisions of workers in regard to union activity in Egypt in the 1930s and 1940s were largely rational, but that workers often attempted to make firms locations in which contractual relations of agency rather than strict subordination through service obtained.

In so doing I will suggest as well that as an empirical matter it was workers, more than owners, who were interested in enhancing productivity. I hope to show that much of the activity of activist workers in plants was intentionally rational: they thought about the courses of action that would benefit them the most. I shall use memoirs by trade union activists for this enterprise; recognizing that all are written after the fact, I believe that all attempted to set down as accurately as possible their beliefs, desires, and intentions at the time described rather than in the present. There is no way to subject such a claim to empirical proof, and it runs counter to both theories of rationality and poststructuralism. In terms of strict rationality workers will never reveal their true preferences, and in terms of strict poststructuralism they do not have anything as strictly separable in their minds as preferences, beliefs, or desires from which an analysis must begin. To accept the arguments of either approach as a definitive way of resolving evidentiary problems, however, is simply to substitute the analyst's preferences for those of the subject and I therefore reject them.[11]

I think my approach will not do so well in explaining where unions come from, either in terms of the collective action to get them under way or in terms of the decision of some individuals to become trade union organizers. Unions are attempts to create a monopoly over labor supply to firms. We should therefore expect to see great temptations to free riding as all workers prefer that other workers pay the costs of union formation. Some workers are willing to pay the costs of union formation, and the decision to do this can be quite rational as long as there are no side payments to cease being a union organizer, but being a union organizer has a deeper wellspring than simple instrumental rationality precisely because employers and officials do resort to bribery. As Marsha Posusney points out in her contribution to this volume there are aspects of labor organization that defy explanation by rationality and there is a sense of moral purpose and even heroic endeavor that must be noted.[12]

Activists themselves believe they are fighting not so much for quantifiable benefits as for dignity. If the establishment of unions involves the struggle for dignity or respect regardless of the price, then we would seem to be well outside the area that social choice theory can explain. There are many things that social choice theory does not explain and this may be one of them. In conclusion I will link the concept of dignity with the role of a trade union in a firm and suggest what is empirically necessary to transform the master-servant relationship into one with elements of the agent-principal relationship.

To recapitulate, I believe Marxist, Weberian, and Durkheimian modernization theories to be fundamentally flawed: capitalists do not appear to be more rational than other people nor do workers appear to be less so. Capitalists including large capitalists (one is almost tempted to say *especially* large capitalists) turn out in certain cases not to be fully rational. They may not, for example, choose the best available mix of labor and capital to compete either in domestic or international markets. They do not necessarily use labor efficiently nor does a purely market mechanism force them to do so. Last, although it is hard to imagine why workers would prefer to be ordered around, it is far easier to imagine that capitalists enjoy telling other people what to do. Consequently capitalists might prefer to maintain manifestly suboptimal efficiency from a strict productivity standard if it allowed them scope to continue to exercise authority over others. Workers, on the other hand, would be more likely to wish to transform any hierarchical relationship into a bargaining relation both for material and nonmaterial satisfaction.

Given my theoretical starting point this should come as no surprise: entrepreneurs make guesses about the allocation of labor within the firm and the degree to which the firm can save on transaction costs in a market by subsuming marketable operations within itself. Because my argument here is about labor history and labor politics rather than blackboard economics there is no reason to assume that capitalists guess right very often.[13] Firms might learn the information about the optimal allocation of labor in the marketplace; that is, from the effects of the guesses of other firms. I leave that possibility to economists. They might also learn about it from those who provide labor. A perverse reality is that "rational" capitalists must be made to listen.

What I wish to do now is to examine some documentary sources regarding employment, training, and personnel turnover in Egyptian factories in the private sector in the 1930s. I hope to suggest ways in which workers were concerned quite directly and self-consciously with who paid the costs of administering the large textile factories, especially Mahallah al-Kubra, and with the problem of how to voice their preferences regarding compensation relatively accurately.

The documentary sources I shall use are almost exclusively memoirs of trade union activists regarding conditions of hire, training, job upgrading, and tenure at large textile factories.[14] I shall also refer briefly to details of an existing union contract to make some estimates of the costs involved. It is hard to imagine what other sources might be available to answer questions about how workers understood the choices before them at the period.

What was the nature of the market for factory labor in the Egypt in the 1930s? It was so underdeveloped that it is hard to think of it as a labor market.[15] In a very real sense the firms incorporated much of what we think of as the labor market within their own operations. The very largest firms tried to attract as many potential workers as they could to the plant gates and then seem to have hired as many of them as possible. Turnover was extremely high.

Labor recruiters toured villagers, explained that factories existed which would hire unskilled youths, and arranged trucks to take prospective candidates back to the large factories in Mahallah.[16] On arrival at Mahallah workers discovered entry-level positions and likely wages for them by quizzing other workers whom they happened to encounter by chance.[17] Although the search for employment brought peasants into the factory, compensation itself seems to have had little impact on workers' effort. A clerk passed through the factory once a day in the afternoon taking attendance and wages were evidently based solely on his entry.[18] Workers recognized the weak incentive provided by a system in which everyone evaded superiors and in which there were no returns to skill, training, education, or effort: "Come along, uncle, here's someone who knows something: he who works is the same as he who doesn't; whoever stands beside the machine all day is equal to someone who screws off all day, those ones who only come at the moment the clerk arrives."[19]

So inefficiently was labor used that it seems not to have been uncommon for workers to wander around the factory like tourists in wonderland, examining the diesels that produced electricity as well as the cloth making and dyeing apparatuses.[20]

Such wandering was not wholly without purpose however. In addition to amusement, wandering provided entry-level workers with information about other positions and (in a rough and ready way) enabled them to apply for them.[21] From the beginning there was serious overstaffing—mandated at least in part by letting workers with very low levels of skill hire on to see if they wanted to work in the plant. Individuals felt their presence was hardly noticable, given the confusion inside the plant itself.[22] The sole control over the workers' presence on the job besides the single visit of the clerk was the locking of the plant gates at 7 A.M. and the exclusion of late workers from the factory (and the day's pay).[23]

Discipline was based on the assumption that the workers were riffraff who needed to be forced into accepting factory organization by the whip.[24] Supervision was inadequate and supervisors appear often to have been technically incompetent. On the verge of fainting Fikri al-Khuli was told by the workmate who was teaching him how to use the machine: "Stand up, stand up by the machine and make yourself more occupied. The director is coming by and Sadiq Bek is a man who doesn't like to see a machine idle; he'll whip you with a shalut but he doesn't care what the machine is doing as long as it's going."[25]

The concern about the director who neither knew nor cared how effectively the workers ran the machines as long as they ran them was augmented by the inability of workers to communicate effectively with the plant administration. Voicing complaints brought corporal punishment and the plant was run by supervisors who were often petty tyrants.[26] An aura of fear in the plant made workers afraid to complain and afraid to seek or share information about how their machines worked.[27]

High levels of ignorance about exactly how the machines worked also often led to fatalities, and the textile mills were no exception. Workers were injured and killed by machines throwing off shuttles, gears, or other pieces and piercing the eyes, heads, or extremities of workers.[28] Associated with plants managed like Mahallah were the relatively high costs borne by workers in terms of training, job search, and the risk to life and limb as well as a long and arduous day in generally very unpleasant conditions.

Owners clearly enjoyed the prerogative of telling workers what to do and seem to have been unwilling in large and small firms alike to allow workers much independence in production. Taha Sa'd 'Uthman in his memoirs describes something similar in his first position at a small textile firm in Bani Suwayf. The foreman belittled his work and exaggerated his errors, initially leading 'Uthman to believe that the foreman feared competition.[29] It later appeared that the owner had instructed the foreman to accustom 'Uthman to life in the factory where obedience was expected and "the spirit of dignity, generosity, and human feelings" would be extinguished.

Our picture of life outside the large plant at Mahallah in which Fikri al-Khuli worked is from interviews with workers in the Cairo area where plants were often smaller, sometimes foreign owned, and where skill levels were somewhat higher. Sometimes (as with 'Uthman) workers learned their skills in trade schools, but it was possible to pick up fairly advanced skills on the shopfloor. 'Abd al-Qadir Hamada describes himself as a lathe operator (*barrad*) with no degrees and only a primary school education. His first job, in 1921, was at Egypt's only sugar refinery, at Hawamdiyya in Giza province, not too distant from Cairo. "There were three strikes: one in 1923 and two in 1924 and I personally participated in those strikes and gave what aid I could to the leaders."

His explanation of the strike is at some variance with the conventional explanations, which tend to focus on relative decline in real wages in the post-World War I inflation, and has primarily to do with dignity:

> The company didn't respect the work rules. It really tyrannized the workers terribly even though the sugar company was among the first to give its workers better than average wages (*ujur ahsan min ghayriha*) and to provide services to a greater than average degree. However the workers had more anger than those of other companies and this undoubtedly pushed them to strikes. Besides, the company favored the administrative staff over the workers and this was a big factor in the anger of the workers. We also see this in our present government.

Although Hamada repeatedly discusses the nationality of the factory owners for whom he worked as critical to his decisions about staying at or quitting a particular factory, evidently it was the quality of labor management that counted. Before coming to the silk weaving company, he tells us,

> I worked in four companies... but I did not stay in any one of them because I hated foreigners (*ahqadu 'ala al-ajanib*) all my life, and the administration in each of these companies was in the hands of foreigners so that a (European) worker in them was haughty (*mutaghatrisan*) and considered himself inherently better (*a'la aslan wa nasban wa hasban*) than these Egyptian workers. Often he would call them "ass" or "cattle." Such a worker might be alone among fifty or sixty Egyptians who would stand and listen carefully to what he said, but could not remain silent, and this was one of the main reasons my career was short in foreign [-managed] companies.

Finally Hamada was able to find employment in the Helwan firm, which was at least Egyptian managed, although it is unclear if it was actually owned by Egyptians at the time he began to work in it. His first job at the plant was under relatively worse conditions than his previous employment, for it was essentially piecework (*ajir saghir ziyadatihi rahna ijadat 'amali*), a condition he accepted because of his self-confidence. He was certain that he could increase production as the machinist in whatever section he was assigned. This indeed occurred, and he must have been a fairly skilled mechanic at the time as well as responsible for the running of the section, for Hamada is specific that the production of the section, not just Hamada's personal output, rose after his assignment there (*wada'uni fi ahad al-aqsam fa-zada intajuha ziyadatan kabiratan*).

Piecerates can provide workers with higher incomes, but they shift some of the risks of production to the worker. Workers are then more directly at risk from a lack of cooperation by other workers and by management shortcomings in terms of availability of material and the like.[30] Nevertheless workers in such a situation can, as individuals, have some bargaining power and must be rewarded as agents rather than as servants: owners and workers must bear the costs of using market institutions rather than firm ones to determine the wage.

By definition not all workers can benefit fully from incentive wages just as not all the children in Lake Woebegone can be above average.[31] On average, most workers do better with a wage that smooths out the differences between workers rather than heightening their competition. Hourly rates, generally preferred by unions, again shift risk back to the firm by making the firm responsible for an average and relatively smoother level of production.

'Uthman thought about average wages as a limit to returns for being an agent. Although in general aware of the importance of his effort for the firms in which he worked, he tells a particularly poignant story of his position at Neumann and Kleiner during World War II. He had been hired by the firm when it sought a skilled mechanic and his work was so good that the owner increased his wage by 2 piasters beyond what had previously been agreed on.[32] The owners then bought new loom machinery and put him on salary. On at least one occasion he was able to save Neumann from disaster by adapting the machinery for nonstandard thread. Neumann expected 'Uthman to act as his agent, and 'Uthman did. He maximized Neumann's welfare: the plant, he says, was in his hands to run without any interference from the owner.[33] 'Uthman's wage remained strictly a matter of Neumann's discretion and had a predetermined relationship to the wage of the average production worker.[34] It was then that 'Uthman recognized his interest in a higher average production wage and trade unions for such workers.

Something other than simple wage calculations was at play, though; in particular, a concern with being treated with dignity by managers. Much as Hamada might have hated Europeans, what made them hateful was not peculiar to them but embedded in the work process, treating potential agents as servants:

> I saw in Egyptians what I had hated in foreigners. I found the same disdain and cruelty from the administrative staff to the workers, and when in such conditions I took on the responsibility of presiding over the union, our demands were not answered. So we sent a request to the Bureau of Labor, and they demanded certain measures that they (the company) carried out and I was selected president of the union.

Of his life at work, Hamada concludes: "If only the company would give some thought to the situation of the worker they would bestow something of their wealth on such a desperate person. After all, the company exhausts the worker of his intellectual and bodily force by this manner, and he deserves work which allows him to earn his sustenance and support his family."

These stories indicate how difficult it often was, when workers were taken as beasts of burden, for them to communicate with management. It is well known that in Mahallah (and other firms) management often provided workers with extensive social services, which often were of extremely low quality. By the 1940s, the Mahallah plant provided workers with subsidized (but not free) housing, hospital care, playgrounds, and cafeteria. Workers evidently did like the company housing, something to be expected given rising rents in Mahallah and the antipathy of local residents to the influx of workers.[35]

Yet some workers resented services and would have preferred higher money wages: "When the worker buys a loaf and sweetmeat at 1½ piaster he will be more satisfied than by eating in the cafeteria. Will it be any good so long as there is rice, a loaf and some cooked vegetables? Certainly not. I know people who eat there but if I knew that eating there was worthwhile I would have eaten there."[36] Many workers preferred money to a significant deduction from their pay for the dubious pleasures of the cafeteria.[37] The firm would not turn in-kind wages into money, however.

One result of the situation in Mahallah was high quit rates. A majority of the maintenance workers in 1952 voiced their willingness to leave Mahallah for better-paying positions elsewhere, and a significant number of workers in other sections did also.[38] Interviews again make the point: "There is a strong feeling among maintenance workers that ability and initiative do not result in advancement or other form of reward. They [maintenance workers] choose to take better jobs in order to receive recognition for their services and to protest against this lack of recognition in the mill."[39] Other workers told the same story, and those most interested in self-advancement were most likely to leave; and this was most pronounced among the semiskilled workers.[40] Managers and owners appear to have wanted workers to act as agents for the owner but to be unwilling to bargain about what agency was worth. They also seem to have enjoyed ordering workers around.

One last source about union organization is an interview done with 'Isam 'Abd al-Mun'im 'Isawi, an important figure in the Mechanized Textile Workers Union at Shubra al-Khayma in the 1940s, whose memoirs were published in *al-Thaqafa al-'Ummaliyya.* 'Isawi did not finish school but this did not prevent him from understanding the world of choice, tactics, strategy, and action. 'Isawi must have begun working in 1928, the first date mentioned in the text. 'Isawi was first a whitecollar worker (*katib*) in the Sornaga company that year, where more than 1,500 clerical and manual workers were employed; he only identifies Sornaga as an "Italian company." 'Isawi was 14 at the time and would have been well into secondary school, relatively advanced for a young Egyptian then. Most of the department heads were foreigners, and the record keeping was in English. The highest administrative staff as well as the ownership was Italian, and their treatment of Egyptians terrible. 'Isawi's report is similar to that of Hamada, for he says the Italians were disdainful and haughty.

Unlike the foreign-owned enterprises described in Hamada, however, here we find low wages and oppressive conditions as well as personal abuse combining to make up an unjust situation (*wa-kan al-zulm yukhayyamu 'ala al-'ummal*). The workday was eleven hours long.

'Isawi and his friends at work decided to try to form a union and began secret meetings to effect a change in the workers' situation. They had two major improvements in mind: first, (in general) to challenge injustice (*zulm*); and second, (more concretely) to effect the ouster of the general manager who routinely employed physical violence with the workers. This manager was presumably the source of injustice or at least its most obvious manifestation. 'Isawi himself was chosen to challenge the manager, a heroic but not enviable position to be in, for the manager was the nephew of the owner. 'Isawi went to the manager's office and told him how displeased he was at the treatment of fellow Egyptians, something that must have come as a shock to the manager, who evidently spoke Arabic. The manager did not accept such criticism, and 'Isawi was fired.

'Isawi moved to Alexandria, where he found work in the same line as in Sornaga. This was a position for which he was fitted by experience, but entry was facilitated because a relative was the manager. To his dismay, 'Isawi discovered that Egyptian management was no guarantee of good treatment: "One of my relatives was a section head, and along with him there was another foreman named Amin Effendi. I found there the same treatment, but worse, than the situation in the Sornaga company. Amin Effendi. . . treated the workers with cruelty. . ."

'Isawi tried to remonstrate with this relative about Amin Effendi's methods and was bluntly told that he had no grounds to complain and would do well to watch what he said and where he said it. 'Isawi was unable to restrain himself as counseled and was consequently fired. His firing occurred after Amin Effendi found out he was trying to organize the workers, and the two men had a confrontation in the foreman's office.

The memoir ends by referring to 'Isawi's published memoirs and by mentioning the return to illegality after the union was dissolved (probably in 1946 although no date is given). The workers resumed meeting in cafes and created committees in every factory, and a new union formed in 1947, the "Textile Workers Union of Cairo and Its Suburbs." 'Isawi contends that two major achievements of the union were in joining unions in the same craft into one large union and in gaining regular wage and benefit increases from 1944 until 1952. He concludes by defining workers as intentional members of a moral community rather than individuals located in an institutional framework: "These were the positions that I defended as the rights of the workers, and I believe I have done this to the maximum today for I have always been a textile production worker because I didn't have the greedy capitalist mentality at the time when several old union comrades got central positions and big salaries."

Identity and moral consequences appear to be more at play here than rationality. Both Hamada and 'Isawi were willing to stand up to the boss and risk firing to speak out for justice.[41] Hamada tells us he "could not remain silent" when Egyptians were being abused, although other Egyptians, in his own testimony, clearly did not speak out. Voicing protests was a fairly risky thing to do because even though no one wanted to receive physical abuse, no structure protected the complainer.[42]

Continuing to voice protests was not only dangerous but brought about other decisions to make. Material self-interest was widely recognized by owners as a way to induce would-be union activists to cease their activity. Taha Sa'd 'Uthman was offered a government sinecure at a much higher income if he would cease his union activity.[43] After thinking about the offer "from all sides" he refused the proposal because it seemed like a betrayal of his psychological integrity and because he feared that God would punish him. This decision, extrarational in its ethical roots, appears rooted in 'Uthman's identity rather than in any larger cultural structure. Both Hamada and 'Uthman had skills that were transferable from one firm to another and therefore could more easily risk firing, but apparently many skilled workers remained distant from union activity.

The question of abuse was everpresent and figured sharply in workers' dreams of a better future. Abuse should be understood to mean a situation in which there is no way to question the power of a superior or to assert that what workers knew or valued mattered. Of course, individual workers placed a real value on their own lives and safety as well as on their ability to support their families. Recalling his mother's prayers that God end his anger at the common people, Khuli ponders a world in which

> if this happened everyone could relax...all evil would be gone...and if that happened everyone could go to work and not find a chief kicking workers in the factory...or a foremen forbidding workers from going to the bathroom...and the district attorney would come to investigate when a worker was killed at a machine...and if this happened surely the doors of heaven would open....[44]

These are surely rather modest demands to provoke the opening of heaven's gates. As in the tale of the emperor's new clothes we need to appreciate the courage (or perhaps the innocence) required to voice that which owners and the state desired to remain unsaid. An analysis of discursive practices seems as far beside the point as an analysis of strategic rationality.[45]

There were issues more amenable to rational analysis but they were intimately connected to the issue of productivity. Determining wages was an acute problem in interwar and postwar Egypt and remains one. Wages were low and so was productivity but managers appear to have believed that low wages were advantageous.

The Mahallah works expanded dramatically during the 1930s and were under intense competition in the domestic and international markets (primarily Palestine in the case of Egypt), especially from Japan. Average monthly Japanese cotton piece exports (with which the firms in which all of these men worked competed) rose from 9.1 million square yards in 1930 to over 21 million square yards in 1934.[46] Japanese exports to Palestine in the gray and printed and dyed categories also soared in this period, largely at Egyptian expense.[47] Egyptian productivity was actually quite low relative not only to Britain and the United States but also in regard to Japan even at this early period. Labor costs as a proportion of output seems to have been as much as five times that in Japan.[48]

One indication that (even though wages were low) labor costs were relatively great is the distribution of skilled and unskilled workers. The basic wage seems to have gone to a completely unskilled worker, the person who performed only the equivalent of heavy lifting.[49] Other wages were based on this base rate: 150 percent of it for "semiskilled" and twice it for "fully skilled" workers. Yet the most fully skilled male workers in the plant—those with the most seniority, training, and likely to earn the highest wages not only in terms of base rates but in terms of productivity bonuses—were expected at most to oversee four looms.[50] Relatively unskilled Japanese women with turnover rates as high as 72 percent in the first five years were already responsible for an average of 2.8 looms each by 1931.[51]

What this suggests is that Egyptian managers were rather poor at managing the labor they employed, something Fikri al-Khuli suggests in regard to the visit of the manager to the shopfloor mentioned earlier.[52] They had not learned the lessons that Japanese employers, anxious to be competitive in world markets, had already learned:

> In cotton weaving the cheapness of labour formerly retarded the adoption of technical improvements such as the automatic loom, since it was long believed that an equivalent advantage could be gained more economically by employing more workers to speed up existing plant and to extend hours of work. This policy was modified...as it became clear that in practice it tended to defeat its own end, for not only were both the quality

and quantity of output *per capita* inclined to deteriorate with the lengthening of working hours but also the necessity to maintain and house a growing body of workers involved increasingly heavy indirect wage costs.[53]

Unfortunately no detailed figures are available, but the best contemporary study of the problem of turnover indicated that yearly turnover at Mahallah from 1934 to 1945 was between 50 and 100 percent.[54] The losses to employers due to high turnover and absenteeism (about 9 percent a year at Mahallah) were well enough understood to appear in the form of the "cost of hiring and training new, unskilled employees, increased wear and tear of machines and tools, increased clerical work in connection with the hiring process, reduced rates of production during early period of employment and increased amount of spoilt work and material by new employees."[55]

Summing up the narratives and the evidence of labor productivity presented thus far it can be said that workers in the Egyptian textile industry suffered from an inability to influence the ways in which management dealt with them, which they conceived (with good reason one might add) as a constant assault on their dignity. Egyptian firms in the textile industry, especially in Mahallah, suffered from low productivity due at least in part to high levels of turnover and absenteeism and the associated costs of an open labor market in the firm, given the low level of qualified workers. It is hard to imagine why individual capitalists would choose to lower profits in their sector by investing in machinery when no one else did.[56] Nor is it easy to understand why competition should have driven capitalists to use cheap labor less efficiently given the costs associated (at least in the short term) with closing the firm labor market.[57] There is good statistical evidence, admittedly drawn from the United States, that quit rates are lowered more due to union voice than to union monopoly power over wages: that "unionized workers quit less and accrue more tenure than otherwise comparable nonunion workers has more to do with the fact that unionism transforms working places through 'voice' than with the fact that it raises pay."[58]

Voice is important precisely because it allows the two sides to communicate or, in Freeman and Medoff's words, to "change the employment relationship from a casual dating game to a more permanent 'marriage.'"[59] To the degree that voice enhances productivity it is not only a collective good (for the workers in the firm) but also a public good (by providing society with greater productivity than would otherwise be the case).

In Egypt those most willing to engage in the struggle to create unions were (in all cases with which I am familiar) able to secure the support of external political entrepreneurs or else were sufficiently independent because they possessed scarce skills much in demand by many firms. They would therefore be "dragon slayers" in terms of public goods provision: those who are willing for their own reasons to provide sufficiently high levels of a public good to benefit all without the free-rider problem arising.[60] Only if someone does something like this, whether as external political entrepreneur or as "dragon slayer," is it likely that both employers and employees will benefit from the reduced quits associated with union organization.

Workers do well enough to understand issues of power within the plant in terms of dignity; we would do well to understand dignity in terms of power within a firm. We would also do well to understand that the ability of workers to voice their concerns and bargain with employers (that is, to choose wage levels while employers choose employment levels) can have important positive social consequences. To be able to voice demands is to have dignity, to be a partner in a discussion.

Dignity so conceived is close to what Amartya Sen calls *commitment*. Commitment is important to production because rationality alone cannot get us to the greatest productivity of which we are capable: "it is certainly costly and may be impossible to devise a system of supervision with rewards and punishment such that everyone has the incentive to exert himself."[61] If we are to take commitments seriously as well as concepts such as dignity we must also cease to look at preferences as *either* revealed utility functions *or* revealed cultural norms. Precisely because we all too often assume that "the only way of understanding a person's real preference is to examine his actual choices, and there is no choice-independent way of understanding someone's attitudes toward alternatives," we substitute our reconstructions of motivation even when people try to tell us about their motivations.[62] Not only economists do this; so do literary critics and followers of Michel Foucault.[63] I suggest (following Sen) that we substitute for reconstructions of other people's inner states their own statements when we have them.

By so doing we can watch as workers attempt to escape the confines of the hierarchical discipline imposed on them not only brutally but often thoughtlessly and for little economic gain. In so doing we must cease to see socialism as the creation of the workers and capitalism as the creation of the capitalists. Modern economies are created by the joint and unceasing efforts, albeit often with unequal power, of capitalists and workers.

Notes

1. See for example Ellis Golderg, *Tinker, Tailor and Textile Worker* (Berkeley: University of California Press, 1986); Joel Beinin and Zachary Lockman, *Workers on the Nile* (Princeton, N.J.: Princeton University Press, 1987); Noureddine Sraieb, ed., *Le Mouvement Ouvrier Maghribi* (Paris: CNRS, 1985); Joel Beinin, *Was the Red Flag Flying There?* (Berkeley: University of California Press, 1990). For attempts to think about the problem in new ways, see especially Charles Sabel and Jonathan Zeitlin, "Historical Alternatives to Mass Production: Politics, Markets and Technology in Nineteenth Century Industrialization," in *Past and Present* (August 1985): 133–176, and Jonathan Zeitlin "From Labour History to the History of Industrial Relations," *Economic History Review* 2 (1987): 159–184.

2. Ronald H. Coase, "The Nature of the Firm," *Econometrica* 4 (November 1937); reprinted in Ronald H. Coase, *The Firm, the Market, and the Law* (Chicago: University of Chicago Press, 1988).

3. Ibid., p. 34. There are a variety of implications to this point, one of which is that arguments that presume inefficiency of artisanal production in the Middle East and the superiority of industrial production miss the boat not only empirically but theoretically as well. I cannot pursue this point here but I intend to in a forthcoming work on the political economy of medieval Islam.

4. Ibid., p. 40.

5. Ibid., p. 54. The hierarchical organization of the firm is identical with Max Weber's bureaucratic type of authority, which is largely defined by its rule-bound nature and the absence of "property" in the performance of assigned duties. Weber considered bureaucratic authority more efficient *by definition* than any other kind, just as most contemporary students of firms and labor in the Middle East consider them *by definition* more efficient. See Max Weber, *Economy and Society*, ed. and trans. Guenther Roth and Klaus Wittich (Berkeley: University of California Press, 1978), pp. 217–219 and 223.

6. There is a difference between household enterprises and firms but there is convincing evidence that the scale effect may begin much sooner than was previously believed. For an analysis distinguishing household from "micro" firms, see Stephen P. Davies, Donald C. Mead, and James L. Seale, Jr., "Small Manufacturing Enterprises in Egypt," *Economic Development and Cultural Change* (February 1992): 381–412. An earlier study is Michael Hoffman, "The Informal Sector in an Intermediate City: A Case in Egypt," *Economic Development and Cultural Change* (1986): 263–272.

7. For an attempt to investigate variations in industrialization along such dimensions, see Yasumitsu Nihei, David A. Levin, and Makoto Ohtsu, "Industrialization and Employment Practices in Asia: A Comparative Study of Ten Spinning Factories in Five Asian Countries," *Economic Development and Cultural Change* (1982): 145–171.

8. See Shams al-Din al-Sarakhsi, *Kitab al-mabsut* (Beirut: Dar al-ma'arifah, n.d.), vol. 19, p. 2. See also Abraham L. Udovitch, *Partnership and Profit in Medieval Islam* (Princeton, N.J.: Princeton University Press, 1970), pp. 44–45 on the *mufawada* contract.

9. Udovitch, ibid., p. 44.

10. For an interesting account of the agent-principal problem in the medieval Mediterranean, see Avner Greif, "The Organization of Long-Distance Trade: Reputation and Coalitions in the *Geniza* Documents and Genoa During the Eleventh and Twelfth Centuries" (Ph.D. diss., Department of Economics, Northwestern University, 1989).

11. They also fly in the face of common sense.

12. For an overview of some of the very important macroeconomic questions and worker strategies raised by Posusney, see Joan M. Nelson "Organized Labor, Politics and Labor Market Flexibility in Developing Countries," *The World Bank Research Observer* (January 1991): 37–56. Worker militancy is closely related to economic expansion, as Posusney suggests in this volume, but it may also be related to expectations of long-term decline.

13. See Coase, *The Firm, the Market and the Law*, p. 19, where "all information needed is assumed to be available and the teacher plays all the parts. He fixes prices, imposes taxes, and distributes subsidies (on the blackboard) to promote the general welfare." For an insight into the dilemmas of rationality for capitalists in Egypt, see Bent Hansen's discussion of the interwar debate on the elasticity of demand for Egyptian cotton in the world market. Bent Hansen, *Egypt and Turkey* (London: Oxford University Press, 1991), n. 3 on p. 108.

14. The two unpublished sources I wish to present were both given to me as photocopies of a handwritten original by Gamal al-Banna in Cairo in 1981. Gamal al-Banna, the brother of the founder of the Muslim Brethren, Hasan al-Banna, was himself a member of the executive board of the Textile Workers Union in 1950. The two memoirs appear to have been dictated in the late 1960s or early 1970s, a time of relatively great interest in the history of the Egyptian trade union movement by Egyptian scholars. The two memoirs with which I shall deal most completely are by "Shaykh" 'Abd al-Qadr Hamada and 'Isam 'Abd al-Mun'im 'Isawi.

15. For a broad review of the issues involved in understanding labor markets, see Subbiah Kannapan, "Urban Labor Markets and Development," *Research Observer* (July 1988): 189–206. Kannapan argues that at present labor markets may well be working efficiently and not perversely and that small-scale manufacturing is of growing importance in Third World countries (pp. 200–201).

16. Fikri al-Khuli, *al-Rihlah* (Cairo: Al-Ghad Publishing, 1987), p. 17. Although subtitled *riwayah*, which usually means a fictional story in contemporary Arabic, this

is clearly an autobiographical narrative and refers therefore to the literal meaning of the root verb *rawa* (to give an account).

17. New arrivals evidently might not even be aware of the meaning of quite common job classifications such as "porter." See al-Khuli, ibid., p. 45.

18. Ibid., p. 46.

19. Ibid., see also p. 102 for an explanation by another worker, Ibrahim, as to why he is not as tired as the other workers: he leaves the factory as soon as his name is placed in the roll by the clerk.

20. Ibid. Note the use of the word *itfarag* for "look at". The same verb appears later, for example, in the context of looking at (and presumably enjoying the sight of) pretty local women, p. 103.

21. Ibid., pp. 47 and 50–52.

22. Ibid., p. 102.

23. Ibid., pp. 110–112.

24. Ibid., p. 112.

25. Ibid., p. 113.

26. Ibid., p.113. *Jabbabir* is the word used.

27. See Goldberg, *Tinker, Tailor*, p. 150.

28. Al-Khuli, *al-Rihlah*, pp. 126–128. See also Goldberg, *Tinker, Tailor*.

29. Taha Sa'd 'Uthman, *Kifah 'ummal al-nasij* (Cairo: Madbuli, 1983), p. 12.

30. For a good account of how piecework systems can operate, see Michael Burawoy, *Making Out* (Chicago: University of Chicago Press, 1979), pp. 48–51.

31. This point seemed obscure to readers for the press. Averages are constructed by adding some number (commonly, n) of values and dividing the total by n. Short of deliberately retaining unproductive workers to keep the average low, many workers would be producing less than it. Assuming any near-Gaussian ("normal") distribution of skills among workers very few would be very much above average and thus very few would benefit much from such schemes.

32. *Kifah 'ummal*, p. 40.

33. Ibid., p. 41.

34. Ibid., p. 41.

35. See William Carson, *The Mahallah Report* (Badr Al-Shayn: Ford Foundation. 1953), p. 58. See also al-Khuli regarding the antipathies between the original local population and newly arrived workers.

36. Carson, ibid., p. 59.

37. Ibid. Whether workers actually would have eaten better on their own is beside the point here. We are talking about voiced worker preferences for money income as opposed to nonmoney income.

38. Ibid., p. 72.

39. Ibid., p. 73.

40. Ibid., pp. 79 and 84.

41. Hamada especially wanted to be a union organizer, for he left one firm that had too few workers to organize.

42. This is the classic prisoner's dilemma, which can be captured in a variety of ways without mathematics. For a clear premodern instance, see the account of belling the cat in *Piers Plowman* (B-text, Prologue, 11. 146–181).

43. *Kifah 'ummal*, p. 36.

44. Al-Khuli, *al-Rihlah*, p. 253.

45. For a more profound look at the methodological question here, see Charles F. Sabel, "Constitutional Ordering in Historical Context," paper presented at the workshop Games in Hierarchies and Networks at the Max Planck Institut fur Gesellschaftforschung and forthcoming in Fritz W. Scharpf, ed., *Games in Hierarchies and Networks*.

46. G. E. Hubbard, *Eastern Industrialization and Its Effect on the West* (Oxford: Oxford University Press, 1935), p. 31.

47. Ibid., p. 41. From 103,000 tons of gray and 38,600 tons of printed cotton piece goods, Japanese exports reached 747,800 and 794,400 tons, respectively; whereas Egyptian exports plummeted from 670,300 kilos to 16,400 in the former group and from 367,600 to 69,300 in the latter. Palestine was a part of the British imperial system, and Egypt was a strategic asset to Great Britain.

48. Assuming that Muhammad Anis's category "net output" is something pretty close to c.i.f. costs for cloth then labor accounted for 8–15 percent of costs in Japan but 56 percent in Egypt. Compare ibid., p. 86, with Anis, *The National Income of Egypt* p. 789. Hubbard evaluated freight costs as not more than 2.5 percent of c.i.f. costs, but even if we place them at 5 percent, it is clear that labor was employed far more efficiently in Japan as a factor of production.

49. See the 'Aqd al-'amal al-mushtarak of the Ahliyya Company and its workers in 1949, pp. 32–39, for the job descriptions.

50. Ibid.

51. Hubbard, *Eastern Industrialization*, pp. 113 and 120. See also Gamal El Din Said, "Productivity of Labor," *L'Egypte Contemporaine* (1945) for an estimate of Egyptian textile labor as being about one-quarter as productive as that of British workers.

52. For a debate at the aggegrate level on this issue, see Gregory Clark, "Why Isn't the Whole World Developed? Lessons from the Cotton Mills," *Journal of Economic History* (March 1987): 141–173, and the rejoinder by Mira Wilkins "Efficiency and Management: A Comment on Clark's 'Why Isn't the Whole World Developed?' " *Journal of Economic History* (December 1987): 981–983.

53. Hubbard, *Eastern Industrialization*, p. 114.

54. Gamal El-Din Said, "Productivity of Labor," p. 502.

55. Ibid., p. 502.

56. State intervention solved this problem in Japan.

57. There is some evidence that the general level of industrialization may cause shifts in employer perceptions of the value of closed or open firm labor markets. See Nihei, Levin, and Ohtsu, "Industrialization and Employment Practices in Asia." See especially p. 170 for an argument about changing employer preferences for internal as opposed to external labor markets over time.

58. See Richard B. Freeman and James L. Medoff, *What Do Unions Do?* (New York: Basic Books, 1982), p. 95. Of course, union wages also reduce quit rates.

59. Ibid., p. 94.

60. See Richard Cornes, "Dyke Maintenance, Dragon-Slaying and Other Stories: Some Neglected Types of Public Goods," talk given to the Economics Department of the University of Washington. Cornes's argument is that the provision of some public goods, including income redistribution, can be not only individually rational but also pareto-optimal under certain conditions.

61. See Amartya Sen, "Rational Fools: A Critique of the Behavioural Foundations of Economic Theory," *Choice, Welfare and Measurement* (Cambridge, Mass.: MIT Press, 1982), p. 97.

62. Ibid., p. 89.

63. Ibid.

Feroz Ahmad

6

The Development of Working-Class
Consciousness in Turkey

With the restoration of the constitution in July 1908 and the establishment of the Young Turk regime there was an acute awareness that the social structure had to be transformed if Turkish-Muslim society were to survive in the unpredictable world of twentieth-century imperialism. Ideologues of the Young Turk movement, especially of its "Union and Progress" wing, were more explicit. Yusuf Akçura noted that "If the Turks fail to produce among themselves a bourgeois class by profiting from European capitalism, the chances of survival of a Turkish society composed only of peasants and officials will be very slim."[1] It is worth noting that Akçura did not consider it relevant to mention the working class (or the declining guilds); but that is consistent with his analysis of modern society: no bourgeoisie, no working class.

Toward the end of World War I, Unionist policies of fostering capitalism had met with some success, and both Turkish and foreign observers noted the emergence of a "national economy" dominated by a new class, the bourgeoisie. Moise Cohen, writing under his Turkish name Tekin Alp, spoke of an emerging capitalist economy and warned the government that "this state of affairs could not fail to provoke the conflict between capital and labor in our country" unless timely measures were taken.[2] Tekin Alp's warning was prophetic and deserved to be taken seriously. Though the measures to industrialize the country had been limited, among the small group of workers—wage laborers outside the guilds—that emerged during these years was an even smaller nucleus, who were conscious of themselves as people who were exploited and whose interests were different from those of their employers.

This consciousness was the result of the political struggle waged against the conservatives after 1908 and especially the propaganda conducted by the Turkish intelligentsia, some of whose members had moved to the Left during the war and came under the influence of

Bolshevism after their seizure of power in November 1917. Large numbers of Turkish prisoners of war were in Russia at the time of the revolution and some of them, especially those in the Turkish-speaking regions, joined the revolutionary movements. Nor should we forget the thousands of workers and students who were sent to Germany by the Turkish government to acquire industrial skills. Many also learned about trade unionism and the class struggle from this experience and even about the revolutionary potential of the working class; some even joined the Spartacus League and participated in the the Spartacist Rising in Berlin in 1919. How many Turks were there among the 400,000 workers who struck in Berlin on 28 January 1918 in support of the Soviet call for peace without annexation and reparations, and for the self-determination for all peoples, and for the workers' participation at the peace negotiations at Brest-Litovsk?

Some of these students and workers, led by Nejat Ethem, founded the Workers and Peasants Party of Turkey in Berlin in 1919; and the first issue of *Kurtulus (Liberation)*, the party's organ, came out in Berlin on May Day. The party moved to occupied Istanbul later in the year and became an active political force in the struggle for liberation. Not surprisingly, munitions workers who had just returned from Germany were the most conscious and took the lead in organizing. In 1919 they set up the Association of the Workers of Turkey (*Türkiye İşçi Derneği*) while some other workers, principally Greek and Armenian, formed the Union of International Workers (*Beynelmilel İşçiler İttihadi*).[3]

It would be unhistorical to exaggerate the level of political consciousness among the Turkish working people. Most of them still had their roots in the countryside and others tended to be more artisans than workers. They lacked the discipline of industrial life and were only in the process of being converted from peasants and artisans to workers. Their loyalty was to their craft rather than their class, to their neighborhood, and to their shaykh and the sufi order to which he belonged. The Unionists had encouraged this tendency by strengthening the guilds for the purpose of political mobilization even though the economic functions of guilds were discouraged. Therefore in various political demonstrations of the constitutional period people marched with other guild members carrying the symbols of their crafts.

During the national struggle of 1919-1922 the workers sided with the nationalists against the sultan's government in Istanbul as well as against the invading Greek army. Their motivation may have been largely patriotic and religious but the element of class solidarity was also present as the demonstrations on May Day 1921 suggest. The first May Day in the Ottoman Empire was celebrated in 1909; thereafter the Young Turk regimes repressed all manifestations of worker solidarity. Strikes were crushed and then forbidden by law. But in 1920, there were May Day demonstrations in the Black Sea port of Trabzon, where workers shouted slogans hailing Enver Pasha and Lenin.[4]

At this point, nationalism and internationalism seemed to go hand in hand. The following year, May Day was celebrated by the workers in nationalist Ankara as well as in Izmir and Istanbul, the last two cities then under foreign occupation. The year 1923 saw the first major mass May Day demonstration led by the Workers and Peasants Socialist party of Turkey, founded in September 1919. More remarkable was the May Day demonstration in the distant port of Mersin, where the people protested against the French fleet anchored in the harbor with slogans like "Long Live May First, Down with Imperialism."[5] The tobacco workers of Istanbul and the munitions workers of Adapazar played a leading role in the demonstrations. As a result, the Istanbul Union of International Workers was closed down, and some workers and socialist intellectuals, including Şefik Husnu, were arrested. Şefik Husnu's political weekly, *Aydınlık (Enlightenment)* of June 1923, published a poem entitled "In Praise of May First."[6] It was written by Yaşar Nezihe, the daughter of an impoverished working man. Crude though it may be as a work of literature, the poem is interesting for the ideological perspectives it provides.

> Oh Worker. . . .
>   Though the right to live free today is yours
>   The bosses have snatched that right from your grasp.
>   You make the parasites wealthy with your labor,
>   Why don't you hate for them from your heart?
>   They live in comfort, you submissive to their will;
>   Though your poverty brings ruin day by day.
>   Pity you share the fruits of your labor with the rich,
>   Make up your mind and break the chain of slavery from your wrist.
>   Raise your head and let him lower his,
>   Let the faces of your offsprings smile a while.
>
> Oh Worker!. . .
> On May First this day of unity
>   Without doubt there is no barrier before it.
>   This mighty world stands passive all around,

Maintain this unity for years to come.
Let the boss appreciate his impoverished worker,
Let him bow his head to you with reverence and respect.
Since you toiled yesterday this world has changed.
Look! the factories are now dormant as though in sleep.
Everyone walks for there is neither train nor tram.
Consider this something in which you can take pride,
When work halts for a day people are perplexed.
Not a sound; every display extinguished like a candle.

Humanity has achieved happiness thanks to you;
But for you, civilization would not have reached these heights.
Cut and cast the yoke of slavery from your neck!
Justice is power. Make known your rights to the unjust.

Mustafa Kemal had recognized the contribution of the workers in the national struggle and gave them representation in the Izmir Economic Congress of 1923, whose motivation was more political than economic. The "Workers' Group," as it was called, proposed its own "Economic Principles," whose fourteenth point was that "May Day be adopted as the festival of the Turkish workers."[7] The Kemalists recognized the potential power of the Turkish workers and the threat they posed to their classless, corporatist vision of Turkish society. In a conversation with Aralov, the Soviet ambassador to the nationalist camp, Mustafa Kemal lamented: "In Russia you have a combative and veteran working class. It is possible for you to rely on it and it deserves to be depended upon. We have no working class. As for the peasant, he carries very little weight."[8]

Mustafa Kemal was correct in stating that there was no working class though he knew from experience that the Turkish workers, though still few in number, were determined to fight for their rights. During the May Day celebrations of 1924, the first since the establishment of the republic in October 1923, the workers demanded an eight-hour workday, a weekly holiday, and May Day as the workers' day. They marched from Cebeci, the working-class district of Ankara, and aired their grievances and demands before the Grand National Assembly building. The government responded by making arrests, proscribing certain pro-labor papers, and closing down the Association for the Advancement of Labor (*Amele Teali Cemiyeti*). The following year, after May Day demonstrations, the government passed a law declaring May 1 as the Spring Festival in the hope that the term *Workers' Festival (İşçi*

Bayramī) would soon be forgotten.⁹ This was the last time workers celebrated May Day in an organized fashion; the next time they would do so would be half a century later in 1976.

The consciousness of Turkish workers may have been limited during the early years of the republic. Nevertheless, during the period after 1908 and especially during the war and the national struggle, they had learned to assert themselves and had seen that common people had a role to play in society. The Kemalist regime's legal and ideological repression against the workers' movement bears testimony to the strength and the potential power of this movement.

The level of consciousness was determined largely by the circumstances of the workers and the vocabulary of the prevailing political discourse. The very size of the working population was small; the census of 1927 showed that 70 percent of all enterprises employed fewer than four people and tended to be artisanal workshops rather than factories. Only about 150,000 of the work force of approximately 1.5 million were employed in places with more than four workers; that is to say, establishments bearing some resemblance to a factory. At the same time, large numbers in this labor force were women and children, and one wonders how class conscious and militant children below the age of 15 tend to be.¹⁰

It is also misleading to project the consciousness of the left-wing intelligentsia represented by people like Şefik Husnu [Dĕgmer] and Nejat Ethem, and journals like *Kurtulus* and *Aydīnlīk*, on the workers and imagine that they understood and shared their ideas of class and class struggle. The potential for such a partnership was there, and that is why the state took measures to curb it. But Yaşar Nezihe's "Ode to May Day" does give an idea of the extent of consciousness in someone who was clearly in the vanguard of the movement.

She was aware of the antagonism between the "boss" (*patron*) and the worker and how the latter enriched the former (described as a parasite) with the surplus from their labor. The workers were seen as poor and submissive, tolerating the "bonds of slavery" that the author wanted them to smash. She called for unity to force the boss to appreciate the impoverished worker. The strike was viewed as an effective weapon that had paralyzed the capital and shaken the people; the author wanted the workers to understand their power and remain united. She recognized that the workers had "the right to live free," that "justice is power," and that something could be achieved by letting the "unjust know of your rights."

What we do not hear in Yaşar Nezihe's passionate voice is the mention of class or class struggle. The call for unity was abstract and not in the context of unions or soviets (Turkey in the 1920s was aware of the soviets and the concept was openly discussed at all levels of society) or under the leadership of a party, even though the poem was published in *Aydınlık*, the organ of the Peasants and Workers Socialist Party. The antagonist was the boss and not the state or government; perhaps at that point there was still hope that the emerging state would support the workers' demand for justice. In short, there is little political consciousness reflected in the poem; the struggle is seen as primarily economic, and the goal is to improve wages and working conditions.

Apart from some members of the intelligentsia who were literate in a foreign tongue, the rest of the population lacked the language to express the ideas of class struggle in its political sense. In a society long divided along the lines of faith, which cut across class lines, the very concept of class did not exist. The term for class in Turkish (*sınıf*) is related to *esnaf*, which means artisan, and even *sınıf* was not widely used during the early republic. Thus the word *zümre* was used in 1920 in "the Political Program of the People's (or Popular) Class" (*Halk Zümresi Siyasi Programı*). The term *tabaka* (layer, stratum) was often used as a synonym for class. Thus *aşağı tabaka* or *yüksek tabaka* described rank or standing in society as lower and upper class, respectively. Even the term for *worker* (as someone who has nothing to sell but his or her labor) had not emerged unchallenged. *İşçi*, which came to assume this meaning, was used alongside *amele, emekçi, and rençber*, whose connotations were those of unskilled laborers or toilers. Later *emek* became virtually synonomous with *İşçi*, and one can find *emekçi* used as proletarian and *emekçi sınıfı* as the working class or proletariat; the two words *işçi* and *emekçi* used side by side as in *işçi/emekçi kitleleri* mean "the working/toiling masses." *Amele* and *rençber* continued to imply laborer and toiler. The leaders of Turkey's workers at the Izmir Economic Congress of 1923 were aware of the problem of terminology; their first proposal in "Economic Fundamentals of the Workers' Group" was that "male and female workers who were designated as '*amele*' should hereafter be designated as '*işçi*'."[11]

The leaders of the socialist movement knew that they had to resolve the problem of terminology if they wanted to accelerate the process of class consciousness among the workers. Nejat Ethem turned his attention to this issue in the first number of *Kurtulus* after its transfer to Istanbul. He posed the question "Who Are the Proletariat?"[12]

After providing the reader with the classical Marxist account of the transition of society from feudalism to capitalism, Ethem noted that the Ottoman ruling class of the nineteenth century had accepted the bourgeois system with the *Tanzimat* reforms. He realized that it would be difficult to explain new ideas like "capital" to workers who might read his article. He used the Turkish *sermaye* as an equivalent, knowing that *sermaye* had many meanings including a prostitute in a brothel. Finally he asked his reader to accept the "international" term *kapital* and *kapitalist* or *sermayedar* so that there should be no confusion. Nejat Ethem then explained that capitalist society was a two-class society: those who owned everything and who made others work, and those who worked; the first were the *kapitalist* and the second the *proletarya*. In an asterisked footnote he emphasized that

> there is no Turkish equivalent for this term. Some people translate it as *halk* (people), *avam* (common people), *ahad-i-nas* (a synonym for *avam* or *fakirler sinifi* (the class of poor) but not one of these is an equivalent. Just as the entire world is using words like *telefon* (telephone), *telegraf* (telegraph), and *sosyalist* for socialist, the proletariat has also been accepted as an international word. We are also obliged to accept it.[13]

> Who are the proletariat? The proletariat [he answers] are the class who spend their life working but who do not earn in proportion to their labor and who have difficulty subsisting.

> . . .

> The proletariat are not only factory workers; in a more general definition they are the classes which constituted the laboring people of the nineteenth century.

> The proletariat, instead of making others work in their place, earn their own livelihood with their own labor. In today's capitalist world there are only two options: to rob or to be robbed....Of the two, all those who are robbed are the proletariat...."Proletariat" may best be understood as those who are forced to live according to an old Turkish saying, "a new day, new food" (*yevmun cedid, rizkum cedid,* or living hand to mouth). The definition of proletariat is so broad that 95 percent of the population is described as proletarian.

Having said all this, Nejat Ethem concluded on a realistic but pessimistic note: "What a pity that the proletariat [in Turkey] which is growing each day under conditions of exploitation, pressure and poverty and is being pushed down does not recognize itself in so many places."[14]

If Nejat Ethem attempted to clarify the term *proletariat*, in another issue of *Kurtulus* Doktor Şefik Husni [Değmer] analyzed the problem of "Today's Proletariat and the Understanding of Class." He noted that among the Turkish people who were broadly defined as the proletariat "there is no feeling of class, no understanding of class, and no class friendships." That is because society has been incorrectly classified as "those who live by private profit and earnings and those, big and small, who work for the State and live off the budget; they are also seen as a privileged stratum (*tabaka*)." These working people in the broadest sense saw themselves as members of another class (especially if they had any contact with the state) and failed to understand their true interests. As a result they remained distant from the workers' movement. On the other hand

> the core of the proletariat, the workers, have totally understood the gravity of the situation and realized that safeguarding their interests depends on the socialist parties. In recent days we have proved this with an experiment. The workers responded very quickly to our initiatives and from the encouragement they received from us they took courage and immediately began to organize.[15]

The socialist intellectuals understood the limitations of the human material they were working with. At the same time, they knew that political gains would be rapid if they forged an alliance between the intelligentsia and the workers. The Kemalists drew similar conclusions about the danger from their Left.

Apart from the poverty and limitations of their own political language, Turkey's workers had to contend with Kemalism's ideological discourse. During the national struggle, the Kemalists adopted a radical posture and described their supporters against the imperialist powers and the old order as the people or *halk*. (Initially their rhetoric was so radical that European observers denounced the Kemalists as Bolsheviks.) Like the Third Estate in France before the revolution of 1789, the term *halk* included the vast majority of the nation and an array of socioeconomic groups, with only unrepentant members of the old order being excluded. The principal goal of this collective was to defeat the old order and its allies and to create a new order of their own. Above all else, this task required solidarity and united action by all the components of this entity, "the people." Class conflict was therefore implicitly excluded. When they began to establish the new state in 1923 the Kemalists described it as "a People's State, the State of the People."[16] The party they formed was called the People's party!

The Kemalists also saw the national struggle as the beginning of a new age for Turkey. They wanted to create a totally new state, a modern society, and a new type of Turk very different from the "Ottoman."[17] Given such ambitions, the Kemalists refused to tolerate any ideological challenge from the Left or the Right. They feared the Left because its alternative vision for the new Turkey threatened to seduce the masses away from Kemalism.

We have noted how leftists were arrested after May Day 1924. But following the outbreak of the Kurdish rebellion in February 1925 and the passage of the Law for the Maintenance of Order of 4 March 1925, all oppositional activity came to an end. Even though the left-wing press supported the government's policy against the rebels, its three main papers, *Aydinlik* (*Enlightenment*), *Yoldaş* (*Comrade*), and *Orak Çekiç* (*Hammer and Sickle*), were shut down along with the papers of the right-wing opposition that had coalesced around the Progressive Republican party. For the next twenty years, the monoparty state monopolized ideology, crushing all manifestations of dissent whenever they arose.[18]

During these years there is little to say about how working-class consciousness fared; one may assume that as Turkey began to industrialize in the 1930s, the increasing number of workers were encouraged to adopt Kemalism, that is to say, corporatist nationalism, as their ideology. However, constant legal repression may also be taken as an indicator that social peace had not been achieved and that the workers were still restless. In 1935, for example, the Penal Code was amended to punish strikes and the Labor Law of 1936 formally banned strikes in certain sectors. The introduction in 1936 of Articles 141 and 142 of the Penal Code proscribed all propaganda on behalf of communism and made it a criminal offence to engage in activity whose aim was to replace the rule of one class by another. Finally, in 1938 the Law of Associations proscribed all bodies organized on the basis of class. These measures suggest that there was an undercurrent of ideological dissent among both the intelligentsia and the workers that the government was determined to stifle.

Until the end of World War II Turkish workers were totally unprotected, with neither a party nor unions to defend their interests. They therefore bore the brunt of wartime inflation and suffering. With the end of the war and the establishment of multiparty politics, the government recognized that workers had genuine grievances and therefore set up a Ministry of Labor to deal with them. Under pressure from the new opposition Democrat party (DP), Article 9 of the Associations Law was amended to permit organizations based on class.[19]

The postwar political liberalization had an immediate impact on the politics of the Left. The Socialist party of Turkey was formed in May 1946, followed by the Socialist Workers and Peasant party of Turkey. In July 1946, some trade unionists set up the Workers' Association of Turkey and gained immediate political significance as both major parties—the ruling Republican People's party (RPP) and the opposition DP—vied for the workers' vote. The ruling party with all the patronage at its command was able to establish its influence over the association. Nevertheless, the workers became so politicized that by the end of the year the martial law regime in Istanbul closed down all the unions as well as the socialist parties, accusing them of being communist front organizations.[20]

The government tried to control the workers by passing a Unions Law in February 1947, which permitted the formation of trade unions without conceding the right to strike or collective bargaining. Far from encouraging unionization, this law alienated the workers from unionism as well as from the ruling party. The opposition took advantage and won over Turkey's workers by promising to restore the right to strike when it won power.[21]

In the 1950s, the workers divided their political loyalties between the two major parties, the ruling Democrats and the opposition RPP. They failed to win any significant rights (essentially the right to strike and to bargain collectively) not because they were ignorant and lacked consciousness (as most writers claim) but because the two parties had tacitly agreed not to make any concessions to the workers. The power of the state as well as the prevailing Cold War ideology made militancy virtually impossible. The government encouraged the apolitical trend among the workers by having the unions organized by American experts. They introduced the notion that unions should have no affiliation with any political party (as they did in Britain); instead (as in the United States) they should lobby and bargain for *economic* concessions with the party in power. The Confederation of the Workers Unions of Turkey (*Türkiye İşçi Sendīkalarī Konfederasyonu*), better known as *Türk-İş*, which was set up in 1952 "with extensive aid and support from the International Confederation of Free Trade Unions (ICFTU)," adopted this philosophy.[22] This kind of unionism soon came to be known as *American unionism*.

The result was a general despondency among the workers, marked by a feeling that the government had let them down and that the unions would achieve nothing on their behalf. Nevertheless, workers did join; and in 1950, of the approximately 375,000 workers covered by the Labor Law, 78,000 or 20.9 percent, were members of eighty eight unions. By 1960 this figure had grown to around 825,000 of whom 283,000 or 34.3 percent were organized in 432 unions.[23] During these years, working-class consciousness lay dormant, waiting to be awakened by a new political conjuncture. Such a conjuncture arrived with the overthrow of the DP government by the military coup of 27 May 1960.

Whenever the political door has opened even a crack to the workers, they have seized the opportunity to fight for their rights. That was the case in July 1908, again in 1919 and 1946. Each time the door was slammed violently in their faces with no substantial gains being made, though experience was gained on each occasion. This time, in 1960, the situation was different, and thanks to the changing climate in Turkey and the world, the door stayed open longer. Were the workers capable of seizing the opportunity after years of repression and manipulation? They were, largely due to the hard core of radical unionists forged by the repression. These people also understood the problems they faced in leading a work force that was politically uneducated, demoralized, and apathetic.

The reportage published in 1963 by Engin Ünsal, a union organizer, provides a lively sense of how a variety of workers were thinking in the early 1960s. Sabri Tiğli, the inspector of a textile union, candidly stated that "the worker still has not grasped the importance of his union. The employer, with the mentality of someone living in the eighteenth century, is hostile to the union and unionized workers."[24]

Kemal Türkler, who played a seminal role in Turkey's working-class movement until his assassination in June 1980, was the leader of the Metal Workers' Union in the 1960s and a founding member of the Workers' party of Turkey (WPT) in February 1961. His analysis of the movement was more fundamental. He noted that one of the major difficulties they faced as organizers was the lack of class consciousness, which he tied to the fact that Turkey's culture had not yet reached the requisite level of development. Consequently, even most organizers were neither well trained nor well versed in the problems of their class. There was a general agreement among union leaders that "the trade unionist is lacking in culture, he does not read enough, he does not know languages, he has hardly any foreign contacts, and he does not know how to communicate with the people he represents."[25]

One of the questions facing the workers' in the early 1960s was how to defend their rights and achieve their goals. Should they try to accomplish this through strong unions or through a workers' party? The unions were divided, even though twelve of them had already set up the Workers' party of Turkey in 1961. The majority supported the *Türk-İş* line of politically neutral unions. Mustafa Tiğli, who was quoted previously, justified this line arguing that "strong unions can protect workers' rights far better. Class consciousness and industry are still not sufficiently developed for unions to play an active role in a party and that could be damaging for Turkey. It's war, economic war [against the bosses]. Strong unions can force the parties to carry out their wishes."[26]

The supporters of "political unionism," men like Kemal Türkler and Rıza Kuas, leader of the Rubber Workers' Union who went on to become a WPT member of parliament in 1965, argued for a two-front strategy for achieving their class goals of social and economic justice. Türkler wanted strong, well-organized unions, and a workers' party that acquired its strength from the working class and the unions that were its organizations. Therefore the laws necessary for effective unions could be passed only if the workers had a voice and votes in parliament. Kuas expressed his views in a more down-to-earth manner: "Just as the human body needs two arms and two legs, the worker needs both a union and a party."[27]

If that is how the leadership thought, how about the rank and file? Ünsal provides us with a sketch of Burhanettin, a textile worker in Istanbul with fourteen years behind the machine who earned 450 liras a month or about $45 at the official rate of exchange at the time. Being single, he said he was able to survive; but many workers raised a family on the same wages. He was a union member and content with the way his union worked for him. But when you talked to him (observed Ünsal) you could not miss the fact that he was from (backward) eastern Anatolia. He was apathetic and had no views about the problems of the country. He said: "Let those at the top [the union leaders] think about these problems. We have to earn our daily bread."[28]

Burhanettin may have been a typical representative of the majority of Turkish workers. But Ünsal also came across workers who were not apathetic; on the contrary, they were acutely aware of their situation and willing to organize and struggle. Surprisingly, he came across such workers in Gaziantep, a town of 120,000 in southeastern Anatolia. In Gaziantep in 1962 there were seven unionized industries with about 4,000 workers, half of whom had joined their unions. More surprisingly, five of the seven unions supported the Workers' party, which had a membership of about 1,200 in the town, of whom 600 were unionized members, the other 600 being peasants and artisans. Why did so many people support the WPT in this "backward" region? Ünsal's respondent, Ahmet Top, replied:

> Because those who sit in parliament are not on the side of labor and the laws they pass do not benefit the worker. If we can put representatives of peasants and workers in parliament then this situation would change and laws to our benefit would be passed. So far we have struggled as unionists but this produced no results. On this issue we are willing to collaborate with intellectuals who are on the side of labor. If we as workers don't gather around a political center, we will achieve success with difficulty.

Asked what he understood by socialism, Ahmet Top replied: "[A system] which takes a society to welfare and happiness by keeping in sight the rights and interests of the labor force and the popular masses as well as capital, and provides everyone an income based on one's work from the national wealth."

How did socialism differ from communism? "Communism is the dictatorship of labor. It comes to power through revolution. It views society as its slave. We are opposed to this."

What did Ahmet Top think of *Türk-İş*? "The administrators of *Türk-İş* are in the position of being organs of the government. People without courage are in power and cannot do anything other than what the government says. On the political side, they do not support the idea of obtaining our rights through a party. This attitude will split Turkish unionism."[29]

The question of fighting for rights through either unions or a union-party coalition has dogged the Turkish working class ever since the 1960s. It is clear from Turkey's experience since the founding of the republic that without the support and guidance of a socialist party the workers have no ideological moorings. That is why governments have constantly proscribed such parties, leaving the workers politically leaderless. In 1952 the government began experimenting through *Türk-İş* with a non-political unionism that a number of trade unionists found unsatisfactory.

As early as 1955, some of the people who went on to form the Workers' party began to discuss the need for such an organization to represent the working class. This was a remarkable initiative, for in the past workers had waited for intellectuals to establish parties to lead and direct their movement. For the first time workers set out to found their own party and did so at an opportune moment, in February 1961.[30]

The Workers party of Turkey was founded officially on 13 February 1961 by twelve trade unionists. It claimed to be the party of workers, peasants, and all exploited people, a radical claim in a country brought up on the principle of populism and the unity of all classes. Mehmed Ali Aybar, who became its leader, notes that the use of class to define the position was considered subversive and created panic in the ruling circles; it was seen as a sign that something fundamental had changed at the grass roots.[31]

It was a reflection of Turkey's political culture, with its alienation from the common people, that the party was not taken seriously while it was led only by workers. Aybar and other Istanbul intellectuals were sought out by the new party's leaders to help write the program and regulations as well as to give advice. After the first meeting in March 1961, Aybar met the unionists regularly. He noted their reserve and realized that they did not trust "the gentlemen's team," they did not enjoy the company of intellectuals and they wondered whether leftist intellectuals who were against the employers could really be trusted. "I believe that they were looking for an answer to that question." Slowly the spirit of confidence grew and workers and intellectuals became more comfortable with each other. Finally, in February 1962, Mehmet Ali Aybar was offered the party's leadership, which he accepted without much hesitation.[32]

Only after Aybar, an ex-law faculty *doçent* who was expelled from the university in 1946, became leader and other intellectuals joined the party did the WPT begin to make its mark. The suspicion of intellectuals remained, especially if they were known leftists like the sociologist Behice Boran, who had been expelled from the university in 1948. In the political culture of Cold War Turkey, such people were regarded as antinational and agents of a foreign power; that is to say, Moscow. Almost all of the founders of the Workers' party were lukewarm toward socialism and positively hostile to communism. Ibrahim Güzelce, who was most open to socialism, did not want the party to be tarred with the brush of communism.[33]

To establish a balance between workers and intellectuals in the party and to prevent leftist intellectuals from establishing their hegemony over the party, it was decided that workers would constitute half of the party's administration and would play an active role in policy making.[34] This was the collaboration between workers and intellectuals that workers like Ahmet Top had talked about.

The workers began to awaken to the new possibilities provided by the 1961 Constitution, the most liberal and democratic constitution of the republic. The right to strike was recognized but there was still no law on strikes. To press their demands for laws on collective bargaining and the strike the Association of Istanbul Workers' Unions organized a mammoth meeting in the city on 31 December 1961. Groups representing various unions around the country came to Istanbul, until over 100,000 were present. Aybar, who was an eyewitness, gives the figure of 250,000 and says that the march stretched 2.5 kilometers.[35] Journalists counted over 5,000 placards, some of which read:

- Everyone has meat in their pot, the workers have only trouble.

- We want the strike against the bosses who dupe us and the state.

- A collective contract for social security, strike for just work.

- No democracy without the strike.

- The foundations of the Turkish economy are in the workers' arms and fingers.

By all accounts, the largest workers' meeting ever organized was conducted with great maturity. The police and security forces were there in full strength but there was neither violence nor arrests as there would be on future occasions. The speeches all emphasized the necessity of laws granting the right to strike and collective bargaining. Only Kemal Türkler attacked the attitude of the bosses and threatened that workers would strike if the right to strike was not legalized.

It would be wrong to think that the workers remained passive while they were denied the right to strike. An examination of the sections on "Workers' Agitation" in *Türkiye İşçi Sīnīfī ve Mücadele Tarihi* [*The History of the Working Class of Turkey and Its Struggle*] reveals that there was some agitation at all times but it increased dramatically after 1960.[36] That is why the claim, made even by people sympathetic to the working class, that it acquired its right without a long struggle is not convincing.

Alpaslan Isikli, who shares this view, quotes Bülent Ecevit, the minister of labor who was instrumental in the passage of the pro-labor legislation, as telling parliament:

> In almost all the Western democracies, the rights we are about to grant the Turkish worker with this law were only acquired after long and bloody struggles....There can be no doubt that by granting the Turkish worker these rights without necessitating such struggles you will have rendered history and society a great service....In countries of the West, application preceeded the laws...; with us, the laws will come first and application will follow.[37]

Given the relative youth of the Turkish working class, the struggle for rights had been long; if it had not been bloody so far that was because state power had been overwhelming and the workers weak. But the workers would have to pay with blood to retain the rights they had just won.

The development of consciousness advanced rapidly after 1963 as the increase in unionization and strikes suggests, as well the growth in the support for the Workers' party.[38] The publication of pro-labor papers and magazines around the country helped the process. But progress was not as rapid as some had hoped. A trade unionist member of the Workers' party, Ibrahim Güzelce, relates a conversation he had with a foreign comrade in Vienna. Asked what percentage of the workers had joined their party, Güzelce replied that the figure was not very large but he was optimistic that the situation would be different in the years ahead. Had the leaders of the unions naturally joined the party, he was asked. No, unfortunately, confessed Güzelce, the large majority of them were still in the parties that defended private enterprise.[39] Most union leaders belonged to Türk-İş, the confederation that opposed "political unionism" and wanted to prevent the politicization of the workers. Such leaders were cultivated by the major parties and some entered parliament on their slates.

The employers had also begun to take measures to prevent the growth of independent unions and stifle political consciousness. This was particularly true in Anatolia, especially in the east. When Şaban Erik went as an observer to a union congress in the east he found that many workers were reluctant to play active roles. They said that by fighting for their rights the unions had angered the bosses who had in turn become even more hostile to the workers. Thus, instead of bringing benefits the union had made the worker's lot worse. A worker told him: "The employers are more powerful than we are. Even though we are organized, we do not like each other, respect each other, or support each other. That is why the employers, even though they are not organized, are more powerful than we are. They support each other. If we go on like this, we shall be oppressed for another hundred years." After speeches and discussion, the workers voted out the old committee and elected the slate proposed by the local employer.[40] The situation in Anatolia resembled what one reads about company towns in America.

The regime, alarmed by the growing militancy among the workers, began to encourage countermeasures from the Right. Again nationalism and anticommunism were mobilized to win back workers to the fold. For this purpose the Association to Struggle Against Communism, a body with close links to the Justice party, was formed in 1962. Attempts were made to subvert the "worker-intellectual alliance." At the party's Diyarbakir Provincial Congress, Aybar issued the warning that "without intellectuals who inform, awaken, and organize, it is impossible for the working people to be saved from exploitation. The purpose of the divisive propaganda is to leave the toiling masses without any organization or to leave them as groups who cannot find their way."[41] At the same congress, Behice Boran, a former sociologist, also discussed the question of ethnicity and class. She cautioned that the issue of race and religion was being exploited by the ruling circles; they were trying to manipulate the differences between Turks, Kurds, Circassians (*Çerkez*), and Abkhazians (*Abaza*), as well as Sunnis and Alevis, to divide the working class, to fragment it, and then to continue exploiting it a little longer.[42] These issues were exploited thereafter by the parties of the Right to encourage Turkish chauvinism and thus to undermine social and class solidarity.

There was, however, room for optimism as well, due to the success of the Workers' party in elections, suggesting that the voters were becoming aware of their class interests. In the municipal election of March 1964 the WPT won in the shantytown of Gültepe in Izmir and elections became an indicator of politicization and class consciousness. The left-wing writer Kemal Bilbaşar, who visited Gültepe, wrote: "In the Aegean region, even in Turkey as a whole, the people of Gültepe have arrived at the understanding that they are workers. Even though the Republican People's party and the Justice party were rooted here for some time, the workers have proved that they have achieved this consciousness by showing such great interest in the WPT."[43]

Aybar has also emphasized that the radio progaganda during the campaign for the municipal elections had a dramatic effect on the development of his party as well as in heightening consciousness among the listeners. Speeches made on behalf of his party were both shocking and influential. Instead of beginning with the conventional mode of address, "Dear citizens," WPT speakers began "Dear workers, peasants, toilers, and exploited people." The listener, initially startled, listened to the party's message with attention. That was particularly true among the peasants and the workers, who then filled the coffee houses whenever members of the party came to address them.[44]

The results of the municipal elections, the first ones in which the Workers' party took part, so alarmed the government that it prevented the WPT from contesting the partial Senate elections in June 1964. When Aybar analyzed the results he noted that, though his party had been kept out of the elections, this had not helped the Republicans, the leading party in the coalition, to make any gains. The RPP's strategists had been convinced that they would win the WPT votes because their party also promised reform. But, commented Aybar, the WPT supporters no longer voted as they were expected to because they had woken up. His party's election speeches on the radio the previous year had made a great impression on people. Though the Republicans had taken a leaf out of the WPT program and spoke of social justice and land reform, they were not taken seriously. Many voters had come to understand that the RPP stood for the status quo, and only the WPT's program promised genuine reform. The Workers' party emphasized that only the people themselves could carry out the necessary reforms; the RPP continued to propose reform from the top. Finally, concluded Aybar, RPP speakers could not imitate their WPT counterparts on the radio, hinting that there was a class difference in the way they spoke, just as in countries like Britain. "For one thing there was a difference in voices; the WPT speakers spoke with an authentic, convincing, and manly voice which could not be imitated [by the bourgeois parties]."[45]

The very existence of the Workers' party had the effect of sharply reducing the voter turnout in the partial Senate elections. Compared to the 81.41 percent vote cast in the general election of 1961, the turnout in June 1964 was only around 45 percent. In Istanbul, the vote for the rival JP and the RPP had been reduced by 35 and 47 percent, respectively. Aybar concluded that the reason for the low voter turnout was that the number of people who understood that the major parties were not on their side was growing rapidly.[46]

The optimism of Workers' party supporters seemed to be confirmed in the general election of 1965. The party garnered 3 percent or 276,000 votes from fifty-four of the sixty-seven provinces in which it had contested the elections, which gave them fifteen seats, thanks to the "national remainder system" in effect at the time. Its campaign had aroused great interest around the country, and the meeting in Istanbul, with the large concentration of workers, had been particularly encouraging. But apart from Istanbul, where the party won 7.9 percent of the vote, it won most of its votes in relatively backward areas such as Diyarbakir (8 percent), Kars (6 percent), Tunceli (5.8 percent), and Yozgat (5.3 percent),[47] where Kurds and Shiites tended to support its secularist, patriotic (rather than nationalist) policies. The industrial regions had not voted solidly for the Workers' party. That is why Prime Minister Süleyman Demirel was able the taunt its deputies in the Assembly. "The Workers' Party of Turkey has nothing to do with the workers except for its name. . . . How many votes did it win in Turkey's industrial regions?, Ask them how many votes they got in Zonguldak where there are 60,000 workers."[48] Demirel had a point. In the mining region of Zonguldak the Workers party won 4,856 in 1964, 7,683 in the 1968 local elections, and 4,638 in the 1969 general election.

The party's fortunes improved in the local elections of 1968 with a vote of around 6 percent, then plummeted in the general election of 1969 when, without the "national remainder system," which the major parties removed from the election law, its representation was reduced to two deputies. Again, with the exception of Istanbul, its votes came from the least developed region of Turkey, the provinces of Adiyaman, Diyarbakir, and Tunceli.[49]

What was the explanation? Why were the workers not responding to "their party's" appeal? There was a variety of reasons, among them the adverse political climate in which redbaiting was a prominent feature. With the beginning of the Cyprus crisis in December 1963, nationalism was aroused to fever pitch and politics of class was relegated to the sidelines. Although selfconscious Kurds continued to vote for the WPT (which explains its success in Diyarbakir) the Alevis organized their own radical and secular Unity party (*Birlik Partisi*) in 1966. Meanwhile, the RPP also moved to the left on the political spectrum with its so-called left-of-center program designed to provide an option for workers. The Workers' party itself split between those who wanted a broadbased coalition of peasant, workers, and intellectuals (the Aybar group) and those who wanted to stick to an orthodox Marxist line of giving primacy to the working class (the Boran-Aren group). Others called for a "national democratic revolution," relying more on "progressive officers" than workers to bring the Left to power (the Mihri Belli group). Such divisions confused politically active students, let alone the workers.

It seems fair to conclude that in the late 1960s the economic struggle was still uppermost in the consciousness of most workers. Since the strike and lockout law had gone into effect in July 1963 and until August 1969, Turkish workers went on strike on almost 400 occasions. Some of the strikes had been long and bitter, and two workers were killed in the Kozlu strike. There were clashes with the security forces during the Mannesman-Sümerbank strike. Factories were occupied during the Derby, Singer, and Silahtarağa strikes, and the workers actually took over and ran the Alpagut Linyitleri works and increased production by 50 percent.[50]

Many workers were frustrated by the so-called above-party unionism advocated by *Türk-İş* and responded by supporting the new Confederation of Revolutionary Workers Unions (*Devrimçi İşçi Sendikalarīi Konfederasyonu*), better known by its Turkish acronym DİSK. Some of the same unionists who had founded the Workers' party in 1961 saw that *Türk-İş* had become the unofficial arm of the ruling Justice party and the Confederation of Employers' Unions known as TİSK. Because the law did not permit an organic link between parties and unions (and the WPT's political leadership did not want such a link anyhow), they decided that an agreement on common political principles would have to suffice. They agreed that DİSK would act on the principle that the rank and file had the last word in making decisions; that DİSK would oppose collaboration between classes; and that DİSK would engage in "class-based unionism." As a direct response to the demand of workers for greater democracy within the unions, it was agreed that there would be secret ballots, public counting of votes, and referenda when called for. The name Solidarity Between Unions (*Sendīkalararasī Dayanīsma*, with the acronym SADA) was considered but rejected for the more radical-sounding DİSK. The founding of the confederation was announced on 13 February 1967, the sixth anniversary of the Workers' party.[51]

Kurthan Fişek, an ex-political scientist who, before his expulsion from the university in 1971 made an extensive study of capitalism, workers, and strikes in Turkey, writes that the working class underwent a radical metamorphosis in the 1960s; it emerged from being a "class in itself" and set out to become a "class for itself." "Just look at the daily paper," he argued; "virtually everywhere in Turkey and every other day worker agitation explodes spontaneously outside the control of their organizations."[52] Just in case we think that this is the discourse of an intellectual and therefore unlikely to be used by workers, we find a textile worker, Şaban Erik, using the same terminology to describe the situation in the late 1960s.[53] During these years, Marxist discourse had become commonplace, at least among literate workers, thanks to the proliferation of left-wing publications from around the world.

The founding of DİSK sharpened the conflict between workers and their employers and hastened the process of politicization. The employers responded by trying to control the unions in their factories by encouraging so-called yellow unions, affiliated to *Türk-İş*. This only discredited *Türk-İş* even more in the eyes of the workers. It was forced to curb militancy among its own rank and file even when it organized demonstrations in support of its own economic demands. Thus the meeting of 24 August 1969 organized in Ankara to protest against the failure of parliament to pass the retirement law for workers was carefully controlled; an estimated 180,000 are said to have participated and *Türk-İş* (and the government) took measures to prevent any spontaneous acts, especially in favor of DİSK. The song that was sung in chorus was "We are patriots, we oppose the extremists and are hand in hand with *Türk-İş*."[54] As the popularity of political unionism associated with DİSK grew, the ruling class represented by both the major parties (the Justice party and the RPP) saw the threat and decided to act. Demirel's government introduced a bill in the assembly to amend the Unions Law so that any union that did not represent at least one third of the labor force in a given workplace would be disqualified. The purpose of this piece of legislation was to destroy DİSK, and the minister of labor was rash enough to boast about that in public. DİSK lobbied to prevent the passage of the bill. But when its efforts failed, it responded by planning a mass demonstration against the measure. Before its plans were complete, it was faced with a *fait accompli*; factory workers around Istanbul laid down their tools and spilled out of the factories into the streets, catching the leadership totally off guard.

The demonstration began spontaneously on Monday, 15 June 1970, on both sides of the city divided by the Bosphorus waterway with about 70,000 workers from over 100 factories. By the following day the protest had more than doubled in size and workers from the Anatolian side began to march toward the sea to board ferries to link up with demonstrators on the European side.

The authorities, initially taken by surprise, mobilized the security forces including the army. Workers were attacked and fired on but the march could not be halted. Workers crossed the police barricades and finally reached Kadïkoy, only to find that there was no ferry service. On the afternoon of 16 June martial law was declared in the Istanbul-Marmara industrial region but not before Turkey had been thoroughly shaken. The workers' protest had been silenced at the cost of three workers killed along with a policeman and a shopkeeper. Hundreds were wounded, and many more taken into custody. Strikes continued in many factories despite martial law, and employers seized the opportunity to fire the "troublemakers." Workers—Turkish and German—also demonstrated in German cities to protest the Turkish government's measures against the working class.[55]

The events of these "two long days that shook Turkey" may be considered the high point of class consciousness achieved by the workers of Turkey and a turning point in the history of the labor movement. It was the first time that the working class had acted for an essentially political reason, though declining wages since 1967 were an important factor in their anger and militancy. The slogans and banners they shouted and carried reflect the mood of those days:[56]

- Independent Turkey.

- NO! to American bases.

- We won't allow the government to crush the freedom of unions.

- Unions are our lives, we'll sacrifice our blood.

- The constitution can't be changed, the new law can't be undone.

- [Prime Minister] Demirel resign!

- We're workers, we're powerful!

- We're right, we're powerful, we're workers!

- The JP government is not our government, it's the bosses' government.

- We've nothing to lose but our chains.

- NO! to amending the Unions Law.

- Long live the working class.

- Damn all [religious] reactionaries and fascists.

- No democracy without unions.

- You can't close our unions.

- Worker and peasant hand in hand.

- We're all soldiers (*mehmetcik;* i.e., English Tommies or American G.I.s].

- Long live DİSK!

- Death, no retreat.

- The working class is our mother.

- We're coming, breaking our chains and the heads of our oppressors

Turkey understood the significance of the dramatic events of 15–16 June, and the various forces acted according to the way they interpreted these events. The adventurist Left concluded that the workers were ready to rise up if only the Left would provide the lead. They therefore began a campaign of urban terrorism designed to light the fuse of revolution. The ruling classes saw the danger ahead in the rising consciousness and growing demands of the working class and decided to curb this trend violently, describing the event in an exaggerated and rhetorical manner as "the dress rehearsal for revolution." The result of the tension created in the period that followed was the military intervention of 12 March 1971. Its goals were to crush the Left and to restructure the country's political institutions in a way that would provide social peace and stability.[57]

The Workers' party was closed down, and no quarter was given to the left-wing intelligentsia that had provided the ideological leadership to the working class. As a result, working-class consciousness, though not destroyed, was channeled in the direction of social democracy which became the dominant ideological trend in 1972 under the leadership of Bülent Ecevit's post-İnönü RPP.

The working class, now without a party but led by DİSK, fought back and the restoration of May Day as Workers' Day became the symbol of its struggle.[58] Workers also began to rally around the increasingly radical RPP, espousing social democracy since 1972. The RPP's electoral victory in 1973 boosted morale and even though Prime Minister Ecevit made a tactical mistake and resigned in 1975, workers remained in a combative mood. The celebration of May Day 1976, for the first time in fifty years, was taken as a warning by the so-called Nationalist Front coalition government in which the neofascists had strong representation. The Right decided to destroy social democracy and remove the only ideological option open to the working class. The following year, the Istanbul meeting on May Day was drowned in blood, with thirty four killed and hundreds wounded. Shots were fired from a government building creating a panic; to this day no one has been brought to trial for triggering this mayhem, whose purpose was to intimidate workers from showing solidarity and fighting for their rights.

For the remainder of the 1970s terrorism became the order of the day. It is worth noting the role of DİSK and the working class in trying to launch the "No! to Fascism" campaign during these years. The struggle was seen as both economic and political and was waged on both fronts. The number of unionized workers continued to increase throughout the 1970s, from 2,088,219 in 1970 to 5,721,000 in 1980. The unions also continued to strike, except for the period of military rule from 12 March 1971 until after the general election of October 1973, when strikes were banned by law.[59]

The military intervention of 12 October 1980 was designed to complete the work of the 12 March regime. This time there were no half measures; everything possible was done to depoliticize the country. Thousands were arrested, and all political parties were closed down, their leaders proscribed from politics for a period of five to ten years. For the time being, the workers were not even given the option to support social democracy. Even more significantly, the DİSK leadership was arrested and put on trial (many on capital charges), accused of conspiring to overthrow the state. The field was left entirely to *Türk-İş*, always willing to collaborate with any regime. Meanwhile, a new constitution and labor laws severely curtailed the rights won by the working class after 1961.

The workers took a terrible beating in the 1980s, literally and metaphorically. Young workers and students in particular were imprisoned and tortured with the goal of forcing them to shun politics; it is doubtful whether this strategy has worked. Without the right to strike the standard of living of the working class plummeted. But the workers continued to resist politically. They failed to be seduced by the right-wing trade union confederations cobbled together by the neofascists (MİSK or the Confederation of Nationalist Workers' Unions) or the Islamists' *Hak-İş*. They voted for the anti-12 October parties and by the late 1980s had made the social democrats the principal political group outside the Assembly. After the defeat of the Motherland party in the 1991 general election, the social democrats entered the coalition with the right-of-center True Path party. One of the principal promises of the coalition has been to restore democratic institutions undermined by the military regime. The workers will benefit from this.

Meanwhile, the Turkish working class has naturally been influenced by events in eastern Europe, especially Poland, where the Solidarity movement has triumphed against the communist state. More workers are now convinced that they too can make gains providing that their struggle also becomes political and is not restricted to economic demands. Asked about "Turkey's Solidarity," Zeynel Coşar, a shipyard worker and and a leader in the recently founded Socialist party, retorted: "Turkey's Solidarity? Solidarity belongs to Poland. Our working class is no less militant than theirs; it possesses enough accumulated consciousness to give a good example of creative activity."[60]

As the grip of the military regime has loosened so the working class has begun to reassert itself to win back the rights it lost since October 1980. The spring of 1989 saw a wave of strikes as workers fought for democracy as well as for higher wages and better working conditions. The monthly *Saçak* in its "Diary of Worker Agition in Spring '89" lists over 224 strikes around Turkey between 7 March and and 18 May 1989, involving hundreds of thousands of workers. These strikes have come to be seen as the beginning of a new phase in the development of the working class.[61]

Saçak also lists the most popular slogans heard during the strike wave; again the slogans provide an insight into working-class grievances and aspirations, including the demand for the restoration of the strike:

- Our right to strike can't be prevented.
- We'll extract our right for a general strike.
- Workers! Hand in hand to the general strike.
- Workers-society hand in hand to the general strike.

There were anti-*Türk-İş* slogans:

- Where are you, union? Aren't you workers?
- Don't sell the worker and take a step back.
- You won't sit comfortably in your armchair.

- Şevket resign! [Şevket Yîlmaz is the president of *Türk-İş*].

- *Türk-İş* resign!

- Down with yellow unionism!

- Workers take over the unions.

And there were the political and economic slogans:

- We are hungry.

- We want bread.

- Where is democracy?

- Down with the police's radio and television.

- End police-employer collaboration.

- A free press.

- Break your chains!

- [Prime Minister] Özal resign!

- Government resign!

- Long live May First!

- We're workers, we're powerful!

- Long live workers' unity!

- Workers unite and take power!

What then is the state of the Turkish working class at the beginning of the 1990s? The military coup battered it and left it leaderless, but, as a result, it has also begun to emerge with a greater sense of self-confidence than ever before. In the spring of 1989, for the first time on its own initiative, it launched a struggle to regain rights taken away by the military regime. It did so without leaders, and the question has been raised as to whether this movement would spawn its own leadership. Without its own leaders the movement would be likely to stall. But the workers were aware of this and also clear that, without an economic and political struggle, the economic gains they would make would be ephemeral. That meant having a party of their own. But that was a major obstacle in the political climate of the late 1980s and the early 1990s.

Equally important was the struggle for democracy within the unions. The workers had no real representation, because their representatives tended to speak either for the central organization or the branches and usually reflected the views of the bosses. Workers complained that they were not permitted to speak in their own workplaces, because the delegate insisted on speaking for them. That too had to change.

At the Workers' Congress organized by the Socialist party in Istanbul on 18 June 1989, it was possible to see the spirit of self-reliance asserting itself among the workers. No longer did they feel in awe of their allies, the intellectuals, though they still had great respect for them. The octogenarian Mehmet Ali Aybar, the grand old man of the Turkish Left who had been invited to open the Congress, was asked to cut short his address by workers in the audience so that they could have time to air their views and ideas. This was done politely, and Aybar appreciated the request because he saw it as a sign of maturing and stepped down with grace.[62] A reflection of this new confidence may also be seen on the mastheads of two recently founded workers' papers, *İşçilerin Sesi* [*The Workers' Voice*] and *İşçiler ve Politika* [*Workers and Politics*], which read: "We are the producers, we'll be the rulers" and "The liberation of the working class will be its own work," respectively. But where will all this lead in the 1990s? That will depend on the development of the political regime that finally emerges after the ravages of the 1980s, and that in turn will depend on Turkey's position in the post-Cold War world.

Notes

1. *Türk Yurdu*, no. 40, 12 Aug. 1333 (1917) quoted in Niyazi Berkes, *The Development of Secularism in Turkey* (Montreal, 1964), p. 426.

2. "Kapitalizm devresi basliyor," *Iktisadiyat Mecmuasi*, 2, no. 67 (8 Nov. 1917) quoted in Feroz Ahmad, "Vanguard of a Nascent Bourgeoisie: The Social and Economic Policies of the Young Turks, 1908–1918," in Osman Okyar and Halil Inalcik, eds., *Social and Economic History of Turkey (1907–1920)* (Ankara, 1980), pp. 345–346.

3. On the Berlin *Kurtulus* (Liberation), see Rasih Nuri Lleri's preface to *Kurtulus* (Istanbul, 1975), pp. 9–22; and Kemal Sülker, *100 Soruda Türkiye'de İşçi Hareketleri*, [Workers Movements in Turkey in 100 Questions] (Istanbul, 1968), pp. 11–12.

4. Şehmus Güzel's article on May Day in Turkey in *Ikibine Doğru* (14 May 1989): p. 33. Güzel has written an authoritative account of the Turkish working class as his

doctoral dissertation in Aix-en-Provence, 1975. It is entitled "Le mouvement ouvrière et les grèves en Turquie: de l'empire Ottoman à nos jours." See also his article on the workers movements during the republic in *Cumhuriyet Dönemi Türkiye Ansiklopedisi*, p. 7: 1848–1876, and "Être ouvrier en Turquie," *Les Temps Modernes* (July–August 1984): pp. 268–288.

5. Nail Güreli, *Iki I Mayis*, (Istanbul, 1979), p. 15; and T. Z. Tunaya, *Türkiye'de Siyasi Partiler 1859–1952* (Istanbul, 1952), pp. 438–439.

6. The poem is given in A. Cerrahoğlu, *Türkiyede Sosyalizm (1848–1925)* (Istanbul, 1968), pp. 208–209, and Güreli, ibid., pp. 15–16. Cerrahoğlu, pp. 209–210, also gives the text of another poem, "May First," which Yasar Nezihe published in *Aydınlık* the following year. He also provides a brief account of the poet's life on pp. 203–214.

7. Günduz Ökçün, ed., *Türkiye İktisat Kongresi 1923—Izmir* (Ankara, 1968), p. 432.

8. S. I. Aralov, *Bir Sovyet Diplomatinin Türkiye Hatiralari*. (Istanbul, 1967), p. 92, quoted in Feroz Ahmad, "The Political Economy of Kemalism," in Ali Kazancigil and Ergun Özbudun, eds., *Atatürk—Founder of a Modern State* (London, 1981), p. 157.

9. Güreli, *1 Mayis*, pp. 16–17; Güzel, *Ikibine*.

10. Alpaslan Işıklı, "Wage Labor and Unionization," in I. C. Schick and E. A. Tonak, eds., *Turkey in Transition*, (New York, 1987), p. 312; for more detailed statistics, see Tum İktasatçılar Birliği, *Türkiye İşçi Sınıfı ve Mücadeleleri Tarihi* (Ankara, 1976), pp. 62ff.

11. Ökcun, *İktisat Kongresi*, p. 430. See also the writings of an early Turkish communist, one of the leaders of the recently founded Communist party of Turkey, who was murdered in 1921, in Mustafa Suphi, *Türkiye'nin Mazlum Amele ve Rençberlerine* (Ankara, 1976).

12. "Proletarya Kimerlerdir?" [Who Are the Proletariat?] *Kurtulus* (Istanbul) no. 1 (20 Sept. 1919), in *Kurtulus* (no. 3): 75–83.

13. Ibid.

14. Ibid.

15. "Bugunku Proletarya ve Sinif Suuru," *Kurtulus*, no. 3 (20 Nov. 1919) in ibid., pp. 170–175.

16. Ahmad in Kazancigil and Özbudun, *Ataturk*, p. 156.

17. Ibid., p. 149.

18. Ibrahim Topcuoğlu, *Türkiye'de İlk Sendika Sarikisla'da 1932* (Istanbul, 1975) discusses labor militancy after 1925, noting that in 1927 Istanbul tramway workers formed an organization and went on strike for five days. But the government intervened and closed down the association, describing these actions as "communistic and contrary to the national interest." In 1932, Topcuoğlu and some workers in Izmir formed an organization that they called a union (*sendika*) for the first time and not an association.

His wife Melek, he writes, became the first woman trade unionist to be sentenced to prison when this union was closed down and its organizers put on trial. For working-class activity during the early republic, see A. Snurov, "Kemalist Devrim ve Turkiye Proletaryasi" (a monograph published in Russian in 1929) in A. Snurnov and Y. Rozaliyev, *Türkiye'de Kapitalistleşme ve Sīnīf Kavgalarī* (Istanbul, 1970), pp. 9–83. See also Sülker, *100 Soruda*, p. 261; and Kemal Karpat, *Turkey's Politics: The Transition to a Multi-Party System* (Princeton, N.J., 1959), passim, for a discussion of the single party period and especially the years after 1945.

19. Sülker, *100 Soruda*, pp. 30–31.

20. Feroz Ahmad, *The Turkish Experiment in Democracy 1950–1975* (London, 1977), p. 43 and passim.

21. Işīklī in Schick and Tonak, *Turkey*, p. 317.

22. Ibid., p. 316.

23. Ibid.

24. Engin Ünsal, *İşçiler Uyaniyor* [The Workers Are Awakening] (Istanbul, 1963), p. 16. Ünsal went on to become a legal adviser to unions.

25. Ibid., p. 17.

26. Ibid.

27. Ibid.

28. Ibid., p. 20.

29. Ibid., pp. 29–29. Even in the 1970s, small artisan shops and workshops were dominant in Gaziantep. For a fascinating picture of Gaziantep in the early 1970s see Raci Bademli, "Distorted and Lower Forms of Capitalist Industrial Production in Underdeveloped Countries: Contemporary Artisan Shops and Workshops in Eskisehir and Gaziantep, Turkey" (unpublished Ph.D diss., Massachusetts Institute of Technology, 1977).

30. Mehmet Ali Aybar, *Türkiye İşçi Partisi Tarihi* [History of the Workers' Party of Turkey], 1, (Istanbul, 1988) pp. 196ff.

31. Uğur Mumcu, *Sosyalizm ve Bagīmsīzlīk: Aybar ile söyleşi.* [Socialism and Independence: Interview with Aybar] (Istanbul, 1986), pp. 25 and 27.

32. Aybar, *İşçi Partisi*, pp. 174–180.

33. Ibid. p. 212.

34. Ibid., pp. 216–217. Aybar writes that the reason why workers were given only 50 percent was because the prevailing political climate was extremely hostile. The party would have been accused of violating the penal code, working to establish class rule, and closed down. In the party he founded in the 1970s, the Socialist Revolution party, the ratio established was 3:2 in favor of the workers.

35. Ibid., p. 190. For an annotated chronology of events of this period, see Feroz Ahmad and Bedia Turgay Ahmad, *Türkiye'de Çok Partili Politikanin Acīklamali Kronolojisi 1945–1971* (Ankara, 1976), p. 243 and passim.

36. Tum İktisatçīlar Birligi, *İşçi Sīnīfī*, pp. 151ff. On the number of strikes after 1963 see Isikli in Schick and Tonak, *Turkey*, p. 325.

37. Isīklī, ibid., pp. 317–318 and his article "Cumhuriyet Doneminde Turk Sendikacīlīgī [Turkish Unionism During the Republican Period], *Cumhuriyet Dönemi Türkiye Ansiklopedisi*, 7: 1831.

38. On unionization and strikes, see İşīklī, ibid., pp. 316 and 325, respectively. On strikes, see Kurthan Fisek's excellent *Devlete Karşī Grevlerin Kritik Tahlili* [A Critical Analysis of Strikes Against the State] (Ankara, 1969).

39. "Ezilenler Uyaninca" [When the Oppressed Awaken], *Sosyal Adalet* (Oct. 1964): 211.

40. Şaban Erik, "Biz İşçiler" [We Workers], *Sosyal Adalet* (Aug. 1964): pp. 16–17.

41. Aybar's speech at the congress, Sunday 8 Nov. 1964, in *Sosyal Adalet* (Dec. 1964): 45.

42. Ibid. On Boran's experience during this period, see her interview with Ugur Mumcu in his *Bir Uzun Yürüyüş* [A Long March] (Istanbul, 1988).

43. "Gültepe: İlk İşaret taşī" [Gültepe: The First Milestone], *Sosyal Adalet* (April 1964): pp. 16–17.

44. Aybar in Mumcu, *Sosyalizm*, pp. 40–41 and 45.

45. "Seçimler ve Otesi" [Elections and Beyond], *Sosyal Adalet*, (June 1964): 2–3.

46. Ibid.

47. Şirin Tekeli, "Seçimler" [Elections], *Cumhuriyet Dönemi Türkiye Ansiklopedisi*, 7: 1815.

48. Aybar, *İşçi Partisi*, vol. 2, pp. 56–57.

49. Tekeli, *Türkiye Ansiklopedisi*, p. 1816.

50. Kurthan Fişek, "24 Agustos," *Emek* [Labor] (24 Aug, 1969): pp. 8–9.

51. Aybar, *Isci Partisi*, vol. 2, pp. 173–176.

52. Fişek, *Emek*, pp. 8–9.

53. Şaban Erik, "Aybar ve Ettikleri" [Aybar and What He Did], *Emek* (1 Dec. 1969): 4–5.

54. The press (25 Aug. 1969); Fişek gives a much lower figure of 20,000 and claims that the demonstration actually fizzled out because the workers were cynical about *Türk-İş's* leadership. See his article in *Emek* (8 Sept. 1969): 4.

55. The best account of the events of 15–16 June is provided in Turgan Arinir and Sirri Öztürk, *İşçi Sinifi, Sendikalar ve 15/19 Haziran*, (Istanbul, 1976) which discusses "the events, their causes, the trials, and provides documents, memoirs, and analysis." Kemal Sülker's, *Türkiye'yi Sarsan İki Uzun Gün* [Two Long Days That Shook Turkey] (Istanbul, 1980), is an insider's account. See also Tum Iktisatcilar Birligi, *İşçi Sinifi*, pp. 189–190 for more information.

56. Sülker, ibid., pp. 98, 106–107, 133, and 136–137.

57. Ahmad, *Turkish Experiment*, pp. 288–362, for a discussion of the early 1970s.

58. Güreli, *1 Mayis*, pp. 18ff.

59. Işikli in Schick and Tonak, *Turkey*, pp. 316 and 325.

60. "Türkiye'nin Welesalari" [Turkey's Walesas], *Ikibine Doğru* (16 June 1989): 8.

61. See Saçak, no. 64, June 1389): 5–13, where strikes are listed along with the workplace, the reasons for the strike, and the number of workers involved.

62. On the Workers' Congress, see the Turkish press of 19 June 1989; and *Ikibine Doğru*. (19 and 26 June 1989).

7

Historiography, Class, and Iranian Workers

This responsibility still rests on the working class to organize itself and the people and by the complete elimination of the exploiters, carry out its task of rebuilding the world. This is the decree of history, and the working class will inevitably accomplish this task.

(*Workers' News*, issue 1, p. 3, 1980)[1]

A worker is one who, obeying the command of God, endeavors to develop the earth and its materials....Thus, the workers are of divine value; and obeying that command is a divine and Islamic duty....The differences in expectations and trades must not divide the various layers of population, must not damage the Islamic brotherhood. The atheist (*ilhadi*) ideologies attempt to use these means to define the workers as a class, so separating them from the Islamic *ummat* (people) and crushing its unity.

(President Khameneii of the Islamic Republic, May Day 1981)

There does not exist, as such, a history of the Iranian working class. There is neither a complete life history of the working class at the national level nor one that covers a short period of it in a particular region. Writings on labor history consist overwhelmingly of accounts of the trade unions with particular focus on the period between 1941–1953, rather than a history of laboring men and women, their work, community, culture, and politics. Labor history, however, is not solely the domain of labor researchers; social historians, political scientists, leftist activists, and religious (Islamic) authorities have also commented on the history and the behavior of the working classes. These less conventional commentators tend to use written histories, political speeches, statements in the publications of left-wing activists, and the various writings of Islamic leaders in Iran as their vehicles of commentaries about labor.

In the first section, I look very closely at a sample of all these types of literature to illustrate how the "working class" has been conceptualized by the commentators: the political scientists, historians, activists, and the state ideologues. The major theoretical assumptions and conceptual schema through which the working class is portrayed will be examined, as will practical implications of the theoretical conceptualization of working class. In general, I identify four historiographical currents represented by the orientalists and modernizationists, labor historians, the left-wing activists, and the Islamic theoreticians, who, on the whole, exhibit an elitist, structuralist, essentialist, and moralist approach to working-class history and behavior.

In the second section, I shall present my own perception of the way the "working class" must be conceptualized in general. In this connection, I will argue that an alternative perspective must transcend the inadequacies of the preceding approaches, in particular the one that defines a worker only in terms of his or her objective position in the class structure (structuralism), and rest instead on the consciousness, culture, and action of workers. Yet, at the same time, problems of "culturalism" and the inadequacy of the portrayal of language as the sole criterion of class expression will also be examined.

The final section is an attempt to present my understanding of the "reality" of the working class in Iran by examining its representation in social and political discourse; that is, by showing the way in which workers were perceived both by the public, especially by the state authorities and the employers, and by themselves. In this regard, the issue of language, in particular Islamic language, is explored. Through a discourse analysis, I will discuss how workers expressed their sense of "classness" and what role Islam, as an ideology, cultural form, and discourse, played in this process.

Four Historiographical Currents

Orientalist and Modernizationist Historiography: Workers Dismissed

Until very recently, Iranian historiography, in general, had been reduced to the history of personalities, institutions, and individual events; it consisted of a narrative and empiricist methodology, highly politicist and individualistic in nature, with a parochial perspective. The political and social developments and conflicts were hardly seen in class terms, nor were they explained according to any historical logic. Instead, they read as a broad historical survey focusing on the impact of international affairs on domestic politics. Many Western writers on Iran seemed to look at the historical developments in Iran from an explicit or implicit orientalist perspective. By emphasizing the "uniqueness" of Middle Eastern societies in general, this perspective tended to focus on such issues as culture and religion as the context of historical continuity and the individuals or elites as the source of change.

Marvin Zonis's *The Political Elite of Iran*, for instance, represents an *elitist* approach to political history of Iran, in which there is little room for social groups, especially social classes, to play a role. Such an approach is based on the theoretical assumption that "the attitudes and behavior of powerful individuals in societies whose political processes are less institutionalized within the formal structures of government are valid guides to political change."[2] Although one cannot deny the role of individuals in political change, and that may occur as well in Western countries whose political processes *are* institutionalized, one must acknowledge the impact of social forces that may affect or even shape the behavior of individuals. In the elitist historiography, the working class along with other subaltern groups are simply dismissed.

Donald Wilber's historical survey, *Iran*, on the other hand, represents an "orientalist" approach with a blend of apologism. Wilber's study is broadly concerned with a "proud heritage, respected traditions, religious conformity, and the cement of a graduated society [that] all served to foster continuity and preserve the country's integrity."[3] What is central to his narrative is not conflict but "public consensus" with "the enlightened goals of authority" that guarantee stability. In his *Iran: Past and Present*, which went into its eighth edition in 1979, Wilber does devote some three pages[4] to "industrial labor" but only to say that the Shah broke "Soviet and Communist domination of the unions" by disbanding them. He continues to claim that the working conditions in the postcoup era improved, as strikes were rare. Wilber fails, however, to mention the coup itself, which brought the workplaces under secret police scrutiny and outlawed strikes.

Joseph Upton's broad survey, *The History of Modern Iran: An Interpretation*, surpasses the shortfalls of elitism and apologism. It attempts to focus on the history of the people. The people, according to him, consists of three broad social categories: the peasants, the townsmen, and the tribesmen. The middle class is later added to the list. The category "worker" rarely appears in the text; and when it does, it is devoid of any analytical value or social significance.[5]

Quite a similar approach is adopted by Ann Lambton, a prominent British orientalist. For Lambton, "Persian society under the Qajars" consisted primarily of the "tribal leaders," "landowners," "the high officials of the bureaucracy," "religious classes," and the "merchant classes." Beyond these were the "masses," both rural and urban, whose main function is described as the payment of "taxes to the government, the local leaders, or both," and whose social state is seen as burdened by disaster and disease while being steeped in religiosity.[6] Again the category "worker" is either dismissed from the book or is enmeshed into the category of "urban masses."

The absence of the category "workers" or "working class" in these historical accounts may indicate an ontological or social absence of the working class in the society. However, it is more likely that orientalist literature, a priori, assumes that the working class lacks any social and political significance. In short, in the elitist and orientalist narrative, the category "worker," as distinct from *isnaf*, or the guild employees, has rarely had an independent existence, but is merged into the broad category of urban masses, which is depicted as destitute, ignorant, and deeply religious.

In recent years, some scholars have also examined modern Iranian history from a "nonclass perspective," but unlike their predecessors, their history is informed by a combination of sophisticated theory and analysis. For this reason we should examine them in some detail. Homa Katouzian provides a serious critique of the historians and social scientists who characterize Iranian history by categories such as "feudalist" and "capitalist."[7] In Katouzian's theoretical assumptions, "class" is simply not applicable to Iranian society in the twentieth century. Briefly, his argument is as follows: the Iranian social formation before the land reform of 1962 cannot be characterized as feudalist, but as a "despotic social formation" defined by arbitrary rule. For Katouzian, "despotism" seems to define not merely pre-nineteenth century Iran, but all of Iranian history up to the present time. The despotism of the twentieth century was, however, further blended with "pseudo-modernism," which refers to the political and economic changes made during the reign of Reza Shah and his son.

Despotism, by definition, dismisses the concepts of legal and political security and certainty in favor of the accumulation of wealth, property, and physical capital. But the inherent weakness of a system of private accumulation of capital, together with an absence of individual autonomy owing to despotism, made for different socioeconomic developments in Iran from those that prevailed in Europe—such as the developments that engendered the emergence of the Industrial Revolution, industrial capitalism, and the subsequent rise of the bourgeois and the proletarian classes. Therefore, Katouzian argues, it is erroneous to characterize twentieth century Iran as capitalist with its attendant class structure and conflict.

Although Katouzian asserts that "Iranian society is not classless,"[8] the term *class* in the book refers simply to the multitude of people and occupations, but carries no social or political weight. And class conflict, according to him, does not play any role in the political development in Iran. Instead, owing to the prevailing despotism, "[d]own to the present day, the clearest line of social demarcation (even stratification) has been that which divides the state (*dawlat*) from the people (*mellat*)."[9] Thus, "working class," in his schema, signifies no more than an aggregate of the individual wage workers employed in industry. Sociopolitically, the workers may assume significance only as part of the *mellat* as opposed to the *dawlat*.

Katouzian's criticism of the wholesale application of Western Marxist concepts to Iran is well taken and shall be further dealt with later (in the third section). However, Katouzian's own model, although hardly original, is not free from conceptual and factual shortcomings. To begin with, he implies that Iran under the Shah cannot be characterized as capitalist because not feudalism but despotism preceded it. Contrary to his assumption, however, capitalism, as a social formation, does not have to originate from feudalism. Anthropologists now record the emergence of capitalist relations from simple egalitarian-communal societies. The prevalence of capitalist socioeconomic systems in a number of postcolonial African countries exemplify this possibility. Yet, capitalism in these societies assumes a particular form, in that it tends to be undermined by the traditional values and precapitalist cultures while simultaneously incorporating them to its advantage. Depending on the cultural traits of each society these values might be different, but perhaps the most common of them include a lack of the liberal values, such as freedom and equality before law (e.g., contract), the prevalence of paternalistic authoritarianism, the desire for rapid turnover, application of trade norms to industrial activities, short-term planning, and the like.[10]

Second, the concept of "despotism," as a *social* formation and not as a political one, implies an unrealistic cycle of continuity in Iranian history, likening, for instance, tenth century socioeconomic conditions to those of the twentieth century. Even if there were a plausible reason for employing the concept "despotism" as merely a *political* form, that is arbitrary rule with or without a constitution, still the despotism of the Shah in the twentieth century was very different from previous forms of it, simply because the Shah's autocracy was constrained by new internal and international forces. Indeed, and that is the third point, this modern type of despotism can coexist with a capitalist economy and social structure. As a matter of fact, and as in many Third World countries, it was largely the state itself that fostered capitalist (pseudo?) modernization, encouraging private accumulation.[11] Arbitrary political interference by the state in economic activities certainly did trouble the capitalists and private business. These restraints, however, were largely *situational*, rather than strategic.

Indeed, the crucial question is not whether or not the Iranian economy under Muhammad Reza Shah, and to some extent under his father, Reza Shah, was characterized by capitalism. One can hardly deny that the economy at this period was essentially capitalistic, although it had incorporated, and at the same time was undermined by, precapitalist culture and traditional values as well as the despotic political form. The crucial question, rather, is whether the prevalence of a capitalistic economy, of the Iranian kind, was sufficient for the making of a working class. It must also be asked how these nonliberal values and "traditional" cultures in the society, such as primordial (religious, kinship, communal) loyalties and identities, affect the development of a working class. A significant historiographical school, that of the Left/Marxist activists in Iran, has, a priori, assumed that the prevalence of a capitalist structure necessarily leads to the development of a working class. It is to this historiographical school that we now turn to discuss its theoretical assumptions.

Marxist Historiography: The Working Class as a Special Class

Although "nonclass," elitist, and orientalist approaches dominate Iranian historiography, the left-wing historians and activists take "class" as a fundamental concept in their historical analyses. These historians have overwhelmingly been either Soviet scholars or Iranians heavily influenced by Soviet Marxist historiography. Their accounts still constitute the main source of historical reference and theoretical approach for most left-wing political organizations in Iran today.

An early major work that deals with the emergence of the working class in Iran is Abdullaev's study (*Iranian Industry and the Creation of a Working Class in the Late Nineteenth and early Twentieth Centuries*, 1963) of which only Chapter 3 has been translated into English. Abdullaev, a Russian historian, discusses the qualitative and quantitative features of the working class, its conditions of work, and political activities. Another Russian historian, M. Ivanov, also devotes sections of his book to a broad survey of the working class up to the early 1960s.[12] This work was translated by the Iranian Tudeh (Communist) party in 1977. After the Revolution, an ideologue of the Tudeh party, Mehdi Kayhan, published segments of his doctoral dissertation written in the former Soviet Union in 1954.[13] The study covers a period between 1941 and 1953, a period of extensive trade union activism. But by far the most influential work within this tradition is *A Survey of the Workers' and Communist Movement in Iran* by Abdossamad Kambakhsh, one of the leaders of the Tudeh party.[14] This work, too, is a survey of the trade union and communist movements in the 1920s and especially the 1940s.

Most of today's left-wing organizations in Iran, especially the ones originating from the left-wing guerrilla groups, have adhered to a similar kind of Marxism. They differ from the Tudeh in terms of their political tactics rather than their theoretical base. These groups have also relied heavily on the historical works supplied by the preceding historians, and although they do not set out to write their own histories of the Iranian working class, they have commented extensively on workers' behavior. Noticeable among such writings are four main texts, which have served as the basis for guerrilla strategy in Iran: *On the Necessity of Armed Struggle and a Refutation of the Theory of "Survival"* (written in 1970), by Amir Parviz Pouyan; *Armed Struggle: A Strategy and Tactic* (1970), by Masoud Ahmadzadeh; *What a Revolutionary Must Know* (1970), by Ali Akbar Safaii Farahani; and *Armed Struggle: A Road to the Mobilization of the Masses* (1973), by Bijan Jazani.[15]

The General Features of Marxist Historiography. Both the historical surveys and contemporary political writings, each written in a Marxist vein, appear to have four general features. First, they seem to be highly ideological and politically biased. For Tudeh historians, for instance, "the leadership of the Tudeh party" is usually depicted as one "of the most fundamental factors of the economic victories and political achievements of the Iranian working class."[16] On the other hand,

Kambakhsh's book combines the history of Tudeh and the workers' movement, stressing the history of the Tudeh party, thereby implying a unity between workers and the party.

Second, the writings derive their theoretical schema and conceptual frameworks from the mechanical Marxism of the Second International, features of which include gross generalizations, simplistic models, and economic reductionism. It is perhaps worth noting that during the 1960s and 1970s, two main Persian texts served as the theoretical education of the young Iranian Marxists. These were Nooshin's *Principles of the Economy* [Usoul-i Ilm-i Iqtisad] and George Politszer's *An Introduction to the Principles of Philosophy*, both notorious for their simplification, economic reductionism, and mechanistic approach to political economy and historical materialism.

Third, despite the use of grand theoretical models, their historiography forces a narrow outlook: institutional, politicist, and structuralist. Members of the working class are viewed primarily at their places of work, whereas their leisure activities, place in the family, community, overall cultural settings, and informal politics are invariably ignored. Ehsan Tabari, the leading theoretician of the Tudeh, attributes the formation of the "working class or the industrial proletariat" to the emergence of capitalism, which occurred with the establishment of factories in the late nineteenth century, during the reign of Naser Eddin Shah, a Qajar king (1840—1890). During this period, a number of workers, such as apprentices of craftsmen, had a "preproletarian and guild character," but the real workers were "those who, by dint of their social position [e.g., their concentration] and the sale of their labor power for a wage, had the greatest resemblance to the industrial proletariat."[17] In addition, he goes on to suggest that, "due to the abnormality of capitalist development in Iran," neither the industrial bourgeoisie nor the industrial proletariat was able to experience full-fledged development.[18] So, for Tabari, the form and the character of social classes are deduced directly from the character, "normality," or "abnormality" of the capitalist structure.

Even in this narrow framework, we are at times confronted with a *reified* history of working people; that is, we are presented with the history of the institutions rather than of the people involved in them. The major assumption is that the working class exists only as a formal grouping in conventional organizations such as trade unions or political parties. In short, these works are not the history of the *working class as such;* that is, the history of working men and women, their life, culture, traditions, ideas, politics, *their* activities in the labor organizations, at the labor process, and in the labor market. Instead, they are histories of their formal *organizations* and the communist movement.

Finally, the historiographies seem to have, albeit in varying degrees, a teleological and essentialist conception of the working class. By analyzing the struggles for wages and conditions of the workers in the 1940s, Mehdi Kayhan wrote in 1954 that, "In an anti-imperialist and anti-feudalist revolution in Iran, the working class is the most consistent fighter against imperialism, and one which is able to resolve the problem of bourgeois-democratic, i.e. anti-feudalist, revolution."[19] There is no historical-empirical evidence to prove this assertion in the context of Iran. Again, over twenty-five years later, a left-wing journal, *Workers' News,* with reference to the struggle of the Iranian workers in the 1979 Revolution, asserted: "This responsibility still rests on the working class to organize itself and the people, and by the complete elimination of the exploiters, carry out its task of rebuilding the world. *This is the decree of history,* and the working class *will inevitably* accomplish this task" (emphasis added).[20] History in the past twelve years has shown that this expectation from the working class has not been realized. The preceding statement is derived not from a historical-empirical analysis of the *concrete* social forces (classes, groups, etc.) in Iran but rather represents a "logical" argument based on an evaluation of the *general* structure of the political economy, the position of the classes, the role of the state, and so on.[21]

Theoretical Assumptions. The "working class" of the Iranian Left represents a highly abstract (rather than a specific) reality, resulting from an abstract analysis of the general sociohistorical conditions of Iran. For the Iranian Left, the "working class" is omnipotent, without defect, sacred, just, and with a historical role. Irrespective of its will, desire, and ability, the working class is depicted as possessing the "responsibility for rebuilding the world," which history has assigned to it. The conceptualization seems to find justification in Marx.

For Marx and Engels, as is well known, "the question is not what this or that proletarian, or even the whole of the proletariat, at the moment considers its aim. The question is what the proletariat is and what, consequent upon that being, it will be compelled to do."[22] Marx's sociohistorical concept and indeed his Hegelian "abstract proletariat" is later amended by his detailed *historical* analysis of the *real* classes in France[23] and his practical involvement in the international working-class movement. Although Marx seemed later to advocate a *contingent* theory of proletarian revolution, his early formulation of an "abstract proletariat" left a powerful impact on later followers. It underlay Lenin's dichotomy of trade union consciousness *vs.* social democratic/class consciousness. Lenin's pamphlet *What Is To Be Done?*, which carried the most systematic formulation of these concepts, was reconsidered by Lenin himself during the revolutionary episodes of 1905 and, especially, 1917. But perhaps it was Lukacs, more than Lenin, who seemed to take Marx's concept to construct his own dichotomy: "actual ideas," which people form about their class, *vs.* "ascribed class consciousness," referring to the ideas, sentiments, and so on, which the agents of class would have if they had grasped their class position in society and the real interests that it engenders.[24] By the notion of "ascribed class consciousness," Lukacs tends to rationalize the behavior of the working class: the proletariat would have developed if it had acted "rationally." This, of course, is a teleology. However, Lukacs, too, who started with the "essentialist" position of Marx in *The Holy Family*, concluded that "the objective theory of class consciousness is the theory of its objective possibility"[25] and that the conditions of this possibility has to be explored by the Marxists.

The traditional Iranian Left, although hardly familiar with Lukacs, is informed by Lenin's *What Is to Be Done* and shares quite a similar essentialist conceptualization of the working class. For instance, Bijan Jazani, a leading Marxist guerrilla theoretician in the early 1970s, grants not only a "specific historical interest" to the Iranian working class, but also a specifically "proletarian ideology." Marxism, according to Jazani, *is* the ideology of the working class. The fact is that Marxism has never been the ideology of the Iranian *workers*—not in the 1970s, nor at present, nor even during the 1940s when the Tudeh party had a great deal of political influence among them. Instead of the working class, as Jazani admits, it was a segment of the "rising petty-bourgeoisie," the intellectuals, who adhered to Marxism.[26]

Furthermore, the Tudeh historians and the contemporary Left activists depict the working class in two contradictory fashions. On the one hand, the working class is depicted as omnipotent, perfect, special, with a historical "responsibility for rebuilding the world." And, on the other hand, it is portrayed as "wretched, deprived, with no rights, down at the lowest social scale, just like the slaves at the time of slavery, deprived of education and literacy, under the devastating burden of labor."[27] How will such a working class "abolish" itself and liberate all of humanity? How are these discrepancies explained in Iranian Marxist literature?

At least four explanations are provided. The first views the growth of the working class in terms of the Marxian concepts of "class in itself" *vs.* "class for itself," as well as "actual power" *vs.* "potential power." The working class, according to this perspective, develops from a premature phase ("class in itself") to the stage of maturity ("class for itself"). Thus, in an evolutionary process, the "potential power" of the working class becomes actualized. To explain the reasons behind the failure of the Iranian workers to achieve their "potential power," Marxist historians such as Ehsan Tabari point to the "abnormality" of capitalist development in Iran.[28] Most commentators, however, focus on the political factors.

Political repression under the Shah, and this is the second explanation, prevented the working class from initiating even "economic" struggles, let alone "political" ones. The Shah's political control served as the major justification for Marxist guerrilla leaders to resort to armed struggles as opposed to "political work among the working class."[29] Pouyan, a leading guerrilla theoretician, wrote in 1970 that the workers "presume the power of their enemy to be absolute and their inability to emancipate themselves as absolute."[30] As we saw in the previous section, other labor historians have also stressed the factor of political control. Although political repression was crucial to the suppression of workers' organization and struggle after the 1953 coup that ousted the nationalist government of Dr. Musadeq, this factor *alone* cannot explain why the working class failed to reorganize. Such an explanation is simply political reductionism, a thesis that will be dealt with critically in the next section.

Third, the working class has not had "true" leadership. The guerrilla organizations blamed the Tudeh party for "betraying" the working class by its "opportunism," quietism, and compromise; and the Tudeh party in turn accused them of "voluntarism" and "terrorism." The Iranian "new Left" accused both of similar charges. Although extremely significant, a theoretical discussion of working-class leadership (i.e., the issues of a vanguard party, spontaneity and the role of the trade unions) goes beyond the scope of this chapter. This absence of "true" leadership (a socialist party?) resulted, according to Iranian Marxist literature, in the working class embracing "religious," "petit bourgeoise," and "populist" leadership especially during and after the Revolution of 1979. This process is believed to have hampered the development of class consciousness.[31]

Finally, the Left has invariably made reference to the lack of class consciousness, or "proletarian culture," and an absence of a "true consciousness." Bijan Jazani acknowledged that, "without a proletarian culture, without a class consciousness and without an experience of struggle, a definition of the proletariat as the most revolutionary class in our society is simply incorrect."[32] A serious historical and contemporary analysis, by the traditional Left, of consciousness and culture among the Iranian working class is indeed rare. One reason, perhaps, relates to the way in which the Left perceives working-class consciousness and culture. A consciousness is presumed to be truly proletarian when it is *secular* and even *socialist*,[33] and the working class is considered to be conscious when it is organized in a "working.class party." This represents a fixed, definite, and a priori assumption of working-class consciousness. By presuming the universality of such consciousness, the commentators and historians of the Left overlook the fact that working-class consciousness and actions can take different and specific forms in different cultures. Such a postulation, therefore, would make unnecessary any historical or sociological enquiries about working-class subjectivity and culture: what is necessary instead, it would seem, are attempts to make the workers secular and "socialist," perhaps by recruiting them into "the working-class parties." In short, the Left wished to have the working class speak their (Left) language, use their terminology, and think along their lines.

An obvious elitism and Eurocentrism shades this understanding of class consciousness and culture. Rather than address the real experiences of life for Iranian workers, this school focuses on the unproblematic extension of the way in which class consciousness was understood (in terms of the organization of the workers in the social democratic parties) in Russia before the 1917 Revolution. The Russian experience had itself been influenced by concepts deriving from the English labor movement.[34]

This approach to understanding working-class consciousness led to the Left's dismissal of Islamic workers after the Revolution as simply *Hezbollahi* (generally pro-regime) and Islamic organizations as "pro-capitalist" and "reactionary."[35] Thus, the Islamic *Shuras* (councils)[36] and Islamic Associations, which played a significant role in working-class organization in the post-Revolution periods albeit along an exclusivist and divisive line,[37] while they waged battles against the "liberal-professional" managements, remained uninvestigated.

In summary, Marxist activists in Iran have conceptualized the working class primarily in terms of its location in the class structure (structuralism), and its essential revolutionary role (essentialism), and by assuming a fixed and abstract "perfect" consciousness expressed in a universal form. By such a conceptualization, they tend to divorce workers from their true selves, their empirical reality.

Social Democratic Historiography: The Working Class as the Labor Movement

A new group of historians, with Marxist and social democratic orientations, has come to the fore by offering serious works of scholarship in labor history. In comparison with the works inspired by Soviet Marxism, the new contributors seem to transcend the simplistic models, economic reductionism, and the political bias of the former historiography. Because the works of these scholars focus overwhelmingly on the "labor movement" aspect of working class history, they may loosely fall under the rubric of the "social democratic" school of labor historiography.

The studies by Willem Floor (*Labour Unions, Laws and Conditions in Iran: 1900–41*), Ervand Abrahamian ("The Strengths and Weaknesses of the Labor Movement in Iran, 1941–53" and *Iran Between Two Revolutions*) and Habib Lajevardi (*Labor Unions and Autocracy in Iran*) constitute a significant shift in labor historiography. As the titles illustrate, these works put together, and especially Lajevardi's, cover almost the entire history of the labor movement in Iran, from its genesis in 1906 to the Iranian Revolution of 1979.

According to these sources, although some sort of labor organizations existed after 1906, "it was not until 1921 that a significant labor movement appeared in Iran."[38] The newly formed Communist and Social Democratic parties brought together the existing unions and established a Federation of Trade Unions with branches in the main cities and the oil fields. The "golden age" of unionism, 1918–1925 according to Floor, was brought to an end with the accession to power of Reza Shah, a move to which the pro-Soviet elements of the labor movement themselves contributed.[39] The unions in general at this time organized employees of small-scale workshops, trade clerks, construction workers, postmen, teachers, and the like. These constituted some 20 percent of the industrial labor force in 1920. The unions published several regular papers, established clubs, organized strikes, celebrated May Day, and were involved in national political activities. In fact, according to Floor, the "primary aim of the labour movement [. . .] was the destruction of imperialism and capitalism."[40]

The new phase of the labor movement began with the Anglo-Soviet invasion of Iran in August 1941, which destroyed Reza Shah's dictatorship. In this relatively free political climate, the labor movement, with the strong influence of the Tudeh party, was revived and developed to become the largest and most militant in the Middle East,[41] as well as the strongest in Asia and Africa.[52] The 1953 coup that toppled the nationalist government of Dr. Muhammed Musadeq and reinstated the Shah brought the organized activities of the Iranian labor movement to an almost complete halt. Thus, the history of labor in the post-coup era, until the revolutionary crisis of 1978, became the history of state suppression, working–class passivity and state-run or corporatist unions.

These studies provide the most systematic and detailed narratives on Iranian workers. My intention here is not so much to examine the factual accuracy of the narratives as to discuss how the authors have viewed and portrayed their subject matter and what implicit or explicit theoretical assumptions inform their stories. Broadly speaking, the studies provide an overwhelmingly *institutional* and *politicist* approach to the study of the labor movement. The working class is depicted as those working *men* who have come together in the labor unions, primarily to pursue the political aim of opposing the government. Yet most of these studies avoid giving the predominant role to the "workers," who are largely ignored, and instead place the emphasis on the labor unions and the leadership or the "elites" of these organizations. This in itself assumes a concept of "labor movement" that implies an inherent unity and harmony between its various segments; that is, the leader, activists, and the rank and file members. We are, therefore, presented with little historical evidence with regard to the possible *conflicts* (of interest and vision) between the rank and file and the leadership of the movement.

Theoretical work on formal and bureaucratic organizations (defined by specialized functions, fixed rules, and hierarchy of authority) emphasizes an "essential" *lack* of harmony between the masses and officialdom. Michels's theory of the "iron law of oligarchy" explains oligarchical control *vs.* mass apathy in terms of "the technical competence which definitely elevates the leaders above the mass and subjects the mass to the leaders."[43] Accordingly, the historian of the trade union movement must look at the *internal structure* of unions and the division of labor, highlighting union democracy or bureaucracy. Because, as Richard Hyman has suggested, the union is "first and foremost, an agency and a medium of power," it is involved not merely in an *external* relationship of control (i.e., in relation to the employers) but also in an *internal* one, with regard to the ordinary members, lay activists, local officials, and national leaders.[44]

In reality, then, complete harmony and unity do not result from a given labor movement; rather tension and conflict exists between top and bottom and among different segments of the rank and file. But how do the historians under investigation treat the issue of unity/conflict in the Iranian context? Floor does point out the conflict of interests between officialdom and mass of the workers, but finds the rank and file to be *subordinated* to the political whims of the "middle-class" leadership. The Marxist leadership, according to Floor, was "more interested in political matters than in bread and butter issues" or other concerns of the rank and file.[45] The appalling working conditions indicate that the unions did not pay much attention to these economic issues. Did the members of rank and file resist or reject those of their leaders who turned the trade unions into their own political apparatus? They did not. Their lack of experience, combined with their isolation, illiteracy, and expectation of paternalism were all contributing reasons why workers accepted the authority of their leaders. "The workers in general had neither the time and energy, nor the understanding and capacity to organise labour activities, let alone a labour movement."[46] In other words, the labor movement hardly represented a movement *of* the workers themselves. It was rather a movement of a movement of a handful of elites, the leadership, which had harnessed the masses. This explains, for Floor, why the labor movement failed when Reza Shah's autocracy took over.

On the other hand, both Lajevardi and Abrahamian seem to be adamant that the workers were not "like sheep who can be swayed in any direction by the demagogue of the day."[47] In fact, Lajevardi asserts that "Iranian workers frequently followed to the end those leaders in whom they believed—suffering hardship, imprisonment, and some cases, loss of life."[48] This conclusion presumes an essential unity of interests, internal cohesion, and strength in the labor movement. What, therefore, caused the demise of the labor movement was not an internal factor, but an external one: political repression.[49] In fact, for many Left and liberal historians and activists, political repression during periods of autocratic rule solely accounts for the defeat and consistent nonorganization of labor, and this is considered especially true of the period 1965–1975.[50] The "political repression" thesis, however, is fueled by questionable theoretical premises, thus rendering it inadequate for an explanation for the failure of the labor movement during the reign of the Shah.

First, this prevailing argument assumes that a labor movement is merely the *formal* and *open* organization of labor, a view that limits its scope to official procedures on a national scale, thus reducing the forms of labor resistence to the conventional forms of stoppages or public demonstrations. This approach obviously ignores the *informal*, unofficial, and (especially) clandestine forms of resistance by workers at the level of the *labor process*. "At least as important, if not more so, [are]," according to van Onselen when describing the workers' consciousness under an African labor-coercive economy, "the less dramatic, silent and often unorganized responses, and it is this latter set of responses which occurred on a day-to-day basis that reveal most about the functioning of the system and formed the warp and woof of worker consciousness."[51]

Under repressive conditions, labor resistance may take the form of absenteeism, sabotage, disturbances, theft, religious practice, and poor quality production. Labor activism of this nature is not necessarily unplanned or purely "spontaneous," as some historians and Marxist revolutionaries tend to suggest.[52] For instance, my interviews with factory workers in Tehran in 1980 suggest that stoppages and strikes in the early 1970s, under the Shah's police state, were carefully thought out and planned.[53]

Second, political reductionism implies a zero-sum relation between the power of the state and the organization of political activities in general and labor in particular: when the state is strong, the opposition to it (including labor organization) is weak or nonexistent; and when the state is weak the opposition to it strong. Goran Therborn has satisfactorily argued that such a conclusion is unjustifiable.[54]

Finally, political reductionism rests on an assumption that establishes a *necessary* link between political conditions (freedom/restriction) and labor activities (organization/nonorganization). Thus, it is taken for granted that in the absence of political restrictions, the labor force will automatically organize itself independently. I have argued that the link between political conditions and labor activities is only contingent.[55] The relationship is mediated by the form of workers' consciousness, the degree of organizational tradition, leadership quality, and the extent of corporate ideology. For instance, where the unions are dominated by the corporatist and paternalist ideology of the workers and the leaders alike, a labor movement can hardly be considered as truly independent, even if it may operate openly. Some corporatist labor movements in Latin America, in Mexico, for example, illustrate the point.[56]

In summary, the new breed of labor historians on Iran has made a significant contribution to Iranian labor studies, in that they have rescued the workers and their movements from the dismissive treatments of the elitist, orientalist, and modernizationist schools of historiography. Also, the studies have transcended the teleological approach and highly abstract generalization, by the Marxist activists, of workers' behavior. The narratives, however, have stopped short of examining the working class beyond the class structure, institutions of the unions, and workers' and workers' links with the formal political parties. The position of workers in the community, family, cultural, and ideological settings has consequently been overlooked. In short, the social democratic current of labor historiography in Iran is informed by structuralist, politicist (an exclusive focus on conventional politics), and institutional perspectives, in which the status of workers' *subjectivity* is, consequently, missing.[57]

An Islamic Historiography: The Working Class as the "Mustazʿafin"

The ideologues and the leaders of the Islamic regime in Iran have advocated two concepts of work and the working class. The first is an *instrumentalist* or pragmatic view. This has been developed in response to the politicoeconomic exigencies of postrevolutionary Iran. The second is one based on the *ideological* (Islamic) orientation of the ruling clergy.

The crisis of productivity in industry, along with ideological control by the state of the working class during the war with Iraq, was combined with the government's Islamic ideology to advocate work as a religious duty. "The hours of work," declared President Khamaneii, on May Day 1981, "are the moments of worshiping of God (*ibadat*), paying debt to martyrs, the deprived people, and the downtrodden of society. Wasting even one moment is equivalent to violating the rights of the deprived and to disrespecting the blood of the martyrs."

Based upon a *hadith* (saying) of the Prophet Mohammed that says that "to work is like jihad in the service of God," the instrumentalist religious conception of work was widely employed by the ruling clergy to secure the cooperation of the workers in raising production. It advocated that the performance of work brings rewards that are not material but spiritual, granted not in this world but in the next. However, the penalty for misconduct is a matter for worldly punishment, as well as God's wrath in the world to come. This view was widely propagated by the special factory clergy, who were dispatched by the ruling Islamic Republican party in the early 1980s to spread the government's brand of Islam in the workplaces.[58]

Accompanying their instrumentalist (tactical) application of work ideology, the ruling clergy also instilled *ideological* conceptions of work. One version shares a great similarity with the work ideology of early Christianity; that is, work serves primarily as a means of promoting the health of the body and soul, guarding against evil, idleness, and decadence. It is in this context that the Ayatollah Khomeini addressed the workers: "One day of your life is worth all the lives of the capitalists and feudalists put together."[59] Also, primarily as a reaction to socialist and radical views on labor, the regime granted great dignity and religious piety to labor and the laborer. The case is exemplified in the widely expressed *hadith* that the "Prophet Muhammed kisses the hands of a laborer" and Khomeni's saying that "Labor is the manifestation of God."

The Islamic ideologues, in addition, have offered two images of the "working class": universal and particular. On the one hand, the *universal image* (the "human dimension" of workers) postulates that "all human beings are the *bandeh* (slave) of God; all are *kargars* [workers]; and every one works for the other. In this way, they set in motion the machinery of life and human evolution. In short, this is the divine conception."[60] This concept is spelt out more clearly by ex-President Khamaneii: "the value of work and the worker in Islam is higher than in any other materialist ideology. Following the Islamic world-view, we view work and worker to hold divine value, not merely material value. A worker is one who, obeying the command of God, endeavors to develop the earth and its materials."[61]

On the other hand, the *particular* image presents the worker as one involved in a wage-labor relationship.[62] But the worker, in this sense, is essentially a mere commodity the procedures for whose exchange, according to the labour minister in 1981, Ahmad Tavakkoli, are to be found in the section on *ijareh* in the Islamic *fiqh*. The term refers to hiring or renting objects and animals. As opposed to *ijareh*, the Perso-Arabic word *istikhdam* (literally asking to do a service, and equivalent to employment) was normally used, in prerevolutionary Iran, to refer to hiring *free* labor.

Although in legal terminology the term *worker* was understood in its *particular* meaning, as an object to be hired for a wage, its *universal* conception tended to be highlighted in public discourse. In the universal conception, the "working class" is stripped of its "classness" and is depicted as an integral segment of the broad category of *mustaz'afin* (downtrodden), the oppressed segment of the Islamic *ummat*. This view of "worker" relates to the model used by the Islamic ideologues to conceptualize social stratification.

As has been mentioned, according to the regime's Islamic thinkers every person in society is a *kargar*, a worker, in one form or another: they are all the "slaves" of God. What distinguishes among them is not the fact of property ownership, prestige, or market capacity, but the degree to which each has incorporated "justice" in his or her work and life; that is, the extent to which one is close to God. According to this view, class distinction, in any system, emerges when those who hold power and property get involved in an "unjust" accumulation of wealth (or *ifraat* and *takathor*). Capitalism, as such, is not an un-Islamic and illegitimate economic system. It becomes so only when accumulation is carried out through such un-Islamic methods as *"riba* [usury], lying, betraying, fraud"* and reluctance to pay a fair wage.[63] Once these evils are removed from the society and when everyone, in whatever "useful" occupation, works justly, then "the conflict between the worker and employer would wither away from the world."[64]

For the ideologues of the Islamic regime, therefore, "justice" is the basis for social demarcation and stratification. The relations of injustice divide society into two broad social groupings: *mustakbarin* and *mustaz'afin*. In the Quran, the term *mustakbarin* refers to the "advantaged" group such as Haroun, and *mustaz'afin* describes the "disadvantaged" groups, such as the people of *Bani-Israel*. The dichotomy, therefore, signifies social status determined by the relations of justice/injustice. In Iran, after the revolution, the term *mustakbarin* was used by the Islamic leaders to refer to all those who have acquired power and property through "illegitimate" and "unjust" channels. They are the enemies of Islam and the Islamic ummat. The mustaz'afin, on the other hand, included all those who were "oppressed" by the injustice of the mustakbarin. These may include the rural and urban poor, the unemployed, shantytown dwellers, and the like, who make up the backbone of the Islamic ummat.

In this concept of social stratification, the "working class" is dissolved within, and represented by, the broader category of mustaz'afin, the downtrodden. As mustaz'afin, the working class would share the same status and significance as the other "oppressed" Islamic masses. In this image, not only did the working class lose its position as a "special" class and its "revolutionary potential," as understood by the Marxists, it also lost its "classness" in terms of its position in relation to the means of production. On May Day 1981, President Khamaneii declared in an address to the workers: "The workers must approach the labour questions through the Islamic view. The differences in interests and trades must not divide the various layers of population, must not damage the Islamic brotherhood. The ilhadi [atheist] ideologies attempt to use these means to define the workers as a class, so separating them from the Islamic ummat (people) and crushing its unity."

The denial of the working class as a class was accompanied by the removal from official discourse of those manifestations and symbols that express it: by changing its name from the word kargar (worker) to karpazir (one who agrees to do work). This seemed, at the same time, a strategy through which the Labor Ministry attempted to end the idea of kargar so widely associated with the term socialism, the Left, and inqelab-i kargari, "workers' revolution."

In short, the ideologues of the Islamic Republic of Iran advocate a populist-moralistic definition of the working class. The working class is depicted not on the basis of relations of property, income, or prestige, nor in terms of consciousness, but in terms of its relation to "justice." The theoretical implication of this assumption is that the working class is subsumed and incorporated into the broad category of the "oppressed or disadvantaged Islamic mass," the mustaz'afin.

Identifying the working class as mustaz'afin displays an interesting model that seems to allow for a conceptual resolution of the problem of the alliance of the "popular classes," because the concept of mustaz'afin includes all those classes (the working class, the peasantry, the urban poor, and the petit burgeoisie, etc.) that are considered to be in a "disadvantaged" position vis-à-vis the mustakbarin, the "upper classes." Such an alliance therefore exhibits an ideal social basis for the Islamic state in Iran today.

The model, however, raises a number of problems. The major problem has to do with the fact that the concept of "injustice" remains vague and undefined. Unlike the concept of exploitation, which has a definite meaning, "injustice" or "unfairness" remains cloudy, unspecified, its meaning changing with time, place, and culture. On the other hand, classifying a large group of people (workers, peasants, the destitute, etc.) on the basis of their shared experience vis-à-vis social "injustice" may certainly differentiate them collectively from other people who lack that experience. But the identity and consciousness that these "disadvantaged" groups may share does not represent a *class* consciousness, but rather some form of social identity similar to that which corresponds to identification of gender, race, or nation. As we will discuss later, the notion of *class* identity is necessarily linked to "class position," or the relationship to the means and conditions of production, although this element alone cannot determine a class.

Conceptualizing the Working Class: Some Theoretical Remarks

None of the preceding historiographical accounts exhibits a sound conceptual ground for a complete history of the Iranian working class. Some tend to ignore its existence by, a priori, denying it as a socially meaningful category (the elitist and orientalist writers). Others assume a predetermined historical character, a political ideology and cultural traits for the working class (the Marxists). They, in fact, tell us what the working class ought to be, rather than what it really is. Still other texts, those of the labor historians, depict only part of its reality. And finally, the Islamic ideologues incorporate it into and identify it with a larger social category, the "oppressed," which comprises not only workers but also other social classes and groups: the peasantry, urban poor, the petit bourgeoisie, and so on.

The perspectives of the overall historical and political writings put together are, thus, shaded by elitism, essentialism, political-institutional reductionism, and moralism. Within these theoretical frameworks, the working class is invariably conceptualized in terms of its position in the social and economic structure: sometimes in terms of its relation to the means of production (among the Left activists and the labor historians), or employment in industry (among the elitist and orientalist writers), or in terms of its position vis-à-vis "justice" (the Islamic theoreticians). Alternatively, a sound historiography would be one that would transcend the inadequacies primarily of structuralism and essentialism by portraying the working class in its totality. To this end, I want to propose that "class" is more than simply class position, the relationship of the agents to the means of production or their market capacity. Rather, it must be seen as a historically specific form of consciousness expressed, within the context of a certain (class) structure, in a complex of discursive fields and practices. In this perspective, class and class consciousness are viewed to be identical.

A structuralist perspective views class as a "thing," the existence of which presumes or is reflected in class consciousness. Thus, the objective position of class, and "objective interests" deriving from that class position, predetermines the class consciousness. The fact, however, is that the notion of "interests," which is meaningful only when it is perceived and articulated, is part and parcel of consciousness. And, in addition, as Stedman Jones has argued, interests do not pre-exist their expression.[65] In other words, class is the same as class consciousness, and class consciousness can be manifested only through language, "since there is no social reality outside or prior to language."[66] Therefore, to make sense of the working class we must start not from the structure and "objective interests" to arrive at a class consiousness, but from the language of the class to characterize its political movement. Similarly, to make sense of the character of a labor struggle, the historian should look at what the participants say or write, instead of assuming that their very class position predetermines the nature of their movement.

One problem with Stedman Jones's concept of language in his historical analysis is the implication that symbols represent definite meanings. This conclusion is problematic, because it is possible to assume that people may deduce *different* meanings from the expression of the same symbols. This is especially true in socially fluid periods in the history of a given society. This problem in Stedman Jones has to do, as Joan Scott notes, with his *literal* perception of language. Stedman Jones "reads 'language' only literally with no sense of how facts are constructed."[67] Attempting to rescue the role of "language" in histori-ography, Scott redefines *language* not simply as "words in their literal usage but [as] creation of meaning through differentiation."[68] In other words, historians should not simply take the words at their face value, but should see what, in fact, the words actually mean. In this sense, class is perceived as an identity resting on a set of differentiations expressed in language defined as a complex process of the construction of meaning.

The conceptualization of class suggested by Stedman Jones and amended by Scott overcomes a great many of the problems attached to a structuralist conception. However, it does not escape a number of difficulties of its own. First, the status of "structure" in the analysis is either totally missing (as in Scott) or treated very cursorily (in Stedman Jones). I would like to emphasize that the element of "class position" is essential for a conceptualization of class, although, as we have shown so far, it is by no means sufficient on its own. If this element is removed from the definition, and class is perceived *only* in terms of an identity resting on a set of differentiations, then "class" can easily be confused with and subsumed into other forms of identity, such as gender, nation, ethnicity, and so on.

Second, Scott's insistence on the role of language, perceived as the creation of meaning, in historiography seems well justified. However, this notion does have certain shortcomings as there can be more than one interpretation of a "text", be it spoken or written. Which interpretation is correct? What criteria can we employ to decode the "language" to arrive at the "true" meaning of text? Here, I believe, the role of the "objective position"—the social background or material conditions—becomes prominent. What is needed, I would suggest, is a conceptualization of class that rests primarily on the notion of consciousness, culture, and identity (expressed in language in action), but also incorporates the element of the "class position." We do not yet possess such a comprehensive model.

E. P. Thompson's notion of "experience" represents an attempt to bridge the gap between the class position and consciousness. According to Thompson, members of a class come to feel and articulate the identity of their interests as a result of their common (class) *experiences*, which are determined largely by *class position*. *Class consciousness* is the way in which these experiences are handled in cultural terms: in traditions, value systems, ideas, and so on.[69]

But how do we identify this consciousness? In other words, at what point can we claim that Iranian workers hold a "class consiousness" and, therefore, constitute a class? This is a no less controversial issue than others we have discussed so far. We noted that the Iranian Marxists, following Lenin, tend to equate class consciousness with secular socialist ideology. Eric Hobsbawm, for his part, subjects a (working) class formation to a set of definite conditions. For him a working class may be recognizable by "the physical environment in which they lived, by a *style of life* and leisure, by a certain class consciousness increasingly expressed in a secular tendency to *join unions* and to identify with a *class party of labour*" (emphasis added).[70] And, as we saw earlier, E. P. Thompson formulates class consciousness in terms of a set of cultural practices.

Are the factors suggested by these historians—that is, secular ideology, organization in the unions and the party of labor, identical styles of life and leisure, secular ideology, and cultural self-activity—*necessary* conditions by which to identify and study the Iranian working class? I contend that they represent *sufficient* but not necessary conditions. Hobsbawm and Thompson (and to some extent Lenin) in fact formulate the particular experience and character of the *English* working class (see note 4). This working class developed in a particular cultural setting characterized by the "freeborn Englishman," liberalism, the traditions of self-help, and so on.[71] Therefore, a generalization of the previous conceptualizations represent either Euro- or, even more precisely, Anglocentrism. The consciousness of the working class, as such, cannot be presumed to be as necessarily secular, or socialist, or manifested in the organization of a party of labor. Workers' consciousness is historically specific and can assume different forms in different historical conditions. Religion, such as Islam, may well be a means to articulate class consciousness among certain Muslim workers.

So what we need is a conceptualization of class and class consciousness that can accommodate the cultural peculiarities of the societies in which workers are studied. To this end, we may speak of a working *class* when the workers come to perceive, and be perceived by others, as having a common and distinctive position and interests among themselves, which differ from (and are even opposed to) those of other people: and when this perception, among the workers and other people, is expressed in social, political, and cultural discourses or practices. A class understood in this way, then, becomes a socially meaningful category and, therefore, an effective social force. Such a perception of class (consciousness) would not be concerned with whether the workers are secular, socialist, or religious, "progressive" or "reactionary." The ideological traits it may uphold—its "reactionary" or "progressive" character, secular or religious tendencies—become a function not of "structural determination" but, simply and significantly, of struggle.

"Workers" and the "Working Class" in Iranian History

In this section, an attempt to depict the Iranian working class in terms of the preceding theoretical understanding is made by tryng to show the way in which workers were perceived both by themselves and in the public and official discourse. I do realize that my analysis is bound to be cursory in view of the fact that the original data needed for this purpose is, at present, inadequate.

The "Workers" in Ancient Iran

Some accounts speak about "workers" as if they have existed continously throughout Iranian history. In such accounts, the working class ceases to be a historical phenomenon. For example, a publication in 1971 by the Ministry of Labor, *The History and the Conditions of Work in Iran: From Antiquity up to the Present* (Tehran), portrays a "class of workers" which had originated during the Sassanian dynasty (A.D. 224–641). This "class of workers" include all those casual laborers (*agir*) involved in nonagricultural production, ranging from handicrafts, construction, and services through "wage work" or "nonwage" labor. Even independent writers, such as Farhang Qasemi, have also extended the concept of the working class to include a social group whose existence dates back to pre-Islamic Iran.[72] The same is also true of Gholamreza Insafpour who speaks of different categories of "workers": "agricultural workers," "free workers," "craft workers," and so on.[73]

It is not totally arbitrary to apply the term *workers* to the pre-Islamic era as well as to other periods that preceded the emergence of capitalism in Iran. In fact, neither the term *kargar* (worker) nor the reality of "wage labor" (*kargar-i mozdour*) is new, as the origins of both can be traced right back to the era of Achaemenids (500 B.C.).

The term *kargar*, the equivalent of "worker" that we use today in Iran to refer to the class of wage workers, originates in the Avesta, the holy book of the Zoroastrians. The Avesta appears to refer to *kargar* as a manual-physical laborer who works on the land. Incidently, the agricultural laborer and indeed agricultural work in general possess a high status in this holy book.[74]

At the same time, in ancient Iran, some sort of "wage work" also existed.[75] Olmstead, a historian of ancient Iran, describes the agricultural labor force during the Achaemenid dynasty in terms of intermediate landlords, the smallholders who might or might not own a few slaves or "free workers," the farmers tied to the land, and finally the vast group of the *khusnashins*. These last constituted a segment of the rural population who were not tied to land, and so enjoyed a certain degree of mobility. It was, by and large, the destitute *khushnashins* who, for the sake of sheer survival, would eventually resort to "wage labor."[76] There were, in addition, other categories of *kargars*: (a) the craft workers (*kargaran-i pishivar*) who were involved in the production of armory, clay cups, rugs, linen, and wooden goods;[77] (b) seasonal laborers: (c) the "free workers" who, in reality, were "owned" by the rural smallholders;[78] and finally (d) the laborers of public works, such as roads, mines, and so on who, in fact, were unfree.

A more recent authoritative work on ancient Iran by Dandamaev and Lukonin offers an exceptional insight into the life of the plebians in Achaemenid period.[79] On the whole, these authors also identify three types of "workers": "free," "semifree," and "unfree." "Certain numbers of skilled craftsmen (weavers, shoemakers, architects, etc.) were also slaves,"[80] and some slaves were also used as houseworkers, although they worked mostly in agriculture. Nor were all laborers slaves, however. Temples and private slave owners were frequently forced to employ skilled and free laborers to perform difficult types of work, for instance, in agriculture, handicrafts, and construction.[81] Large numbers of these workers were not exactly "free," because they would be "subject to punishment by the king" if they refused to work for such "employers" (as, for instance, the temple of Eanna). Some laborers worked specifically in the royal household and the households of Persian nobles.[82] These were called *kurtash*, and were, by and large, free.

As for the concept "wage" it seems that it was overwhelmingly in kind, in the form of goods such as wine, sheep, grain, flour, and beer.[83] But as money per se developed in the economy, the reward for labor could also be in terms of a money wage, especially silver.[84] In fact, Olmstead reports that some evidence from Persepolis suggests that the wages of each class of workers—children, women, wage workers, or craftsman—were precisely specified by the authorities.[85]

So far, it is clear that the term *kargar*, "worker," had emerged long before, and that some sort of wage labor also existed in ancient Iran. Yet it seems equally clear that the meaning of the word *kargar* and the nature of wage work in ancient Iran were quite different from those in Iran today. And therefore the continuity that some historians have implied for the prevalence of the category of wage labor throughout Iranian history simply does not hold. In the Avesta, the term *kargar* referred simply to manual-physical work, primarily in agriculture. And the kinds of work relations in ancient Iran that are described by historians as *kar-i mozdouri* (literally, wage labor) or *kar-i azad* (literally, free laborer) can hardly be compared to today's free-wage labor. In ancient Iran, "wage labor" represented some kind of physical labor carried out by those who did not control the conditions and outcome of their work, but whose relationship to the "employer" varied a great deal: from being "free," semi-free (debt bondage, indentured labor), to partly or fully a slave. In addition, a free market with the principle of free contract between two free individuals, normal today, hardly existed then.

The Turn of the Century: From Amalajaat to Kargars

Following the Islamic conquest of Persia in the seventh century a vast number of Persian terms were replaced by Arabic words. Therefore from the beginning of the Islamic era up to the end of the Qajar dynasty, in the first decade of the twentieth century the word *kargar* was almost absent from the public and official languages. The prevalence of Islam in Iran changed fundamentally the rigid "class structure" of the Sassanid period. After a few centuries of instability and chaos, the Irano-Islamic class structure established itself with the emergence of the Safavid dynasty. The main elements of this class structure, which continued until the end of the nineteenth century, included the ruling class, the bureaucratic middle class, the merchants and industrialists, the clergy, laborers, peasants, and nomadic people.[86]

Toward the end of the Qajar dynasty, the elements of the social hierarchy, in the language of the First Majlis after the Constitutional Revolution, comprised the Qajar royal family; *ulama* (the clergy); *ashraf* (the nobles) and *a'ayan* (the notables), including the *ummal* of the government; *tojjar* (the merchants); *mallakin* (the landlords); *fallahin* (the peasants); and *isnaf* (the "guilds").[87] It appears from this that the *kargars*, as a coherent social category, did not exist or at least was not recognized officially. We know, however, that certain "economic classes," according to Abrahamian, "objectively" existed in the Qajar period; and these included (a) "the landed upper class," which comprised the Qajar dynasty and local elites, (b) the "propertied middle classes" (merchants, craftsmen, and the clergy); (c) "urban wage earners"; and (d) the rural population, that is, the peasantry, and the tribal masses.[88]

In this list, the category of "urban wage earners" refers to the casual, seasonal, and unskilled construction laborers. At this time, this kind of labour force was widely referred to as *amalajaat*, not *kargars*.[89] *Al-Maathir Va Al-Athar* (1886/1984), by M. H. Itimad Al-Saltaneh, represents perhaps the best available source on the economy of the period, as it contains a detailed classification of occupational categories of employees in the ministries and the Royal Court. This official document describes, for instance, the janitors, mule and camel attendants, carriage drivers, warehouse employees, and so on as *amalajaat*.[90] The term, therefore, was used to identify the general category of urban laborers, but particularly a category of low-status, unskilled manual workers. Nowhere in these documents, memoirs, and official writings does one encounter the word *kargar*. It remained in the background, most notably in the *Shahname*, the epic work of the Persian poet, Ferdowsi.[91]

The term reappeared in public discourse only with the development of the "modern" manufacturing industry, toward the end of the Qajar period. The term specifically referred to the wage workers of the newly established factories. The first wave of industrialization began in the 1890s through the initiative of indigenous merchants such as Haj Amin Al-Zarb and foreign, especially Russian and German, capital. These industries concentrated on silk, textile, oil, wood, sugar, soap, oil, and the like. By the turn of the century, some sixty-one factories had been established, in which 1,700 workers were employed.[92] The labor force engaged in "modern industry," including oil and railways, reached some 6,700 by 1910, but this number still could not match the labor force of over 100,000 in the handicraft workshops.[93] "Modern industry," however, continued to grow rapidly in subsequent periods, particularly the 1930s, 1950s, and, at an accelerating rate, the 1970s.

The reappearance in general usage of the concept *kargar* as a social category seems to have been initiated by the Social Democrats, the left-wing intellectuals of the Constitutional Revolution (1905), people like Mirza Aghakhan Kirmani. These intellectuals were influenced by nineteenth-century European socialist thought, in which the "working class" was a main element.[94] Other protagonists of Social Democratic thought included Mirz Malkum Khan and Abdul-Rahim Talebov, both of whom, advocated "land to the tiller."[95] Thus, their interest in the "workers" derived not from the presence of a strong working class, but from the theoretical significance attached to the "workers" in the European socialist literature that these intellectuals had adopted. Yet most of these intellectuals focused their attention and advocacy on the conditions of the peasantry, which given the predominantly agricultural nature of the economy in Iran in the 1900s was perhaps logical.

According to Adamyyat, the historian of the Mashruta, "it was in *The Principles of the Science of the Wealth of the Nations*, written by Mirza Muhammad Ali Khan Foroughi (1323 A.H.L. or 1900), that a reference was first made to the *kargaran* (plural form of *kargar*) as a new social class."[96] The focus on "workers" as a social force came later, especially in the 1920s, primarily through communist activists such as Soltanzade who spoke of the *kargaran* as a significant social class, which existed along with "the peasantry, petit bourgeoisie (industrial and small landholders), feudal lords [landowners], the intermediate bourgeoisie, the big bourgeoisie, and the industrial bourgeoisie, which, quantitatively, is still small."[97]

For these intellectuals and activists, "classness" was a function of economic structure. The left-wing thinkers of the Mashruta had learned from the experience of the European socialist movement that the "working class," especially those members of it in modern manufacturing industry, were the prime agents of socioeconomic change. Applied to the social framework of Iran, the term *working class* could include only a tiny fraction of the population. Yet its emergence into the vocabulary of the people of Iran indicated an historically novel social group.

1940s: The Development of a Class Consciousness?

But did this group of workers constitute a social *class*? The truth is that although the left-wing writers referred to *kargaran* as a class, they really imported this concept from Europe. The nonideological writings on workers, such as an unpublished piece by Man Khanan (*Risala-i Siasi*, manuscript, 1314 A.H.L. [1893]) still described the "workers" in terms of *amala* and *fa'ala*;[98] and terminologies like *taa'ifa* (kin), not *tabaqa* (class), still were used to describe the workers in their collectivity.

During the following years, especially the 1940s, however, certain indications of a development of a class consciousness among the Iranian workers were evident. The decade of the 1940s followed a new wave of industrialization under Reza Shah, which increased the physical number of modern factory workers. In the period between 1930 and 1941, Reza Shah had set in motion a $260 million industrial program, and a similar amount had been invested in the railways.[99] So the number of modern industrial workers also increased during the same period, reaching, in 1940, an estimated total of 263,000, compared with 250,000 laborers in the traditional craft industry.[100]

Three developments represented a sense of classness among the workers of modern sector at this conjuncture: trade union organization, affiliation to a "party of labor," and voting behavior. These served as the institutional mechanisms through which the workers would articulate the identity of their economic interests. The first sign of trade unionism dates back to 1906, but it was not until 1921 that a significant labor movement appeared in Iran.[101] The period between 1918–1925 is described, by Willem Floor, as the "golden age" of unionism.[102] After over a decade of inactivity due to Reza Shah's repression, trade union organizations reemerged vigorously. Following the collapse of Reza Shah's regime after the Anglo-Soviet invasion of Iran in 1941, a new free political climate was created, and the labor movement, under the banner of the United Central Council of the Unified Trade Unions of Iranian Workers (C.C.F.T.U.), with the strong influence of the Tudeh party, was revived and developed to become the largest and most militant in the Middle East. This state of affairs lasted until the coup of 1953 that toppled the nationalist government of Musadeq, after which an era of repression prevailed in the country until the 1979 revolution.

The workers were also organized as a political unit, in the Tudeh (Communist) party. The Tudeh, which claimed to represent the interests of the working class and other masses of the people, became the strongest opposition party in the 1940s. It was able to send its own representatives to the *Majlis*, the Iranian Parliament; secured a great deal of influence in the army; had prominent sympathizers among the intellectuals, artists, and writers; and, perhaps most important, exerted an effective power in the streets and the factories.[103]

Finally, the political differentiation and conflict between the workers and their employers (as a social group) manifested itself also at the electoral level. Ervand Abrahamian reports how, in the early 1950s, the class division within the bazaar (considered to be dominated by paternalistic labor relations) was manifestly revealed during the elections when employees consistently voted for the Tudeh party and the employers in general supported the conservative and liberal politicians.

[A]n electoral survey submitted to the prime minister in 1951 showed class lines divided almost all the craft and trade guilds of the Tehran bazaar. For example, the shoe manufacturers backed a pro-British politician, but their 5,000 workers sympathized with the Tudeh: the owners of barber shops supported Mosaddeq and Kashani, whereas their employees leaned towards the Tudeh; the 400 bathhouse owners favored the Imam Jom'eh, while many of the 4,000 bath attendants were affiliated with C.C.F.T.U.; the 250 clothes manufacturers helped conservative candidates, but their 8,000 tailors backed the Tudeh; and the 1,914 coffeehouse keepers endorsed Mosaddeq, Kashani, and the Imam Jom'eh, whereas their 4,500 assistants and waiters favored the C.C.F.T.U.[104]

These three developments—organization in the labor unions (C.C.F.T.U.) and in the party of labor (Tudeh party), as well as political partisanship (voting behavior)—seem to fulfill some of the conditions that Eric Hobsbawm attaches to the development of a working-class consciousness in England between 1880–1914. However, an additional condition, uniformity in life-styles or cultural practices, remains. This factor seems to be a major indicator of class consciousness in Hobsbawm's scheme. As for Iran the labor historians do not provide us with any evidence of this sort. We do not know to what extent, if any, the workers shared a common way of life, traditions, institutions, and value systems as the cultural manifestation of their shared experiences. In addition, one must ask to what extent the traditional forms of identity such as communalism, ethnicity, regionalism, age, and gender hindered the development of a common identity among the workers during this period. Although a seemingly strong trade union movement certainly existed, we do not know whether the C.C.F.T.U. was a union *of* the workers, reflecting the economic desire of the masses of the rank and file, or whether it was simply an instrument in the hands of the official leaders. The same set of questions can be posed with reference to the Tudeh party, if it is seen to represent the Iranian workers in the 1940s and the early 1950s. One should perhaps hesitate to consider voting behavior as a historical document if, for example, the voters are bussed to the polling stations by the promise of a free meal or the fear of losing jobs. I am in no way intending to suggest that the Tudeh voters were so persuaded, but simply insisting that these issues have to be clear for the historian. In short, a record of exactly what the masses of the workers themselves felt about their leaders and their organizations, about themselves and the other social classes, would be significant and best discovered by examining their discursive expressions in the political, social and cultural fields. Only through such sources may an understanding of working-class consciousness be possible.

The Postcoup Era: Growth, Suppression, and a Sense of Classness

The coup of 1953 totally eliminated those material-"institutional" indicators (in Hobsbawm's formulation) of working class consciousness; that is, the trade unions and the Tudeh Communist party. The postcoup regime in Iran forbade the workers to join independent unions and to join their own chosen political organizations. Instead, the state launched its own corporatist and factory-based workers' syndicates, which were infiltrated by the secret police, or SAVAK, agents.[105] The role of "language" as a tool of historical study of class (consciousness) becomes evident especially in conditions prevailing at times such as those during postcoup Iran, where the institutional manifestations of classness were forcefully eliminated by repression. That said, a discussion of the particular features of working-class consciousness under the Muhammad Reza Shah's dictatorship follows.

Writers such as Homa Katouzian have argued that notions of class (as consciousness) and class conflict are totally irrelevant to the Iranian situation. Class conflict, according to Katouzian, played no role in the political development of Iran. Instead, for him, owing to despotism, "Down to the present day, the clearest line of social demarcation (even stratification) has been that which divides the state (*dawlat*) from the people (*mellat*)."[106]

Katouzian's reference to the *mellat/dawlat* dichotomy as a language of stratification and conflict in contemporary Iran is significant, because he goes beyond a simple structuralist deduction of conflict from class position. However, some evidence in the realm of social discourse points to the prevalence of some form of class demarcation and conflict among the *mellat*, the "people" themselves, notably between workers, on the one hand, and employers and the state, on the other.

During the twentieth century the definition of the words *kargar* and *karfarma* (boss or capitalist) has been the cause of a long struggle. During Reza Shah's rule, and as a reaction to the activity of the newborn labor movement, a Majlis deputy totally denied the existence of workers (*kargaran*) in Iran. "We do not yet have workers in Iran," he declared. "Every one is an employer."[107] In the early 1940s, during the reemergence of a militant trade union movement under the Tudeh party, the use of the term *kargar*, "worker," was banned.[108] It continued, however, to be used. Later, in the 1970s, during the heyday of economic development as well as the anti-Shah armed struggles, the state ideologues declared that the term *proletariat* (then used widely in Iranian Marxist literature) was no longer appropriate to Iranian workers; only the Western working class had launched a "class war." Similarly, it was suggested that, the "boss" was no longer a *"karfarma* which is reminiscent of class privileges," but a *"karamaa* which is appropriate to the hearty cooperation of all groups in the new system of production. . . in the era of [White] Revolution."[109] The postrevolutionary Islamic ideologues were no exception. In fact, even more than their predecessors, they attempted to obscure the identity of the workers by giving the latter a new name, *karpazir* (one who agrees to do work) instead of *kargar*, and incorporating it into the broad category of the *mustaz'afin* (the downtrodden).

In addition, workers came to be viewed by other social groups, especially the state authorities, as a *tabaqeh-i ijtimaii*. a social *class*, in the sense of a group of people with a common identity. Historically, the term *tabaqeh* (class) was used loosely, and perhaps for the first time, during the first Majlis (1906–7), to describe any social category (such as a religious minority) and social orders such as *ashraf* (the nobles), *a'ayan* (notables), *ulama* (the clergy), *tojjar* (the merchants), and so on.[110] It was not until the late 1940s and 1950s that the term *tabaqeh* came into general public (not merely the left-wing intellectual) usage, indicating socioeconomic differentiation and conflict. Abrahamian reports that in the sixteenth Majlis (1948–1958), some twenty two deputies described their society as divided into conflicting classes.[111] Perhaps the impact of the Tudeh party and the militancy of the industrial workers who seemed to be struggling through the language of *tabaqeh* (class) and conflict, should be emphasized.

During the 1960s and the 1970s, notwithstanding the suppression of independent labor unions and political parties, the working class experienced such "unprecedented growth" that, in the words of Asadulla Alam, minister for the imperial court in 1976, it became "one of the [socially] effective classes in our society.[112] The development of the working class as the major "economic force" in society was invariably acknowledged publicly by the state officials. The pages of *The White Revolution*, authored by the late Shah, contains a recognition of this economic power in various forms. The government funded research and publications to deal with this new economic force. One such publication, *Kargar-i Irani dar Iran-i Imrouz* [The Iranian Worker in Today's Iran] by Fereydoun Kavousi, was recommended by the royal court. Acknowledging the economic and social significance of the working class and that it "will soon constitute the largest social group" in Iran (p. 125), the book advocates the adoption of appropriate policies to recognize the status of workers.[113]

An important aspect of these publications is a tacit recognition by them of the danger of "class conflict" in Iranian society. Therefore, in his writings and speeches, the Shah frequently referred to "class conflict" and "class privileges" in Iranian society, when addressing the issues relating to "social justice" and the "White Revolution."[114] Discussing the principle of "workers participation in the ownership of the industrial establishment," the Shah, in his late years, attacked the Tudeh party for its "opposition to this principle," because this decree of the White Revolution, he argued, would "resolve the class conflict" in Iran.[115]

Finally, Iranian workers themselves also came to perceive themselves as a group of individuals with a common and distinct position in the economy and society. However, the manifestation of this (class) consciousness has by no means been straightforward, nor has its historical development been cumulative and evolutionary. Rather, both the process of its development and the forms of its expression have been complex.

The industrialization of the 1930s created a class of "modern" manufacturing workers who, in the decade that followed, launched a flurry of industrial actions and refined their skills of organization (in the labor unions and the Tudeh party). However, during the postcoup years, not only were these experiences rendered futile due to stringent state suppression, but the working class itself was also "diluted." In other words, the extensive policy of industrialization in the late 1960s and 1970s further diversified the industrial labor force in terms of its regional and cultural backgrounds. As new industrial units were established, they fostered a new wave of rural-urban migration. Between 1967 and 1976 some 330,000 people migrated to the cities each year. Rural laborers from different parts of the country poured into the newly established factories. From the late 1960s until 1977, the average annual growth rate of manufacturing labor was 8 percent. This figure was higher in the industrially concentrated cities. Thus, the number of workers in mining and manufacturing, including the small-scale workshops, increased from 816,000 in 1956 to 2.5 million in 1977. Coming largely from the Turkish-speaking areas of Azerbaijan, Hamadan and Zanjan, the Gilani-speaking regions of the Caspian Sea, and from the central provinces, this immigrant labor force lacked almost any experience of industrial and (modern) organisational activities. In short, in the two decades prior to the 1979 revolution, the manufacturing workers came to be characterized by a hierarchy of experience and age, ethnic diversity, and relatively high labor turnover.[116] These features certainly constituted some aspects of workers' self-consciousness, although we do not know how central they were to it.

Yet from the mid-1970s things started to change. By this time, the new workers of the 1960s had acquired a fair amount of experience in industrial work and urbanism. Therefore, by the eve of the revolution, the industrial working class shared a common experience in at least one arena: industry. The result was the development of an "industrial consciousness"that derived its elements from an industrial setting, an urban life-style, and industrial work. This industrial consciousness manifested itself in a series of demands and covert strikes in the mid-1970s—a development lacking during the 1960s.[117]

Beyond industrial awareness, the workers also developed a more general form of class consciousness in terms of the expression of identity and differentiation. A survey of workers in an industrial settlement in Tehran, carried out by Ahmad Ashraf in 1969, pointed to the rise of such an awareness among the workers. In this settlement, a member of the industrial working class "identifies himself as a worker, and makes a sharp distinction between his class and the traditional working class [artisans] and the lumpen proletariat. To make this distinction clear, instead of a three-class terminology use by the upper classes, they usually use a four-class terminology, and thus identify themselves with the members of the *third class* while identifying the lumpen proletariat with the fourth class."[118]

As I understand it, the way in which the Iranian workers expressed their understanding of classness in "language" was, in general, through identifying themselves with the *singular* word *kargar*, or "worker." Notice the following statements made by different workers about different issues in a conversation with me during 1980 and 1981 in Iran:

> **Worker A.** The syndicate normally takes care of the *kargar*'s economic interests; it does not care about the country's social and political interests. . . . The syndicate would defend the *kargar* in money terms. . . . The *kargar* would say: "I only want this [wages and conditions], and that's it."
>
> **Worker B.** The employer attempted to divide the *kargar* into three parts. . . . He would keep one group at the top [economically], one group at the middle, and the rest were destitute and under his thumb.

Worker C. The *shuras* [workers' councils] must try to see what's wrong with the *kargar*. . . .

Worker D. [Before the Revolution], as soon as the *kargar* reacted [to the employers' pressure], they would be fired; [they] *did not have* unity among themselves, because, [the employers] would not allow them to. But when this revolution occurred, the *kargar* came to develop some unity. . . .We, all the *kargaran*, demand a *shura*, in order to work resolutely for us, the *kargaran*.

In all of these statements (except the last sentence), not the plural form (*kargaran*), but the singular one, *kargar*, is used to refer to the plurality of workers. Worker D even uses a *plural* pronoun ("they") with its corresponding verb with a *singular* subject (the *"kargar"*). This inconsistency is not a grammatical issue but an epistemological one.

The fact is that the singular noun, *kargar*, in the language of these workers has a connotation of collective identity and wholeness: whereas the plural form carries a meaning of diversity and particularity. The concept of *kargar*, as a singular noun, connotes totality, generality, and abstraction. Those whom I interviewed considered the individual workers as being so identical with one another that the name and characteristics of one represented those of all. By contrast, the use of the plural form (*kargaran*), as in the last sentence of Worker D, signifies a *numerical ensemble* of *different, diversified, and concrete* workers. In this sentence, Worker D, by using the plural form (*kargaran*), refers to the *specific* workers of his own factory and not the working class in general. In short, the singular noun *kargar*, for the Iranian workers, signifies a totality of workers who share a common identity among themselves and, thus, represents the Iranian working *class*.

Conclusion: An Islamic Class Consciousness?

The preceding discussion suggests that Iranian workers by the 1970s and the early 1980s had developed a sense of "classness"—a feeling of identity of position among themselves and differentiation from (and conflict with) other classes. But what were the constituent elements of such a consciousness? On what shared experiences was such an awareness based? Was it in the workplace, the political institutions, or in cultural settings?

We noted earlier that the organization of workers in both independent labor unions and political associations was prohibited.

Although it can be asserted that workers did share a common experience at work, one product of which was the development of an "industrial consciousness," knowledge of their experience outside of work remains relatively unknown. In fact, the sphere of nonwork has not attracted much attention from social scientists in Iran. Only a few cursory works such as those of Javadi Najjar[119] and Ershad[120] have touched on some aspects of workers' lives outside their workplaces. Yet study of the way of life of workers outside work is immensely important for a crucial reason: capitalistic and authoritarian workplaces by nature nurture conflict and friction; it is, largely in the, sphere of nonwork that the hegemony over the working class of bourgeois culture, as well as that of the precapitalist values, are achieved.

Even simple data would indicate that the diversity of ethnic backgrounds, regional origins, communal affiliations, gender relations, and leisure activities of workers well may not lead to common nonwork experiences among them. There is, however, one exception. Iranian workers, whatever their differences, do share a common religion: Islam.

Islam, by its very nature, represents not simply a set of personal ideas, but also plays a significant part in the cultural and day-to-day practices of the majority of the Iranian people. In Iran, the three Arabic months of Muharram, Ramazan, and Safar are months full of religious activities. Shite Muslims in the working-class neighborhoods attend mosques, *hay'ats*, and *nazries*[121] almost every evening. On these occasions, not only are religious duties performed, but socializing with fellow Muslims also plays an important role. Islam thus constitutes a significant part of the workers' subjectivity and consciousness, which is expressed in their social and political discourses. And Islamic ideology and language play a vital part in articulating a form of working-class consciousness. The following statement, for instance, illustrates how a factory worker in Tehran in 1980 perceived "exploitation of labor" in Islamic terms:

> The Revolution that we made was an Islamic Revolution. We didn't make a Communist Revolution. Therefore [the members of factory councils] must act within the Islamic framework and ideology. The objective must be to implement an Islamic economy which is neither a capitalist economy nor a socialist one. It is an economy based on itself. . .and, that means "to each according to his labor." In a communist country people must work for the state. And in capitalist countries there is [a minority] of people in whose hands capital circulates. And in the communist system

capital belongs to the state that exploits people and pays them something. But Islam says: "No! the worker who works should get the fruits of his labor."[122]

Islam, in fact, was reinterpreted by the industrial workers to express their own immediate and class interests. This was so because in a historical situation when a secular modern political language has not become popular, the language, terms, and symbols of the predominant popular culture, in this case religion, becomes political. Political behavior is clothed in religious language, slogans, and even in sermons. Here religion is no longer simply an instrument of class domination, as some tend to see it, but rather an arena of social struggle.[123]

In sum, by the early 1980s, Islam had become a key element in workers' subjectivity. But its role in articulating class consciousness seemed rather complex and contradictory. Not only did Islam serve as an ideology and discourse to express common needs, at the same time it contributed both to exclusivism and blurring of class lines.

Religious ideology among the working class, as Eric Hobsbawm has noted,[124] is by nature exclusivist. For it represents, more than anything else, a belief system that tends to differentiate and divide its holders from nonbelievers or followers of other religions. This exclusivism and division undoubtedly act against class unity. The Islamic workers' associations in postrevolutionary Iran broadly exemplified this feature of religious ideology. The militant Muslim workers considered Jewish, Bahai,[125] and secular workers belonging to socialist organizations as their enemies.

Not only was Islamic consciousness divisive, it tended also to spread a "populistic" ideology among the working class. Populism, by emphasizing the concept of the "people," is an ideology that works against the development of a *class* consciousness and the idea of class division in society. How did Islam tend to spread populism among the workers in Iran? The ruling clergy shared an Islamic language with the workers, albeit with a populist content. According to this populist Islam, the working class was to be seen not as an independent class, but as a segment of the Islamic *ummat*, the "people," sharing similar characteristics with other members of this social category. The eight-year war with Iraq undoubtedly contributed to this process by developing intense patriotic sentiments among the population, including workers.

Islam serves as a central element in articulating working-class consiousness in Iran. It remains, however, to be seen what form of consciousness the Iranian workers will acquire when Islam ceases to be a state form and when the conjunctural ideological influences such as nationalism and populism give way to an "open–door" policy and economic austerity.

Acknowledgments

Various friends and collegues have assisted me in preparing this chapter. Asghar Feizi, Mustafa Vaziri and Touraj Atabaki helped me by providing an access to the materials necessary in writing this study. I have benefited from the substantive comments made by Joel Beinin, Zachary Lockman, Dipesh Chakrabarty, Nicholas Hopkins, Ali Mirsepassi and the three anonymous reviewers of SUNY Press. Linda Herrara did a painstaking job of editing the early drafts, and Lucy Cooper cleaned up the final version. My special thanks to them all. Finally, I would like to acknowledge the financial support of the Conference and Research Grant Committee of the American University in Cairo in preparing this chapter. Obviously, none of them is responsible for any errors this chapter may contain.

Notes

1. *Workers' News* was an ad hoc newsletter published by an exiled Left group in London during the Iranian revolution of 1979.

2. Marvin Zonis, *The Political Elite of Iran* (Princeton, N.J.: Princeton University Press, 1971), p. 5.

3. Donald Wilber, *Iran* (London: Thames and Hudson, 1963), p. 4.

4. Donald Wilber, *Iran: Past and Present* (Princton, N.J.: Princeton University Press, 1979), pp. 312–314.

5. Joseph Upton, *The History of Modern Iran: An Interpretation* (Cambridge: Cambridge University Press, 1961).

6. Ann K. S. Lambton, *Qajar Persia* (London: Tauris, 1983), p. 106.

7. Homa Katouzian, *The Political Economy of Modern Iran, 1926–1979* (London: Macmillan, 1981).

8. Ibid., p. 354.

9. Ibid., p. 16.

10. See Dipesh Chakrabarty, *Rethinking WorkingClass History: Bengal, 1890–1940* (Princton, N.J.: Princeton University Press, 1989), for an excellent discussion. See also Hisham Sharabi, *Neo-Patriarchy* (Oxford: Oxford University Press, 1988).

11. Here, Katouzian seems to have in mind a rational and "real" model of modernization, according to which Iranian modernization becomes "pseudo." This ideal type, however, is not spelled out in the text.

12. M. Ivanov, *Tarikh-i Novin-i Iran* [A Modern History of Iran] (Stockholm, 1977), trans. from Russian.

13. Mehdi Kayan, trans., *Barrasi-ye Elmi-ye Sharayet-i Kar va Zendegi-Ye Kargaran-i Nassaji dar Iran* [A Scientific Analysis of Working and Living Conditions of the Textile Workers in Iran] (Tehran, 1980).

14. Abdossamad Kambakhsh, *Nazari beh Jonbesh-i Kargari va Kommonisti dar Iran* [A Survey of the Workers' and Communist Movement in Iran] (Stockholm, 1975), 2 vols.

15. There are other Marxist-oriented scholars that I have, intentionally, excluded from this category because as scholars, their perspective and methodology differ from the left-wing activists. Notable among them are Ervand Abrahamian and Khosrow Shakeri.

16. Kayhan, *Barrasi-ye Elmi*, pp. 198–199.

17. Ehsan Tabari, *Foroupashi-ye Nizam-i Sonnati va Zayesh-i Sarmaye-dari dar Iran* [Disintegration of the Traditional Socio-Economic System and the Rise of Capitalism in Iran] (Stockholm: Tudeh Party, 1975).

18. Ibid.

19. Kayhan, *Barrasi-ye Elmi*, pp. 197–198.

20. *Workers' News*, 1 (1980), p. 3. For similar remarks, see Masoud Ahmadzadeh, *Anche yek Enqilabi Bayad Bidanad* [What a Revolutionary Must Know] (London, 1974), p. 47.

21. My own contention that "We must draw a qualitative distinction between the nature and forms of the working class struggle and the struggle of the other masses" also represents a structuralist and essentialist understanding of the consciousness and politics of the working class. See Assef Bayat, *Workers and Revolution in Iran* (London: Zed Books, 1987), p. 79.

22. Karl Marx, *The Holy Family.* (Moscow: Progress, 1956), p. 53.

23. These analyses may be traced in Karl Marx, *The Eighteenth Brumaire of Louis Bonaparte*, in *Selected Works*, vol. 1 (Moscow: Progress, 1962), and his *Class Struggle in France, 1848–1850* in *Selected Works*, vol. 1 (Moscow: Progress, 1962).

24. See George Lukacs, *History and Class Consciousness* (London: Merlin Press, 1971).

25. Ibid., p. 79.

26. Bizhan Jazani, *Chegouneh Mobarize-ye Mosallahaneh Toudeii Mishavad* [Armed Struggle: A Road to the Mobilization of the Masses] (London, 1978), p. 31.

27. *Kargar-i Kommonist* (publication of a Marxist-Leninist organization in Iran), 2 (1981): 8.

28. Tabari, *Foroupashi-ye Nizam*, p. 100.

29. See Amir P. Pouyan, *Zarourat-i Mobareze-ye Mosallahaneh va Radd-e Teory-e Baqa* [On the Necessity of Armed Struggle and the Refutation of the Theory of Survival] (London, 1975); Jazani, *Chegouneh Moubareze*; and Ahmadzadeh, *Mobareze-ye Mosallahaneh*.

30. Pouyan, *Zarourat-i Mobarezeh*, p. 52.

31. See, for instance, *Nazm-i Kargar* (publication of the Organization of Socialist Tendency) 1 (1980): pp. 16–17: and Pouyan, *Zarourat-i Mobareze*, p. 166.

32. Jazani, *Chegouneh Mobaeze*, p. 29.

33. See, for instance, Val Moqaddam, "Industrial Policy, Culture and Working Class Politics: A Case Study of Tabriz Industrial Workers in the Iranian Revolution," *International Sociology* (June 1987): p. 169.

34. We know that the Bolsheviks, in particular Lenin, borrowed and used some major concepts (e.g., trade union consciousness, class consciousness, labor aristocracy, etc.) from the experience of the English labour movement through Sidney and Beatrice Webb's *The History of Trade Unionism* (London, and New York: Longmans Green and Co., 1894).

35. See, for instance, *Kar* (a publication of the Feda'in Organization), no. 164, p. 10; *Paykar* (a publication of the Marxist-Leninist Peykar organization), no. 58.

36. The *Shuras*, or *workers councils*, were the workplace organizations that sprang up immediately after the revolution of 1979 in Iran. As elected bodies, they aimed to exert control over management and democratize the work environment. The *Shuras* differed from each other in terms of the ideologies of their members and activists. For instance, the Islamic *Shuras* were distinguished from the "independent" ones in that the former adhered to Islam as their principal guideline and were supported by the ruling clergy. For a detailed study of the *Shuras* in Iran, see my *Workers and Revolution*.

37. Let us note that the craft unions, e.g., the powerful British Engineering Union, in the late nineteenth century and early twentieth century, were clear manifestations of labour organizations. Yet, they were exclusivist and sectarian, refusing the entry of the unskilled workers and women into their unions; see James Hinton, *The First Shop-Stewards' Movement* (London: Allen and Unwin, 1973).

38. Ervand Abrahamian, "Strengths and Weaknesses of the Labor Movement in Iran, 1941–1953," in M. E. Bonnie and N. Keddie, eds., *Continuity and Change in Modern Iran* (Albany: State University of New York Press, 1981), p. 182.

39. Willem Floor, *Labour Unions, Law and Conditions in Iran* (Durham, England: University of Durham, Centre for Middle Eastern and Islamic Studies, 1985), pp. 22–23.

40. Ibid., p. 3.

41. Ali Ashtiani, "Sheklgiri-ye Tabaqe-ii Karger dar Iran" [The Formation of the Working Class in Iran], *Nazm-i Novin* 5 (Fall 1984).

42. Fred Halliday, *Iran: Dictatorship and Development* (London: Penguin Books, 1979).

43. Robert Michels, *Political Parties* (Glencoe, Ill.: The Free Press, 1958), p. 84.

44. Richard Hyman, *Industrial Relations: A Marxist Introduction* (London: Macmillan, 1975); see also Richard Hyman, "The Politics of Workplace Trade Unionism: Recent Tendencies and Some Problems for Theory," *Capital and Class* 8 (1979)
I am aware that these historians did not intend to write a *complete* history of the working class in Iran. Rather, they aimed to focus on certain aspects of labor history, e.g., trade union movement (Abrahamian, Floor), autocracy and the labor unions (Lajevardi). Throughout the present section, my critique is directed not against *these historians'* approach and focus, but rather against these existing historical *texts* and their conceptual underpinning.

45. Floor, *Labour Unions* p. 2.

46. Ibid.

47. Habib Lajevardi, *Labor Unions and Autocracy in Iran* (Syracuse, N.Y.: Syracuse University Press, 1985), p. xvii.

48. Ibid.

49. Abrahamian, however, does point to some other factors (in addition to political repression) that contributed to the decline of the labor movement after 1946, such as the relative success of the rival state-sponsored unions in attracting a number of workers and a fall in the inflation rate and rise in the level of unemployment after the war; see Abrahamian, *Iran Between Two Revolutions*, pp. 366–367.
These contentions are partially supported by Willem Floor in his review of Lajevardi's book (*Labor Unions and Autocracy*) in *Iranian Studies* 20 (1987). But he is particularly emphatic on the impact of political control.

50. See, for instance, Lajevardi, *Labor Unions*, p. xiv: Abrahamian, "Strengths and Weaknesses," pp. 192, 200–201; Ashtiani, "Shekigiri-e Tabaqe-ye Kargar," p. 84; and Pouyan, *Zarourat-i Mobareze*.

51. Charles van Onselen, *Chibaro: African Mine Labour in Southern Rhodesia* (London: Pluto Press, 1976), p. 227.

52. See, for instance, Lajevardi, *Labor Unions*, p. 206; Ahmadzadeh, *Mobareze-ye Mosallahaneh*; and Pouyan, *Zarourat-i Mobareze-ye Mosallahaneh*.

53. See Assef Bayat, "Capital Accumulation, Political Control and Labour Organization in Iran, 1965–1975," *Middle Eastern Studies* 25 (April, 1989).

54. Goran Therborn, "Why Some Classes Are More Successful Than Others," *New Left Review* 138 (1983).

55. Assef Bayat, "Capital Accumulation, Political Control and Non-Organization of Labour, 1965–1975," paper presented to the Middle East Studies Assoiation of North America (MESA), Boston, 1986.

56. Ian Roxborough, "The Analysis of Labor Movements in Latin America: Typologies and Theories," *Bulletin of Latin American Research* 1 (1982).

57. It must be stated that Abrahamian does acknowledge the significance of an understanding of the working class according to culture and consciousness. A quotation from E. P. Thompson's *The Making of the English Working Class* points to the "culturalist" bias of Abrahamian. However, one is not sure to what extent his narrative in *Iran Between Two Revolutions* is informed by such a perspective.

58. Dipesh Chakrabarty, writing on the history of the jute mill workers in Bombay (in *Rethinking Working Class History*), has done valuable work in bringing the issue of "culture" into the discussion of industrial relations, an area conventionally argued to be determined both by the rationale of industry and the logic of capital, such as the productivity drive, and by the formal and informal organizations of employees. It is highly relevant to consider the influence of culture on the industrial policy in the postrevolutionary Iran. Yet I would still stress that industrial relations under the Islamic Republic were characterized not merely by the employee-employers culture, nor simply by the ideology of the Islamic state, but rather by a tension between these cultural and ideological factors, on the one hand, and the rationale of industrial organization, on the other.

59. Ayatollah Khomeini's speech on May Day, 1981.

60. Hojjat al-Islam Imami Kashani in *Jomhuri-e Islami* 29 April, 1982, Appendix, p. 2.

61. Ex-President Khameneii, May Day, 1981.

62. Imami Kashani, *Jomhuri-e Islami*, p. 3.

63. Ibid.

64. Ibid. This model of social stratification appears to incorporate elements of functionalism (when the division of labor in society is assumed to be natural) and neoclassical economy (when "exploitation" is assumed to occur in the realm of exchange) into the Islamic notion of justice. The model, in addition, reflects the position of the Quran on social stratification; see the *Quran* 43:32; 16:71.

65. Gareth Stedman Jones, *Languages of Class*, (Cambridge: Cambridge University Press, 1983), p. 21.

66. In Joan Scott, *Gender and the Politics of History* (New York: Columbia University Press, 1988), p. 56.

67. Ibid., p. 55.

68. Ibid.

69. Thompson, *The Making of the English Working Class,* pp. 9–10.

70. Eric Hobsbawm, *Workers: Worlds of Labor* (New York: Pantheon Books, 1984), pp. 194.

71. I am indebted to Dipesh Chakrabarty who brought these points to my attention.

72. See *Sandikalism dar Iran, 1284–1320* [Syndicalism in Iran, 1905–1941] (Paris: publisher unknown, undated].

73. See his *Tarikh-i Zendegi-ye Iqtisadi-ye Roustaiian va Tabaqat-i Iitimaii-e Iran* [A History of Rural Economic Life and Social Classes in Iran] (Tehran: Shirkat-i Sahami-ye Intishar, 1974).

74. Zamyad-yasht, clause 45, in ibid., p. 125.

75. A. T. Olmstead, *The History of the Persian Empire* (Chicago: Chicago University Press, 1948), pp. 78–79, 81.

76. Ibid., cited in Insafpour, *Tarikh-i Zendegi,* p. 242–243.

77. Insafpour, *Tarikh-i Zendegi,* p. 346.

78. Ibid., pp. 242–243.

79. Muhammad Dandamaev and Vladimir Lukonin, *The Cultural and Social Institutions of Ancient Iran* (Cambridge: Cambridge University Press, 1989).

80. Ibid., p. 153.

81. Ibid., p. 157.

82. Ibid., p. 158.

83. Omstead, *History of Persian Empire,* p. 177.

84. Dandamaev and Lukonin, *Cultural and Social Institutions.* p. 158; and Insafpour, *Tarikh-i Zendegi* p. 213.

85. Olmstead, *History of Persian Empire.* p. 177; Insafpour, *Tarikh-i Zendegi,* p. 213.

86. James Bill, *The Politics of Iran: Groups, Classes, and Modernization,* (Columbus, Ohio: Merrill Publishing, 1972), pp. 2–7.

87. See Ahmad Ashraf, "Maratib-i Ijtimaii dar Dawran-i Qajarieh" [Social Status in Qajar Period], *Kitab-i Agah* 1 (1981). The term *ummal* in the classification refers only to the officials of the state bureaucracy.

88. See Abrahamian, *Iran Between Two Revolutions.* p. 33; also Ahmad Ashraf, "The Roots of Emerging Dual Class Structure in Nineteenth Century Iran," *Iranian Studies,* 14 (Winter–Spring 1981); Ashraf, "Maratib-i Ijtimaii."

89. See, for instance, Husseinqoli Khanshiqaqi, ed., *Khatirat-i Mumtahen al-Dawlah* [The Memoirs of Mumtahen al-Dawlah] (Tehran: Amir Kabir, 1974), pp. 141–142.

90. Mohammad Hasan Khan I'timad al-Saltaneh, *Al-Maathir va Al-Athar* (Tehran: Nashri Farhang, 1984), pp. 377, 391, 394–395.

91. The word *kargar* appears more than ten times in the *Shahname* by Ferdowsi, who strived to maintain and revive Persian culture and language against the Arab domination of Persia. See Fritz Wolff, *Glossar Zu Firdosis Shahname* (Berlin: Gedruckt in der Reichsdruckerei, 1935), p. 627.

92. Ahmad Ashraf, *Mavane'-i Tarikhi-ye Roshd-i Sarmayedari dar Iran: Doure-ye Qajar* [Historical Obstacles to the Development of Capitalism in Iran: The Qajar Period] (Tehran: Intisharat-i Zamineh, 1980), p. 97.

93. Willem Floor, *Industrialization in Iran: 1900#1941*, (Durham, England: Durham University, Centre for Middle Eastern and Islamic Studies, 1984), p. 5.

94. Fereydoun Adamyyat, *Ideologi-ye Nehzat-i Mashrutyyat-i Iran* [The Ideology of the Constitutional Movement in Iran] (Tehran: Amir Kabir, 1976), p. 270.

95. Ibid., p. 273.

96. Ibid., p. 82.

97. In Khosrow Shakeri, *Isnad-i Tarikhi-ye Ionbesh-i Kargari, Social Demokracy va Komonisti-ye Iran* [Historical Documents About Workers', Social Democratic, and Communist Movement in Iran] (Tehran, undated), vol. 2, p. 190.

98. See Adamyyat, *Ideologi-ye Nehzat*, p. 282.

99. Floor, *Industrialization in Iran*, p. 35.

100. Ibid., p. 28.

101. Abrahamian, "Strengths and Weaknesses." p. 182.

102. Floor, *Labor Unions*, pp. 22–23.

103. Abrahamian, *Iran Between Two Revolutions*.

104. Abrahamian, "Strengths and Weaknesses," p. 191.

105. Bayat, *Workers and Revolution*, Chapter 3.

106. Katouzian, *Political Economy of Iran*, p. 16.

107. In Lajevardi, *Labor Unions*, p. 16.

108. Cited from Anwar Khameii, in Lajevardi, *Labor Unions*, p. 34.

109. Resolutions of the Eighteenth National Conference on Labor, May 1979, Clause 1, in Fereydoun Kavousi, *Kargaran-i Iran dar Iran-i Imrouz* [The Iranian Workers in Today's Iran] (Tehran 1976), p. 164.

110. Abrahamian, *Iran Between Two Revolutions*, p. 10.

111. Ibid., p. 23.

112. In Kavousi, *Kargaran-i Irani*, Preface.

113. Ibid., p. 125.

114. See Mohammad Reza Pahlavi, *Qanoun va Idalat az Nazar-i Shahanshah Arvamehr* [Law and Justice from the Viewpoint of Shahanshah Aryamehr] (Tehran: 1967).

115. Mohammad Reza Pahlavi, *Pasokh beh Tarikh* [Answer to History] (unknown place, no date), p. 138.

116. Compared to the manufacturing sector, the oil industry had a relatively stable labor force for a long time due to the age of this sector.

117. Bayat, "Capital Accumulation," p. 202.

118. Ahmad Ashraf, "Iran: Imperialism, Class and Modernization from Above." (Ph.D. thesis, New School for Social Research, 1971), p. 345.

119. Zahra Javadi Najjar, "Barrasi-ye Nahve-ye Gozaran-i Awqat-i Faraqat-i Kargaran-i Karkhanejat-i Gharb-i Tehran" [A Survey on the Leisure Time of the Factory Workers of Eastern Tehran] (B. A. thesis, University of Tehran, 1974)

120. F. Ershad, "Migration and Life-Style: Work and Leisure in an Industrialized City (Arak)" (M.A. thesis, London, 1978).

121. A *hay'at* refers to a religious sermon. *Hay'ats* are normally organized on the basis of common ethnic or geographical origin of the members (e.g., the *hey'ats* of the Azeri Turks) in Ramazan, (the month of fasting), and Muharram (a holy month in which the *Shiite* Muslims commemorate the killing of the grandson of the Prophet Muhammad, Hussein, in the early years of the emergence of Islam). A *nazri* refers to the ritual of giving charity in Iran.

122. My field notes collected in 1981 in Iran.

123. A number of empirical studies on the working class in the African context have also proven how political and class consiousness are historically specific and that it may well be expressed in religious language. Van Onselen's classic *Chibaro: African Mine Labour in Southern Rhodesia* and Robin Cohen's study of black African workers have shown how different forms of protest ranging from adopting a religious belief to industrial sabotage and theft can be the manifestation of worker consciousness. See Robin Cohen, "Hidden Forms of Consiousness Amongst African Workers," *African Review of Political Economy* 18 (1980). More recently, Paul Lubeck's impressive study on "the making of a Muslim working class" in northern Nigeria emphasized the role of Islam in articulating the cultural-ideological traits of workers and their feeling of classness. See Paul Lubeck, *Islam and Urban Labor in Northern Nigeria: The Making of a Muslim Working Class* (Cambridge: Cambridge University Press, 1986).

124. Hobsbawm, *Workers*, chapter 2.

125. *Bahaiis* are members of a religious sect who have gone through a series of persecutions by the Islamic government in Iran.

Marsha Pripstein Posusney

8

Collective Action and Workers' Consciousness in Contemporary Egypt

Introduction

With apologies to the historical emphasis of this volume, this chapter deals with contemporary Egypt.[1] It begins with the 1950s and focuses in particular on the period from the advent of *infitah*, or economic opening, in 1974 through the late 1980s. In it I attempt to infer workers' consciousness from the patterns of protest behavior they have exhibited.[2]

Implicit in this approach is the assumption that whether or not workers possess class consciousness, in the traditional Marxist sense or in some other form, is an empirical question. As Zachary Lockman suggests in his Introduction, the attitudes of workers towards their jobs, their employers, and the larger economic and political context in which they live cannot be assumed a priori from the nature of the work they perform or their relationship to their employers.

At the same time I continue to uphold the essence of dialectical and historical materialism. Properly understood, Marxism does not argue that economics uniquely determines politics, only that it sets the stage on which the political game is played. Likewise, although a worker's relationship to the means of production does not determine his or her ideas, it does limit the possibilities. Given this, I was troubled by the the "postmodernist" emphasis of the Harvard conference, reflected here in Lockman's Introduction and especially in his own chapter. Postmodernism posits the supremacy of culture, making structure contingent on ideas. One implication is that class itself is only a function of the subjective consciousness of workers.[3] Language and culture certainly do influence, not merely reflect, the way workers think, and may form part of the explanation for the failure of proletarian movements to develop as Marx envisioned. But class remains an objective construct, independent of its recognition by workers or others.

From a methodological perspective, discursive analysis of workers' use of language can clearly provide insights into the attitudes and beliefs of workers and how these change over time.[4] However, in the Middle Eastern context such rich empirical material is rarely available, due to the conjoined problems of widespread illiteracy, political repression of workers, and restrictions placed on foreign researchers by host governments.[5] A different way to investigate workers' consciousness is to examine collective actions by workers, such as strikes, slowdowns, factory occupations, and public demonstrations.

Such social protests can provide clues to workers' consciousness in several ways. First, the frequency of such actions, as well as the degree of participation in them, are indications of the extent to which workers recognize the need to act together to achieve their goals. Second, collective actions are manifestations of workers' dissatisfaction with the status quo. The expression of their demands suggests the extent of their grievances—are they limited to an particular shop or industry or do they include broader political and economic concerns? Demands may also reveal how workers view their employers. Finally, the political and economic context in which strikes occur can point to underlying causes that may not be explicitly expressed in demands. In particular, whether strikes occur more frequently in good economic times or bad, and in more or less favorable political circumstances, is a further indication of the attitudes and motivations of their participants.

Social science literature contains numerous, and contradictory, theories that associate workers' beliefs with different aggregate patterns of strike behavior. Unfortunately, many of these arguments derive from analyses of Western countries and embody suppositions that are inapplicable to the Middle East. It is presumed, for example, that strikes are planned activities, organized by union leaders as a tactic in collective bargaining negotiations. In Egypt, however, strikes have been officially banned since 1952; elsewhere in the region, unions as well may be illegal. Some theories also portray strikes as an economic weapon to be used instead of, or in conjunction with, political action at the voting booth.[6] But the parliamentary democracy that workers enjoy in the advanced industrial countries is not available to those in the Middle East.

Arguments relevant to Egypt can be grouped into three competing perspectives. The first of these is traditional Marxism. Although Marxist arguments should not, as suggested earlier, be upheld a priori, neither should they be rejected out of hand. The point is to test what Marxist theory would lead us to expect against the concrete experience of Egypt.

Short of a proletarian revolution, Marxism anticipates a fairly steady growth in the frequency of strikes and the number of workers involved in them as capitalism progresses. More and more workers should come to recognize and seek to change the terms of, or end, their exploitation. Moreover, as workers increasingly realize their common interests as a class, we should expect to see more acts of solidarity; individual factory protests should blossom into industrywide or general strikes.[7] There should also be evidence of more frequent or larger struggles erupting at plants where Marxists are at work endeavoring to raise the class consciousness of workers.

In Egypt, however, free-market capitalism gave way to a mixed system beginning in the late 1950's. Gamal Abd Nasser brought the largest enterprises in the country under state control and instituted a system of profit sharing and workers' representation in management. Nasser labeled this new economic system socialism, but given that private enterprise continued to exist in Egypt, that the market remained the main means of distribution of goods, and that state ownership signified little in the way of actual workers' *control* over the means of production, numerous analysts have referred to it instead as state capitalism or state socialism. Michael Buroway has argued that such a system will still engender working-class solidarity; workers will recognize that they have a collective interest in opposition, not to private capitalists but to "the authorities."[8] This reasoning would be supported by the steady growth of a workers' movement after the July 1961 socialist decrees, with the demands raised in labor protests reflecting increasing hostility toward the state.

In the moral economy view, collective actions are a response to violations of norms and standards that the subaltern class has become accustomed to and expects the dominant elites to maintain. Rather than reflecting some emerging new consciousness, then, protests under a moral economy aim at resurrecting the status quo ante. The goal is not to negotiate and redefine the terms of exploitation, but to reinstate them after they have been abandoned. Moral economy arguments are most commonly associated with agrarian societies and peasant rebellion,[9] but have been used to explain workers' protests as well: E. P. Thompson demonstrates that eighteenth century English workers were moved to protest violations of their notions of fair practices in the marketplace for grain, and Charles Sabel shows how Third World immigrant workers in Europe would strike when angered by insults to their dignity or infractions of the principle of "a fair day's work for a fair day's pay"; Peter Swenson illustrates how, even in advanced industrial economies, workers' views of just wages are influenced by distributional norms, the upsetting of which can precipitate strikes.[10] Thus, evidence for a moral economy in Egypt would be collective action by workers that follow a "stability-disruption-protest" pattern, with demands that are restorative or exhibit notions of fairness and patron-client relationships.[11]

Rational choice theory holds that all social phenomena must be understood as the consequence of individual behavior, with individual decisions based on expected outcomes according to an ordered set of preferences that can be formalized in a utility function.[12] Much of the literature also presupposes that these preferences are shaped by selfishness. The application of these principles to industrial relations suggests that workers evaluate whether or not to strike by weighing the expected costs, in terms of foregone wages and possible job loss, against the expected benefits of higher pay. This calculation should lead to increased protests when the labor market is tight, because under these circumstances workers will anticipate fewer risks from striking and expect to wring more concessions from their employers; although workers may have grievances, strikes are precipitated by a perception of opportunity, not an increase in discontent.[13]

Since the seminal work on the "free rider" problem by Olson, an important focus of this literature has been on how collective actions can occur in spite of the tendency of rational individuals to refrain from risking the cost of participating in actions from which, if successful, they will reap the benefits nevertheless. For workers, Olson's answer revolved around the ability of union leaders to provide money incentives selectively, whereas others have emphasized nonmaterial rewards for participation.[14] The illegality of strikes in Egypt, along with consistent government interference in union leadership selection, should make the free rider problem especially difficult to overcome.[15] It removes the formal union structure as a vehicle to selectively provide material or psychic incentives and means that wildcat strikes can bring the additional costs of imprisonment, beatings, or job loss. However, provided that the likelihood of punishment is constant with regard to changing economic conditions, strikes should still be more likely in better economic times when more financial gains are anticipated. Therefore, a variable pattern of protests, with increasing activity in prosperous times and significantly fewer strikes during economic downturns, should be the signpost of utility–maximizing behavior on the part of Egyptian workers.

Ellis Goldberg uses a different interpretation of rational choice theory in his discussion of Egyptian workers. He suggests that their skills were largely plant specific, making tenure at the place of employment a priority over higher wages; therefore workers were generally risk averse and disinclined to strike, especially in industries considered most likely to lay off employees if a strike were to occur. Nasser's socialist measures, by providing job security, eliminated this impediment. According to Goldberg, however, they had the simultaneous effect of removing the motivation for strikes, because the state was now meeting the workers' basic needs. Neglecting repression as a disincentive for protest, Goldberg sees this as the explanation for the apparent quiescence of Egyptian workers in the 1960s, as well as for their disenchantment with unions during that time.[16]

This study argues that, since the 1960s, Egyptian workers have viewed themselves in a patron-client relationship with the state. The latter is expected to guarantee workers a living wage through regulation of their paychecks as well as by controlling prices on basic necessities; the government should also ensure equal treatment of workers performing similar jobs. Workers, for their part, provide the state with political support and contribute to the postcolonial national development project through their labor.

Evidence for this type of moral economy can be found, first of all, in the overall connection between economic conditions and workers' actions. Although the available evidence prohibits precise correlations, it is apparent that labor protests occur more frequently when the economy is deteriorating. This is suggestive of restorative protest, aimed at preventing erosion in the workers' standard of living.

Second, the immediate causes of wildcat protests show the significance of workers' feelings of entitlement. In many cases, workers were not raising new demands, but rather seeking to regain earnings that had been taken away, again indicating restorative protest.[17] Moreover, where workers were seeking actual raises, it was most often in the context of seeking parity with others who had just been granted the increase. Thus it was a preexisting egalitarianism that workers were seeking to restore. Feelings of entitlement are also evident in protests that erupted as a result of unmet promises by management or the government.

Third, in almost all incidents, the workers' demands were directed against the state. Most protests broke out in public sector enterprises, so the fact that the state was the target is an objective function of its ownership of the means of production. But even in private-sector protests, as well as in mass demonstrations as opposed to plant-based actions, the targets have often been symbols of the state—the Parliament building, the ruling party's headquarters, the President's mansion—and the slogans have reflected a belief by workers that the government is responsible for their plight and obliged to satisfy their perceived needs.

Fourth, workers revealed their view of their own obligations in the symbolic nature of their protests. Actual work stoppages have been rare. More commonly, protests have involved factory occupations during which management and foremen are evicted while workers continue to perform their jobs, or abstention from cashing paychecks. Through symbolic actions such as these workers signal that they remain loyal to the cause of production, even while feeling aggrieved.

E. P. Thompson has argued that the entitlement expectations of the English "crowd" limited the flexibility of that country's rulers.[18] The apparent constraints it places on the Egyptian government is the fifth aspect of the Egyptian moral economy described here. Although moving quickly to suppress workers' protests with force, Egyptian authorities have almost always given in to some or all of workers' demands. At the same time, only the largest incidents are ever covered in the official press, and these are customarily blamed on outside agitators. Preventing any escalation of the protest and maintaining an image of national harmony and worker satisfaction seem to be far more important to Egypt's rulers than minimizing financial concessions.

Wages, Working Conditions, and the Frequency of Labor Protests

Numerous difficulties are associated with collecting accurate data about wages and employment levels in Egypt, and statistics regarding strikes are even more problematic.[19] Consequently this section makes no attempt at precise correlation between the two. However, the evidence available does suggest that Egyptian workers are most likely to protest when economic conditions are in decline, thus contradicting rational choice predictions and lending support to the moral economy view. There is also some indication that the overall level of protests that occur when real wages are falling is increasing, so that Marxist arguments cannot be ruled out on this basis alone.

The socialist decrees of July 1961, and subsequent modifications of them, brought immediate material improvements in workers' living standards along with an elevation of their status in society.[20] The industrial workweek was reduced to six days of seven hours per day, and the minimum wage was doubled for many workers. Pensions, injury compensation, and health insurance were also improved. There were additional benefits for industrial and service workers in the public sector. Twelve different job categories, each with a set minimum salary, were defined, with annual raises guaranteed for all workers who perform satisfactorily. The state provided for worker representation on the board of management of all public sector firms and gave public sector workers a share in company profits. In 1965, wages for public sector workers were switched from a daily to a monthly basis, effectively increasing their minimum wage again. The effects of this legislation on real wages is shown in Table 8.1.

Table 8.1

Real Wage Index and Hours of Work, 1959–1967

Year	Hours worked per week	Hourly real wage index	Weekly real wage index
1959	50	na	143
1960	49	na	141
1961	48	147	140
1962	47	151	141
1963	45	177	159
1964	44	190	168
1965	53	157	166
1966	52	161	167
1967	49	162	158

Source: Mahmoud Abdel-Fadil, *The Political Economy of Nasserism* (Cambridge: Cambridge University Press, 1980), p. 33. Base year is 1950. Based on the Survey of Employment, Wages and Working Hours (hereafter SEWWH), published by CAPMAS. The SEWWH includes salaries for managerial, technical, and clerical employees, which were generally higher than those of industrial workers during this period. It excludes establishments employing less than ten persons, where wages were generally lower. We focus on nominal wages in Egyptian piasters per week going to blue-collar workers.

The Nasser government also took on a distributive function by subsidizing the cost of many essential food items, as well as energy, and controlling the prices of many other goods. In addition, the government obligated itself to ensure the compliance of private capitalists with minimum wage standards and other laws protecting workers. While public-sector workers depended on the state for their very livelihood, these other factors together served to institutionalize the economic dependence of private-sector workers on the state in other ways.

Nasser explicitly promoted the idea of reciprocal rights and responsibilities. He expected that workers would show appreciation for these measures with greater enthusiasm toward their jobs, thereby increasing productivity. This was sanctified in the National Charter of 1962: "Every citizen should be aware of his defined responsibility in the whole plan, and should be fully conscious of the definite rights he will enjoy in the event of success."[21] Unions were formally charged with educating workers about the new national ethos and expected to forego any role in making economic demands.

Protest activity remained quite low during the early 1960s, with only a few documented incidents through 1964. As we have seen, Goldberg attributes this quiescence to the satisfaction of workers' concern for job security. This analysis, however, cannot explain the lack of militance during the 1950s, before these measures were implemented, nor the low level of 1960s protests in the private sector, where workers did not benefit from the new protections.[22] It also cannot account for the increase in collective action that coincided with economic downturns later.

In fact, Egypt's retreat from socialism came soon after the initial experiment began. After the middle of 1965, as balance of payments difficulties set in, no new social legislation was introduced. Instead, investment expenditures were cut and a forced savings plan was implemented, where one-half a day's pay per month was deducted from all public employees' salaries and put into a special account; there were also some price and tax increases and several factory closures. A 1965 revision in the labor code allowed paid overtime, although it did not make it mandatory.[23]

After Egypt's defeat in the 1967 war the government initiated another round of price and tax increases, and there were renewed calls for workers to sacrifice for the "battle" (al-maʿraTa). The workweek was increased from forty two to forty eight hours without compensation

Table 8.2

Real Wage Index (RWI) in Manufacturing, 1966–1973

Year	RWI
1966	100
1967	95
1968	98
1969	106
1970	103
1971	99
1972	108
1973	107

Source: See Gerald Starr, "Wages in the Egyptian Formal Sector," Technical Papers no. 5, *Employment Opportunities and Equity in Egypt* (Geneva: International Labour Office, 1983), p. 17. Calculated from the SEWWH.

to workers, forced savings were increased from one-half to three-quarters of a day's pay per month, and additional measures, such as cancellation of paid holidays or "donation" of compensations, were attempted in some plants over the course of the next year.[24] In the manufacturing sector, real wages fell in 1967 and remained below their prewar levels the following year (see Table 8.2).

The increase in protests that accompanied this retreat counters the general rational choice expectation of an inverse relationship between strike activity and economic conditions. By Goldberg's analysis, workers should have remained quiescent, because the new job security provisions in the public sector were not rescinded. Yet Hussein reports a number of strikes breaking out at the end of 1966 in response to the renewal of overtime, as well as cases of workers evading disciplinary measures, slowing down work, and even paralyzing or breaking machines to express their anger at the deteriorating economic and political situation.[25] There were numerous protests against the forced salary deductions in 1968.[26]

Wages recovered in 1969 and 1970, and there is no record of labor incidents during those years. Helwan, the most industrialized city in Egypt, did become a center for incipient labor activism at the time.

Mass meetings organized by leftists for workers to discuss political and economic issues grew to include 4,000–5,000 workers. Harsh criticisms were leveled at both Arab Socialist Union (ASU) officials and company managers, and in 1969 the minister of the interior ordered the Socialist Institute where the meetings were held closed. Labor activists then organized smaller meetings of workers around different plant or occupational issues.[27]

However, not until 1971, when wages were eroding again, did this groundwork materialize into the actual protest activity that challenged Sadat after he assumed power. That year saw at least five incidents, the largest involving 30,000 workers at the Helwan Ironworks; and the following spring workers struck several textile factories in Shubra al-Khayma. These actions correspond roughly to another period of declining real wages; in the latter half of 1972 and throughout 1973, when wages were improving, there is again no record of protest activity (see Table 8.2).[28]

In the immediate aftermath of the 1973 Arab-Israeli war, Sadat's government again increased forced savings. This time deductions rose from three-fourths of a day's pay to one full day's pay per month. Then, in the spring of 1974, Parliament passed the *infitah* (econmic opening) law, confirming Egypt's new openness to Western trade and investment. Inflation, spawned by demobilization after the war, was exacerbated by the resultant influx of imports. Real wages fell in 1975, and remained below the prewar level the following year as well (see Table 8.3).

The beginning of 1977 saw Sadat, under pressure from the IMF, announce the partial removal of subsidies on a wide range of items. Prices skyrocketed, and on January 18 and 19, Egypt erupted in rioting which left 79 dead and 1,000 wounded, with widespread destruction of property and 1,250–1,500 arrests.[29]

Although workers remained quiet in the first year after the war, they responded to the aggravated inflation by renewing, and later intensifying, protest activity. This reaction began in the fall of 1974, which saw four strikes. At least as many incidents occurred the following year, with some larger factories involved. There was also a demonstration against the government's new economic policies at a central Cairo train station. The workers' chants at the demonstration reveal their dissatisfaction with their eroding earnings: "Where is our breakfast, hero of the crossing?" (the latter phrase is a reference to Sadat) and "In the days of defeat, the people could still eat." The year 1976 saw a slight

Table 8.3

Sectoral Wage Trends, 1973–1987

Year	Nominal wages/real wage index Public sector[a]	Nominal wages/real wage index Private sector[a]	Wage Ratio Public/Private[b]
1973	491/100	421/100	1.17
1974	556/101	432/92	1.29
1975	576/94	473/90	1.22
1976	663/97	596/102	1.12
1977	813/108	744/115	1.09
1978	897/104	842/114	1.06
1979	1054/114	1022/129	1.03
1980	1289/113	1204/123	1.07
1981	1576/121	1418/127	1.11
1982	1928/127	1671/129	1.15
1983	2271/123	2120/134	1.07
1984	2613/128	2569/147	1.02
1985	2800/121	2800/141	
1986	3100/108	3100/126	
1987	3400/99	3400/115	

[a] Nominal wages in Egyptian piasters per week. From the SEWWH; covers blue-collar workers in establishments of ten or more workers only. Figures for the years after 1984 are rounded off by CAPMAS. I am grateful to Ragui Assaad for supplying me with this data. The real wage index is from Ragui Assaad and Simon Commander, "Egypt: The Labor Market through Boom and Recession," World Bank, 1990, p. 26.

[b] Calculated by author. The ratio for 1985–1987 was not computed because of the rounding off of the nominal data.

increase in the number of protests, including a strike by bus drivers that paralyzed parts of Cairo for several days.[30]

When the prices rose in January 1977, workers walked off their jobs in industrial establishments throughout the country. As with the January 1975 demonstration, the workers' chants reflect a feeling that things had been better in the past. There were cries of "Down with Sadat," "Nasser always said, 'Take care of the workers,'" "It's not enough that they dress us in jute, now they've come to take our bread away," and the simple word, "Nasser." The rioting ended only when the government reinstated the subsidies.[31]

Numerous other measures to appease labor followed shortly thereafter. Meanwhile, hundreds of thousands of Egyptians left for jobs in the Persian Gulf oil states. Migration bid up the cost of labor in the formal private sector, causing nominal wages there to surpass those in the public sector for the first time. Real wages recovered in 1977 to surpass their prewar levels, and grew more or less steadily through 1981 (see Table 8.3).[32] Workers did not take advantage of the new prosperity to push for even more gains, as rational choice theory would lead us to expect. On the contrary, there is written documentation of only one incident between 1977 and 1981.[33]

Husni Mubarak, who came to power in October 1981, was initially not as forthcoming with workers as his predecessor. Mubarak seemed bent on reducing the burden of social welfare programs on the state treasury. There were no new increases in the minimum wage, and in 1983 he announced that there was no money to pay for workers' raises; budget tightening measures were introduced in some individual parastatals as well.[34] Nevertheless the increase in real wages continued during his early years, as shown in Table 8.3. Labor protests did resume in 1982–1983. Although there was no repetition of large public demonstrations as in 1975–1977, the number of incidents during these years does rival the earlier period.[35] The coincidence of these actions with a time of rising wages makes this the only period that does correspond to rational choice, rather than moral economy, expectations. But the events of the subsequent years confirm the general correspondence between worker protest and deteriorating, rather than improving, economic conditions.

By 1984 oil prices were softening and some of Egypt's expatriate workers in the Gulf were losing their jobs; Mubarak intensified his efforts to reform the economy. There were some price increases in 1984, along with an attempt to increase the workers' contributions to insurance plans. A new round of price hikes, especially on energy products, came in 1985 as Egypt once again entered negotiations with the IMF and currency reform began. These measures accelerated inflation, and real wages began to fall in 1985. There were also frequent calls in the official press for privatization and public-sector reform, threatening the benefits enjoyed by workers in the parastatals.[36]

Workers reacted with a marked upsurge in walkouts, factory occupations, and other actions. The level of struggle overall was considerably higher than in the mid-1970s; in 1986 alone, fifty incidents were reported. Some of these protests were quite protracted, prompting opposition members of parliament to demand an inquiry into the causes of labor unrest. With the economy continuing to deteriorate, this strike wave was still in progress at the end of 1987.

Entitlement Protests: Reaction to Takeaways

The relationship between strike frequency and economic conditions is too murky to discern definitively among the three perspectives, but the superiority of the moral economy approach becomes clearer when one investigates the specific causes of workers' protests. Virtually all of the incidents reported earlier grew out of a sense of injustice among workers, a feeling that they were being denied something to which they were entitled. One such form of entitlement protest is action that results when part of workers' customary income is either taken away or not paid when expected.

One of the few strikes to occur in the early 1960s, at the Tanta Tobacco Company, was prompted by management's withdrawal of bonuses.[37] We saw earlier that the takebacks that accompanied the crisis of 1965 also engendered numerous protest actions. Workers' discontent was manifested in other ways as well; when the leaders of the Egyptian Trade Union Federation (ETUF) urged members to work harder and sacrifice a portion of their earnings, there was resistance, and implementation of the ETUF's specific proposals was spotty at best.[38]

Egyptian workers did intially respond to the calls to sacrifice after the 1967 war. But when corruption and mismanagement in both the military and the public sector were exposed in its wake, workers began to question the sincerity of the "battle" and resent its burdens. Sabir Barakat, who was involved in organizing one of the protests at that time, explains how participants were motivated by a sense of injustice: "A law was issued in 1968 to deduct 25 percent of workers' compensations for what was called at the time the war effort. We were surprised when we discovered that this was being applied to our salaries which were really only pennies that didn't suffice—it fed us only because it had to. We couldn't bear any deductions so when this took us by surprise we started to resist it."[39]

Opposition to takeaways also provided the opening salvo of the period of heightened activism which accompanied the *infitah*. In September 1974 workers occupied the Harir textile factory in Helwan, protesting the forced savings, which they declared were no longer necessary; with disengagement talks under way, the rationale for workers' sacrifice in the name of fighting Zionism had disappeared. They won a change in the savings plan for workers throughout the country: the deductions were reduced by almost 60 percent to 1.5 percent of salary, and now applied only to workers earning more than 30 pounds per month.[40]

A 1974 strike at the private-sector Tanta Tobacco Company occurred when the owner suddenly switched workers from a monthly to a daily pay rate, resulting in about a 30 percent decline in wages. Workers sat in at a public-sector plant that year after being denied their annual production reward because the production plan was not met, despite company acknowledgment that the shortfall was not their fault.[41] The bus drivers who struck in 1976 were incensed over the company's delays in paying their traditional holiday bonus; their walkout ended when the bonus was issued.[42]

In 1982, Kafr al-Dawwar textile workers occupied their local union headquarters protesting reductions in their incentive pay. Workers of the #36 factory in Helwan sat in in 1983, demanding a cost of living increase and payment of incentives that had been withheld. Four thousand workers occupied the Nasr Pipe Manufacturing Company plant in 1984, demanding payment of production incentives and rewards and the resignation of the new management that had changed overtime rules; most of the workers' economic demands were met. In March of that year, workers staged a series of protests related to the refusal of the Daqhaliyya Textile Factory to pay overtime; in April 4,000 workers occupied the Shubra Company for Engineering Products, charging that poor management had led to a decline in their incentive pay.[43]

The major national takeaway of 1984 was a new law doubling the workers' contribution to health insurance and pensions, first issued in the early summer. Implementation resulted in workers at the Nasr Car Factory and several other large plants refusing their paychecks and an in-plant demonstration in Alexandria; at the Transport Authority a strike was threatened. These incidents led the prime minister to halt further application of the law and form a committee to reexamine the issue. Parliament reissued the law in late September, but this time implementation was staggered to avoid simultaneous protests. The deductions hit first in Alexandria, where more than 10,000 workers in two large textile factories refused their paychecks. They began in Kafr al-Dawwar two weeks later and coincided with a decision by Mubarak to raise prices on a number of subsidized items. The result was three days of strikes and riots in the city reminiscent of January 1977, as workers and other townspeople cut telephone lines, blocked transportation, destroyed rail cars, and set fires.[44]

Al-Ahali charges that a high government policy committee called on public-sector managers to lower supplemental pay in 1985, and a upsurge in antitakeaway protests that year lends support to this accusation.[45] At the Miratex Company in Suez, workers struck for three days in February over declining incentives; the company closed the plant so the action would not spread to the other factories. A new protest broke out there in September over the company's failure to pay the traditional bonus for the opening of the schoolyear. Night shift workers at the Suez Company for Petroleum Refining occupied their plant in July over declining incentives; and in that same month there was a two-day sit-in over incentives at the Talkha Fertilizer plant. In July, workers at the East Delta Bus Company refused their paychecks, protesting reductions of up to 50 percent in take-home pay; a similar action later occurred at the Southern Flour Mill in Alexandria because of declining incentives and overtime pay. A one-day work stoppage at the Bani Suwayf Weaving Company brought management promises to restore wages and purchase new equipment so that production, and hence incentive pay and bonuses, could increase.

In Mahalla al-Kubra, 3,000 workers struck the Sigad plant in May 1985, protesting management's failure to pay the May Day bonus; the action broke up when the company promised to issue the checks. Then in October, 1,200 workers at the large Misr Spinning and Weaving (hereafter MS&W) plant refused their paychecks for three days because of declining wages. This protest resumed in February 1986, with a demonstration of 500 workers in front of the local headquarters calling for the union to adopt their demands.[46]

Some of the most prominent and prolonged protests over takeaways in the mid-1980s were at wholly private-sector or joint-venture enterprises that had been created under the auspices of the *infitah* laws. When the tax incentives they had been granted expired, various of these companies began to scale back operations or cut workers' salaries. Thus some 700 workers sat in for three days at Arabb, an electrical products joint venture, in February 1986, objecting to declining compensation and incentives. At the Arab Wood Furniture Factory (Atico), management stopped paying workers' salaries in May 1986 and announced in July that the factory would close, laying off 920 employees. The parliamentary committee that must approve such closures rejected the company's request, but the company refused to honor the committee's decision. On August 12 and 13, more than 650 workers occupied the headquarters of the ETUF, demanding back pay from May and the reopening of the plant. Despite a court ruling in their favor, workers had not received any of their back pay by the end of 1987 and were threatening a new round of sit-ins.

A similar situation developed with the American-owned McDermott Company, which had requested permission to suspend operations in July 1985 and began to dismiss workers before receiving an answer. In January 1986, in a measure workers charge was aimed at forcing them to quit, McDermott cut the wages of its remaining workers by 50 percent, in addition to deducting one-third of their salaries for the previous two months. In the fall, workers began a series of protest actions aimed at company as well as government targets. The McDermott case continued into the spring of 1987, when a court ruled that the company must rehire 300 workers and sell assets to provide them with back pay. When the company refused to implement the ruling, the workers began a new round of sit-ins.[47]

Entitlement Protests: The Demand for Parity

A second type of entitlement protest revolves around notions of fairness in the wages earned by different types of laborers. Distributional norms reflect workers' evaluations of how much they contribute to production in relation to others. Egyptian workers have demonstrated a belief in parity; that is, that similar work should yield similar rewards. They have also exhibited opposition to widening disparities between the wages of manual workers and those afforded to civil servants and company managers.

After the 1961 socialist decrees, the discrepancies in benefits and protection available to public versus private-sector workers became an issue for the latter. The smaller incidents of the early 1960s reflect this concern. They occurred in the private-sector Tanta Tobacco Company, as the workers sought and ultimately won the new minimum wage that had been declared for the public sector. There were several sit-ins and work stoppages around this demand in 1961 and 1962.

In the winter of 1972 the cabinet agreed in principle to entitle workers in private sector establishments to the same minimum wage, working hours, and holidays that public-sector workers received.[48] But the Ministry of Industry delayed issuing the law limiting working hours. Believing that the government was reneging on that issue, hundreds of workers in Shubra al-Khayma walked out of several textile factories on March 21 and marched through the town. A second march ensued the next day, when the papers published the minister's decree and the workers returned, only to find themselves locked out of the plants by employers who were hostile to the new legislation. Private-sector employers continued to resist Law 24, and disputes over implementation and interpretation of the law led to several other strikes by private-sector workers over the next few months.[49]

Expectations of parity with public-sector workers were also implicit in the demands of workers in the *infitah* companies mentioned previously, because such layoffs could not have occurred in the parastatals. Some of the incidents also involved explicit demands for other forms of protection afforded to government workers. The workers at Arabb, in addition to seeking restoration of their previous pay levels, also objected to the company's overall labor policies, which included arbitrary firing, false work contracts, oppression of temporary employees, and restrictions on union activity. Some 7,800 workers at the Johns Company, an American concern, struck for one day, demanding various types of compensation and the application of Egyptian labor laws to foreign companies.

Parity protests have also emerged within the public sector, when workers at one plant see their counterparts at another receive an increase in the discretionary component of wages. Therefore the most prominent concern behind the 1971 action at the Harir factory was the demand for a 5 percent "exceptional" raise, which had been granted to workers at a similar plant in Imbaba.[50] Later that year, when the government was negotiating with the Helwan steelworkers, the president of the ETUF went to the nearby Harir plant and promised its workers parity with whatever the steelworkers won, to preempt any new outbreaks of militancy there.[51]

A 1975 protest at the MS&W factory in Mahalla al-Kubra was the culmination of a prolonged effort by returning servicemen to receive full wages for time spent on the battlefront. The employees who worked during the war earned an hour per day overtime, but the returning soldiers had received only a straight seven hour per day compensation. After months of complaining to union, ASU, and management officials, the workers heard that a decree in their favor had been issued, and that their counterparts in Harir had already begun to receive the overdue money. When management denied these reports, workers sat in at the local union headquarters demanding an investigation, and shortly thereafter they occupied the factory itself.[52]

That same year workers occupied the Shubra al-Khayma cableworks, demanding parity in incentives and compensation with the nearby Delta Ironworks employees.[53] And although the bus drivers who struck in 1976 were seeking their traditional holiday bonus, they were moved to action only after learning that their counterparts in Heliopolis had recently received two such grants.[54] Spinners in Minya occupied their factory in 1983 seeking pay parity with workers in other shops. In 1986, after workers at the Esco textile factory in Shubra al-Khayma won a prolonged battle for holiday pay (see later), the protesting workers at the MS&W plant added this to their own list of demands. Their victory in turn sparked a series of similar actions in Mahalla al-Kubra.

The socialist ideology of the 1960s praised the contributions made to society by manual workers. Workers signalled their receptivity to these ideas when they objected to government measures which would have created, or widened, discrepancies between themselves and white-collar government employees, including company managers. Sabir Barakat's account of the 1968 protest against takeaways at Delta Ironworks reveals how egalitarian ideas contributed to the workers' actions:

> We had senior civil servants and workers who used to get something called gas compensation—if someone took their own car to work he got a compensation of 25 pounds per month. In those days a skilled worker earned only 12 pounds a month. So we made a campaign around the issue, saying "if there is a serious need to expand the Treasury, in front of you is an amount that can be borne by the people who can afford it. The worst that will happen is that they won't come to work in a private

car and will have to come in company cars like the rest of us—which is really no sacrifice—yet you demand from us a very hard life". . .They gathered us in the cafeteria of the company and gave rhetorical socialist speeches to us, saying "If you have in your hand a piece of bread don't you give your brother a bite? Even if all you have in your hand is one piece and it isn't enough to satisfy you, you have to sacrifice a bite to the army for the war." The response of the workers was: When we have in our hand a piece of bread and our brother is hungry, but we have a third brother who has an expensive cake, it's very natural that he who has the cake gives up half of it, then I'll give up a bite.

As we have seen, the January 1975 demonstration in Cairo was a response in part to the new ostentatiousness of the wealthy under the *infitah*. It was also precipitated by the prospect of increasing disparities between blue and white-collar public servants. Toward the end of 1974, parliament had begun discussing an employment reform bill that proposed long-delayed promotions for thousands of civil service workers and revised the job classification scheme to eliminate the lowest paid categories. Union leaders serving in parliament pushed to have the reforms extended to the public sector as well, but 'Abd al-'Aziz Higazi, the prime minister, spoke against the union's proposals. 'Abd al-Rahman Khayr circulated copies of Higazi's remarks among Helwan workers, charging that they reflected a hostility toward manual laborers characteristic of the new government. His coworkers not only agreed, he said, but were also incensed by newspaper advertisements for expensive and luxurious New Year's Eve celebrations at Cairo's fancy hotels, one of the first manifestations of the new flamboyance of the upper class. Khayr and others therefore planned their protest for the morning of January 1, at the time when the party goers would be heading home from one of the nearby ritzy hotels. They demanded extension of the employment reforms to blue-collar workers.[55]

The reform issue also had a role in the 1975 incident at MS&W in Mahalla al-Kubra. After the workers' initial action, the company president promised to release the soldiers' checks. But before the disbursements were made, the news that parliament had decided on the employment reform for civil servants broke; workers took over the factory the following day, demanding overtime pay, extension of the employment reforms to industrial workers, and improved health conditions. When security forces stormed the plant three days later, the workers' families and other townspeople raided the homes of the companies' managers and put their luxury goods out for public display, thus also reflecting a sense of injustice at the income disparities between manager and employee.[56]

Entitlement Protests: Unmet Promises

A third type of entitlement protest is one that does involve new demands. These are, however, demands to which workers feel entitled because of promises made by company management, the government, or the courts. Generally, protests have broken out around such demands only after a prolonged period of patient waiting by workers. Thus, developing anger over unmet expectations is the impetus to workers' action.

The largest incident of the early 1960s, at the MS&W plant in Kafr al-Dawwar, was such a protest. Prior to nationalization, the company's owners had routinely deducted a portion of workers' salaries for an insurance fund. After the state assumed this responsibility, workers expected that these back deductions would be returned to them. When they were unable to win this demand through months of negotiation with the plant's new managers, they occupied the factory: the three-day protest ended with an agreement by the company for immediate partial repayment of the deductions.[57]

Unmet promises were particularly involved in the incidents of the 1980s. The February 1983 sit-in at the Nasr Company for Chemicals and Pharmaceuticals occurred after the company had reneged on verbal promises to meet the workers' demands for increased incentive pay, and compensation for lunch and back shift employment. March 1984 saw 400 workers sit in for several hours at a military plant in Heliopolis, demanding payment of a previously announced raise. The afore-mentioned protest at the Johns Company was primarily in response to the company's failure to fulfill a two-year old promise to provide workers with health insurance.

At the Esco textile factory, 1985 saw workers awaiting a decision on a court case, arguing that a 1981 law entitled them to one paid day off per week. An initial ruling issued in their favor in October 1984 had been rejected by the management, which appealed the case. The situation boiled over in January 1986 after an appeals court again found in the workers' favor. When the company failed to recognize the ruling, workers refused their paychecks. That action brought no result, and on January 30 about 10,000 workers—more than half the company's total employment—took over the factory. The strike ended on February 2 with the establishment of a ministerial "committee of five," including representatives of the local union and textile federation officials, to examine the issue; workers left their blankets in the plant to facilitate resumption of the occupation if they deemed it necessary.

The committee of five announced a compromise decision to pay Esco workers for two days off per month. Workers rejected this, refusing their February paychecks, and won a new decision that two additional days off would be paid beginning the following year. The holiday pay would not be retroactive to the issuance of the 1981 law, however. Many workers accepted the deal only reluctantly, and several months later, in the context of continued tense relations between employees and management, there was a new occupation demanding the retroactive pay. This sit-in was smaller than the previous one, but nevertheless involved thousands of workers. After it was smashed by police, workers began to collect donations to take the back–pay case to court.[58]

A train drivers' strike in the summer of 1986 is especially illustrative of how protests can erupt from prolonged official frustration of workers' expectations. The wildcat strike grew out of demands originally raised by the workers in a 1982 slowdown.[59] The drivers waited for three years and got no response from either the government or their federation officials. Finally, in December 1985, the minister of transportation and the head of the Railway Authority met with them. These officials promised on the spot to resolve some of the issues and investigate the others and meet with the workers again. Four months later nothing had changed, and the workers began a renewed campaign of sending telegrams to the authorities. After ten more weeks elapsed with no official response, the drivers and conductors announced a sit-in at the headquarters of their league on July 2.[60] The occupation ended later that night when the deputy minister of transportation came and promised that his superior would meet with the workers again on July 7. That day about 1,000 workers gathered for the meeting, only to learn that it had been put off because the minister was busy again. The council of the league sent an urgent telegram to Mubarak, the prime minister, and the minister of the interior, expressing their anger and frustration. Only when there was no reply did the trains stop running.[61]

Workers With and Against the State

Many of the incidents cited occurred in public-sector establishments. As such, they were objectively directed against institutions of the state. When parastatal workers raise demands, they reveal expectations of what renumeration *the government* is obligated to give them. Significantly, though, even private-sector workers have often targeted the government in their protests, suggesting that they too view the state as the guarantor of their livelihoods.

The first large action by private sector workers after the socialist decrees was the 1972 walkout by textile workers in Shubra al-Khayma. As we saw earlier, it was directed against the government, which was charged with reneging on promises to upgrade their benefits. On the second day of the protest workers blocked a motorcade carrying the prime minister.

In the 1980s the ruling National Democratic party (NDP) was sometimes targeted as a manifestation of the government. Therefore, after the insurance deductions were increased in 1984, workers at one textile factory in Alexandria demonstrated in their plant, with chants of "down with the NDP." Elsewhere antigovernment slogans were chanted in marches to the local headquarters of the NDP, and several government offices.[62] McDermott workers' protests included sit-ins at the NDP offices in Suez and visits to the minister of labor at his home. When they were denied the annual production bonus in October, 500 workers occupied the company's headquarters in Cairo and later sat in in front of parliament. When the company refused to implement the spring 1987 court ruling, the workers began a new round of sit-ins at NDP headquarters, and also caravaned from Suez to the president's palace in Cairo.[63]

Because of the interference of the government in union elections, the fact that most senior union officials are affiliated with the NDP, the historic conjoining of the posts of ETUF president and minister of labor, and the frequent unresponsiveness of these union officials to wildcat protests, some workers have come see the confederation itself as an instrument of the state; hence, the sit-in at confederation headquarters by the Atico workers. Also, in many of the smaller incidents cited here, workers occupied the office of their local chapter seeking official union support for their demands.

But if workers expect the government to ensure that they are compensated justly for their labor, they also believe that they have an obligation to the state. In particular, the nature of labor protest in Egypt suggests that workers did adopt the Nasserist ideology of the 1960s, stressing reciprocal rights and obligations. Workers see their responsibility lying in production, to contribute to the postcolonial modernization and development of their country. The evidence can be found in the relative scarcity of actual strikes, in favor of protests that exhibit dissatisfaction while not interfering with work. Indeed, the astute reader may have noticed that I have generally avoided the use of the word *strike* in describing workers' protests, in favor of *sit-in, incident,* or *action*. This reflects the fact that workers themselves have eschewed actual work stoppages, using them only as a last resort.

The most common alternative to strikes is the in-plant sit-in, during which management is ejected or ignored but workers continue running the factory on their own. The factory sit-in was initiated in the 1963 incident at Kafr al-Dawwar. For several days, the workers continued round the clock production to prove their loyalty to the country, but electrified the fence around the plant to prevent security forces or government officials from getting in. The sit-in ended when the various officials involved agreed to immediate partial repayment of the deduction.

In the largest action of 1971, 30,000 Helwan steelworkers elected strike committees and maintained production while sitting in at the factory. Harir workers demonstrated inside their plant for parity demands in 1971, and their 1974 protest against forced savings was also a factory occupation. The 1975 sit-in at Mahalla al-Kubra lasted three days, during which time production continued. Likewise, the workers who occupied the Shubra al-Khayma cableworks in 1975 kept production going, while refusing to allow government or union officials to enter.[64] In the first action of 1984, at the Nasr Pipe Company, the workers actually doubled output during their occupation. When the Esco workers occupied their plant in 1986, they continued working for two days. Only on the third day, when no responsible officials had come, did the workers cut off production.

A second symbolic technique is a boycott on cashing paychecks. It is used particularly in the public sector, where workers say it is effective because it interferes with government accounting procedures. The boycott was first used by the workers of Delta Ironworks in their 1968 protest against salary deductions. By refusing their paychecks, but continuing to work, the workers demonstrated that they remained loyal to the "battle." The next documented use of this tactic was when 2,600 workers at the Tura Cement Factory refused their paychecks for two days in February 1982. As we have seen, some 10,000 workers in Alexandria boycotted their checks in 1984 after parliament issued the new law on insurance deductions; the tactic was also used to protest takeaways and parity disruptions at several large factories in 1985 and 1986.

Another form of protest involves sending telegrams to government officials seeking redress of grievances. In addition to showing the workers' reluctance to strike, such messages can also provide insights into workers expectations of themselves and the state. Thus the initial reaction of workers at Delta Ironworks to Sadat's 1977 removal of subsidies shows both their fear of, and disgust with, the government:

> I suggested that we send a telegram to the officials denouncing them, but the other workers...were afraid of denouncing the government. So in the end we decided to send a very satirical telegram. It read:
>
> To the President of the Republic:
> We thank you for increasing prices, and raise the slogan, "more price hikes for more hunger and deprivation." May you always be a servant of the toiling workers.

The protest organizers collected signatures and a small contribution from 600 workers in the plant to send this message.

Railway workers first wired their concerns to the president, the prime minister, and other high government officials in 1982, and continued to press their case in this manner over the next four years. The urgent telegrams sent to Mubarak in an effort to ward off the strike are particularly revealing of their moral economy beliefs. It concluded, "We are all waiting here at the league headquarters.... Some of the trains have already stopped running *in abandonment of our responsibilities.* The situation is getting more serious. It is almost 2 P.M. and at 6 P.M. this evening all of the trains will stop running" (emphasis mine).[65]

Significantly, even when workers have raised aggressive demands they have used symbolic protest to press their case. The best case for rational choice theory is that some of the incidents of 1982–1983, which occurred during a time of rising real wages, also centered around new concerns. Yet no work stoppages were involved. This includes a 1982 sit-in by 6,000 workers at the Talkha Fertilizer Plant, demanding a lunch compensation and revision of salary and promotion schedules. That same year railway workers used a slowdown to demand a cost of living adjustment, insurance against accidents, an increase in the compensation for uniforms, and elimination of the requirement that drivers be personally responsible for paying compensation to train accident victims. The largest incident of 1983, a protest demanding a nature-of-work compensation at the Helwan Light Transport Factory, was another factory occupation.[66]

Government Response to Labor Protests

Despite sharp differences in overall economic strategy, the Nasser, Sadat, and Mubarak regimes have pursued very similar policies with regard to labor protest. The actions have been quickly put down by a combination of repression and concession. The apparent goal of the government's behavior is to contain labor protest, to prevent incidents from one plant from inspiring protest at another.

Virtually every incident recorded here involved some arrest of workers. When only a small, single plant was involved, the immediate fate of the detainees was usually left to the discretion of local police, with national security agencies and government figures called in only if the protests could not be quickly broken up. However, protests that involved issues of national policy, large numbers of workers, or more than one plant brought rapid intervention from the highest levels of government.

Therefore when the Tanta workers sat in in the early 1960s, the company summoned local police. The workers were beaten with rifle butts, and their union leaders were blindfolded and taken to the police station where they were kept concealed. Ultimately, federation officials summoned from Cairo negotiated their release, along with a contract in which workers won restoration of the bonuses as well as other, new benefits. But the workers who refused their paychecks at Delta Ironworks a few years later were taken away immediately by state security police. Their intimidation had an effect, as Barakat relates, but here too concession was also involved in ending the protest:

> They arrested twenty two workers. . . .They came back two days later completely silent and went to pick up their checks. We tried to get them to talk but they refused to say a word. After that the stand of the workers

began to weaken. But 'Abd al-Nasir [Nasser] in those days was smart—on the same day he sent orders that these deductions shouldn't harm the salaries of the workers and they returned the deductions to us—and that ended the situation.

Around the same time, the minister of defense repealed a decision to deduct the transportation compensation and any salary increases due to promotions from workers at another military plant; all back deductions were returned.[67]

Local police sometimes treat workers with particular brutality. Three of the leaders of the 1971 Harir protest were tied to their cell doors and periodically beaten with clubs and whips. Only the intervention of Muhammad Haykal, then editor-in-chief of *al-Ahram*, brought an end to the beatings and medical care for the victims, who still bear scars from this incident.[68] After police arrested workers during the 1985 Sigad strike, one woman was beaten in front of her husband, and the arrest of a male worker while his wife was in labor caused her to name the baby "Ifraj" (release). The Sigad detainees were placed in cells flooded with sewer water, forcing them to stand until arraignment.[69]

Not suprisingly, though, the volume of arrests appears to be greater in the more prominent incidents. When security forces stormed the Helwan Ironworks plant in 1971, some 3,000 workers were arrested. Seventy-six of the protesters who blocked the prime minister's motorcade in 1972 were detained. Attempts by security forces to suppress peaceful protests have also contributed to their escalation into violence. The 1975 New Year's demonstration turned into a mini-riot when police attempted to prevent the protesters from marching to a nearby government building; dozens of arrests and a witchhunt for the action's organizers ensued. When security forces raided the MS&W plant in Mahalla al-Kubra in 1975, 2,000 were arrested; 50 workers may have been killed that day.[70] Barakat argues that police initiated the violence in January 1977: "On the second day we struck at the factory....We went out and demonstrated. They tried a tactic on us—they said they would search us as we were leaving. They took workers in their cars to examine them. There are three bridges near the plant....They dropped workers off at each one, in order to divide us. The result was that there was a demonstration at each bridge, and while each group was marching it was attacked by the police."[71]

But each of these events was also met with significant concessions. Sadat, who condemned the 1971 Helwan sit-in as an "undemocratic act," quickly promised to investigate and ameliorate workers' grievances. In June 1975, following the series of protests documented earlier, the employment reform measures were approved for public-sector workers.[72] And although the government officially blamed the 1976 bus drivers' strike on communist agitation, Sadat met immediately after it with leaders of the drivers' federation—his first meeting with mid-level union officials—to discuss the workers' other grievances. A similar meeting was held between the minister of transportation and leaders of the railway workers' federation, and it resulted in an increase in their annual production reward.[73]

After the "bread riots" there was a marked increase in the repression of the Left and labor militants. The leftist press was shut down, and virtually every leftist involved in the trade union movement was imprisoned at some point between 1977 and 1981.[74] But as we have seen, Sadat quickly repealed the decision to lift subsidies. Furthermore, soon thereafter he held his first formal meeting with ETUF leaders since before the 1973 war and agreed to demands not only for wage increases, but also for greater union input into management and government decision making. In addition the minister of labor issued a number of new directives aimed at speeding the settlement of individual and collective workers' complaints and generally improving industrial relations. Periodic wage increases in both sectors continued over the next few years.[75]

This trend continued into the Mubarak era. At the Helwan Light Transport Factory, security forces armed with tear gas, clubs, and electric prods surrounded the plant and broke up the occupation, but management did agree to the workers' demand.[76] Three workers died in clashes with security police in the 1984 Kafr al-Dawwar riots, and there were over 120 arrests. As a result of the riots, though, Mubarak repealed the price hikes on pasta and cooking oil.[77] At the MS&W plant in Mahalla, security forces raided the wool factory where workers were sitting in and arrested 160. The next day, the company closed the plant, putting the workers on forced vacations, and another 257 workers were arrested outside the factory.[78] The second Esco sit-in was likewise smashed by the police, who stormed the plant on the third day of the protest, arresting over 500 protestors.[79]

The heaviest hand was reserved for the train drivers. The government called out the army to run an emergency bus service and the central security police to attack the striking workers. They were clubbed, kicked, and beaten, and over 100 were arrested. Security police

238 / Workers and the Working Classes in the Middle East

continued to hunt down the leaders of the action, and those who were arrested were dealt with harshly. Some were denied food and bedding for two days. Unlike any other case cited here, the workers were charged with violations of the emergency laws and arraigned before supreme state security courts, which are empowered to impose indefinite sentences; these courts are supposed to deal only with cases of armed terrorism. The speed and severity of this response would seem to reflect the centrality of the services suspended by the drivers, and the high visibility of a railway strike relative to the protests at individual industrial establishments. Nevertheless, after the strike was broken the minister finally found the time to meet with groups of workers. Most of their demands were met, and some were given financial rewards for agreeing to return to work.[80]

It is instructive to contrast this with the government's response to the protests at the *infitah* companies. None of the incidents in foreign-owned firms were met with the same official repression visited on workers in wholly Egyptian-owned facilities. This suggests that the regime considered the conduct of foreign firms in Egypt to be a sensitive issue and did not want to risk inflaming public sentiment by appearing to side with the companies.

Conclusions

With the possible exception of the January 1977 riots, one could choose any given point in time over the thirty-five years covered here and observe, with accuracy, that the great majority of Egyptian workers were not engaged in any form of collective protest. If this inactivity is the phenomenon one wishes to understand, rational choice certainly offers a plausible explanation. But inertia does not make change; collective action does. And when we seek to explain those occasions when workers did take action, the rational choice perspective is contradicted. There is little to suggest that the protests cited here were the result of a detached and dispassionate calculation by workers that the conditions had changed to make the potential benefits of action exceed its probable costs. If that were the case, we should have seen the most actions occur in times of expansion, when the labor market was tight. And these should have been actual work stoppages, as workers sought to press their advantage. Instead, we found periods of prosperity associated mainly with relative labor quiescence. Only the incidents in 1982–1983 can be cast as aggressive, and these were marked by the same symbolism as the clearly restorative actions.

Finally, the fact that workers are able to act collectively at all, given the severe repression in Egypt, should give rational choice proponents pause. Only a "perverse utility function" that places a high value on martyrdom or a strong belief that individual participation in such action matters, combined with a deep commitment to the goals, could lead utility maximizers to join protests under these repressive circumstances.[81] But these assumptions imply collective, rather than individual, rationality and still cannot account for the nonopportunistic timing of the Egyptian actions.

The evidence here indicates that collective actions had an emotional rather than a dispassionate trigger: anger provided the impetus. And this anger was caused by the violation of workers' sense of justice, by the denial of something to which they felt entitled. This cannot, in and of itself, refute the notion that rational calculations are behind the *absence* of such protest. But it does suggest an alternative explanation: that quiescence indicates a basic sense of rightness, a belief in the fairness of the status quo.

In that sense, these findings also contradict the Marxist expectation that workers will seek to renegotiate, rather than restore, the terms of their exploitation, and will do so increasingly over time. Relatedly, there is no evidence of a growing sense of solidarity among workers; the twenty-seven-year span covered here saw only one explicit solidarity action.[82] Nevertheless, Marxists can find some reason for optimism in the information presented here. It must be remembered that the status quo workers are seeking to preserve does embody socialist principles of public ownership of the means of production and equity among workers. Thus, even their defensive protests arguably reflect some form of class consciousness. Furthermore, the evidence points to two ways in which Marxists appear to have influenced the course of workers' struggles in Egypt. First, it appears that more protests occurred at those plants where there was a history of leftist presence, such as Harir and Delta Ironworks. This suggests that the efforts of Marxists to promote class consciousness do help to instill a sense of collective identity among workers. Relatedly, the periods of most intense struggles, the 1974–1976 and 1984–1987 strike waves, coincided with the times that leftists had the greatest freedom to operate. The leftist press in particular appears to have played a role in spreading the news of incidents that went uncovered in the official newspapers, enabling workers to realize that they can score victories against the state. Thus, even though workers' struggles continue to be defensive and restorative, it is not unreasonable to suggest that they will increase in volume and intensity and that the influence of the Left among workers will grow, if Mubarak continues to mix limited political liberalization with efforts to impose market-oriented reforms on the economy.

Notes

Portions of this chapter appeared, in revised and expanded form, as "Irrational Workers: The Moral Economy of Labor Protest in Egypt," *World Politics* vol. 46 no. 1 (October 1993).

1. This chapter is based on dissertation research conducted in Egypt from June 1987 through July 1988. I am grateful to the American Research Center in Egypt, Fulbright-Hays, and the Social Science Research Council for generous financial support of my research and writing. I would also like to thank Ellis Goldberg, Zachary Lockman, and Peter Swenson for helpful comments on earlier drafts of this chapter. Any errors, of course, are my own.

2. Again with apologies to the intent of this volume, this time with regard to the effort to broaden the conception of the working class, my use of the term *workers* here refers primarily to the industrial proletariat. As a political scientist my concern, at the broadest level, is with the interaction between governments and the societies they govern. An underlying assumption of my research is that the state in most postcolonial socieites takes economic development, and particulary industrialization, as one of its central goals. Accordingly, it must endeavor to influence the behavior of workers toward the achievement of this aim. Whether and how workers respond to these attempts will affect not only the success of economic development plans but also the legitimacy of the government that promotes them.

This perspective privileges urban workers, especially the industrial proletariat, as a group essential to the unfolding political economy of developing countries. Capitalism need not be embraced by the state, nor classical Marxism by the analyst, for the centrality of workers to the political and economic future of the country to be recognized.

The reader should note that my use of the term *workers* here is not meant to be synonymous with "working class," as I would include in the latter dependents of workers as well.

3. See, e.g., the quote by Joan Scott in the chapter by Zachary Lockman, which argues that unless class consciousness can be demonstrated, workers do not constitute a class.

4. See Scott Lach and John Urry, "The New Marxism of Collective Action," *Sociology* 18, no. 1 (February 1984): 43–46.

5. For the same reasons, we cannot generally conduct attitudinal surveys of workers.

6. A useful summary and critique of the Western-based theories can be found in Michael Shalev, "Industrial Relations Theory and the Comparative Study of Industrial Relations and Industrial Conflict," *British Journal of Industrial Relations* 18 (1980): 26–34. See also the typology offered by Michael Shorter and Charles Tilly, *Strikes in France 1830–1968* (Cambridge: Cambridge University Press, 1974), pp. 10–12.

7. On the importance of solidarity to the Marxist notion of class consciousness, see Douglas E. Booth, "Collective Action, Marx's Class Theory, and the Union Movement," *Journal of Economic Issues* 12, no. 1 (March 1978): 163–185, especially 168–169.

8. Michael Buroway, "The Contours of Production Politics," in *Labor in the Capitalist World Economy*, ed. Charles Bergquist (New York: Sage, 1984), pp. 41–42. See also the application of Buroways's arguments to Egypt in John S. Henley and Mohamed M. Ereisha, "State Control and the Labor Productivity Crisis: The Egyptian Textile Industry at Work," *Economic Development and Cultural Change* (1987): 491–521.

9. An excellent summary of the peasant-based literature can be found in Samuel Popkin, *The Rational Peasant* (Berkeley: University of California Press, 1979), especially Chapters 1, 2, and 9.

10. E. P. Thompson, "The Moral Economy of the English Crowd in the Eighteenth Century," *Past and Present* no. 50 (February 1971): 79–136; Charles Sabel, *Work and Politics: The Division of Labor in Industry* (Cambridge: Cambridge University Press, 1982), pp. 128–136; Peter Swenson, *Fair Shares* (Ithaca, N.Y., Cornell University Press, 1989), pp. 11–108.

11. On the use of the stability-disruption-protest model by pluralist theorists, see David Greenstone, "Group Theory," in Fred I. Greenstein and Nelson Polsby, eds., *Micropolitical Theory* (Reading, Mass.: Addison-Wesley, 1975), pp. 243–317.

12. For expanded discussions of the meaning of rational choice, see Jon Elster, *Sour Grapes* (Cambridge: Cambridge University Press, 1983), especially pp. 1–42; and Barry Hindess, "Rational Choice Theory and the Analysis of Political Action," *Economy and Society* 13 (1984): 255–277.

13. For a review of empirical studies that support this argument, in the Western context, see Andrew R. Weintraub, "Prosperity vs. Strikes: An Empirical Approach," *Industrial and Labor Relations Review* 19 (October 1965): 231–238; Bruce E. Kaufman, "Bargaining Theory, Inflation, and Cyclical Strike Activity in Manufacturing," *Industrial and Labor Relations Review* 34 (April 1981): 333–355; and Michael Shalev, "Trade Unionism and Economic Analysis: The Case of Industrial Conflict," *Journal of Labor Research* 1 (Spring 1980): 133–173.

14. Mancur Olson, *The Logic of Collective Action* (New York: Basic Books, 1971); see also Russell Hardin, *Collective Action* (Baltimore: Johns Hopkins University Press, 1982).

Critics argue that rational individuals can recognize the free rider dilemma and adopt a "collective rationality" that values group rather than individual benefits; a Marxist analysis suggests workers should be especially prone to such collective rationality. See, *inter alia*, Edward N. Muller and Karl-Dieter Opp, "Rational Choice and Rebellious Collective Action," *American Political Science Review* 14 (June 1986): 471–487; John E. Roemer, "Neoclassicism, Marxism, and Collective Action," *Journal of Economic Issues* 12 (March 1978): 147–161; and Booth, "Collective Action."

15. The details of this interference are provided in Marsha Pripstein Posusney, "Workers Against the State: Actors, Issues, and Outcomes in Egyptian Labor/State Relations, 1952–1987" (Ph.D. diss., University of Pennsylvania, 1991), Chapters 1–3.

16. Ellis Goldberg, "The Foundations of State-Labor Relations in Today's Egypt," *Comparative Politics* 24, no. 2 (January 1992): 1471–162.

17. I use the terms *new* or *aggressive demands* to refer to those that seek increments to real wages, or improvements in working conditions, that do not grow out of comparisons with the past.

18. Thompson, "The Moral Economy," p. 79.

19. I use real wage indices to indicate changes in workers' earning power. There are a number of different sources of nominal wage data in Egypt, each with a different scope and methodology. On the limitations of this data, see Ibrahim al-'Issawi, "Labour Force, Employment and Unemployment," Technical Papers No. 4, *Employment Opportunities and Equity in Egypt* (Geneva: International Labour Office, 1983), pp. 2–3. Real wage calculations also hinge on the accuracy of the deflator employed. The sources cited here used either the general or the urban consumer price index (CPI), based on a marketbasket heavily weighted with domestically produced and price-controlled items to calculate the CPI. Since the 1970s, as consumer preferences have turned toward imports and controlled items have become more difficult to find, the CPI has increasingly understated inflation.

No reliable time series on strike frequency was available. The statistics published in the annual *Yearbook of Labor Statistics* (Geneva: International Labour Office) are supplied by the government and appear to reflect the fact that strikes are illegal and officially frowned upon; no incidents at all are reported from 1960 to 1968, for example, despite documented evidence to the contrary. Furthermore, as will be shown later most of the protests by workers have not involved actual work stoppages and hence would not be reflected even in accurate data on strikes. I relied instead on press accounts and interviews with individuals active in the labor movement.

20. Robert Mabro and Samir Radwan, *The Industrialization of Egypt 1939–1873* (Oxford: Oxford University Press, 1976), pp. 135–137; 'Abd al-Mughni Sa'id, "Nidal al-'Ummal wa Thawrat 23 Yulyu," *Al-Silsila al-'Ummaliyya*, no. 30 (Cairo: Institite for Workers' Education, 1968), pp. 79–92; Muhammad Khalid, *'Abd al-Nasir w'al-Haraka al-Niqabiyya* (Cairo: Cooperative Institute for Printing and Publishing, 1971), pp. 44–54.

21. Cited in Hrair Dekmejian, *Egypt Under Nasir: A Study in Political Dynamics* (Albany: SUNY Press, 1971), p. 140.

22. On the 1950s, see Joel Beinin, "Labour, Capital and the State in Nasirist Egypt, 1952–1961," *International Journal of Middle East Studies* 21 (February 1989): 71–90.

23. John Waterbury, *The Egypt of Nasser and Sadat* (Princeton, N.J.: Princeton University Press, 1983), pp. 93–97, 409; Mahmoud Abdel-Fadil, *The Political Economy of Nasserism* (Cambridge: Cambridge University Press, 1980), pp. 33–34.

24. *Al-'Ummal* (hereafter U), August 1967, pp. 4–5, 18–19; *al-Ahali*, October 24, 1984. Compensation, usually for meals, uniforms, shift work, or dangerous jobs, are in addition to workers' basic pay and granted at the discretion of management.

25. Mahmoud Hussein, *Class Conflict in Egypt, 1945–1970* (New York: Monthly Review Press, 1973), pp. 234–237.

26. U, March 23, 1968, p. 5.

27. Sayyid Fa'id interview, July 1988.

28. The rise in real wages shown in 1972 followed an increase in the minimum wage ordered by the government in March of that year. See Gerald Starr, "Wages in the Egyptian Formal Sector," Technical Papers no. 5, *Employment Opportunities and Equity in Egypt* (Geneva: International Labour Office, 1983), pp. 13–14.

29. Raymond Hinnebusch, *Egyptian Politics Under Sadat* (Cambridge: Cambridge University Press, 1985), p. 71; and Raymond Baker, *Egypt's Uncertain Revolution Under Nasser and Sadat* (Cambridge: Harvard University Press, 1978), p. 165.

30. Interview with 'Abd al-Rahman Khayr, October 1987.

31. Husayn 'Abd Al-Raziq, *Misr fi 18 wa 19 Yanayir* (Cairo: Shuhdi Publishing House, 1985), pp. 80–84; *MERIP* no. 56 (April 1977), p. 6; Baker, *Egypt's Uncertain Revolution*, p. 165. See also Ghali Shoukri, *Egypt: Portrait of a President 1971–81* (London: Zed Books, 1981), p. 323.

32. The trend shown in this table is confirmed by numerous workers from both the public and private sectors.

33. *al-Ahali*, April 12, 1978, (hereafter Ah). It is possible that more job actions did occur, but went unrecorded because of a clampdown on the leftist press after the riots. One leftist told me there were as many wildcat strikes during these years as in the 1974–1976 period. However, he was in prison most of this time and could not provide details, and I was unable to unearth any corroborating evidence.

34. *Middle East Economic Digest* (hereafter MEED), 1982 and 1983 volumes.

35. The leftist weekly *Al-Ahali* was my primary source of information on the frequency, causes, and nature of labor protest in the 1980s. Hereafter only supplemental references are cited.

36. *MEED,* 1984–1987 volumes.

37. *Al-Tali'a* (hereafter T), August 1976, pp. 55, 58. Subsequent references to the 1960s incidents at this plant are from the same source.

38. For details, see Posusney, "Workers Against the State," Chapter 4.

39. Barakat interview, October 1987. The incident described occurred in the Delta Ironworks plant; all subsequent information concerning actions at this plant is from the same interview.

40. Fa'id interview; U, February 3, 1975, p. 1; Ah, October 24, 1984.

41. T, September 1976, p. 55; al-'Amal (hereafter Am) no. 141 (February 1975): 10–11.

42. Al-Ahram (hereafter A), September 21–22, 1976; U, September 27, 1976, p. 1, October 18, 1976, p. 1; Ruz al-Yusuf (hereafter RY) no. 2520 (September 27, 1976), pp.4–5; Khayr interview.

43. Al-Sha'b, April 27, 1984.

44. MEED, October 19, 1984.

45. Awraq 'Ummaliyya, no. 5, January 1986, pp. 6–7.

46. Al-Akhbar, February 10, 1986.

47. A compromise agreement was finally negotiated between the Ministry of Labor, company officials, and workers' representatives in October 1987. Al-Ahram al-Iqtisadi, October 26, 1987.

48. Like the 1962 legislation, this was limited to the largest industrial establishments. Also, for workers younger than 18, the minimum wage was set lower.

49. U, October 16, 1972, and November 6, 1972. Subsequent references to the 1972 incident are from the same sources.

50. Fa'id interview. Public-sector workers usually receive an annual raise provided that their performance is satisfactory, whereas exceptional raises are generally granted by government only in response to labor discontent. Unlike incentive pay, bonuses, and compensation, an exceptional raise ('ilawa istithna'iyya) is considered part of the workers' basic pay when future percentage increases are calculated.

51. Ibid. The key demand of the steelworkers was a "nature of work" compensation.

52. Am, no. 144 (May 1975): 10–14; A, March 22–23, 1975.

53. Shoukri, Egypt; Barakat interview. Incentive pay is a monthly addition to workers' basic wages. It is based on production, but decided by management within a range set by law. In addition to compensation, workers' basic wages can also be supplemented by an annual production reward and periodic special grants, usually given at the start of the schoolyear, May Day, and on major religious holidays.

54. A, September 21–22, 1976; U, September 27, 1976, p. 1, October 18, 1976, no. 1; RY, no. 2520, (September 27, 1976), pp. 4–5; Khayr interview.

55. Muhammad Khalid, *al-Haraka al-niqabiyya bayn al-madi w'al-mustaqbal* (Cairo: Institute of the Cooperative House for Printing and Publishing, 1975), pp. 130–131; interviews with 'Abd al-Rahman Khayr, October 1987, and 'Abd al-'Aziz Higazi, March 1988.

56. Am, no. 144 (May 1975), pp. 10–14; A, March 22–23, 1975; Shoukri, *Egypt*, pp. 240–241.

57. Interviews with M. Mutawalli al-Sha'rawi, March 1988, and M. Gamal Imam, October 1987; Fernand J.Tomiche, *Syndicalisme et certains aspects du travail en République arabe unie (Égypte) 1900–1967* (Paris: 1974), p. 80. All subsequent references to this incident are based on the same sources.

58. *Sawt al-'Amal* no. 5 (August 1986): 27–34.

59. Ahmad Sharaf al-Din, Sabir Barakat, and Ilhami al-Mirghani, "Kifah 'ummal al-sikka al-hadid fi thamanin 'am, 1916–1986," *Sawt al-'Amil* notebooks, no. 1 (1986).

60. The leagues are informal rivals to the official trade union movement, which originated in the 1950s when civil service workers were not permitted to unionize. See Posusney, "Workers Against the State," Chapters 1–3.

61. Sharaf al-Din et al., "Kifah," pp. 28–30.

62. *MEED*, October 19, 1984.

63. *Al-Ahram al-Iqtisadi*, October 26, 1987.

64. Barakat interview.

65. Sharaf al-Din et ar, "Kifah," pp. 28–30.

66. *Sawt al-'Amal*, no. 3 (October 1985): 5.

67. U, March 23, 1968.

68. Fa'id interview.

69. RY, March 17, 1986, p. 5.

70. Shoukri, *Egypt*, pp. 240–241; Khayr interview.

71. Barakat interview.

72. U, June 23, 1975.

73. A, September 21–22, 1976; U, September 27 and October 18, 1976; RY, no. 2520 (September 27, 1976), pp. 4–5.

74. Khayr and Barakat interviews.

75. For details, see Posusney, "Workers Against the State," Chapter 5.

76. *Sawt al-'Amal* no. 3 (October 1985), p. 5.

77. *MEED* October 19, 1984.

78. *Al-Akhbar*, February 10, 1986.

79. *Sawt al-'Amal*, no. 5 (August 1986), pp. 27–34.

80. See also *al-Akhbar* and Reuters, July 9, 1986.

81. See Roemer, "Neoclassicism," p. 155; and Muller and Opp, "Rational Choice."

82. In 1982, workers at the Nasr Fertilizer Plant in Suez occupied one of the plant's administration buildings in support of the Talkha workers.

Joel Beinin

9

*Will the Real Egyptian Working Class
Please Stand Up?*

Ask harshly
Every reader of books
If ever one of them would have believed
That despite ignorance and lifelessness
The sense of the people would return before
Any thought or voice?

This is the great Egypt!
Oh my beloved
This is Egypt

Ahmad Fu'ad Nigm[1]

In one of his last publications to appear before his death, the
Egyptian Marxist political activist and historian Ahmad Sadiq Sa'd
proposed a revised interpretation of the significance of the
demonstrations and riots that swept Egypt on January 18 and 19, 1977,
shaking the foundations of the regime of Anwar Sadat.[2] This angry
eruption of Egypt's subaltern masses was an early example of a now-
familiar pattern in Third World countries. In an effort to overcome the
structural limitations of the Nasserist import–substitution industrialization
strategy, Egypt entered a period of economic adjustment culminating
in Anwar Sadat's proclamation of a new open door (*infitah*) economic
policy in 1974, heralding the intention to reopen the country to the
capitalist world market. The transition from a centrally planned to a
market economy has been marked by a chronic crisis whose first
manifestations were the recession of 1965–66: a consequence of the
Nasserist economic strategy based on increasing both consumer
consumption and investment in industrial development simultaneously.
Faced with an internationally uncompetitive industrial sector, a shortage

of hard currency, mounting foreign debt, government budget deficits due to an inflated bureaucracy, and the need to subsidize basic consumer goods to contain popular discontent, the Egyptian government called in the International Monetary Fund, which, in accord with its ideological commitment to the supremacy of the market, proposed as the price for its economic assistance government budget cuts including reducing subsidies on basic consumer goods and other measures that placed the burden of economic adjustment on those least able to bear it.

January 1977: Defensive Reaction or Revolution Manqué?

Following the IMF's prescriptions, on January 17 the veteran technocrat, deputy prime minister for financial and economic affairs, Dr. 'Abd al-Mun'im al-Qaysuni, presented the new government budget to the People's Assembly and announced that the total subsidy for basic consumer goods would be cut by half, from £E 554 million to £E 276 million. This would result in sharp price increases for bread (50 percent), sugar (25 percent), tea (35 percent), and bottled gas (50 percent), as well as significant increases for rice, cooking oil, gasoline and cigarettes. To soften the blow, increases in public-sector wages and pensions were also announced, but at less than the projected rate of price rises. On that day, in response to the government's capitulation to the IMF *diktat* and the actual increase in market prices that morning, before al-Qaysuni's speech, the first gatherings and other expressions of popular protest erupted, followed by two days of the most widespread collective outrage witnessed in Egypt since the burning of Cairo on January 26, 1952. The demonstrations were punctuated by numerous acts of destruction directed against buildings housing institutions of the regime and commercial private property servicing the extravagantly Westernized taste of the nouveau riche and recycled monarchy-vintage pashas who had come out of hiding to enjoy the social and economic opportunities of the open door economic order.

The government and the official media attributed the demonstrations and riots to "a criminal plot" by Marxists and other left opposition elements aimed at "seizing control of the Egyptian people's revolution and turning it to their interests. . .a naked plot aimed at catapulting the plotters to power through violence."[3] The government charged both the legal Left—the National Progressive Unionist party

(Tagammuʿ)—and the four illegal communist parties with incitement and arrested dozens of Nasserist and Marxist students, journalists, trade unionists, and political activists *after* the disorders had subsided. The Tagammuʿ weekly, *al-Ahali* (*The People*), was closed, as was *al-Taliʿa* (*The Vanguard*), the monthly journal edited by prominent Tagammuʿ leader Lutfi al-Khuli, which had been the leading public forum of the Marxist intelligentsia since its inception in 1965.

The official response of the Tagammuʿ defended the party by asserting (correctly) that the mass actions had not been organized in advance by its cadres. Rather, the people had been "surprised" by the government's economic decisions following on several years of increasing cost of living and growing disparity between the rich and the poor. The January events were "an automatic reaction by the masses...an attempt to express their rejection of these decisions."[4] Lutfi al-Khuli's lead article in *al-Taliʿa* asserted that the primary popular response to the new government policy was "spontaneous peaceful mass demonstrations" and emphasized that little or no violence accompanied the protests on January 18.[5] The "reaction of the bricks" (i.e., trashing property), he argued, was a response to police repression of the demonstrations; and he explained that the targets of the rioting—illuminated advertisements for luxury goods and display windows of boutiques offering high-priced imports for sale—were chosen because the outrageous prices of these goods were "provocative to the weak purchasing power of the masses."[6] Al-Khuli's partial justification of the collective acts of property destruction depended on representing them as a defensive reaction to flagrant violations of the accepted norms of moral economy by the beneficiaries of the open door. Even this limited defense of violence, according to Sadiq Saʿd, prompted the regime to close down *al-Taliʿa*.

The illegal communist parties, though their analysis of the consequences of Sadat's economic policies since 1974 led them to expect a mass response of some sort, did not anticipate either its scope or its radical thrust. Their evaluation of the events and the role of left activists in them as presented in their underground publications did not differ substantially from that of the Tagammuʿ and its supporters. Former *al-Ahali* editor Husayn ʿAbd al-Raziq's detailed study, *Egypt on the Eighteenth and Nineteenth of January* (in Arabic), elaborates on the basic theme established by the first official Tagammuʿ reactions, supported by 160 pages of documents, statements, and testimonies from government, legal, and illegal opposition sources. As ʿAbd al-Raziq is commonly believed to be a member of the Communist Party of Egypt, his book can be considered an expression of the joint views of an important component of the Tagammu' and the Communist party. The underground Marxist organizations all asserted, like the Tagammu', that their members organized neither the demonstrations nor the acts of property destruction. In fact, during the court proceedings against them, the government offered no evidence connecting any of those arrested and charged with membership in illegal organizations to vandalism, arson, or violence on January 18 or 19.[7]

The rhetorical strategy of the Left's defense implied that on January 18 and 19 the initiative was entirely in the hands of the regime. The demonstrators were motivated primarily by their immediate economic needs. Their original intention was to march to the People's Assembly and demand a redress of grievances. Only the government's failure to permit expressions of protest transformed the issue into a question about the legitimacy of the entire regime.[8] The masses were surprised and provoked. Acts of violence—smashing illuminated advertising signs and display windows of stylish boutiques; trashing casinos and buildings of the government, the ruling party, and other symbols of the regime— were acknowledged to have taken place. But they were represented as defensive and reactive responses to provocations by the police, who attempted to restrict freedom of expression by attacking the demonstrations with unnecessary force. Lutfi al-Khuli's use of the passive voice—"*wa-intalaqat al-sharar*" (and sparks were set off)—to describe the moment when the violence intensified due to arrests of left activists is emblematic of the reactive posture of the organized Left.[9]

In contrast to the government's unfounded accusations against the Left on the one hand and the defensive stand of the Left itself on the other, Sadiq Sa'd contended that the demonstrations and riots were an extraordinary popular uprising marked by "a state of raised mass social and political consciousness."[10] Although there can be no doubt that the mass actions were initially an unrehearsed response to the government's budget announcement, in Sadiq Sa'd's view, as the movement in the streets developed the crowd seized the tactical and political initiative. Especially on January 19, the demonstrators advanced beyond declaring disapproval of the specific economic policies that had prompted the demonstrations to challenge the legitimacy of the entire regime and its restructuring of Egyptian society as embodied in the open door policy. The slogans raised by the demonstrators began to articulate a vision of an alternative social order.

Table 9.1

Workers' Collective Action, 1971–1976

Date	Place	Action
May 21, 1971	Misr Helwan Spinning & Weaving	Sit-in demanding wage increase
August 1971	Iron and Steel Co.	Sit-in, strike
October 1971	Cairo taxi drivers	Strike
February 1972	Private sector textile workers in Shubra al-Khayma	Demonstration
September 1972	Iron and Steel Co.	Strike
January 1, 1975	Helwan workers at several enterprises	Demonstrations over ecomonic demands at Bab-al-Luq train station
March 25, 1975	Misr Spinning & Weaving, Mahalla al-Kubra	Strike lasting at least three days over work rule changes
April 1975	Kablat Co., Shubra al-Khayma	Strike
April 1976	Military Plant #45, Helwan	Demonstration for increased meal allowance
June 1976	Nasr Transport Co.	Sit-in
November 1976	Cairo Joint Transport Authority	Strike

Sources: Taha Sa'd 'Uthman et al., "bi-taklif min maktab al-'ummal al-markazi li-hizb al-tajammu' al-watani al-taqaddumi," *100 'amm min al-nidal: fi dhikra al-mi'awiyya li'l-'id al-'alami li'l-'ummal, mayu 1886–mayu 1986* (Cairo, 1986), pp. 54–55; Mustafa Kamil al-Sayyid, *Al-Mujtama'wa'l-siyasa fi misr: dawr jama'at al-masalih fi al-nizam al-siyasi al-misri, 1952–1981* (Cairo, 1983), p. 74; Ahmad Sadiq Sa'd, "Hajatuna ila istratijiyya ishtirakiyya jadida: qira'a thaniyya fi ahdath yanayir 1977," *al-Tariq* 46, no. 4 (1986): 15.

Sadiq Sa'd correctly situated the uprising of January 1977 in the context of the upsurge of working-class resistance to the open door policy during 1975 and 1976 expressed by a series of demonstrations, sit-ins, and strikes. The leadership and prominent participation of industrial workers employed in the public sector on January 18 support the view that the demonstration and riots should be considered an extension of their earlier efforts to resist the open door policy (see Table 9.1) rather than a limited protest against increased food prices.

In greater Cairo, workers of the Misr Spinning and Weaving Company in Helwan initiated the demonstrations by leading other workers in a march around the industrial suburb, chanting demands for cancellation of the price hikes and the ouster of the government, and expressing particular enmity to President Sadat and his family. Police tried to isolate Helwan from the capital, and some workers, for their part, blocked the roads and railway tracks leading to Cairo, perhaps to prevent police reinforcements from arriving. Other workers from Helwan reached Cairo, where they joined demonstrators from various neighborhoods and from 'Ayn Shams University. In the northern industrial suburb of Shubra al-Khayma, workers struck and occupied their plants. In Alexandria on January 18, the demonstrations were begun by workers at the Naval Arsenal, where tensions were already high due to an earlier rash of dismissals. Joined by workers from other enterprises, they marched toward the headquarters of the Arab Socialist Union, chanting antigovernment slogans and throwing stones at the police and security forces. Some university students joined the demonstration. Cars, trams, and buses on the route were destroyed, as were the rest houses of the president and vice-president of the republic. A police station was stormed; a movie theater, buildings of large companies, and a consumer cooperative rumored to engage in favoritism and bribery were set ablaze; and many display windows were shattered. On the morning of January 19 workers at the Misr rayon mill and Military Plant No. 45 in Helwan left work, cut transportation links between Cairo and Helwan, and demonstrated throughout Helwan. Other demonstrations that day were initiated by workers of the Sugat textile mill in Hada'iq al-Qubba and the Shurbagi textile mill in Imbaba.[12] Later that day the demonstrations spread throughout Cairo, and acts of violence became more widespread.

Sadiq Sa'd also noted the radical character of the chants raised in various demonstrations throughout Cairo. Slogans shouted by communist students were taken up by many others. Industrial workers in particular exhibited their pro-Nasserist sentiment by carrying pictures of the former president in demonstrations and chanting "Nasser, Nasser" and "Abdel Nasser used to say 'Be mindful of the workers'" and the satirical ditty, "Oh, our rulers in 'Abdin, In the name of justice and religion, Where is justice and where is religion?" (*Ya hukkamna fi 'Abdin, bism'l-haqq wa-bism'l-din, fayn al-haqq wa-fayn al-din?*).[13]

The most distinctive element of Sadiq Sa'd's interpretation is that, in contrast to other leftists who regarded the violence of the crowds as incidental to the political and social character of the popular movement or merely a defensive reaction to police provocations, he argued that "the core of the uprising and its overall direction was direct and violent resistance to the reduction of the standard of living of the popular classes, that is, an open challenge to the dominant wealthy class."[14] He embraced the impetuous assault on the symbols of the regime's power and ostentatious displays of the wealth of the ruling elite as a more radical challenge to the legitimacy of the regime by the unorganized masses than the peaceful protests directed toward the People's Assembly led by students and trade unionists.[15] Though the presence of many undisciplined elements—the unemployed, youth, workers in small-scale craft and service enterprises, recent migrants from the countryside— caused some misdirected excesses, act of violence were the essence of the mass actions for Sadiq Sa'd and expressed a collective statement of refusal to continue to obey governmental authority. He also noted that intellectuals who participated in the demonstrations had advised those destroying property to desist, but were rebuffed and told that this was how the people expressed their feelings.[16] In sum, Sadiq Sa'd argued that both during and after the events the organized Left was reformist, limiting itself to supporting the demands of the masses and defending the legitimacy of their actions, whereas the actual movement and consciousness of the masses were revolutionary. "The political direction of the uprising was more correct than the political direction of the Left," he concluded.[17] The evidence about the character of the demonstrations compiled by Sadiq Sa'd appears to confirm both their exceptional nature and structural character as a continuation of workers' resistance to the open door policy. His argument also constitutes a criticism (and self-criticism) of the Left intelligentsia—the principal source of leadership for the organized Left—for being isolated from workers and other popular strata in whose name and for whose interests they purport to speak. Though it is not the case that the organized Left had no working class and peasant supporters, its national leadership and sense of political priorities had long been dominated by an internally divided but nonetheless socially distinctive circle of Cairene intellectuals with

Western-style educations and cultural mores, including many from elite backgrounds. Would it then be valid to draw the conclusion, strongly suggested by Sadiq Saʿd's description and analysis, that the timidity and social isolation of the Left intelligentsia were responsible for missing a revolutionary opportunity (or at least for limiting the political potential of the popular uprising?

For those who sympathize with Egypt's subaltern strata and hope for their economic and social liberation there is a strong temptation to embrace this conclusion because it unproblematically explains the limitations of the popular resistance to the open door policy by the betrayal of the intelligentsia, whereas the working class and its potential allies remain pure and unsullied as the true revolutionary subject. Indeed, there are many elements of truth in Sadiq Saʿd's representation of the January events and their import. His emphasis on the extraordinary confrontational character of the rebellion and the centrality of the popular violence to its significance and historical impact seems justified; and his criticism of the Left intelligentsia is well-founded.

The Marxist Left and the Working Class

Although historically the Marxist intelligentsia encouraged the formation of trade unions and other forms of working class organization and struggle, it also imposed its own agenda on the working class and consistently subordinated class struggle to the anti-imperialist national struggle.[18] This was not the consequence of opportunism or betrayal, but of Marxist orthodoxy—the firm belief in a determinist and teleological Soviet-style Marxism alloyed with the Maoist theory of "new democracy." Intellectuals from most trends in the communist movement actively participated in organizing the labor movement as a political force during the last decade of the monarchy and encouraged workers to develop their leadership skills. But the immediate significance of the working class as a historical and political subject was considered to be its potential contribution as the vanguard of a national united front whose objective was to free Egypt from military occupation by Great Britain and economic domination by Europe and its local "feudalist" allies. Because the Left conceptualized workers' economic struggles mainly as a component of the national struggle against foreign capital, there was no contradiction between the immediate interests of the working class and the national movement. When the stage of national liberation was completed, the working class would proceed to fight for its class interests in its own right. By so restricting the role of the working class as a historical actor to a script whose final acts became unplayable on the Egyptian stage, the Marxist Left inadvertently contributed to the disorganization and disorientation of the labor movement during the regime of Abdel Nasser.

The corporatist policies of the Nasser regime demobilized the organized working class by integrating trade unions into the structure of the state. Leaders of the labor movement who objected to the movement's loss of civil autonomy were subjected to harsh repression. At the same time, the policy of encouraging large-scale industrial development increased the size, concentration and significance of workers in the national economy, while the ideology of Arab socialism legitimated concern for workers' well-being in the national political discourse. Under these conditions it was reasonable for most workers and trade unions not to pursue a strategy of confrontation with their employer—the state for an increasing number of them—especially as their erstwhile allies, the Left intelligentsia, agreed with or were unable to oppose effectively the government's view that militant struggles by workers against capital hindered the development of the national economy. The combination of corporatist integration, repression of the militant Left, enhanced public status and significant improvements in the living and working conditions of organized workers in the public sector during the Nasser era bureaucratized the trade unions, increased their influence on public policy within the parameters acceptable to the regime, drained them of their fighting spirit, and made them incapable of confronting Sadat's open door policy with the same level of organization, consciousness, and combative élan that characterized, for example, the militant struggles of unionized textile workers in and around Shubra al-Khayma from the late 1930s to the early 1950s.

The working class was not only structurally transformed and organizationally demobilized during the Nasser era, its subject position in national politics was also discursively reconstructed. As Zachary Lockman argues in Chapter 4, the working class became a legitimate subject in Egyptian political discourse because of the role assigned to it in the nationalist project as articulated by the urban *effendiyya* (urban middle strata with a modern, Western-style education). Workers assumed more or less importance in the national movement depending on whether the vision of the *effendiyya* was bourgeois Wafdist, Nasserist or Marxist; but in this respect the relationship of the Marxist intelligentsia to the working class differed little from that of Wafdists or Nasserists. With the apparent realization of the goals of the nationalist project in the 1950s, strikes and other manifestations of class struggle disappeared from the legitimate vocabulary of nationalist politics. Because it accepted many of the premises of Nasserism and because in any case it was too weak to elaborate an alternative political vision and practice, the Left did not undertake the task of articulating a new conception of the working class subject in postindependence Egypt. Workers certainly continued to struggle against capital, but the previous discursive framework for representing, organizing, and consolidating these struggles in a comprehensive political strategy was no longer regarded as legitimate. The few strikes and other manifestations of working-class collective action from 1954 to 1967 were widely considered aberrant phenomena requiring, at best, a benevolent administrative resolution.

For several years after the dissolution of the two Egyptian communist parties in 1965, the Marxist intelligentsia all but ceased to concern itself with working-class issues and concentrated on integrating itself into the Nasserist regime: publishing *al-Tali'a* under the auspices of the semiofficial daily *al-Ahram*, joining and assuming leading positions in the Arab Socialist Union and its secret Vanguard Organization, and participating prominently in the direction of the regime's mass media and ideological-cultural apparatus.

Following the death of Gamal Abdel Nasser in 1970, many Marxist intellectuals at first believed that his successor, Anwar Sadat, because he possessed less charisma and personal power than the hero of Arab nationalism and Arab socialism, would of necessity be more receptive to their influence and participation in the new regime. This expectation was heightened when Sadat appointed two former leading members of the Communist party, Fu'ad Mursi and Isma'il Sabri 'Abd Allah, to cabinet posts in the government—a level of prominence and toleration far beyond what was possible during Abdel Nasser's era. Even after Sadat's "corrective revolution" of May 15, 1971—a coup against prominent pro-Nasserist government figures signaling the first stage in Sadat's abandonment of Arab socialism and reorientation of Egypt toward the United States—misapprehension of the direction of the new regime prevailed.

Thus, in January 1972 Lutfi al-Khuli, as the leader of an Egyptian delegation to the congress of the Communist Party of Lebanon, asserted that Egypt was enjoying a "definite democratic atmosphere." When asked about the violent clash between police and workers during the August 1971 sit-in at the Egyptian Iron and Steel Company in Helwan, where 6,000 workers were employed, al-Khuli described the police intervention and subsequent confrontation with the workers as a response to the attempt by 15 porters, who might have been directed by nonworkers, to prevent workers not participating in the sit-in from entering the mill. Summarizing the discussion of this affair by the Central Committee of the Arab Socialist Union, he concluded that the most important aspect of the incident was "confirming the necessity of solving problems in a democratic manner in the framework of an alliance of the working people's forces and the importance of the working class within [that alliance]."[19]

This unenthusiastic and somewhat myopic report of the steel workers' struggle framed wholly within the orthodox Marxist-nationalist conceptual universe is an example of the insensitivity of many leading figures of the Marxist intelligentsia to the untransformed nature of social relations at the point of production under Arab socialism and their disinterest in the concrete, but necessarily untidy, manifestations of class struggle that were unleashed by the economic downturn of 1965–66, Egypt's defeat in the June 1967 war, and the death of Abdel Nasser. Industrial workers' disappointments over the shortcomings of Arab socialism were expressed by a significant revival of large-scale collective action during 1971 and 1972—the first instance of more-than-episodic working-class militancy since the early 1950s (see Table 9.1). Al-Khuli's attitude toward the iron and steel workers and the position of two prominent former Communist party leaders in the government heading ministries with responsibilities for economic affairs seemed to confirm the continuing distance of the Marxist intelligentsia from workers' economic struggles in the first years of Sadat's presidency. The workers' protest movement of 1971 and 1972 could not be assimilated into the prevailing nationalist political discourse since it was directed against the shortcomings of Arab socialism and the economic burdens of the 1967 war as well as the first tentative steps toward the open door policy. Hence, the response of the main body of the Marxist intelligentsia was passive, hesitant, or even critical.

This movement was suspended in deference to the call for national unity during and immediately after the October 1973 war. But after Sadat officially proclaimed the open door policy in late 1974, a second outbreak of workers' sit-ins, strikes, and demonstrations erupted in 1975 and 1976. The Left intelligentsia was more supportive of workers in this movement of resistance because it was now clear that the open door was a key component of Sadat's scheme to abandon both the economic strategy and international orientation of Nasserism. Once again, workers' struggles were represented by the Left as a component of the nationalist project, a front in the battle for economic self-determination. But demobilized and detached from workers since the mass arrest of communists and other leftists in January 1959 and the dissolution of the two communist parties in 1965, the Left intelligentsia was too weak to contribute effectively to workers' active opposition to the open door. The organized Left was also preoccupied with reforming its ranks—the Communist Party of Egypt was reestablished only in 1975 and the Tagammu' was founded in 1976, when multiple political parties were legalized for the first time since 1953. Organizational weakness and fear that the regime would reverse its decision to abandon the single-party system were factors in the Left's response to the uprising of January 1977.

Historical Rereading and Political Prospects

Sadiq Sa'd's purpose in attempting to revise the Left's interpretation of the uprising of January 1977 was to forge a more powerful and united movement of resistance to the open door and all that was associated with it. This required overcoming the historic gap between the modernist, secular culture of the radical intelligentsia and the popular culture of the subaltern strata, which is just as Western-influenced but in very different ways. Sadiq Sa'd's emphasis on the central role of collective acts of violence in January 1977 was an effort to apprehend the specific consciousness and social practice of Egypt's subaltern strata. The untutored resistance emerging from what he considered their innate political instincts was, he thought, "more correct" than that of the organized Left, which should, he implied, learn from the people.

Sadiq Sa'd's historical interpretation is a significant improvement over those of the organized legal and illegal Left parties, yet it also contains several problematic aspects with both historiographical and political implications. His account relies heavily on synechdoche— ascribing the actions and consciousness of a part of the working class to the whole uprising. Certain aspects of the collective actions, which in retrospect seem to have considerable significance, are deemphasized; and there is no effort to ask, nearly ten years after the events, why nothing of a similar nature has recurred. Sadiq Sa'd tended to essentialize the working class and identify only the particular form of militant resistance manifested in January 1977 with its authentic character. Finally, he did not explicitly locate his account of January 1977 in its political context, perhaps because of the continuing threat of political repression against opposition activists.

As the compilation of collective actions in Table 9.1 and Sadiq Sa'd's narrative of January 1977 confirm, popular resistance—to both the crisis of the Nasserist system and the preliminary expressions of the open door policy—was sporadic and concentrated sectorally among organized workers in large-scale, public-sector enterprises and geographically in a small number of heavy industrial areas. Such workers were among the principal beneficiaries of Nasserism and potentially big losers from the open door policy. Their social relations of production, above average level of skill and education, concentration in industries perceived as vital to the national economy, and relatively privileged conditions gave them the greatest capacity to organize themselves outside formal trade union structures or transform local trade union committees into organs of struggle. Industrial areas like Helwan are in part a product of Nasserism, and therefore it is not surprising that many workers employed in enterprises located there still lionize the former president. The strong undercurrent of popular indignation over the growing gap between the rich and the poor, the conspicuous consumption of imported luxury goods, and similar phenomena of the open door era flowed into the demonstrations initiated by these workers to produce the explosive outburst of January 1977.

However, areas of concentrated heavy industry like Helwan and Shubra al-Khayma do not define the limits of the working class or the possibility for radical social change in Egypt. Along with the militant collective resistance to the open door policy manifested in January 1977, millions of Egyptians sought, and at least temporarily found, individual solutions to economic hardship by migrating to the oil-producing countries and working at jobs paying wages five or six times more than they could have earned at home. Even unskilled peasants were employed as construction workers in the Persian Gulf at extravagant rates of pay, by Egyptian standards, which allowed their families to improve their living standards substantially and acquire hitherto unimaginable consumer goods. Some who remained in Egypt found relatively well-paying jobs in the new financial, tourist, and commercial import enterprises and even the small number of industrial projects established as a result of the open door policy. A vastly larger number of potential workers who remained in Egypt, finding no regular employment at all, remained unorganized and unorganizable as they were scattered throughout the interstices of society in that vast and indefinite location often antiseptically termed the "informal sector".

The militancy of public-sector workers in large-scale enterprises, the physical absence of other workers employed in oil-exporting countries, and the quiescence of yet others were all components of the structure of the Egyptian working class in the 1970s and 1980s. This heterogeneity is an aspect of the uneven character of capitalist development in Egypt, where large-scale industrial production coexists interdependently with small enterprises preserving many precapitalist social practices. Even within the modern industrial sector, management and labor organizers sometimes employ precapitalist social and cultural practices both to discipline workers and organize them for resistance. Uneven development fragments the working class socially and culturally. Politically, the failures of secular liberalism, Nasserism, Marxism, and Islamism to offer a decisive resolution to the protracted economic and social crisis of subordinate capitalist development have partially discredited all of these orientations while allowing each of them to persist and maintain a certain following.

Consequently, those who actively participated in the collective actions of January 1977 did not share a unified understanding of the cause of their oppression or the solution to it. Although embracing the violent actions of the crowd, Sadiq Sa'd nonetheless regarded certain forms of violence as misdirected and attributed them to undisciplined social groups, not employed workers. But the presence of "impure" elements in the uprising should not be minimized by representing them as extraneous to its real working-class subject. No social movement can be unitary in composition, and the inchoate rage of the street people was as much a part of its character as the most politically disciplined and directed actions of industrial workers. For, as Gayatri Spivak has argued, "the oppressed under socialized capital have no necessarily unmediated access to 'correct' resistance."[20]

Similarly, Sadiq Sa'd treated the trashing of the casinos on the Pyramids Road simply as an exaction of revenge against the wealthy beneficiaries of the open door. However, the prominence of these sites, historically targeted as dens of iniquity by the Muslim Brothers and other Islamists, suggests that at least some sections of the crowd were inspired by a consciousness shaped by the radical Islamist movement and identified gambling, liquor, dancing, and other morally disapproved behavior as the fundamental causes of Egypt's misfortunes. The intensified activity of armed Islamist radicals during the remainder of 1977 and beyond and the increasing influence of Islamist political groups during the 1970s and 1980s suggest that the Islamist component of the January 1977 uprising deserves more attention than Sadiq Sa'd allotted to it.

The structural heterogeneity of the working class, the absence of an effective oppositional discourse reconstructing an appropriate role for workers and their potential allies among the subaltern strata in the new Egyptian social and political order, the sharp antagonism between Islamist and secularist cultural orientations among the opposition forces, and the availability of individual solutions within the framework of the capitalist restructuring of Egypt (at least until the sharp economic downturn precipitated by the collapse of oil prices in the mid-1980s), more than the timidity of the intelligentsia and the organized Left, overdetermined the limits of the January 1977 uprising. This moment did not open the way toward a coherent movement of militant opposition and a radical change in Egypt's economic and political direction. Rather, the uprising fits a more common pattern in twentieth century Egyptian politics: a tumultuous upheaval that could not be sustained because of inability to forge enduring political alliances among the diverse components of Egypt's subaltern strata.

Nonetheless, Sadiq Sa'd was correct to criticize the organized Left for underestimating the effectiveness and purposefulness of the mass actions of January 1977. Although the crowds were not organized in advance by regular political bodies, their collective action nonetheless achieved substantial gains.[21] The announced price increases were cancelled on the afternoon of January 19 and the international pressure on the Egyptian government to eliminate the subsidies was temporarily relieved. Beyond this immediate accomplishment, the potential for popular collective action continues to inspire fear in the hearts of Egypt's rulers, and apprehension about renewed food riots constrains the options of the government to this day.

Thus, although January 1977 was a partial and temporary victory representing a certain potential, but not necessarily a viable long-term political strategy, it demonstrated that Egypt's workers and other disenfranchised strata assert a powerful, if diffuse, presence in political life, even as the regime has attempted to structure their exclusion from its officially recognized political institutions. Can we write about this presence without essentializing subaltern subjects or transforming them "into autonomous subject-agents, unitary consciousnesses possessed of their own originary essences in the manner we now understand to be the creation, very largely, of Enlightenment humanism's reconstruction of Man?"[22] To do so we must refrain from reifying their experience and attributing to their consciousness an unsullied authenticity that alone can unlock the secret to liberation. The historiographical and political aspects of this problem are interconnected, as is apparent from recent efforts to reassert the centrality of the working class in Egyptian politics by leftist political activists relying heavily on a particular reading of labor history.

Workers' History and Workers' Politics in the 1980s

The context of Sadiq Sa'd's rereading of the events of January 1977 both amplifies its significance and underscores its weaknesses. There was a marked decline in workers' collective action after January 1977. After his accession in 1981, President Husni Mubarak was compelled to relax Sadat's repressive measures against the forces opposing the regime, including trade unionists and left activists, in order to establish his legitimacy and distance himself from the policies of his predecessor. Then, from 1984 on, as workers returned from high-paying jobs in the oil-producing countries, unemployment increased, prices rose relentlessly, and concerns about the security of employment spread due to fears that the government was preparing to sell off public-sector enterprises. Workers resorted to strikes, sit-ins, and demonstrations to achieve economic demands centered around wages, benefits and hours with increasing frequency. According to the Tagammu', there were at least fifty strikes during 1985 and the first third of 1986.[23] The most notable labor actions of this period were the strike and uprising at the Misr Fine Spinning and Weaving Company in Kafr al-Dawwar in September–October 1984, the protracted struggle of workers at the Esco textile firm in Shubra al-Khayma during the first half of 1986 (including a strike and a sit-in), the strike at Misr Spinning and Weaving Company in

Mahalla al-Kubra in February 1986, and the exceptionally militant strike of railroad engineers and stokers in July 1986. The strike and protests at the Egyptian Iron and Steel Company in Helwan in July–August 1989 were also part of this movement. Once again, unionized workers in large-scale public-sector enterprises, especially those located in major industrial centers, were most prominent in this upsurge of workers' collective action.

The labor struggles of the 1980s were often directed by local activists, not necessarily members of Left opposition parties, independent of the trade union bureaucracy. Though the organized Left rarely initiated strikes or protests, it regarded militant workers' collective action as an expression of popular opposition to the open door policy, usually (but not always) supported workers' demands, and organized legal and material assistance. Sometimes the Tagammu' responded timidly because some of its leaders hoped that the government would expand democratic rights and perhaps even legalize strikes if the political opposition demonstrated restraint and "responsibility" and did not simply exploit labor militancy for partisan gains. Although strikes were not legalized, they achieved a certain de facto social legitimacy and could no longer be considered aberrant or exceptional phenomena. Workers' dissatisfaction with the results of the open door policy, their fears about further deterioration in their living and working conditions, and their criticism of the failure of the existing trade union apparatus to defend their interests became well-known to the public and the government, which has been compelled to consider them when deliberating its policy options.

As a result, the working class as a political subject assumed a new discursive prominence. In 1985 the Central Labor Bureau of the Tagammu' began to issue an irregular magazine, *Awraq 'Ummaliyya* (Workers' Papers), followed by several pamphlets and booklets, including one commemorating the centenary of the May First international workers' day.[24] *Al-Ahali* introduced a regular labor affairs column. In February 1985 a group of veteran trade union activists, several younger workers, and labor lawyer Ahmad Sharaf al-Din began irregular publication of *Sawt al-'Amil* (Worker's Voice).[25] During 1986 several local workers' papers based on a specific region or enterprise began to appear.[26] In 1987 the Marxist theoretical journal, *Qadaya Fikriyya* (Ideological Issues), published an issue on the Egyptian working class.[27] Sadiq Sa'd's study of January 1977 appeared in late 1986 and was a component of the Left's desire to reassert the role of the working class in Egyptian politics and rethink its relationship to other social forces.

Many of these writings incorporate an element of nostalgia for the golden era of working-class struggle, the 1940s to 1952, when textile and transport workers were the center of gravity of a labor movement that made a substantial contribution to the national struggle and imparted to it a radical social content that was partially realized in the populist measures of the Nasserist regime. By reminding workers and others of the historic origins of the labor movement as a component of the national movement and the contributions of workers' militant collective action to the national project, they sought to establish the patriotic legitimacy of strikes and other forms of workers' struggle in the present. In this context, the historic relationship between workers and the Left intelligentsia assumed immediate tactical political significance.

The renewed importance of the working class in the political discourse of the Left, the recent upsurge in working class struggles, and the writing of labor history are closely linked in the recent activities of Taha Sa'd 'Uthman, a labor activist since the late 1930s, a long-time comrade of Ahmad Sadiq Sa'd, and an editor of *Sawt al-'Amil*. At a 1987 conference in Cairo on Commitment and Objectivity in the Writing of Modern Egyptian History, Taha Sa'd presented a paper on how to write labor history and directly addressed the problem of the gap between the Left intelligentsia and the working class. Despite generously acknowledging that Left intellectuals (even foreigners including myself) have made worthwhile contributions to writing Egyptian labor history, he complained that the intellectuals "missed the spirit of life and the details that might appear insignificant but whose influence is great on the course of events and their outcome and the fighting spirit of the working class."[28] Therefore, despite their factual correctness, Taha Sa'd considered the writings of the intellectuals to be merely "among the principal sources of raw material" for a proper history of the Egyptian working class, which should rely primarily on the memoirs, documents and testimonies of veteran labor activists.

Taha Sa'd's insistence on the absolute autonomy of workers' experience as the central requisite for writing labor history, like Sadiq Sa'd's interpretation of January 1977, suggests that Left intellectuals cannot apprehend the essence of the struggle and consciousness of the Egyptian masses, which can be authentically expressed only in an unmediated form in labor activists' representation of their own history or in the popular violence of the uprising of January 1977. The intellectual and political project implied by this critique would be, as

Taha Sa'd proposed, to retrieve the authentic voice of workers and other subaltern elements and to privilege it as the starting point for understanding Egyptian history and reshaping Egyptian society. Indeed, Taha Sa'd has followed his own advice and written three volumes of memoirs and historical writings (books that could not have appeared in Egypt during the Nasser era, it is worth noting) in addition to his participation in *Sawt al-'Amil.*[29]

Taha Sa'd's historical writing is an important component of the political style and outlook of *Sawt al-'Amil*. His contributions to the magazine typically consist of capsule biographies of deceased trade union activists, retrievals of political statements of earlier militant labor organizations and summary accounts of historic struggles, such as the lengthy strike at the Misr Spinning and Weaving Company in Mahalla al-Kubra in 1947. *Sawt al-'Amil* has been more sharply critical of the absorption and repression of the labor movement by the Nasserist state than other currents on the Left.[30] Ahmad Sharaf al-Din's series of articles on the strike and riot of 12–13 August 1952 at the Misr Fine Spinning and Weaving Company in Kafr al-Dawwar defended the workers against the false allegations of the military tribunal established to try them by the Revolutionary Command Council and concluded with a demand for a retrial of the unjustly convicted and executed workers. Biographies of veteran trade unionists by Taha Sa'd and others often mentioned that they had been jailed and subjected to harsh treatment from 1959 to 1964, a veiled indication that they were communists or cooperated with communists. One editor even wrote an article calling for legalizing the establishment of a working-class party (a formulaic expression for a communist party).[31]

The apparent function of both nostalgia and the more critical view of Nasserism for *Sawt al-'Amil* has been to assert the continuous historic existence of a working-class political subject independent of any other social force, including the Nasserist state. Although some of the editors are also Tagammu' members, *Sawt al-'Amil* has a much more worker-centered outlook than the publications of the Tagammu'. By appealing only to an audience of workers, *Sawt al-'Amil* can avoid the limitations that the anti-imperialist national united front strategy of the Tagammu' and the historic defense of Nasserism, to which some of its elements are committed, impose on workers' self-expression and collective action. The implication is that the working class is capable of organization and action without the assistance of the Left intelligentsia and need not be bound by its agenda or its disabilities—a conclusion similar to the one that emerged from Sadiq Sa'd's analysis of January 1977.

Self-Criticism

Taha Sa'd's historical prescriptions describe fairly closely the sort of project that Zachary Lockman and I had in mind when we began to think about researching and writing the history of the Egyptian working class. We were committed to placing class struggle at the center of our narrative, and I believe we succeeded in presenting a more comprehensive and nuanced account of the struggle between labor and capital and its impact on Egyptian politics than was previously available. Like many new Left historians, we were greatly influenced by reading E. P. Thompson's *The Making of the English Working Class*, and our original impulse was to apply its insights and method to Egypt. That is why, in anticipation of Taha Sa'd 'Uthman's advice, the second part of *Workers on the Nile* relies extensively on interviews with veteran trade unionists, including Taha Sa'd himself.

We rejected a mechanistic Marxism, in part because we knew that in the second half of the book it would be necessary to explain an important problem in labor history that had been ignored by Egyptian labor historians, especially of the Marxist school, who had written before us: if the consciousness and organizational capacity of Egyptian workers were increasingly enhanced by the spread of capitalist relations of production and the growth of large-scale transport and industry, why was the organized working class so easily integrated into the corporatist structure of the Nasserist state after 1954? A conception positing a self-constituting working-class subject developing a cumulatively higher level of class consciousness as capitalist relations of production spread throughout the economy could not account for this outcome.

Ultimately we rejected both the Thompsonian notion that the working class made itself and the structuralism of Althusser and his adherents, adopting instead as our guide Adam Przeworski's proposition that "class formation is a perpetual process. . . . Classes as historical actors are thus the 'effects' of struggles which are structured by the totality of economic, political and ideological-cultural relations."[32] But we did not fully succeed in implementing this theoretical conception throughout the narrative. Instead we tended to homogenize and reify the working class as a historical subject and regard only those who engaged in collective struggle as real workers, despite our presentation of evidence that the historical experience of workers was diverse and that the political and cultural contest over its meaning persisted throughout the period we addressed.

Our rejection of Thompson was partly dictated by practical considerations and therefore incompletely developed. Despite the large numbers of interviews used to write the second part of *Workers on the Nile*, we thought that we lacked access to sufficient sources of the kind required to write a history of the experience of Egyptian workers. Therefore, *Workers on the Nile* became a book focused on the institutional and political history of the labor movement in which we sought to expose the mechanisms in Egypt's political economy that concurrently enabled and constrained the struggles of the workers we wrote about.

Our cordial and empathic relations with many veteran trade unionists led us to believe that we could ally our research skills with their local memory in the form of their testimony about their experiences and effect "an insurrection of subjugated knowledges" to produce "a historical knowledge of struggles."[33] Having access to many oral history accounts led me to slip into a tendency to attempt to recover the voice of a working-class subject whose essence was the experience of militant class struggle. Highly self-conscious veteran leftist trade union activists like Taha Sa'd 'Uthman, 'Atiyya al-Sirafi, Muhammad Mutawalli al-Sha'rawi (all editors of *Sawt al-'Amil*), and others eagerly told me about struggles they had participated in. Other former workers who were less politicized or did not regard the working class as having a unique historic role had weaker memories, were less articulate and harder to locate, and seemed to have less "interesting" things to say.

The testimony of the Left activists, though it is certainly "real" and "truthful"—much more so than narratives omitting workers from the history of modern Egypt altogether, I still maintain—distorted my vision in two ways. First, most of my informants had long before processed their experience through a political filter that eliminated or minimized aspects of it that tended to contradict their own world outlook and political commitments. Second, believing that these activists were *the* authentic workers led me even further away from understanding the experience, consciousness, and structural position of those workers who were not engaged in economic or political struggles in an organized framework over a protracted period of time. Although we characterized the militant transport and textile workers as the center of gravity of the labor movement in a conscious effort to avoid conceptualizing them as a vanguard, we nonetheless tended to fall into a form of vanguardism.

Some of these weaknesses in *Workers on the Nile* are also present in Ahmad Sadiq Sa'd's rereading of January 1977, in Taha Sa'd 'Uthman's methodology for writing labor history and in the political practice of those who have recently attempted to reassert the presence of the working class as an independent historical subject in Egyptian politics. Is there a way to celebrate the historical legacy of workers' militant struggles and preserve it as a resource for those seeking to reshape the present without homogenizing and reifying the working class and promoting illusions about the purity of its authentic impulse to resist exploitation? Rosalind O'Hanlon has proposed a strategy: "to recover the presence of the subordinate without slipping into an essentialism, by revealing that presence to be one constructed and refracted through practice, but no less 'real' for our having said that it does not contain its own origins within itself."[34]

Therefore, Lockman and I might have taken more seriously our own statement that "before there could be a struggle among classes there had to be a struggle about class."[35] We might have conceived of the orientation of transport and textile workers toward militant struggle as one pole in the contested terrain of popular culture. Without adopting an absolutist rejection of holistic conceptualizations, without which understanding and politics are impossible, we might have placed more emphasis on disaggregating the working class and on the continuing effects of bourgeois and prebourgeois forms of domination on the consciousness of many workers and given more attention to the particular way in which the working class was discursively constructed as a historical subject. These alternative approaches might have made the political conclusions to be drawn from the book less certain. But avoiding this uncertainty only encourages evasion of issues that must be confronted.

Notes

1. Ahmad Fu'ad Najm, "Risala raqm 1," *al-'Anbara* (Cairo, 1982), pp. 189–195. My English translation is adapted from Kamal Abdel-Malek's in *A Study of the Vernacular Poetry of Ahmad Fu'ad Nigm* (Leiden, 1990), p. 162.

2. Ahmad Sadiq Sa'd, "Hajatuna ila istratijiyya ishtirakiyya jadida: qira'a thaniyya fi ahdath yanayir 1977," *al-Tariq* 46, no. 4 (1986): 10–47.

3. Speech of Prime Minister Mamduh Salim to the People's Assembly, January 29, 1977, quoted in Husayn 'Abd al-Raziq, *Misr fi 18 wa 19 yanayir: dirasa siyasiyya watha'iqiyya* (Beirut, 1979), pp. 8–9, 127–158, especially pp. 129, 132.

4. "Bayan min hizb al-tajammu' al-watani al-wahdawi al-taqaddumi ila jamahir al-sha'b al-misri," January 19, 1977, in 'Abd al-Raziq, *Misr*, p. 164.

5. Lutfi al-Khuli, "Jamahir yanayir bayna al-hukuma wa'l-yasar," *al-Tali'a* 13, no. 2 (February 1977): 7, 9.

6. Ibid., p. 8.

7. 'Abd al-Raziq, *Misr*, pp. 93ff.

8. Al-Khuli, "Jamahir," p. 9.

9. Ibid., p. 10.

10. Sa'd, "Hajatuna," p. 11.

11. Ibid., pp. 24–26.

12. Ibid., pp. 27, 28.

13. Ibid., pp. 26–27.

14. Ibid., p. 35. See also p. 17.

15. Ibid., p. 27.

16. Ibid., p. 27.

17. Ibid., p. 45.

18. The next several paragraphs summarize arguments made more extensively in Joel Beinin, *Was the Red Flag Flying There? Marxist Politics in Egypt and Israel and the Arab-Israeli Conflict, 1948–1965* (Berkeley, Calif., 1990); "Labor, Capital and the State in Nasserist Egypt, 1952–1961," *International Journal of Middle East Studies* 21, no. 1 (February 1989); and "The Communist Movement and Nationalist Political Discourse in Nasirist Egypt," *Middle East Journal* 41, no. 4 (Autumn 1987).

19. *Al-Nahar* [Beirut], January 6, 1972.

20. Gayatri Chakravorty Spivak, "Can the Subaltern Speak?" in *Marxism and the Interpretation of Culture*, ed. Cary Nelson and Lawrence Grossberg (Urbana and Chicago, 1988), p. 307.

21. Sa'd, "Hajatuna," pp. 12, 45.

22. Rosalind O'Hanlon, "Recovering the Subject: *Subaltern Studies* and Histories of Resistance in South Asia," *Modern Asian Studies* 22, no. 1 (1988): 197.

23. *Awraq 'Ummaliyya*, no. 6 (April 1986): 1.

24. For example, Amina Shafiq, *al-Idrab* (Cairo, May 1986); Amina Shafiq, *al-Tabaqa al-'amila al-misriyya: al-nash'a, al-tatawwur, al-nidalat* (Cairo, January 1987); Taha Sa'd 'Uthman et al., "bi-taklif min maktab al-'ummal al-markazi li-hizb al-tagammu' al-watani al-taqaddumi," *100 'amm min al-nidal: fi dhikra al-mi'awiyya li'l-'id al-'alami li'l-'ummal, mayu 1886–mayu 1986* (Cairo, May 1986).

25. *Sawt al-'Amil* also published a booklet in solidarity with the strike of the railroad engineers and stokers: Ahmad Sharaf al-Din, Ilhami al-Mirghani, and Sabir Barakat, *Kifah 'ummal al-sikka al-hadid fi thamanin 'amman, 1906–1986* (Cairo, 1986).

26. Among them are *al-Sanaya'iyya* [The Workmen] for the Helwan Iron and Steel Company; *al-Fajr* [The Dawn] for Mahalla al-Kubra and Gharbiyya province; *al-Ard* [The Land] for the Talkha fertilizer plant; and *'Ummal Shubra al-Khayma* [Shubra al-Khayma Workers] for the Shubra al-Khayma area.

27. *Qadaya Fikriyya* (al-Tabaqa al-'amila al-misriyya: al-turath, al-hadir, afaq al-mustaqbal), no. 5 (May 1987). The editor of *Qadaya Fikriyya*, Mahmud Amin al-'Alim, is considered to be a leading member of the Communist Party of Egypt.

28. Taha Sa'd 'Uthman, "al-Iltizam wa'l-mawdu'iyya fi kitabat ta'rikh al-tabaqa al-'amila al-misriyya," in *Ta'rikh misr bayna al-manhaj al-'ilmi wa'l-sira' al-hizbi: a'mal nadwat "al-iltizam wa'l-mawdu'iyya fi kitabat ta'rikh misr al-mu'asir," 1919–1952, al-qahira, 1987*, ed. Ahmad 'Abd Allah (Cairo, 1988), p. 289.

29. Taha Sa'd 'Uthman, *Min ta'rikh al-tabaqa al-'amila al-misriyya: mudhakkirat wa-watha'iq*, 3 vols.: *al-kitab al-thani* (Cairo, 1982); *al-kitab al-awwal: kifah 'unmal al-nasij* (Shubra al-Khayma, 1983); *al-kitab al-thalith: al-tabaqa al-'amila wa'l-'amal al-siyasi* (Cairo, 1988).

30. For example, the editorial of *Awraq 'Ummaliyya*, no. 6 (April 1986): 1, obliquely defended the prohibition of strikes by the Nasserist regime.

31. Ahmad Sharaf al-Din, "Asrar madhbahat Kafr al-Dawwar," *Sawt al-'Amil* nos. 3–5 (October 1985, January 1986, April 1986). These articles are based on extensive historic research, and the author intends to see an expanded version published as a book. On the call for a workers' party and further criticism of the Nasserist regime, see Muhammad 'Abd al-Salam, "Wad' al-tabaqa al-'amila fi misr," *Sawt al-'Amil* no. 6 (May 1986): 11–17.

32. Joel Beinin and Zachary Lockman, *Workers on the Nile* (Princeton, N.J., 1987), pp. 4–5. Przeworski's current attraction to rational choice theory would probably lead him to reject this formulation now.

33. Michel Foucault, "Two Lectures," in *Power/Knowledge: Selected Interviews and Other Writings, 1972–1977* (New York, 1980), pp. 81, 83.

34. O'Hanlon, "Recovering the Subject," pp. 202–203.

35. Beinin and Lockman, *Workers on the Nile*, p. 8.

Eric Davis

10

History for the Many or History for the Few?
The Historiography of the Iraqi Working Class

One of the most radical working-class movements to appear in the Middle East developed in Iraq between the early 1930s and the 1958 Revolution. Encompassing workers from all sectors of the Iraqi economy, the movement exhibited a level of worker solidarity unparalleled in the region. Following the 1958 Revolution, labor radicalism began to decline and the Iraqi working class lost its prominent role in Iraqi politics. With the massacre or imprisonment of thousands of Iraqi communists and leftists following the 1963 coup d'etat that overthrew 'Abd al-Karim Qasim, the movement lost many of its leaders, and labor activism declined still further. Following the seizure of power in 1968 by a Ba'th party faction controlled by Saddam Husayn, workers became even more tightly controlled, particularly by state-dominated labor organizations formed to ensure worker quiescence.

The significance of the Iraqi working class lies not just in the rise and decline of its political power but also in the vision it proffered for Iraq's political, social, and cultural development. Put differently, the cooperation among the diverse ethnolinguistic and confessional groups that formed the Iraqi working class represented a view of Iraqi society that emphasized social justice and tolerance of cultural difference, what is referred to later as the progressive discourse of the Iraqi working class. Although fully supportive of Iraq's Arab character and committed to independence from British colonial control, working-class organizations emphasized the primacy of class over nation and the need for a cross-class alliance as a means of addressing Iraq's multiethnic and multi-confessional character. In their view, true democracy could be achieved only if Iraq were freed from colonial domination, class inequality, *and* cultural repression.[1]

In light of the chauvinist nationalism used by the Iraqi state to justify the recent invasions of Iran and Kuwait, the history of the Iraqi working class assumes added significance. The emphasis of working-class organizations on cross-cultural and multiethnic alliances stands in stark contrast to the thinly veiled racism and politics of exclusion promoted by the state under the Arab Socialist Ba'th party. Understanding why the Ba'th party's vision of society prevailed over that advocated by the Iraqi working class, the Communist party, and their leftist supporters requires a historical analysis and answers to a number of prior questions.

First, how was it possible for such a high degree of worker radicalism to develop during the prerevolutionary period? If politics in Iraq is in fact governed by ethnic and confessional cleavages, how were labor organizations able to recruit workers from such a wide variety of ethnolinguistic and confessional backgrounds? Equally important, why did worker radicalism dissipate so quickly after the 1958 Revolution? What are the implications of these developments for the role of workers in politics, not only in Iraq but elsewhere in the Arab world? For those who have argued for an inexorable march in the Middle East toward greater political participation and equality following the overthrow of monarchies and their replacement by radical nationalist regimes espousing leftist ideologies, the history of the Iraqi working class may be less than encouraging. Nevertheless, despite its ultimate failure to enact its vision, Iraqi working-class history offers great inspiration not only to those political movements that oppose the Ba'thist regime in Baghdad but to labor movements outside Iraq as well.

Rethinking Working-Class History: Concepts and Method

As implied by this volume's title, rethinking working-class history entails an reexamination of past research, offering alternative ways of viewing such research, and posing new conceptual frameworks for the study of labor activism. Beyond these concerns, the history of the Iraqi working class poses an additional question. If the decline in this class's political activism represents a historical experience specific to Iraq—an "internal problematic" as it were—then the question remains what those who are not part of this experience, such as Western academics, hope to accomplish through studying it. Clearly, scholars studying working-class movements in the Middle East (and elsewhere in the Third World) hope their work will encourage greater distribution of wealth and political power and increased life chances for the poor, women, and culturally oppressed minorities. The choice of working-class movements as a topic of study, then, reflects a desire to contribute toward positive social change in the Middle East. What contribution can research and writing by those outside Iraq make, and what form should this take? Why are we writing about workers whose cultures and political practices are very different from our own? Who constitutes our audience(s), and what do we wish to convey to it (them)? In short, what do we hope to accomplish through our writing?

Cynics might argue that Western academic interest in Middle Eastern workers represents a subtle form of Orientalism. Although the object of study differs from the classic concerns of Orientalists, it might be seen as yet another form of the "escape into the exotic." This would be especially true if such study allowed academics to enjoy vicarious political participation through the action of Middle East workers given declining participation and relative political passivity in the West. This form of "Third Worldism" could be seen as pernicious if it were meant to leave to Third World workers the role of active agency in bringing about progressive social change while abdicating a responsibility to enact social change "at home."

To avoid confusion, Western researchers need to make explicit how they view their subject and what they hope to accomplish in examining it. One way of achieving this end is through linking our writing on Iraqi or other Third World workers to American society. Workers in the West and those who advocate a "politics of tolerance" have much to learn from the Iraqi working class. In making such linkages, we offset the potential, however unintentional, to construct more binary oppositions juxtaposing "us" to "them" and to transform Iraqi workers into yet another exotic element of Third World culture that remains beyond comprehension, thereby "proving" once again the impenetrability of Third World society. In my view, the problematic of the Iraqi working class is centered around the issues of oppression, cultural difference, and participation: oppression in the sense that workers in Iraq as in most other countries have suffered greatly both from existing working conditions and the consequences of their own efforts to improve these conditions; cultural difference in the sense that opposition to working-class demands represents a metaphor of the refusal of successive groups that have controlled the Iraqi state to accept the notion of Iraq as a multiethnic, multiconfessional, and multilinguistic society; and participation in the sense that workers have largely been excluded from political and economic decision making in Iraq.

Our efforts should be directed at expanding Western consciousness about the relationship between what transpires in Iraq and what occurs in our own society. With the end of superpower conflict and the threat of thermonuclear war, the global cleavage pitting the industrialized "North" against the underdeveloped "South" has assumed greater prominence as demonstrated by the recent Gulf War. Considering the everincreasing economic interrelationship of the two regions, it behooves citizens of advanced industrialized countries to adopt at least an empathetic if not sympathetic perspective toward non-Western societies. If only on practical, if not on moral-ethical, grounds, the continued economic deterioration of the Third World, of which the oppressive conditions of workers and other sectors of the lower classes represent the most serious manifestation, bodes ill for the continued economic prosperity of the advanced industrialized countries.

More directly, it has been argued that the United States has intervened in the internal politics of Iraq on numerous occasions. From the formative American role in establishing the 1955 Baghdad Pact, to the alleged role played by the Central Intelligence Agency in the overthrow of the Qasim regime in 1963, and the significant contributions by the Reagan and Bush administrations (as well as other European states) to the economic and military strength of Saddam Husayn's regime prior to the August 1990 invasion of Kuwait, the United States bears its share of responsibility for political developments in Iraq.[2] In this respect, far from representing an "exotic other" that bears no relationship to American society, the Iraqi working class, and the larger society of which it is a part, has suffered from the United States' complicity in backing repressive regimes in Iraq.

Marxism and the Study of Working-Class History

The shadow that has haunted all studies of working-class history in the Middle East is Marxian political economy. For many Marxist theorists who have studied the Middle East, the development of capitalist relations of production, the region's integration into the world market, the spread of nationalism, the overthrow of monarchies and their replacement by republican regimes, the nationalization of foreign and domestic industry, and perhaps most important the radicalization of sectors of the working class, peasantry, students, and intelligentsia all augured well for the ultimate development of socialism.[3] However, actual historical change has not borne out this optimism. The ascendancy of Nasserism in Egypt, Ba'thism in Syria and Iraq, Algerian socialism, and other forms of radical Arab nationalism such as Mu'ammar al-Qadhdhafi's blend of Arabism and Islam have not necessarily led to a more liberatory politics in these societies or a more equitable distribution of economic wealth. In certain respects, workers, peasants, and students possessed greater autonomy to engage in political protest prior to the coming to power of purported revolutionary regimes than afterward.[4] With the rise of what 'Issam al-Khafaji has called *state capitalism* [*al-ra'smaliyya al-dawliyya*] and its attendant "parasitic bourgeoisie" [*al-burjuwaziyya al-tufayliyya*], social inequality and standards of living in the Arab countries that experienced radical nationalist revolutions have not changed significantly since the overthrow of the ancient regimes.[5]

A core problem that has afflicted many studies of working-class movements and broader political economies of the Middle East that were strongly influenced by Marxism is the notion that the understanding of social change in the region could be derived from the application of "science" and the development of "laws" of historical movement. This understanding is highly reified and ethnocentric because it is based on the historical model presented in *Das Kapital*, which in turn is derived from the Western tradition, particularly the British experience. Recent works such as Chakrabarty's study of Indian jute workers demonstrate all too clearly the fallacies inherent in the attempts to apply uncritically Western models of social change that are based in universalistic-scientific notions to an understanding of worker consciousness, activism, and solidarity.[6] If anything, workers today play a more diminished role in Arab politics than they did during the 1940s and 1950s, if strikes, political demonstrations, and the number of independent worker organizations are used as indicators of political participation.[7] In Egypt, Syria, Iraq, and Algeria, replacing the ancien regime with radical nationalist elites did not lead to greater social equality but rather to the rise of new bourgeoisies closely tied to the state.

Making sense of the Iraqi working class necessitates the "deconstruction" of much of the teleological thinking in the Marxian paradigm as it has been applied to the Middle East. One of the first Marxists to grasp the importance of transcending a narrow class analysis in an effort to understand the potentialities for workers and members of the lower classes to confront political and economic oppression was Antonio Gramsci. In attributing great significance to the impact of nationalism, Gramsci not only called attention to the need to situate workers in a broader social context but also to the need to integrate culture and ideology into any study of social change.

In many respects, Gramsci's analysis of *risorgimento* Italy is highly relevant to the Middle East, particularly Iraq. Rather than confronted with a working class struggling to expand its political freedom and economic power within an established nation-state and well-defined system of hegemony, Gramsci instead faced a labor movement that functioned within a nascent political community in which there was considerable dissent over the definition of national identity. The lack of agreement over the concept of the Italian nation-state, strong regional loyalties that countervailed allegiances to a central state, and the significant geographical discrepancy of wealth between the northern and southern portions of the country remind us of many of the problems faced by twentieth century postcolonial Arab countries. Because the contours of the Iraqi nation-state were being debated in the 1920s at the same time as the formation of the Iraqi working class (paralleling the Italian situation somewhat earlier), class and national consciousness were intertwined. As both countries were also seeking to shed foreign domination, clearly each case requires a focus on both class and nation when analyzing working-class consciousness.

Among Gramsci's most important contributions for understanding social change are his notions of the "historical bloc," the "organic intellectuals," and the "war of position."[8] The notion of a historical bloc is based on the premise that no political regime can rule for long if it is unable to convince subaltern groups that its interests coincide with their own. This structure of thought expands the ideological-cultural component of class struggle and draws us away from simply envisioning this process in terms of overt conflict. For Gramsci, subaltern groups must internalize the ideology of the ruling class if that class is to exercise what he calls *hegemony*.

The notion of the "organic intellectuals" is thus key to Gramsci's thinking because each class must have members who articulate its interests and aspirations. These organic intellectuals engage in a "war of position" in articulating contending visions of the future that compete in the public sphere for the allegiances of social groups. In this conceptual framework, history and myth become intertwined as ruling groups in particular seek to promote a socially constructed past that serves their interests while simultaneously obscuring the contributions of the subaltern classes to historical change and social development. In trying to understand the development of working-class politics in Iraq, a key question would be the extent to which the organic intellectuals of the working class were able to articulate a vision that not only appealed to workers but also to potential allies among other classes or social groups. To what extent were they able to forge a counterhegemonic "historical bloc?"

In arguing that much if not most historical writing is socially constructed, Gramsci anticipated many elements of more recent phenomenological and poststructuralist writings. Because historical writing has been dominated largely by the ruling classes, it conforms more to myth than to some notion of objective truth. As such, it must be "deconstructed" for subaltern groups to gain a better sense of their own place in history.[9] The organic intellectuals of the working class are key in helping to promote this understanding. A number of questions that need to be asked in the Iraqi context are how has the history of the Iraqi working class been constructed, why has it been constructed in certain ways, and what has been the impact of this construction both on the working class's ability to improve its situation and the larger society of which it is a part?

For Marxist theory, the impact of Gramsci's writings has been to both enrich the study of working-class movements and in a curious sense, to undermine it. Gramsci's statement that "every man (woman?) is a philosopher" indicates his rejection of the image of the industrial worker that pervades socialist realism, both in its literary form and in visual representation. In place of the heroic worker who unquestioningly follows the vanguard party's directives in the struggle for socialism, an image that dominated Leninist and Stalinist readings of Marx, Gramsci substitutes a more fluid scenario in which workers assess their own interests and provide indicators to their leaders as to when efforts to bring about revolutionary transformation are appropriate.

Gramsci's approach endows Marxism with greater flexibility, but it erodes its more traditional (and positivist) linear form by demonstrating that the outcome of history is not preordained. The potential for multiple levels of consciousness historically relativizes processes of social change. Within this analytic framework, class consciousness is no longer shaped and molded in some rigid and fixed sense by "material conditions." Because workers act on historical forces as much as they are acted on by them, the trajectory of "history" can no longer be that confidently predicted. In other words, the logical outcome of a humanist as opposed to a Leninist reading of Gramsci is to chip away at notions of teleology and "scientific" understanding of the role of the working class in social change.[10] If we examine Gramsci's writings on Italy, it is clear that he was well aware of the possibilities of regional, religious, and nationalist identities acting as cross-cutting cleavages to undermine working-class solidarity.[11] Thus working-class consciousness, the direction of social change, and the potential for worker solidarity all become more problematic than in "economistic" readings of Marxist theory.

In seeking to free the study of working-class history from the shackles of economism and positivism, does not Gramsci's theoretical fluidity ultimately deny the working class any privileged position in the process of social change? In other words, if worker responses to material conditions are not predetermined and are open to wide variation, in what sense does "the working class" retain its significance as an object of study? The problem of theoretical arguments that profess universalistic application has been compounded by recent anti-Orientalist, post-structuralist, and postmodernist critiques. Although the critique of Orientalism seems first and foremost an attack on ethnocentrism in Western research, the efforts of poststructuralism and postmodernism seem more closely tied to attempts to break down binary oppositions, linear notions of progress, and male-centered theories while simultaneously introducing greater conceptual anarchy into the approaches brought to the study of social and cultural change. The impact of these critiques has been to erode the notion of a unified vision or predetermined historical outcome. From feminist and Third World perspectives, the notion of "a vision" is often seen as an exercise in power whereby white, economically privileged Western men impose their own understanding of the force and direction of social change under the guise of objective theory.[12] In examining workers, how can an implicit teleological argument that somehow history is being made by the working class and will ultimately lead to the implementation of socialism be avoided?

A volume on Middle East labor history necessarily privileges workers, if only by making them the central focus of study. What form does this privileging take? Certainly, Western scholars' interest in workers reflects a reaction to the emphasis of Orientalism and modernization theory on the role of "Great Men of History" and political, economic, and cultural elites. There has been an attempt to rectify the shortcomings of "top-down" history with history from the "bottom up." The focus on excluded groups fills important lacunae, but how does studying workers assist in transcending the conceptual shortcomings of prior paradigms? If the study of workers is not limited to performing an "additive function," namely, filling in the empirical or descriptive gaps left by the prior research of Orientalists and modernization theorists, then students of labor movements in the Middle East need to be concerned with developing new conceptual approaches as well.

In understanding social change in a capitalist or nascent capitalist economy, Marxian political economy privileges workers in at least two ways. First, following the labor theory of value, workers are conceptualized as residing in the "bowels of the whale." Put differently, because workers are most intimately linked to social reproduction by producing surplus value through their labor power, they, more than any other social group, experience society's tensions or contradictions most directly and severely. Through studying workers, then, one presumably obtains the most authentic understanding of the fundamental stresses and strains of a capitalist system, whether nascent or fully developed.

This assumption makes sense because an understanding of the Iraqi working class's development tells us much about why Iraq has experienced such violence during the twentieth century, why the Iraqi Communist party was able to acquire such a large following, and why the country has experienced revolutionary upheaval. Not only did the Iraqi working class experience many of the social tensions of Iraqi society but it also actively strove to bring about social change through strikes, by participating in mass demonstrations and educational programs, and in supporting forces seeking to bring about social change.[13] Thus Iraqi workers can be seen as both reflecting social tensions and as agents seeking to bring about change to relieve these tensions.

However, to argue that the study of workers allows the researcher to grasp fundamental characteristics of ongoing social change does not necessarily require acceptance of the labor theory of value or a teleological view of history. It does not necessarily mean that, in some abstract or reified sense, workers are more important than, say, women, or confessional or ethnolinguistic groups, in understanding social change or that they will necessarily at some point in the future seize control of the state.

The application of other concepts of Marxist theory are also problematic. The notion of the development of the forces of production has served an important heuristic function as well as an empirical function. One of the most obvious examples is the introduction of the assembly line into modern industrial production, which led Gramsci to formulate his concept of "Fordism."[14] However, to attempt to derive a projection of working-class behavior and consciousness from a change in the forces of production is highly problematic. The mode of production—the more inclusive concept from which the forces of production is drawn—can also be problematic if efforts are made to deduce the types of behavior that workers should be expected to engage in given the level of development of the (capitalist) mode of production.

In summary, a study of Iraqi working-class history will not necessarily yield any predictions about the future. No teleology can be derived from the study of Iraqi workers. Indeed, to attempt to do so is, at one level, to rob workers of their own agency. Care must be taken not to confuse what is seen as scientific prediction with a normative imposition of what we feel Iraqi workers "should" do. We should even be skeptical of the notion of *the* history of the working class, as if it were some type of objective reality in a positivist sense. Instead, I would suggest the contingent nature of all existing histories in that each is socially constructed and each reflects, in the elements or events it emphasizes, its own normative proclivities. Because access to these histories is largely filtered through "organic intellectuals," whether of the state or the working class itself, it behooves us to examine the role of intellectuals in the presentation of histories of the Iraqi working class.

These arguments do not represent a plea for theoretical anarchy or even solipsism. They neither deny the utility of Marxist concepts, which often serve important heuristic functions, nor do they suggest that we avoid making predictions. Rather the thrust of the arguments is for the need for a broader epistemological and conceptual terrain within which to understand workers and their actions. It was precisely the narrowness of the Iraqi Communist party's conceptualization of the Iraqi working class that helps answer a question posed earlier. In assuming that the revolutionary overthrow of the Iraqi monarchy in 1958 represented a major step forward in an inevitable coming to power of the working class and other subaltern groups such as the peasantry, the Iraqi Communist party seriously underestimated the extent to which large segments of the middle and lower middle classes opposed such an outcome. The massacre and imprisonment of thousands of communists and leftist sympathizers, labor leaders, and workers in 1963 following the overthrow of the Qasim regime was the ultimate and tragic demonstration of the shortcomings of this thinking.

What these observations indicate is the crucial character of Cramsci's notion of the "war of position." How a sociopolitical group or movement views the world and its ability to articulate that vision to the larger society is crucial to its success or failure in achieving its goals. The Iraqi working class possessed tremendous political support during the 1940s and 1950s but was unable to ultimately translate this support into political power. Without reducing the Iraqi working class's historical experience to the realm of conceptualization, many of its problems resided in its faulty vision of social change. Conversely, the vision of radical Arab nationalism in the form of the Ba'thism, however unattractive, proved more effective in capturing the political mood and imagination of the postrevolutionary era. With these thoughts in mind, what do competing historiographies of the Iraqi working class tell us about the visions and strategies that contending political forces in Iraqi society have used in relation to the working class and how they affected its fortunes?

Competing Historiographies of the Iraqi Working Class

In making conceptual sense of Iraqi working-class history, existing writings may be divided among three historiographical approaches.[15] Chronologically, the first to appear is what we might term the *Orientalist* historiography of the working class. Expressed in British and American consular reports, in studies by colonial officials and businessmen, in Western newspaper articles, and in incidental comments in travelogues, this perspective most often viewed Iraqi workers with disdain and condescension.[16] A second historiography emerges from the writings of Iraqi communists and leftists. Articulated in pamphlets, speeches, and newspaper articles during the 1930s, 1940s, and 1950s, this literature portrayed the Iraqi working class as the vanguard of social change in ridding Iraq of Western imperialism and developing a democratic society in which minority rights would be respected. Since the 1970s, this writing has taken the form of longer articles, primarily in the Iraqi Communist party's journal, *al-Thaqafa al-Jadida,* in the journal of the Center of Socialist

Research and Studies in the Arab World, *al-Nahj*, and in a number of book-length studies.[17] A third type of historiography has been defined largely by Ba'thist ideology. This represents the most recent writing on the Iraqi working class and has taken the forms of newspaper and journal articles, a limited number of monographs, and most recently, an examination of the portrayal of workers in Iraqi literature.[18]

Who Is a Worker?

In these writings, what exactly is meant by the Iraqi working class? If little has been written on Iraqi workers considering their significant role in twentieth century Iraqi politics, there has been even less reflection on what the term *worker* or *working class* actually connotes. Whether in Orientalist, Marxist, or Ba'thist writings, petty merchants, artisans, industrial workers, and service workers are often lumped together conceptually as an undifferentiated mass. Although all sectors of the working class exhibited radicalism from the 1930s onward, industrial and service workers sustained a higher level of political activism over time than petty merchants and artisans, who are also categorized as workers. Conceptual reflection on what it means to be a worker is not an issue treated systematically in the existing literature.

How are we to understand the concept of worker in Iraqi society? This is not an abstract question as different types of workers demonstrated varying levels of political activism. Why, for example, did railway workers, port workers in Basra, oil workers, and workers on British military bases exhibit a more sustained level of radicalism than workers in the traditional craft and small industrial sectors in urban areas, especially Baghdad?

Gramsci's notion of the historical bloc is instructive here. The closer ties of urban artisans and craftsmen to members of the commercial middle class, due especially to a certain level of shared financial interests, meant that it was easier for nationalist ideas to penetrate this stratum of workers. Because more prosperous (but by no means wealthy) merchants often appropriated the role of organic intellectuals for artisans and craft workers, class consciousness seems to have been increasingly subordinated among these laborers to the more corporatist form of nationalism articulated by the urban middle classes during the 1930s and 1940s. A good case in point is Ja'far Abu Timman—a representative of middle-level merchants in Baghdad, president of the chamber of commerce, and the leader of the nationalist Ahali group—who was able to assume the role of spokesman for artisans and crafts workers.[19] Unfortunately, among the three historiographies, only Ba'thist writings discuss the appropriation of the oppositional voice of workers by other groups or social classes. However, this concern is treated ideologically rather than analytically. That is, Ba'thist historians' concern with this issue extends only to asserting that Ba'th party members played key leadership roles in strikes and other labor actions in helping workers achieve their goals. Their comments shed little light on why some workers actually allowed their goals to be articulated by organic intellectuals from outside their ranks.

Viewed from "the bottom up," it can be argued that, having often been urban residents for at least several generations, many artisans and craft workers did not experience the sense of dislocation experienced by workers in more recently established sectors of the Iraqi economy, such as the rail system, the port of Basra, military bases, and oil installations. The development of a significant labor force outside the traditional craft sector began with a short section of the Iraqi state railways that was completed prior to World War I as part of the German effort to construct a Berlin to Baghdad railroad. It was only after the war that the railway began to expand throughout the country and a large work force was hired. Likewise, economic activity in the port of Basra increased dramatically after the war's end with Great Britain's occupation of the country, leading to an increase in the size of the work force there as well. Similarly, once Iraq was placed under mandatory status by the League of Nations, the establishment of military bases led the British to recruit large numbers of Iraqi workers to service these installations. However, the Iraqi oil industry produced the largest increase in workers. By the end of the 1920s, the Iraq Petroleum Company (formerly the Turkish Petroleum Company) had significantly increased its production following the signing of a concessionary agreement with the Iraqi government in 1925. Large numbers of workers were needed not only to operate the oil fields but also to lay the lengthy pipelines needed to transport the oil to terminals.[20]

In discussing the rise of working-class consciousness, little effort has been made to link its development to the weak sense of nationhood that existed in Iraq during the formative period of the working class. Apart from the urban artisan and crafts sector, the vast majority of workers in newly established industries and British military bases were peasants who were recent migrants from rural areas, particularly southern Iraq.[21] These peasants, who were forced to migrate to urban areas by the deterioration of the agricultural sector and oppression by tribal shaykh-landlords, brought with them very little loyalty to any national boundaries or national consciousness. Many already had a history of political activism, having been involved in the 1920 Iraqi Revolution against the British, in struggles with the shaykhs and their agents, the sirkals, or in struggles with other tribes over agricultural land.[22] In light of their participation in previous conflict and their lack of or weak ties to urban social structures, peasants who became workers were particularly susceptible to developing incipient forms of class consciousness and, conversely, often not susceptible to internalizing forms of consciousness derived from classes higher up in the social order. In short, these workers often demonstrated greater class solidarity than support for the Arab nationalism of the middle classes.[23]

The impact of rural-urban migration on the formation and development of the Iraqi working class still waits to be explored. Did migrant peasants retain their sense of rural origins once they entered the industrial labor force?[24] To what extent did prior conflict with tribal shaykhs condition them to adopt radical political perspectives? Was worker solidarity strengthened by the fact that peasants from particular areas tended to congregate in certain industries, thereby combining preexisting ties, particularly clan identity, with new forms of solidarity? Because migration continues unabated and is considered potentially threatening by the state, as evidenced by its efforts to return peasants to the countryside, this issue requires far more analysis than it has received to date.[25]

Social Differentiation of the Iraqi Working Class

Apart from scattered references by communist intellectuals, the question of gender is largely absent from definitions of who is a worker.[26] Most (male) writers assume that to discuss an Iraqi worker means a male worker. The extent of female participation in the labor force remains largely unexamined. Nor has the relationship between family structure and worker radicalism been explored. To what extent did the deprivations that Iraqi workers suffered at the hands of foreign companies and the Iraqi government adversely affect the family and how did this in turn influence workers in their ability to organize themselves? Put differently, the lack of any systematic study of the interaction between public and private spheres and its impact on worker activism and solidarity demonstrates an insensitivity among both Arab and non-Arab students of the Iraqi working class to the impact of gender relations and family structure.

One of the most contentious issues in discussing Iraqi society is its ethnolinguistic and confessional composition. Communist intellectuals strongly emphasize that party-led worker organizations that opposed the British and the monarchy drew upon workers from all social strata of Iraqi society. Indeed, one of the party's strongest claims to legitimacy derives from its argument that, alone among contending ideologies, its ideology offered the only means to integrate Iraq's major ethnic groups through emphasizing solidarity based on class rather than Arabism. Nevertheless, among publically available documents, only Western diplomatic correspondence and reports openly discuss the issue of ethnic diversity. As might be expected, diplomatic documents use ethnolinguistic and confessional differences to construct a conceptual prism through which all political and social behavior is evaluated.[27] The analytic silence on this issue is striking in both Marxist and Ba'thist historiography. For Marxists, social difference is simply overcome within the working class (and peasantry) through class solidarity. Ba'thists refuse to recognize that social difference has ever been politically salient in Iraqi society. To the extent that it is recognized, Ba'thists argue that such consciousness resulted from colonial attempts to divide and conquer the populace. Because colonial domination has ended, so too has the problem. The failure of both Iraqi and Western writers of varying ideological perspectives to systematically examine internal differentiations among Iraqi workers represents another serious shortcoming of existing studies.[28]

Periodization

Although often implicit in their writings, the issue of periodization is rarely made explicit by students of the Iraqi working class. The most comprehensive study of the Iraqi working class, the lengthy doctoral thesis by 'Abd al-Razzaq Mutlaq al-Fahd, focuses on the period between 1922 and 1959.[29] Al-Fahd divides his study into two sections: the first covers the period between 1922 and 1937, during which workers directed their efforts at organizing unions or syndicates (*al-niqabat*), and the second encompasses the years between 1944 and 1958, when workers began to play a more active role in politics. (The war years are not treated because they are said to constitute an exceptional or atypical period for the working class, which is highly peculiar given the level of strikes and demonstrations during the war.) The other comprehensive study is that by Kamal Mazhar Ahmad, who concentrates on the formation of the Iraqi working class and the beginnings of its political activities during the early 1930s.[30]

Sympathetic to a Marxist perspective, both al-Fahd and Ahmad see a working class that formed in reaction to imperialism and made a major contribution to the nationalist struggle against colonial domination. Both studies offer a tremendous amount of documentation, particularly on the manner in which workers were affected by socioeconomic conditions such as the impact of foreign capital, the decline of agriculture, and its impact on rural-urban migration and urban unemployment. Despite an impressive command of empirical data and strong sympathies for their subject matter, a linear quality pervades these studies. The model proffered suggests that changing material conditions led workers to reflect on their lives and move to organize unions to protect their interests. The authors seem to assume that once British colonial rule and the ancien regime were defeated, the working class was destined to achieve true liberation. Despite the benefit of hindsight, nowhere is the authors' analysis sensitive to the multifaceted character of workers' struggles. For example, what types of problems were developing within the Iraqi nationalist movement, particularly between workers and the middle classes, during the 1930s and 1940s? It is understandable that, with attention focused on ridding Iraq of British colonial domination and overthrowing the monarchy and the corrupt parliamentary regime, those writing during the 1930s, 1940s, and 1950s might have been less aware of the potential contradiction between workers and sectors of the lower middle and lower classes, but the absence of any sense of such a tension in writings of the 1970s and 1980s is striking. This problem assumes even greater significance considering that the middle classes would later usurp the power of the workers once radical nationalist regimes came to power. Indeed, one of the major shortcomings of the working class's leadership, particularly that element drawn from the Iraqi Communist party, was its inability to protect the flanks of the labor movement through developing more ties to nationalist elements of the middle class. Unfortunately, Ahmad and al-Fahd's method of periodization, as with most other leftist and Marxist writers, offers limited analytic insights because, organized around dates corresponding to worker efforts to organize unions and mobilize strikes, it remains largely descriptive.

Ba'thist Historiography: The View of the State

Ba'thist historiography of the Iraqi working class faces a number of problems. First, unlike the Iraqi Communist party, the Arab Ba'th Socialist party cannot draw on a long history of support for and leadership of the working class. In the numerous strikes and demonstrations in which workers participated prior to the 1958 Revolution, it was invariably the Iraqi Communist party that provided a crucial leadership role. Viewing this history in retrospect, Ba'thist intellectuals in Iraq can draw only on party proclamations supporting worker rights that began to be issued in Iraq during the early 1950s. Furthermore, much of the Ba'th party's support of worker rights occurred not in Iraq but in Syria and Lebanon.[31] Given the inability of the Ba'th party to compete with the Iraqi Communist party for historical legitimacy in supporting the advancement of worker rights, how do Ba'thist intellectuals confront this problem?

One mechanism is to organize the periodization of working-class history around the 1952 Intifada and the period thereafter because, apart from written documents expressing support, this was the first time that the Ba'th party actively intervened in labor struggles.[32] Another means is to conflate class and nationalist struggles. In this reading of modern Iraqi history, workers played a crucial but not decisive role in the events that led up to the overthrow of the monarchy in 1958. In other words, class struggle is in no way given a privileged position in the process of historical change. Because Iraqi communists would argue that workers dominated the political space in which opposition to the ancien regime was organized, an argument with which I would largely agree, to see workers as just one among many social forces that struggled against the monarchy and British colonial control is to downplay their historical contribution. In their own rendering of working-class history, Ba'thist intellectuals emphasize the primacy of nation and national consciousness. The question of whether these concepts obscure class or group interests is never raised. Quotes from the writings of Ba'thist ideologues such as Michel 'Aflaq, Ilyas Farah, and Shibli al-'Aysami, from party conference reports, and from the speeches of Saddam Husayn are deemed sufficient proof that party and working class interests are synonomous.

Another characteristic of Ba'thist historiography is to subsume worker activity under the leadership of other groups. During the postrevolutionary period, especially after 1963 and even more so after 1968, this takes the form of Ba'th party leadership that supposedly instills in workers an understanding of their class interests and national responsibilities.[33] In treating the pre-1958 period, an even more pernicious form of rewriting labor history is to portray worker political activism as merely an extension of the manipulative politics of competing factions of the corrupt parliamentary elite that ruled in conjunction with the monarchy. A prominent example of this type of historiography is a study of the 1931 general strike protesting a law by the British that imposed a series of municipal fees or taxes on urban merchants, artisans, and vendors (*qanun rusum al-baladiyyat*). Although accepting the standard historical interpretation that the strike was organized by the Association of Iraqi Artisans (*jam'iyyat ashab al-sana'i'*), the author, Sami 'Abd al-Hafiz al-Qaysi, argues that, once the association's president, Muhammad Salih al-Qazzaz, requested help from Yasin al-Hashimi, the leader of the parliamentary opposition, against the prime minister at the time, Nuri Sa'id, the strike was transformed from "a worker demonstration to a political weapon in the hands of the parliamentary opposition."[34]

Despite its revolutionary pretensions, Ba'th party emphasis on the central role of elites rather than the workers themselves in its own interpretations of working-class history demonstrates a curious conflation of Orientalism and Leninism. Ba'thist writings parallel those of British and American diplomats in Iraq during the prerevolutionary period who constantly observed that, were it not for outside agitators, particularly communists, workers would not have engaged in violent activity or held out for "unreasonable demands.[35] Both Orientalist and Ba'thist historiography implicitly deny the working class the right of agency to determine its own future. Workers are viewed as childlike and politically immature and hence incapable of undertaking any independent political activity on their own. This view also dovetails with the Leninist principles on which the Ba'th party was modeled in which the vanguard party imparts revolutionary consciousness to subaltern groups. In both structures of thought, little or no effort is made to view the world from a perspective gained from consultation with workers themselves such as espoused, for example, by Gramsci.

A third characteristic of Ba'thist historiography of the Iraqi working class is what may be termed *formalism*. In discussing the period following the 1963 overthrow of 'Abd al-Karim Qasim, the emphasis is not on actual working conditions but rather on laws implemented by successive governments under the Ba'th to improve working conditions. The few Ba'thist studies of Iraqi working-class history manifest a curious dualism. Following the traditional chronology of worker activism against British colonial rule and the monarchy prior to 1958, they employ an empirical approach, albeit one that downplays the leadership role of the Iraqi Communist party and the achievements of worker organizations independent of nationalist political elites. In writing about the period after 1958, and especially after 1963, empirical analysis gives way to a formal-legalistic approach that assumes that class conflict and exploitation no longer exist and that the interests of the state and the working class converge. A patronizing tone imbues these writings, as workers are admonished to live up to their national responsibilities, particularly through striving to increase levels of productivity in Iraqi industry.[36]

The analyses of Ba'thist intellectuals, both those writing directly about the working class and those writing about Iraqi industry, demonstrate the impact of Western writings on industrial management. These writings are distinguished by their emphasis on abstract notions of efficiency and their complete ahistoricism.[37] In this respect, Ba'thist conceptions of politics spill over into the socioeconomic sphere. Political history as well as socioeconomic history begin in 1963, once the first Ba'thist regime came to power. After 1968, history is replaced by abstract conceptions of utility, rationality, and efficiency. That is, all group and individual interests are subordinated to the needs of the corporatist nationalism of the Ba'th in which the highest emphasis is placed upon economic and military growth and greater efficiency in political repression (although, of course, the latter goal is never officially stated). If Iraqi Marxism bears witness to the shortcomings of teleological thinking, Ba'thism offers us the ahistoricism of a neo-Taylorism. In this latter discourse, working-class history is lost altogether.

Other forms of Ba'thist writings that bear upon Iraqi workers likewise assume a patronizing and instrumentalist perspective. For example, workers are discussed in relation to illiteracy campaigns and how they may be enticed (forced?) to join them.[38] Programs of reverse migration are discussed for peasants and unemployed workers, who are seen as better served by returning to the countryside.[39] In the name of revolutionary ideology, the Ba'thist regime has worked to obliterate the historical memory of Iraqi workers, which is a prerequisite for the type of abstract categorizing of workers that allows them to be ideologically channeled in directions that benefit those who control the state.

The Progressive Discourse of the Iraqi Working Class

If studying Iraqi working-class history does not allow us to model the future, to make any necessary predictions about the direction of social change in Iraq, in what sense does it contribute to a more liberatory politics inside and outside of Iraq? I would suggest that a study of Iraqi workers underlines the fallacies inherent in Eurocentric notions of history, particularly Orientalist discourse. It also helps us to better understand the current regime's efforts to rewrite the history of the Iraqi working class in ways that are intended to manipulate workers and increase their subordination to the state. Progressive discourse, then, signifies that the history of the Iraqi working class provides us with a deeper understanding not only of the main contours of social change in twentieth century Iraq but also of the possibilities for greater social justice in Iraqi society.

The Fallacy of the Sunni-Shiite-Kurdish Triad

An examination of Iraqi workers during the twentieth century demonstrates the fallacy of viewing Iraqi society through a conceptual lens that portrays historical change as governed by an unholy trinity that pits Sunnis, Shiites, and Kurds against one another. Contrary to Orientalist understandings of Iraqi society in which the logic of collective action is reduced to essentialist notions of ethnolinguistic and confessional identity, studying Iraqi workers demonstrates that, to the extent that confessional differences have divided Iraqi society, they have been most influential among the *upper and middle* and not the lower classes. Indeed, it was the "liberal" politicians of the monarchical period and the factions of the military, Ba'th party, and Nasserists that came to power after 1958, rather than workers and peasants, who attributed the most significance to these categories. Indeed, this is overwhelmingly substantiated in Western diplomatic sources and leftist studies of the working class.[40]

What is again striking about the working class is that ethnolinguistic and confessional differences did not play a significant role in breaking down worker solidarity or impeding political activity. In the worker activism documented by al-Fahd during the late 1940s and early 1950s in the oil fields, in the Iraqi state railways, in the port of Basra and on British military bases, what is most striking was the inability of the British or Iraqi authorities to use social difference as a mechanism for dividing workers. The strength of class solidarity demonstrated by workers, particularly during strikes, buttresses the Iraqi Communist party's claim that class solidarity can transcend ethnolinguistic and confessional cleavages.

In many ways, then, the working class has historically displayed much greater "rationality" than the Iraqi bourgeoisie. In attributing causal primacy to a tripartite conflict centered around sociocultural differences that are conceptualized as immutable, Orientalist discourse implicitly tars the Iraqi populace with the brush of irrationality. In other words, Iraqis are seen as responding first and foremost to "primordial instincts" that take precedence over "rational calculations." To the extent that this model has any explanatory validity (and for reasons other than those posited by Orientalists), it applies most closely to the political elite of the pre-1958 era, which was composed of factions that coalesced around economic and political interests that defined themselves in sectarian terms. This same type of model could be applied to the post-1958 period, where regional-sectarian cleavages also help to explain elite behavior. Sunni-Takriti domination of the Iraqi state is the most prominent case in point. Where the Orientalists are wrong is in reducing all behavior to a sectarian dimension without realizing that sectarian, political, and economic interests are inextricably intertwined and to separate out one from the other yields only a partial analysis.

Where Orientalists are even more shortsighted is in including sectors of the lower classes under the sectarian rubric. In none of the strikes and worker demonstrations that I have examined did ethnolinguistic or confessional differences play any significant role in dividing worker loyalties. Indeed, Western diplomatic records, largely unsympathetic to worker demands, underline the tremendous amount of worker solidarity throughout strikes and demonstrations despite the use of armed force to bring them to an end.[41] Prior to 1958, the Iraqi working class maintained a corporate identity in formulating goals and maintained solidarity in achieving these goals to a much greater degree than did any of the political elites that have controlled the Iraqi state (or even the leadership of the Iraqi Communist party).

The Iraqi Working Class and the Notion of "Rational Choice"

If the historical experience of the Iraqi working class erodes the notion of Iraq as a society guided by immutable ethnolinguistic and confessional identities, then it also casts doubt on theories of rational choice that have gained popularity in recent years in the study of working-class movements.[42] As noted previously, one of the most striking characteristic of the Iraqi working class, especially prior to 1958, was its radical character. By radical I mean the struggle to gain an independent voice for labor organizations and to link the activities of these organizations not only to immediate working-class interests but also to larger questions of social, economic, political and cultural equity. The political activities of Iraqi workers help erode the notion of Third World peoples as passive, unaware of their vital interests, and unable to act collectively in "rational" ways designed to achieve specified ends. They thus raise questions as to whether rational choice theory, in which the concept of utility understood in an individualistic sense is given conceptual primacy, is really ethnocentric and ideological. The concept can be seen as ethnocentric, given its derivation from the Western historical experience (where its applicability is open to question), and ideological, as it is more normative than empirical, that is, rational choice becomes what ought to be and not just what is. In this sense, rational choice theory could be viewed as a form of neo-Orientalism. Unless Iraqi workers act according to an individual calculus based on acceptable Western norms, they are not viewed as engaged in "rational" behavior.

In many instances, strikes occurred where it would have been "rational" for workers to accept higher wages and improved working conditions and declare an end to their labor action. One example is the strike of oil workers in the Kirkuk oil fields in July 1946. Approximately 200 miles northeast of Baghdad, this region is particularly interesting given its ethnic mix of Kurds, Arabs, Turkomans and Assyrians. According to the predictions of rational choice theory, oil workers should have ended their strike once they achieved an improvement in material benefits. A rational calculus of costs and benefits should have bounded the strike. Nevertheless, workers frequently refused to return to work until what may be called political demands were met by foreign companies or the Iraqi authorities. These included such demands as the reinstatement of workers fired from their jobs due to political activism.[43] Clearly, this demand in no way advanced the material or other interests of striking workers who retained their positions. Furthermore, this demand runs against the notion of the "free rider" mentality that Mancur Olson and others have argued afflicts all collective organizations, particularly those organized around Marxian notions of class solidarity.[44]

Other demands included greater control by workers over the work environment; for example, a diminution of the power of supervisors and foremen to discipline workers. Workers consistently called for an end to the British occupation of Iraq and rule by corrupt politicians. Indeed, workers provided the backbone of the two largest uprisings against the Iraqi monarchy, the Wathba of 1948 and the Intifada of 1952. Thus demands for immediate improvements in material conditions were invariably tied to larger nationalist goals of independence and social equity.

It is true that the renegotiation of the concessionary agreement between the Iraqi state and the Iraq Petroleum Company in 1952 (in large measure possible due to working-class militancy, which the state used as a weapon to induce concessions from the consortium) led to a decline in the number of strikes as a result of expanded state spending and a decline in unemployment, but the Iraqi working class struggled for goals throughout the 1930s, 1940s, and 1950s that would, by the definition of rational choice theory, not be in their rational interest to pursue. An example would be the frequent refusal of workers to return to work despite offers of higher wages and better working conditions; instead workers (often drawn from diverse ethnolinguistic and confessional backgrounds) refused to return to work until fired union leaders and strike organizers were reinstated in their jobs. Further, the notion of the "free rider" so prominent in rational choice theory fails to explain why workers exhibited such a high level of solidarity and cooperation.

The historical experiences of Iraqi workers point to the dangers of rational choice theory. In its refusal to historicize its subject and its reduction of consciousness to a simplistic means-end dichotomy, rational choice theory reflects many of the same problems as the neo-Taylorism of contemporary Ba'thist theorizing. Technology, efficiency, and "science" become the highest goods and thus ends in themselves. The recent attempt by some Marxist theorists to base their analyses of working-class behavior on rational choice models is, I believe, fraught with many dangers because it can never remain true to the systemic holism that Marx saw as so central to his work.[45]

Iraqi Workers, Agency, and Social Difference

To the extent that some of the characteristics of Iraqi workers can be conveyed to Western audiences, it is perhaps simultaneously possible to break down some of the pernicious stereotypes that prevail about Third World peoples. It is also perhaps possible to speak to Westerners about problems of social and cultural difference. In other words, what does the story of Iraqi workers tell us about our own efforts to overcome differences based on race, ethnicity, gender, sexual preference, and regional cultures?[46] It is particularly significant for American workers that Iraqi workers were so successful in overcoming the cleavages that those in power sought to create in their ranks because, in the American context, race and gender have been manipulated on numerous occasions to "divide and conquer" labor solidarity. In telling a story about Iraqi workers, then, a crucial dimension should, in my opinion, be the Western backdrop against which this narrative is developed.

One of the most prominent characteristics of contemporary American society is the retreat from the gains in social equality that were achieved during the middle and late 1960s and early 1970s. One of the most important efforts in this regard has been the attempt to erode the confidence of workers and members of minorities in their ability to take control of their lives. Retrenchment in government funding, elimination of state institutions that offered marginalized groups greater opportunities for self-empowerment, and legal decisions circumscribing the power of workers have all been used to roll back progressive gains. Following a long American tradition, ethnic groups, social classes, men and women, and minorities have been set against one another while corporate and state policies that have adversely affected them have largely remained unchallenged. The experience of Third World workers such as those in Iraq—workers with far fewer economic and legal resources at their disposal than their American counterparts—needs to be conveyed to union leaders and union members in the West. It can provide an example of how the salience of social difference can be reduced among workers striving to achieve greater social justice. This is a task to which Western intellectuals should, in my opinion, devote more effort.

The Iraqi Working Class and the Rewriting of History

Perhaps the most profound example of the impact of the Iraqi working class on Iraqi society can be seen in the massive effort currently underway by the state to reinterpret Iraq's history and popular culture. Although the factors that led up to this effort are complex, it is no exaggeration to say that it is in large measure a response to worker and lower class radicalism. One of the central concerns of the state in pursuing the "Project for the Rewriting of History" (mashru' i'adat kitabat al-tarikh) is to restructure historical memory. Of all the aspects of Iraq's past, the most threatening to the state is worker radicalism and the close ties of the Iraqi working class and labor organizations to the Iraqi Communist party. The very fact that the state feels it so essential to reinterpret the way in which Iraqis understand twentieth century labor history, and the effort it has made to remove the Communist party from any role in that history, indicates the potential threat that it still feels from radical sectors of the working class.

An important contribution of Gramsci's writings has been to enhance our awareness of the fact that not all power is exercised through force and overt coercion. Gramsci's concept of hegemony calls attention to the efforts of those who control the state to attempt to obscure notions of class interests through processes of socialization that can occur in the family, the educational system, religious institutions, and under the influence of the mass media. In this model, the concept of historical memory looms large because one of the keys to achieving hegemony is to convince subaltern groups to believe in the historical construction of political community propagated by the ruling class. Anticipating Foucault, hegemony theory as articulated by Gramsci argues that control through self-discipline by subaltern groups themselves is a much more efficient form of domination that the exercise of force and violence. Thus it is possible to see current efforts by Ba'thist intellectuals to rewrite the history of the working class as just as dangerous as the efforts of the colonial state to use force and violence to suppress attempts by workers to implement greater social justice.

Although I have discussed the reinterpretation of history and popular culture in modern Iraq in greater detail elsewhere,[47] suffice it to say here that one of the key components of this effort is to replace class with nationalist consciousness. Attempts have been made to penetrate Iraqi history at several critical periods beginning with the country's ancient Mesopotamian civilizations, as well as its pre-Islamic Arab past, the 'Abbasid period, and the period of colonial domination following World War I. To give history a more populist character, more recently a strong emphasis has been placed on folklore. The attempt to demonstrate a continuous national identity in Iraq over time is made through an emphasis on the love of the land as expressed in such cultural idioms as poetry and folktales.

Although the more recent effort to promote concern with folklore bestows a more populist aura on the state, the appropriation of the past, whether in terms of the "high culture" of written discourse or the "low culture" of folklore, is part of the attempt to construct hegemony. In reexamining history and popular culture, the state uses intellectuals to impose interpretations that alter traditional understandings, exclude others that are seen as threatening, and in many instances, create wholly new readings of the past. This is especially true regarding attitudes toward Iran and Persian culture fostered by the state following the Iran-Iraq War. Efforts to reinterpret the historical relations between Iraqis and Iranians in excessively conflictual terms (perhaps best exemplified in the "Qadisiyyat Saddam" campaign) represents not only an effort to foster chauvinist feelings but also an effort to further deny social difference in Iraqi society.[48] In other words, hostility toward Iranians becomes a metaphor for rejecting the notion of Iraq as an ethnically and linguistically heterogeneous society.

The struggle to counter the attempt to restructure the historical memory of the Iraqi working class as well as the country as a whole continues to be carried on by the Iraqi Communist party, leftist elements of the Kurdish community, and, to a lesser extent, by Shiite religio-political organizations such as the al-Da'wa al-Islamiyya. Complaints by Iraqi officials of low productivity in Iraqi industry indicate the persistence of resistance by workers albeit outside an organizational context. Perhaps most difficult for students of the Iraqi working class is the ability to gain access to oppositional folk culture generated by the masses, such as folk poetry and music. One of the (difficult) tasks of future research will be to determine the degree and effectiveness of lower class resistance to Ba'thist efforts to impose their hegemonic ideology on Iraqi society as a whole.

Notes

1. Ibrahim Husayn, *Lamahat mu'jaza min tarikh al-haraka al-niqabiyya al-'iraqiyya* [A Concise Overview of the History of the Iraqi Working Class] (n.p.: Manshurat al-Thaqafa al-Jadida, 1982), p. 6.

2. See, for example, Middle East Watch, *Human Rights in Iraq* (New York and London: Yale University Press, 1990) pp. 102–114; Adel Hussein and Gregory Alexander, *Unholy Babylon* (New York: St. Martin's Press, 1991), pp. 50–51, 63, 65–66, 68–70, 93–94, 152–153; and Committee Against Repression and for Democracy in Iraq (CADRI), *Saddam's Iraq: Revolution or Reaction?* (London: Zed Press, 1986), p. 32, where it is argued that the CIA helped the Ba'th party overthrow 'Abd al-Karim Qasim in 1963. See also my "The Persian Gulf War: Myths and Realities," in H. Amirahmadi, ed., *The United States and the Middle East: New Directions in Foreign Policy* (Albany, State University of New York Press, 1993), pp. 251–285, for a discussion of support by the Reagan and Bush administrations to Saddam and the Ba'th.

3. For examples of this perspective, see Bill Warren, *Imperialism: Pioneer of Capitalism*, (London: New Left Books, 1980); Samir Amin, *The Arab Nation* (London: Zed Press, 1978); and Mahmoud Hussein, *Class Struggle in Egypt, 1952–1970* (New York: Monthly Review Press, 1973).

4. For an analysis of the rise of authoritarian regimes espousing variants of radical Arab nationalism, see Khaldoun Hasan al-Naqeeb, "The Rise of the Authoritarian State in the Arab East," in E. Davis and N. Gavrielides, eds., *Statecraft in the Middle East: Oil, Historical Memory and Popular Culture* (Miami: Florida International University Press, 1991), pp. 36–70.

5. 'Issam al-Khafaji, *al-Dawla wa'l-tatawwur al-ra'smali fi'l-'iraq, 1968–1978* (Cairo: Dar al-Mustaqbal al-'Arabi, 1983), pp. 16, 165–184; and *Ra'smaliyat al-dawla al-wataniyya* (Beirut: Dar Ibn al-Khaldun, 1979), pp. 173–201.

6. Dipesh Chakrabarty, *Rethinking Working Class History* (Princeton, N.J.: Princeton University Press, 1989).

7. This would seem to apply to the non-Arab states of the region as well such as Iran after the 1978–79 Revolution, Turkey after the rise of the military, and Israel following the decline of the Labor party after 1977.

8. Antonio Gramsci, *Selections From the Prison Notebooks* (London: Lawrence and Wishart, 1971), pp. 6, 12, 15–16, 20, 56, 366, 377, 418.

9. Of course, this raises the thorny issue of what constitutes an objective basis for the individual or group seeking to deconstruct a myth or myths.

10. For a Leninist reading of Gramsci, see Christine Buci-Glucksmann, *Gramsci and the State* (London: Lawrence & Wishart, 1980).

11. Antonio Gramsci, *Il Vaticano e l'Italia* (Rome: Editori Riuniti, 1974); *Il Risorgimento* (Rome: Editori Riuniti, 1977), especially pp. 86–117, 131–133, 137–139; *The Modern Prince and Other Writings* (New York: International Publishers, 1957), pp. 28–51.

12. Terry Eagleton, *Literary Theory: An Introduction* (Minneapolis; University of Minnesota Press, 1983), pp. 131–132, 142; Joan Wallach Scott, *Gender and the Politics of History* (New York: Columbia University Press, 1988), pp. 21, 36–37, 63.

13. There is a large body of writing in Arabic on the Iraqi working class. By far the best and most comprehensive study of the Iraqi working class is 'Abd al-Razzaq Mutlaq al-Fahd, "Tarikh al-haraka al-'ummaliyya fi-l-'iraq, 1922–1958" (unpublished doctoral diss., Cairo University, 1977).

14. Gramsci, *Prison Notebooks*, pp. 279–318.

15. It will be noted that nothing is said about religiopolitical thinking as a possible fourth historiographical school. This is not to argue that Islamicists or Islamic radicals, particularly from the Shiite community, were not sympathetic to the plight of workers. Certainly many were. However, religiopolitical discourse has had relatively little to say about the working-class movement in Iraq.

16. See, for example, John Dos Passos, *Orient Express* (New York: Harper and Brothers, 1927), esp. Chapter 9, "Baghdad Bahnhof," pp. 103–113; also Freya Stark, *Baghdad Sketches* (New York: E. P. Dutton, 1938). See also British Foreign Office documents, e.g., F.O.371/16923, "R.A.F. Monthly Intelligence Summary, Iraq, for Sept., 1933", F.O.371/24562, "Iraqi Personalities for 1939", F.O.371/68459, Basra Consulate-General Monthly Summary, December, 1947", F.O.371/110896. VQ1011/1, "Political Conditions in Iraq, 1953", and United States Consular documents, e.g., 890.G00/176, Sloan to Secretary of State, Feb. 3, 1932; 890G.00/277, "Political Situation in Iraq—Shiah-Sunni Factor," Sept. 26, 1933; and 890G.917/1-345, L. Henderson to Secretary of State, Jan. 3, 1945.

17. See, for example, al-Fahd, *Tarikh al-haraka*; Kamal Mazhar Ahmad, *al-Tabaqa al-'amila al-'iraqiyya: al-takkawun wa-bidayatal-taharruk* [The Iraqi Working Class: Its Formation and the Beginning of its Mobilization] (Baghdad: Ministry of Culture and Information, Dar al-Rashid li-l-Nashr, 1981); Ahmad al-Nasiri, "Hawl al-tufayliya wa namuha fi-l-'iraq" ["On Parasitism and its Growth in Iraq"], *al-Nahj*, no. 2 (November 1983): 234–278; 'Issam al-Khafaji, "al-Tatawwur al-ra'smali wa-l-tabaqa al-'amila al-'iraqiyya" ["Capitalist Development and the Iraqi Working Class"], *al-Nahj*, no. 4 (May 1984): 228–254; "Min al-nidal al-niqabi ila-l-thawra" ["Revolution Through Working Class Struggle"], editorial, and Rajih Mustafa, "al-Tabaqa al-'amila fi zill al-hukm al-diktaturi" ["The Working Class Under Dictatorial Rule"], *al-Thazaqa al-Jadida*, no. 120 (May 1980): 23–24 and 25–32 respectively; Abu Dhikri, "Nazara fi qawanin wa-tashri'at al-'amal fi-l-'iraq" ["An Overview of Labor Laws and Legislation in Iraq"], *al-Thaqafa al-Jadida*, no. 157 (August 1984): 97–107; and Ibrahim Husayn, *Lamabat*.

18. See, for example, Razzaq Ibrahim Hasan, "al-Haraka al-niqabiyya al-'ummaliyya fi-l-'iraq" ["The Labor Union Movement in Iraq"], *Afaq 'Arabiyya*, no. 9 (May 1976): 19–43; 'Abd al-Razzaq Ibrahim Hasan, *al-Shakhsiyya al-'ummaliyya fi-l-qissa al-'iraqiyya* (Baghdad: Dar al-Huriyya li-l-Tiba'a, 1977); Razzaq Ibrahim Hasan, *al-Sihafa al-'ummaliyya fi-l-'iraq* (Baghdad: Ministry of Culture and Arts, Dar al-Rashid li-l-Nashr, 1979) (kitab al-jamahir) [a book for the masses], no. 32; Khalid Muhsin Mahmud al-Rawi, *Tarikh al-tabaqa al-'amila al-'iraqiyya, 1967–1975* (Baghdad: Ministry of Culture and Information, Dar al-Rashid li-l-Nashr, 1982). See also the various issues of the official publication of the General Union of Iraqi Labor Syndicates [al-Ittihad al-'Amm li-l-Niqabat al-'Ummal], *Wa'i al-'ummal*.

19. Hanna Batatu, *The Old Social Classes and the Revolutionary Movements of Iraq* (Princeton, N.J.: Princeton University Press, 1978), pp. 295–297.

20. E. A. Kinch, "Social Effects of the Oil Industry in Iraq," *International Labor Review* 75 (Jan.–June 1957), pp. 194–195, 199; Hamid Ja'id,. *al-Haraka al-'ummaliyya fi-l-'iraq* (Baghdad: Dar al-Salam Press, 1974), pp. 9–10; al-Fahd, *Tarikh al-haraka*, pp. 447–471, 485–503, 505–509, 547–558; Marion Farouk-Sluglett and Peter Sluglett, "Labor and National Liberation: The Trade Union Movement in Iraq, 1920–1958," *Arab Studies Quarterly*, 5, no. 2 (Spring 1983): 152–153.

21. For an explanation of the factors that caused peasants to migrate urban areas, see Makki Muhammad Azeez, "Geographical Aspects of Rural Migration from Amara Province, Iraq, 1955–1964" (unpublished doctoral thesis, University of Durham, April 1968), especially pp. 182–196; al-Fahd, *Tarikh al-haraka*, pp. 22–31.

22. Wamidh J. O. al-Nazmi, "The Political, Intellectual and Social Roots of the Iraqi Independence Movement" (unnpublished doctoral diss., Durham University July, 1974), pp. 221–224; Batatu, *The Old Social Classes*, pp. 143–144, 146, 151, 152.

23. For documentation of this point, see al-Fahd, *Tarikh al-haraka*.

24. A number of studies conducted by graduate students in the Department of Sociology at Baghdad University during the 1970s suggest that peasants did retain ties to their rural origins. See, for example, Ibrahim Mushab al-Dulaymi, *"al-Hijra al-mu'akisa: Dirasa ijtima'iyya li ahwal al-muhajirin min madinat Baghdad"* [Reverse Migration: A Sociological Study on the Conditions of Migrants from Baghdad] (unpublished masters thesis, Baghdad University, 1976); and Muhammad Harbi Hasan, "Aham al-mushakil al'-ummaliyya fi masani' Baghdad" [The Most Important Workers' Problems in Baghdad Factories] (unpublished masters thesis, Baghdad University, 1974).

25. On efforts to encourage peasants to return to rural areas to join agricultural cooperatives, see the study of the experimental project of 1876 participants in five cooperatives in al-Wasit province by al-Dulaymi, "al-Hijra," especially pp. 127–128.

26. See, for example, Yusuf Salman Yusuf (Comrade Fahd), *Min watha'iq al-hizb al-shuyu'i al-'iraqi: kitabat al-rafiq Fahd* [From the Documents of the Iraqi Communist Party: The Writings of Comrade Fahd] (Beirut: Dar al-Farabi, 1976), p. 409; on the role of women in strikes, see "Liqa' ma' al-rafiq Nasir 'Abbud: ta'sis niqabat 'ummal al-muwani, idrabat, muzahirat iyyar fi-l-Basra," ["An Interview with Comrade Nasir 'Abbud: The May Strikes and Demonstrations in Basra"], *al-Thaqafa al-Jadida* no. 152 (March 1984): 54.

27. See note 12.

28. Only al-Fahd, *Tarikh al-haraka*, and Batatu, *The Old Social Classes*, contain the beginnings of such an analysis.

29. Al-Fahd, ibid.

30. Ahmad, *al-Tabaqa*.

31. Following the Ba'thist tendency to commit the sin of omission, an official version of the history of the working class largely ignores the period prior to the coming to power of the current regime. See Khalid Muhsin Mahmud al-Rawi, *Tarikh al-tabaqa al-'amila al-'iraqiyya, 1968–1975* [The History of the Iraqi Working Class, 1968–1975] (Baghdad: Ministry of Culture and Information, Dar al-Rashid li-l-Nashr, 1982); it is also interesting that the first volume of the official history of the Ba'th Party, which covers the years between 1943 and 1949, contains no entries relating to the working class. The articles are largely oriented toward Syria and Lebanon. See *Nidal al-ba'th* [The Ba'th's Struggle], al-juz al-awwal (Beirut: Dar al-Tali'a li-l-Tiba'a wa-l-Nashr, 1963).

32. al-Rawi, ibid., pp. 20, 51–63.

33. Ibid., p. 76.

34. "Afaq min al-haraka al-wataniyya: al-idrab al-'amm sanat 1931 fi'l-'iraq" ["Perspectives on the Nationalist Movement: The 1931 General Strike in Iraq"], *Afaq 'Arabiyya* 9 (May 1976): pp. 72–75.

35. Representative of the British view about worker activity is the following comment on the strike against the Iraq Petroleum Company's facilities in Kirkuk during July 1946: "The Embassy in Baghdad report and the Company confirm that there was no genuine disorder among the Oil Company workers, and that the strike was instigated by agitators. . . many of whom came from Baghdad and the majority of the remainder of whom had only been in the employment of the Company for a month or two harangued the workers and so brought about the strike." FO 371/52456 E9317 16 September 1946. However, it should be also be noted that British officials outside Baghdad, such as consular officials in Basra, were less prone to dismiss worker grievances as merely the products of outside agitation.

36. See, for example, *The 1968 Revolution in Iraq: Experiences and Prospects*, The Political Report of the Eighth Congress of the Arab Ba'th Socialist Party in Iraq, January 1974, (London: Ithaca Press, 1979), p. 87; and al-Rawi, *Tarikh al-tabaqa*, pp. 78–129, where the author discusses numerous conferences organized by the state-controlled General Federation of Worker Syndicates (*al-ittihad al-'amm li niqabat al-'ummal*) and laws passed by the state regulating working conditions in Iraq.

37. See, al-Rawi, ibid., pp. 33–38; and 'Adnan Ra'uf, *Dirasat fi iqtisad al-'amal* [Studies in Labor Economy] (Baghdad: Mu'assasat Dar al-Kutub li-Tiba'a wa-l-Nashr, 1978), especially pp. 50–56, which covers the entire period of the working class prior to 1968, never once mentioning the role of the Iraqi Communist party.

38. For a critique of Ba'thist policies of combating illiteracy, particularly their ideological dimensions, see Thabit al-Mushahidi, "Hawl mahwa al-ummiya fi-l-'iraq" ["On the Eradication of illiteracy in Iraq"], *al-Thaqafa al-Jadida* no. 125 (October 1980): 8–22.

39. See al-Dulaymi, "al-Hijra."

40. See, for example, FO 371/110991/VQ1015/83, Troutbeck (Baghdad) to Eden, December 9, 1954.

41. See FO 371/110998/VQ1015/3, Troutbeck (Baghdad) to Eden, January 6, 1954, which discusses worker demands for political and not just economic concessions; FO 371/52456 E8553 and E7455 "Strike at Kirkuk"; FO 371/23000 E366, where Squadron Leader H. Hendle-Jones discusses the political situation in Iraq with the Iraqi Chargé d'Affaires in Cairo, January 14, 1939; the Monthly Summaries—Basra Consulate-General, August 1946 through December 1954; and al-Fahd, *Tarikh al-haraka*, p. 447.

42. See, for example, Jon Elster, *Making Sense of Marx* (Cambridge: Cambridge University Press, 1985).

43. Al-Fahd, *Tarikh al-haraka*, pp. 449, 486, 495.

44. Mancur Olson, *The Logic of Collective Action* (New York: Schocken Books, 1968), p. 21.

45. For a critique of the attempt to apply rational choice theory to Marxian political economy, see Alan Carling, "Rational Choice Marxism," *New Left Review* 160 (November–December 1986), 24–62.

46. For an excellent discussion of these issues, see Mike Davis, *Prisoners of the American Dream* (London: Verso, 1986).

47. E. Davis and N. Gavrielides, "Statecraft, Historical Memory, and Popular Culture in Iraq and Kuwait," in Davis and Gavrielides, eds., *Statecraft in the Middle East*, especially pp. 132–140.

48. For a more extended discussion of this point, see my "State Building in Iraq During the Iran-Iraq War and the Gulf Crisis," in M. Midlarsky, ed., *The Internationalization of Communal Strife* (New York and London: Routledge, 1992), pp. 69–91.

11

The History of the Working Classes in the Middle East: Some Methodological Considerations

Until recently, modern Middle Eastern history has been conceptualized as largely the affair of the elite, with little room left for other actors. We are still in the process of discovering what it might do to our understanding of the history of the modern Middle East to rethink it from the standpoint of nonelites.[1] Over the last several decades, the burgeoning of Middle Eastern social history has begun the process of recovering the lost peoples' history of the Middle East. Middle Eastern labor history is central to this research agenda, because it demonstrates that the actions of elites, far from dominating events, were often responses to deeply rooted processes of social and economic change.

The recent collapse of many of the basic political and intellectual understandings that sustained social thought since the end of World War II makes the present context a favorable one for such a retrospective survey. With the collapse of the edifice of Soviet power in Eastern Europe in 1989–1990, a new political gameboard has emerged that opens up previously closed options for would-be global strategists and potentially changes the terms of reference for all. Looking back to the recent past, the failed Lebanese and Afghan revolutions in the 1970s and the 1978–1979 Islamic revolution in Iran now seem like prefigurations of what was to come. As the curtain descends on a world dominated by superpower rivalries and on the heroic age of Arab nationalism in the Middle East, it is now possible to rethink the ideologies that justified and sustained the old political system. Global political changes provide one explanation for the current intellectual ferment.

However, by themselves they are inadequate to fully explain it. For a more complete understanding, we must also note the collapse of the dominant paradigms that sustained postwar social thought. Modernization theory, androcentric social theories, and orientalist discourses which previously held unquestioned sway have been seriously eroded by the intellectual ferment in the human sciences in 1975–1990. Although these critiques were fueled by the 1960s Third World movements of national liberation, as well as the women's movement and the new politics of ethnicity, they also reflected autonomous parallel intellectual developments. Finally, the erosion of the old pillars of social thought was deeply rooted in philosophical critiques of Marxism and positivist social science, which had their origins in nineteenth century European thought.[2] For social historians, certain strands of poststructuralism have been especially subversive of older political and social ideas, notably the work of Michel Foucault and Antonio Gramsci.[3]

As a result of this critique, historians have become aware of the existence of other "subaltern" discourses alongside the "master discourses" that have previously shaped our understanding of history. Basic Enlightenment categories such as "the nation," "class," and "the state," which had informed the social sciences, are now being called into question. In the ensuing debacle, we have witnessed the melt-down of established discipiines and methodologies, the blurring of genres, and the splintering of the subject.[4]

As is clear from a reading of the chapters in this volume, the history of the Middle East has not been not exempt from these trends. Indeed, in various ways some essays experiment with these new approaches. The old paradigms around which the history of the modern Middle East was organized (modernization theory and the development of nationalism, both of which are about the same subject: the creation of the modern state) continue to carry much *mana*, even though they face increased criticism.

However, there are good reasons to doubt the receptivity of most scholars of the Middle East to the interpretive turn of postmodernist thought. Thus although some historians of the working classes of the Middle East are asking, "can one do working class history any more?" others ask, perhaps more pertinently, "how can we understand the place of Islam in the struggle for justice and dignity of workers?" Because the two sides agree on neither the initial premises nor the subject, the debate as posed cannot reach a conclusion.

The lack of symmetry between political and intellectual trends in the history of Middle Eastern workers is clear. As the region remains in a prolonged political crisis there is little likelihood of change. But the questions raised by those espousing the new methodologies will not disappear either. The present intellectual trends are too deeply rooted for this. Indeed, the more we learn about the manifold ways the Middle Eastern working classes are composed of groups of workers segmented in a host of different ways from other workers, the more doubt is cast on the ability of so large a concept as class to explain anything by itself. Thus the accumulation of empirical research itself helps to undermine portmanteau concepts like class.

Labor History in Perspective

We can obtain a better idea of what a reinvented history of the working classes of the Middle East might look like from a brief look at the changes that U.S. labor history has undergone in the last generation. Earlier generations of U.S. historians had discussed the emergence of working class protest in New England in the late nineteenth and early twentieth centuries as shaped by the ways work was organized in the factory. For these historians, the concepts of class and the state were central, and the factory floor was the crucible in which an American working class was forged.

If we seek to locate historically the development of labor history as a field, we find that it is connected to the nineteenth century idea of progress, which portrayed elites as the bearers of modernization and opponents of these changes as benighted demogogues who completely misunderstood the direction of history. This emergent workers' counter-discourse sought to legitimize their struggle.

Where elite historians tended to view worker opposition as perverse, or to leave out labor altogether, the emerging field of labor history sought to reinject the workers back into the story. Labor organizers, the villains of capitalist histories, became the heroes of the new labor histories. The sense of labor history as "movement history" is never far from the surface.[5]

Classic labor history viewed its subject as the history of factory workers and saw the revolutionary class as the proletariat. Factory workers led the strikes and work stoppages that for the sake of social peace eventually compelled the capitalist bosses to make provisions for a fair wage, reasonable hours, and job benefits, thereby preserving the dignity of the ordinary worker. The debate over the primacy of structures or experience in the emergence of working-class politics was given a powerful impetus by the publication of E. P. Thompson's *Making of the English Working Class.*[6]

Thompson's work shifted the attention of labor historians from the material circumstances in which the labor movement emerged and the debate over whether the wage rate was rising and falling (industrialization as a material process) to the terrain of workers' experience (industrialization as a cultural process). It continued to assume with the older literature that the modal worker was a male factory worker and that he was employed in a large industrial enterprise. The Marxist thesis that industrialization was marked by the proletarianization of labor remained unquestioned by Thompson. Against the devastating certainties of the new political economy and its new definitions of time, work, and discipline, Thompson contrasted the culture of a bygone age, marked by the doctrine of the rights of free-born Englishmen and the preindustrial moral economy. The result was to change the terms of debate. Instead of increasingly sterile distinctions about whether the rate of profit was rising and falling and how worker wages may or may not have been affected, Thompson's intervention valorized culture and workers' experience.

What the new working-class history has done is to foreground the question of the unit of analysis: is it workers on the factory floor or in their lives outside of the factory? The idea that the true worker is a male factory worker is deeply rooted in the teleological certainties of modernization theory in its liberal and Marxist variants. Yet it is increasingly difficult to accept at face value the factory worker model of "the worker." This debate resurfaced at the workshop (to which I will turn in the next section).

In the 1970s a revisionist trend set in, in response to Thompson. Alan Dawley, in his classic analysis of the Lynn, Massachusetts, shoemakers' strike, adopted a more community-centered approach. For Dawley, what went on in the workplace was only one of the factors involved. He argued that workers drew on preexisting artisanal traditions and popular traditions of republicanism to justify their protest. Dawley argued, like Thompson, that "class happened" in specific historical and cultural contexts rather than as a manifestation of a putatively universal dialectical process.[7] Soon Thompson had many imitators.[8] Sean Wilentz's *Chants Democratic* similarly stressed the role of artisans in the formation of the American working class, and Gary B. Nash's *The Urban Crucible* sought to specify how worker politics intersected with U.S. politics generally.[9] The broadening of perspective extended the vision of labor historians from the union hall and the shop floor into the community. From the history of labor (a study focused on what workers did together on the job site) the focus expanded to the history of the working classes (including all aspects of the lives of workers in their communities).

Another way of phrasing the difference between the two approaches is to see them as divided between those that stress structures and those that stress experience.[10] The recent literature on the European labor movement in the nineteenth century has queried both the assumption that the worker was a factory worker (the proletariat) and that factory workers took the lead in worker organization and the emergence of social movements. New studies stress instead the central role played by artisans in working class activism.[11] We will see later whether these findings have been taken up by the Middle East labor historians represented in this volume.

As scholars have become aware of the essentialism inherent in class, new categories of analysis, such as gender and ethnicity, have emerged (and they themselves have in turn been critiqued).[12] Crucially, the assumption that the modal worker was a white man came into question. With the emergence of women's labor history, the field was further transformed in the 1970s and 1980s in Britain, France, and the United States. One target was E. P. Thompson's *Making of the English Working Class*. Critics noted that although female workers dominated many employment sectors, especially in the textile trade, they were scarcely to be found in Thompson's account.[13] The work of Tom Dublin, Mary Blewett, and Ardis Cameron (among others) on Massachusetts textile workers has done much to redress the balance, by showing the central role played by female workers.[14] Similarly, Christine Stansell's work on women in New York in the nineteenth century has made important contribution in showing the importance of neighborhood networks,[15] while Alice Kessler-Harris has established the importance of women wage workers.[16] In the process, their work has destabilized the category of the artisan, which occupied the center of the story for Dawley and Wilentz.

As organized labor acquired the status of "vested interest" in our society in the 1970s, the search for militant labor became attenuated, and the subject began to slip out of focus. It will perhaps not come as a surprise to learn that the result has been a challenge to the founding concept of the field, class.[17] Following Benedict Anderson, one can see the working class as in some senses an "imagined community" (i.e., whether the category *class* is in fact a "natural" one or a socially generated one).[18]

Sources

The splintering of the subject of labor history calls for a rethinking of the basic approaches, context, and sources of the Middle Eastern field. The chapters in this volume in different ways lend themselves to just such a reconsideration. In the rest of these comments, I would like first to discuss the different conceptualizations of the field as they emerge from the essays collected here. Next, I will comment on what seemed to me the most important debates that arose at the workshop. Finally, I reflect on what was left out of our deliberations in terms of approaches, topics, and the definition of the field.

First, let us consider the sources. Middle Eastern labor history thus far is largely an artifact of the sources on which it is based. Few scholars are able to work in more than one of the four major languages of the region: Arabic, Hebrew, Persian, and Turkish. Those who work on the history of the working class in Egypt have tended primarily to read one another and not those working on the same subject elsewhere in the region. Similarly, those who work primarily on Iran or Turkey have tended not read the literature outside "their" country. The result has been a field that is longer on promise than on delivery, theoretically more sophisticated than the data on which it is based. That is why this volume is potentially such an important one: it breaks down those walls and makes it possible to see that there is a subject here, apart from a nationally defined one.

As historians begin to draw on new sources, they are able to ask more sophisticated questions and become more self-conscious about their research strategies. In general, three principal types of sources have been employed by labor historians of the Middle East. Each has given rise to a distinctive type of labor history.

One group of studies has focused on labor unions and workers' parties, or what we might call *movement histories*. Based chiefly on the records generated by worker organizations, this approach has highlighted institutional and political history. Examples include recent works by Ervand Abrahamian, Eqbal Ahmad, Joel Beinin and Zachary Lockman, and Jacques Couland, to name but a few.[19] The fallacy of this was evident at the conference. Beinin's lament captured the general mood: having set out to write a work inspired by Edward Thompson's *Making of the English Working Class*, he said, he found that given the materials at his disposition and their particular origins—some or most being generated by worker parties and unions—it was very hard to fight past official discourse to get to culture, to get to consciousness.

A second group of studies approach the study of workers via the records of employers (private enterprises or public-sector companies). Such records allow researchers to trace worker protest and radicalism, as well as working conditions, pay scales, and worker productivity.[20] For the most part, due to difficulty of access and gaps in the record, this approach has been less utilized. The documents that Quataert foregrounds in his chapter are featured for a reason: there are not very many other examples to which one can look. It is indeed frustrating to have these few tantalizing documents and so many interesting questions. To move beyond this stage poses a problem to the field.

A third approach utilizes the records of agencies charged with registering, supervising, and repressing worker organizations and activities—labor ministries, health and safety bureaus, police agencies. For labor historians of Europe and the United States, this has been an especially important basis for many fine studies. For Middle Eastern labor historians, gaining access to governmental records has been difficult in the present context.[21]

In the European and American fields, worker memoirs and autobiographies have increasingly been recognized as a crucially important source, especially as the focus has moved to worker consciousness. There are signs that those who work on Middle Eastern labor history are also looking in this direction. In his contribution, Ellis Goldberg draws on a number of Egyptian worker memoirs. In the discussion that followed his paper, it became apparent that worker memoirs and autobiographies, although rare, also exist for other parts of the region. A project that catalogued these memoirs for each country (perhaps eventually across the entire region) could greatly assist in drawing scholarly attention to this precious source.

Finally, some of the contributions to this volume have drawn on working-class poetry and other direct expressions of worker mentality. Generally this kind of material has been the province of folklorists. For example, Feroz Ahmad's essay includes a moving quotation from a poem by a Turkish woman worker. Such poems say more about the actual conditions confronted by workers than a ton of sociological statistics. Although rare, it is infinitely precious: the more we can hear the voices of poor and powerless people, the more convincing what we have to say will be. It is this that made Eric Hobsbawm's *Primitive Rebels* into a classic.

Debates

When we begin and end stories suggests a lot about implicit teleologies and the ways in which we think about things. One question that generated a great deal of discussion at the workshop was the connections between the nineteenth century *ta'ifa* origins of the working-class movement in Egypt and the full-blown unionization of the industrial work force in the twentieth century. There was an important exchange on this subject between Sherry Vatter, on the one hand, and Joel Beinin and (mostly by implication) Zachary Lockman, on the other hand. For Vatter, as well as to some extent for Goldberg and Quataert, the distinction between modern factory workers and artisans makes increasingly little sense. Elsewhere she argues that historians need to take artisan protest more seriously.[22]

Part of the tacit refusal of Beinin and Lockman to accept Vatter's argument about an alternative starting point for Egyptian labor history seems connected to their still being influenced by the Egyptian nationalist school of historiography. It assumed a parallelism in the development of the working-class movement in Europe, the United States, and the Middle East, which in retrospect seems forced. The mood of reassessment is captured very well by Joel Beinin, who speaking self-critically of his earlier work on Egyptian workers remarks, in a wonderful phrase, that the Marxist script for this play (grounded in Soviet notions of how history operates through the role of the working class) was unplayable on an Egyptian stage.

If the workers consist principally of industrial factory workers, as is assumed to be the case by Beinin and Lockman among others, there is indeed a major problem. For the facts are that workers in the modern sector in the Middle East (as elsewhere in the Third World) are a privileged aristocracy in comparison to the mass of others. This lies at the root of the debate between Vatter and Beinin and Lockman. There is some reason indeed to question the supposed primacy of the factory worker in European working-class militancy. Contrary to Marxist assumptions that factory workers and proletarians led the worker's movement, recent studies have demonstrated conclusively that artisans, not proletarians, played the central role in worker protests and organizing.[23] If the proletarian model does not work even for Europe, then it certainly needs to be reexamined in the Middle East.

Another important topic of debate at the workshop was the relationship of structure and culture. In the Marxist tradition,

consciousness could simply be read out of structure. (A factory worker is a factory worker, whether in Lille or Helwan.) Here the critique of E. P. Thompson had evidently struck home.[24] In response, participants adopted a variety of strategies in their presentations and workshop discussions. No one viable strategy emerged, but the work of the Italian theorist Antonio Gramsci was clearly attractive to a number of participants.

Because Gramsci focused on Italy, a Mediterranean society with a history, structures, and political culture in some ways analogous to those of the Middle East, and because although a Marxist Gramsci's intervention sought to lay bare the structures of culture domination, which he calls *hegemony*, many have been inspired by his work. Eric Davis's chapter on Iraq went the farthest in appropriating Gramscian categories. Clearly part of the attraction is that Gramsci allows one to be Marxist but also to be sensitive to culture. Without calling for the abandonment of Gramscian approaches, I find a certain ahistoricism in Gramsci's key concepts. "Hegemony," "historic bloc," and "organic intellectual" perform rapid moves that need to be unpacked and examined historically. They also operate at a level of abstraction that cuts against the close-grained study of worker's lives that is one of the dominant trends otherwise of the new social history. The attempt to specify the contexts that together shape workers' lives—class, gender, religion, ethnicity, neighborhood, sociability and cultures—needs also to be foregrounded surely. How this can be done in a Gramscian framework remains unclear.

The reaction against a sterile structuralism, in many ways a salutary development, may have gone too far. With the exception of Marsha Posusney's and Salim Nasr's contribution to the workshop, there were no structural approaches to the working classes of the region. Posusney's study seeks to uncover the structural constraints on Egyptian worker activism. How much can be expected of Egyptian workers, she asks, given their place in Egyptian society? In arriving at her rather pessimistic conclusion, she traces the structural determinants of political action—placing particular stress on the fact that most Egyptian workers are not organized. Salim Nasr's macrosociological and historical view of the working-class movement in Lebanon, which unfortunately could not be included in this volume, develops a carefully calibrated breakdown of the social composition of the working class, sector by sector, and factored for gender as well as linguistic and religious ethnicity. Against the background of the war and societal breakdown, one finding of potential interest is the striking growth of unionization in the 1980s.

A number of papers invoked the concept of moral economy as a way of coming to grips with the concern to validate workers' consciousnesses. I share many of the reservations that were voiced by Joel Beinin—and more. Taking on this term means taking on a lot of baggage one may not want—not only the problematic way in which the concept is appropriated and used by James Scott,[25] out of Thompson,[26] but also Thompson's extraction of it from the language of the Manchester school and use of it for his own devices, and then all of the critiques that these positions have been subjected to since then. Insofar as it provides a way of talking about dignity and justice, which are centrally important subjective concepts for worker movements, the term nonetheless may continue to have some utility.

Gaps

Although there were some important and wideranging debates over issues arising from different assumptions and approaches to Middle Eastern labor history, in comparison to the recent literature on the history of working class of the United States and Europe some significant gaps and silences can also be observed. It is worthwhile to briefly chronicle some of the more important ones here.

One that has major theoretical implications is what I call the "shadow of the West" problem—the quasi-colonial context in which working-class movements developed throughout the region. In part it has to do with the political context for worker activism. In part it has to do with the broader issue of how to situate the worker's movement in its world historical context. Not only were workers in the modern sectors of the Middle Eastern economy privileged in comparison to the great majority of others in that society, workers also did not contend just against capitalist bosses. Because most of the factory owners were tied to European capital, working class militancy was fatally inflected from the outset by the colonial situation. Mostly the contributions to this volume do not adequately consider the implications of the colonial auspices of class formation and industrialization.

One place this comes out is in the relationship between the nationalist project and the Marxist project, between nationalism and the working-class movement. If we add, "and between both of them and Islam," then we have delimited a major area of research that is only glancingly touched on in most of the chapters. This takes us back to the discussion of culture alluded to earlier. Assaf Bayat's contribution takes us very usefully into the issues. In the case of Iran, he notes the existence of competing discourses about the place of workers, each citing impeccable Islamic sources as legitimation and documentation. How does Islam, not conceived of as the pronouncements of the 'ulama but as the lived lives of Muslims, that is to say on the level of popular culture and political ideology, help shape people's political and moral actions?

The relationship of the class struggle to the national struggle was therefore a central dynamic of worker politics most places in the area until independence. As Beinin, Davis, Goldberg, and Lockman have shown for Egypt and Iraq, the resultant politics were vastly complicated—especially in Egypt, where the efforts of the Ikhwan al-Muslimun (the Muslim Brothers) to organize the working class led to three-cornered rivalry between Islamists, nationalists, and communists in the 1940s.[27]

The shadow of the West problem also raises the deeper epistemological question of the relationship between imperialism and industrialization, imperialism and modernity. Is it appropriate or useful analytically to distinguish between modernity as something that was imposed by the West on the rest of the world and modernity as a global process? There was no resolution of these issues during the workshop but most participants recognized that there had been a tendency to write the history of the working class as part of the biography of the state and that only a more methodologically self-critical approach which sought to insert the region into its full historical context was ultimately viable.

Although the history of women and work has played a big role in the reinvigorization of the history of the working classes in Europe and United States, and was much invoked in our discussions, gender is mostly absent in the contributions to this volume. (Feroz Ahmad's contribution is one of the few to refer to women workers at all). Here, it is clear, there is much to be done. While the history of women in the Middle East has made important strides in the last decade, labor history has lagged behind. Basic sources are lacking, and few models exist. Nonetheless the potential for important breakthroughs is there.

One place to look is in the role of women in textile production, where as the result of the gender division of labor in the region they have tended to play a historically important, if little noticed, role. Certain categories of textile goods (rugs) and certain phases of the production process of particular items have generally been associated with female labor. For example, in nineteenth century Tunisia most of the processing and felting of the wool used in the manufacture of *shashiyas* (the general term for types of wool felt hats, notably including the fez) was done by women, while the master hatters were invariably men.[28] Similarly, although cloth weavers were generally male, spinners (as for example in Lebanese silk production) tended to be female. Although we know a great deal about the transformation of silk production in Lebanon between 1830 and 1860, the relevance of this gender division of labor for the social history of Lebanon has been little explored. Yet since mechanization primarily affected spinners (who were female) the impact of these changes on the family economy and the strategies of individual women must have been considerable.[29] Additional research on work and gender in the Middle East can be expected to yield important dividends.[30]

The role of ethnicity in class formation and the working-class politics of the area is another issue relatively little explored in this volume and largely untheorized in the wider field of Middle East history. The subject is broached in the chapters by Lockman, Quataert, and Vatter, but otherwise largely ignored. As a result of the Left presumption that workers have no country as well as the legacy of imperialist efforts to use divide and rule tactics to control the politics of the area, ethnicity has been but little explored in the context of Middle East labor history. Recent work in American and South African labor history have increasingly sought to explore the ethnic dimensions of working-class culture, as well as the ways in which ethnic tensions have helped shape the role of labor in American and South African politics.[31] The South African example seems potentially helpful in rethinking the politics of colonial Algeria and Palestine, where a split labor market similarly helped to divide workers of settler and indigenous origins against one another and prevented the emergence of a class-based politics of workers against capitalists.[32]

If one begins with the notion that labor history in Europe and the United States has had a deep and productive engagement with economic history,[33] then the divorce from economic history in the contributions to this volume is particularly regretable. There is not enough integration of the study of the history of the working class into the emerging economic history. For Turkey in particular, that economic history is really beginning to add up to something.[34]

Virtually all of the contributions to this volume take as their object of inquiry the specific histories of specific countries. By their very diversity, the contributions to this volume raise the question: what can we hope to learn from one another? If Middle Eastern labor history is studied in a comparative, cross-regional way, it may be possible to discover new sources and new questions, as well as to remap the dimensions of old problems. Why, for example, were tram workers one of the earliest groups to become organized across the area? The comparative history of tram worker organizing—in Cairo, Alexandria, Tunis, and Istanbul—can shed light on this subject. Similarly, the history of another early militant group, the dock workers, might be examined comparatively. Studies of Istanbul and Beirut can be compared with one another as well as with those of other Mediterranean cities, like Marseilles.[35]

To do a comparative history of the region, it is vital that one's definition of the area not be arbitrarily limited. More cases lead to more fruitful comparisons and eventually to better understanding. Here the absence of studies of the colonial Maghrib must be noted. Because the working classes of the Maghrib arguably played the greatest role in the national struggle of anywhere in the region and worker militancy and working class organizations were among the most developed there, the North African experience is an important source of comparative examples. Moreover, North African labor history is relatively well developed— especially with regard to Tunisia.[36]

Comparative history works best when it is connected to an effort to situate the subject in the broader global context in which the working classes of the Middle East emerged—for this occurred not only in response to specific political, economic, and cultural determinants in each locale, but also to the constantly changing interactions of the local scene and the world market. Yet the sources, by their nature local, do not provide much access to this broader context. Indeed, in most of the contributions to this volume it is largely offstage, although the dialectic between local and global was one of the strengths of the Marxist tradition.

Notes

1. For an attempt to see it from the angle of ordinary people's lives, see Edmund Burke III, ed., *Struggle and Survival in the Modern Middle East* (Berkeley: University of California Press, 1992).

2. For an introduction to these issues, see Peter Novick, *That Noble Dream: The "Objectivity Question" and the American Historical Profession* (Cambridge: Cambridge University Press, 1988), and Joan Scott, "History in Crisis? The Others' Side of the Story," *American Historical Review* 94 (1989): 680-692.

3. See Michel Foucault, *The Archeology of Knowledge* (New York: Harper, 1972), and Antonio Gramsci, *Selections from the Prison Notebooks*, ed. and trans., Q. Hoare and G. N. Smith (New York: International Publishers, 1973).

4. In the last chapter of this volume Dipesh Chakrabarty discusses the contribution of the Indian "Subaltern Studies" school. For another view of these intellectual changes, see Clifford Geertz, "Blurred Genres: The Refiguration of Social Thought," in *Local Knowledge: Further Essays in Interpretive Anthropology* (New York: Basic Books, 1983), pp. 19-35.

5. One finds it, for example in journal titles, like *Le mouvement social* or *Social History*.

6. London: Penguin, 1963. More recently, the concept of experience itself has come under critical scrutiny. See Joan Scott, "The Evidence of Experience," *Critical Inquiry* (Summer 1991): 773-797.

7. Alan Dawley, *Class and Community: The Industrial Revolution at Lynn* (Cambridge, Mass.: Harvard University Press, 1976).

8. See especially Herbert Gutman, *Work, Culture, and Society in Industrializing America* (New York: Alfred A. Knopf, 1976), and Eric Foner, *Politics and Ideology in the Age of the Civil War* (New York: Oxford University Press, 1980).

9. Sean Wilentz, *Chants Democratic: New York City and the Rise of the American Working Class, 1788-1850* (New York: Oxford University Press, 1984), and Gary B. Nash, *The Urban Crucible: Social Change, Political Consciousness and the Origins of the American Revolution* (Cambridge, Mass.: Harvard University Press, 1979).

10. For a few programatic statements, see the review essays by David Brody, "The Old Labor History and the New in Search of the American Working Class," *Labor History* 20 (1979): 111-126; and Sean Wilentz, "Artisan Origins of the American Working Class," *International Labor and Working Class History* [hereafter cited as ILWCH] 19 (Spring 1981): 1-22. For a view on how this debate works itself out in Latin American labor history, see Emilia Viotti da Costa, "Experiences versus Structures: New Tendencies in the History of Labor and the Working Class in Latin America—What Do We Gain? What Do We Lose?" ILWCH 36 (Fall 1989): 3-24 and the debate that follows in the same issue.

11. See, among others, the essays by Mark Traugott, Robert Bezucha, Gareth Stedman Jones, and Craig Calhoun in *Global Crises and Social Movements: Artisans, Peasants, Populists and the World Economy*, ed. E. Burke, III (Boulder Colo.: Westview Press, 1988).

12. Joan Scott, *Gender and the Politics of History* (New York: Columbia University Press, 1990). On women's history and gender history, see also Ava Baron, "Gender and Labor History: Learning From the Past, Looking to the Future," in *Work Engendered: Toward*

a New History of American Labor, ed. Ava Baron (Ithaca, N.Y.: Cornell University Press, 1992), pp. 1–46.

13. Joan Scott, "Women in *The Making of the English Working Class,*" in *Gender and the Politics of History,* pp. 68–90.

14. Thomas Dublin, *Women and Work: The Transformation of Work and Community in Lowell, Massachusetts, 1826–1860* (New York: Columbia University Press, 1979); Mary Blewett, *Men, Women and Work: Class, Gender and Protest in the New England Shoe Industry, 1780–1910* (Urbana: University of Illinois Press, 1988), and Ardis Cameron, "Bread and Roses Revisited: Women's Culture and Working Class Activism in the Lawrence Strike of 1912," in *Women, Work and Protest: A Century of U.S. Women's Labor History,* ed. Ruth Milkman (Boston: Routledge and Kegan Paul, 1985), pp. 42–61.

15. *City of Women: Sex and Class in New York, 1789–1860* (New York: Alfred A. Knopf, 1986).

16. *Out to Work: A History of Wage-Earning Women in the United States* (New York: Oxford University Press, 1982).

17. See for example, William Reddy, *Money and Liberty in Modern Europe* (Cambridge: Cambridge University Press, 1987), and Lynn Hunt, ed., *The New Cultural History* (Berkeley: University of California Press, 1989).

18. Anderson's title, *Imagined Communities* (London: Verso, 1986), refers of course to the nation.

19. Ervand Abrahamian, *Iran Between Two Revolutions* (Princeton, N.J.: Princeton University Press, 1982); Eqbal Ahmad, "Politics and Labor in Tunisia" (Ph.D. diss., Princeton University, 1967; Joel Beinin and Zachary Lockman, *Workers on the Nile* (Princeton, N.J.: Princeton University Press, 1987); Jacques Couland, *Le mouvement syndical au Liban* (Paris: Editions sociale, 1970).

20. Some firm-centered studies include Ellis Goldberg, *Tinker, Tailor, and Textile Worker* (Berkeley: University of California Press, 1986), and Donald Quataert, *Social Disintegration and Popular Resistance in the Ottoman Empire, 1881–1908* (New York: New York University Press, 1983).

21. A notable exception is Hanna Batatu, *The Old Social Classes and the Revolutionary Movements of Iraq* (Princeton, N.J.: Princeton University Press, 1978).

22. Sherry Vatter, "Journeymen Textile Weavers Lives in Nineteenth Century Damascus: A Collective Biography," in Edmund Burke, III, ed., *Struggle and Survival in the Modern Middle East* (Berkeley: University of California Press, 1993).

23. For an introduction to a large literature, see the debate over 1848 in Burke, ed., *Global Crisis and Social Movements.*

24. Among the critiques, see Scott, *Gender and the Politics of History,* Chapter 4. Also Alan Dawley, "E. P. Thompson and the Peculiarities of the Americans," *Radical*

History Review 19 (1978–1979): 33–59; William Sewell, Jr., "How Classes Are Made: Critical Reflections on E. P. Thompson's Theory of Working-Class Formation," in *E. P. Thompson: Critical Debates*, ed. Harvey Kaye and Keith McClelland (Oxford: Oxford University Press, 1987); and Ellen Kay Trimberger, "E. P. Thompson: Understanding the Process of History," in *Vision and Method in Historical Sociology*, ed. Theda Skocpol (Cambridge: Cambridge University Press, 1984), pp. 211–242.

25. James Scott, *The Moral Economy of the Peasant: Rebellion and Subsistence in Southeast Asia* (New Haven, Conn.: Yale University Press, 1976). See also the critiques by Samuel Popkin, *The Rational Peasant: The Political Economy of Rural Society in Vietnam* (Berkeley: University of California Press, 1979), and Jeffery Paige, "One, Two or Many Vietnams? Social Theory and Peasant Revolution in Vietnam and Guatemala," in *Global Crises and Social Movements*, ed. Burke, pp. 145–179.

26. Edward P. Thompson, "The Moral Economy of the English Crowd in the Eighteenth Century," *Past and Present* 50 (1971): 76–136.

27. In addition to their chapters in this volume, see also the contributions of Beinin and Goldberg in *Islam, Politics and Social Movements*, ed. Edmund Burke, III, and Ira M. Lapidus (Berkeley: University of California Press, 1988). Also Joel Beinin, *Was the Red Flag Flying There? Marxist Politics in Egypt and Israel and the Arab-Israeli Conflict, 1948–1965* (Berkeley: University of California Press, 1990).

28. Sophie Ferchiou, *Techniques et sociétés: example de la fabrication des chechias en Tunisie* (Paris: Institut d'ethnologie, 1971); Lucette Valensi, "Islam et capitalisme: Production et commerce des chechias en Tunisie et en France aux xviiie et xixe siecles," *Revue d'histoire moderne et contemporaine* 16 (1969): 376–400.

29. On this, see the forthcoming Ph.D. dissertation of Akram Fouad Khater (University of California at Berkeley). Also see his M.A. thesis, "Silk, Shaykhs, Peasants and Merchants: The Impact of Silk Production on the Society of Mount Lebanon in the Nineteenth Century" (University of California, Santa Cruz, 1986).

30. For some of the possibilities, see Donald Quataert's "Ottoman Women, Households and Textile Manufacturing, 1800–1914," in Beth Baron and Nikki Keddie eds., *Women in Middle Eastern History: Shifting Boundaries in Sex and Gender* (New Haven, Conn.: Yale University Press, 1991), pp. 161–176.

31. An early comparative study is by George Frederickson, *White Supremacy: a Comparative Study in American and South African History* (Oxford: Oxford University Press, 1981). A stimulating study on class and ethnicity in the United States is by Gwendolyn Mink, *Old Labor and New Immigrants in American Political Development: Union, Party and State, 1870–1920* (Ithaca, N.Y.: Cornell University Press, 1986). For an overview of recent South African labor history, see the essays in the special issue of *Radical History Review*, "History From South Africa," 46–47 (Winter 1990).

32. On mandatory Palestine, in addition to Beinin, *Red Flag*, see the recent studies by Cershon Shafir, *Land, Labor and the Origins of the Israeli-Palestinian Conflict, 1882–1914* (Cambridge: Cambridge University Press, 1989), and Ella Shohat, "Sephardim in Israel: Zionism from the Standpoint of Its Jewish Victims," *Social Text* (Fall 1988): 1–35.

33. See, for example, William Reddy, *The Rise of Market Culture: The Textile Trade and French Society, 1750–1900* (Cambridge: Cambridge University Press, 1984).

34. Jean-Louis Bacque-Grammont and Paul Dumont, eds., *Economie et societes dans l'empire ottoman (fin du xviiie–debut du xxe siecle)* (Paris: Editions du CNRS, 1983); Huri Islamoglu-Inan, ed., *The Ottoman Empire and the World Economy* (Cambridge: Cambridge University Press, 1987); Charles Issawi, *An Economic History of the Middle East and North Africa* (New York: Columbia University Press, 1982); Caglar Keyder and Faruk Tabak, eds., *Landholding and Commercial Agriculture in the Middle East* (Albany: SUNY Press, 1991); Resat Kesaba, *The Ottoman Empire and the World Economy: The Nineteenth Century* (Albany: SUNY Press, 1988); Roger Owen, *The Middle East and the World Economy 1800–1914* (London: Methuen, 1981); Sevket Pamuk, *The Ottoman Empire and European Capitalism, 1820–1913* (Cambridge: Cambridge University Press, 1987).

35. Donald Quataert, *Social Disintegration and Popular Resistance in the Ottoman Empire, 1881–1908* (New York: New York University Press, 1983), Chapter 5; Couland, *Mouvement syndical au Liban*; William Sewell, "Social Change and the Rise of Working Class Politics in Nineteenth Century Marseilles," *Past and Present* 65 (November 1974): 75–109.

36. See Eqbal Ahmad, "Politics and Labor in Tunisia," and "Trade Unionism in the Maghreb," in *State and Society in Independent North Africa*, ed. Leon Carl Brown (Washington, D.C.: Middle East Institute, 1964), for an English language introduction to the field. On the early period in Tunisia, see Tahar al-Haddad, *al-'Ummal al-tunisiyyun wa zuhur al-haraka al-niqabiyya* (Tunis, 1927); Ahmed Ben Milad, *M'hammed Ali: la naissance du mouvement ouvrier tunisien* (Tunis, 1984); and Mustafa Kraim, *Nationalisme et syndicalisme en Tunisie, 1918–1929* (Tunis, 1976). Also Claude Liauzu, *Salariat et mouvement ouvrier en Tunisie: crises et mutations (1931–1939)* (Paris: Editions du CNRS, 1978); Rene Gallissot, ed., *Mouvement ouvrier, communisme et nationalismes dans le monde arabe* (Paris: Les editions ouvrieres, 1978); Noureddine Sraieb, ed., *Le mouvement ouvrier maghrebin* (Paris: Editions du CNRS, 1980); Albert Ayache, *Le mouvement syndical au Moroc, 1919–1949* (Paris: L'Harmattan, 1982).

12

Labor History and the Politics of Theory: An Indian Angle on the Middle East

A broad agreement runs through this collection: that a rigid, universalistic Marxism is of little or no help today to historians of labor. A Marxism that sees history as a story of progress, determined (and therefore restrained) by a preordained script in which the cultural sphere, for all the talk of its relative autonomy, is always obliged, at least in the notorious last instance, to be but a pale shadow of the political-economic, stands justly discredited in the 1990s. Accounts of working-class histories shaped by the teleology of an inevitable, if not ultimately victorious, struggle for socialism, can only provoke incredulity after the collapse of the Soviet Union. Eric Davis's insistence that the march toward broader political participation and more egalitarian societies is by no means inexorable in the Middle East and Assef Bayat's strictures against the "mechanistic Marxism of the Second International" should not therefore generate much disagreement today. Beinin and Lockman's (auto)critique(s) of their *Workers on the Nile* where, in Beinin's words, they "tended to homogenize and reify the working class as a historical subject and regard only those who engaged in struggles as real workers" express, once again, a spirit in tune with Davis's critique of both Orientalist and Ba'thist-nationalist historiography, and his call for an open-ended, more Gramscian view of history.

These sentiments are characteristic of what has been hailed in some quarters as "the new humanities" of the 1990s.[1] I share these sentiments, but the object of this exercise is to situate them on a more (self-)critical ground. I speak as an outsider to the field of Middle Eastern history. This preliminary and provisional critique therefore owes itself—as perhaps does any parasitical enterprise such as criticism—to the very objects it criticizes. But although acknowledging this debt, I would like to think that my critique develops out of a historiographical agenda that Indian historians share with scholars engaged in thinking about other non-Western cultures. If, as Heidegger once put it (in discussing Japanese language), the "complete Europeanization of the earth and of man" only reinforces a constantly present temptation among philosophers "to rely on European ways of representation and their concepts," how do we—historians of labor in "modern" yet non-Western settings—find languages and categories adequate for a representation of the people we write about?[2]

The problem is obviously of significance to more than just the field of labor studies, and I want to take it up in the concluding part of this chapter along with the question of "open-ended" and Gramscian narratives. I start, however, by highlighting, in the contributions to this volume, areas in which I find traces of the very theoretical positions that our authors would be otherwise careful to avoid.

I

Two tendencies strongly characteristic of much written labor history are present in this collection as well. One is thinking of the state as something external to the process of the formation of a working class. The second is one I will call the problem of *economism* in historical explanation. Let us consider them in turn.

In some of the essays here the state is seen—when our authors write in this mode, for not all of their statements are thus blemished—predominantly in an adversarial role, as a repressive organ whose actions hinder the development of self-consciousness on the part of a working class. In this view, workers, in the process of acquiring class consciousness, necessarily get involved in fighting the state; that is, in fighting for their own political space within a class and state structure seen, within this framework, as predominantly repressive. The workers' struggles are interpreted as so many different exercises in demystification; that is to say, they are assigned the function of making visible, both to the workers themselves and to the narrators of their histories, the thousand and one ties that bind the state to the interests of the ruling classes.

Passages in Marsha Posusney's essay are illustrative in this regard. Posusney argues that whereas a moral economy argument can help to explain the localized and spontaneous nature of Egyptian workers' protests, it is also essential to understand the nature of wage determination in Egypt and the structure and history of the Egyptian labor movement.

The latter, in turn, adds a new dimension to the fact that workers' struggles are struggles against the state. Public, political actions by Egyptian workers in the years 1974–1987 are categorized by Posusney as having been, by an overwhelming majority, directed against the state. This was, in part, an objective function of state ownership of the means of production, but by no means, we are cautioned, was this a particularly Egyptian development. Posusney suggests that it is in fact common to many lesser developed countries, thanks particularly to the predominant role that the public sector often plays in Third World economies.

It is true that many Third World governments play a key role in their national strategies for economic development, but Posusney's position on the state is not determined by a reading simply of the Third World experience. The state is never *internal* to working-class histories as she conceives of them here. It exists within a history that is logically, if not empirically, separate from that of the working class, and it exists primarily as an adversarial force. Posusney's prose has the aim of helping the reader see through the games that the state plays. The "combination of repression and concession" with which the post-Nasser Egyptian state has met workers' revolts suggests to her that these regimes have been anxious to avoid any escalation of workers' protests, and at the same time to maintain their legitimacy in the eyes of the working class. This "legitimacy," however, can never, in Posusney's analysis, be a point of identification between the worker and the state. The worker, in other words, exists as an identity, an agency, a subject, that has to negotiate the state but only as an externality to itself. As categories, the state and the worker are separate; history connects them but only as adversaries.

It should be said, however, that Posusney states explicitly only what some other contributors on occasions take for granted. One can find parallels, for example, in Feroz Ahmad's or Assef Bayat's chapters. In Ahmad's discussion of the history of working-class consciousness in Turkey, the state remains, primarily, an organ of repression. The state is cast in this narrative in the role of one of the major historical obstacles that the Turkish workers have had to deal with in their "evolution" as a class. Ahmad's chapter recalls the "legal and ideological repression" of the Kemalist regime, the measures adopted by the Turkish state to prevent "partnership" between "left-wing intelligentsia" and the workers, the "power of the state" (and Cold War ideology) in the 1950s that made "militancy virtually impossible," and the government's paranoid act of excluding the Workers' party from the Senate elections of 1964.

Assef Bayat takes to task the "many Left and liberal historians and activists" who have seen "political [i.e., state] repression" as the sole factor accounting for the "passivity" of labor, for "the defeat and consistent nonorganization of labor [in Iran], especially in the period. . .1965–1975." His reply, however, is more a critique of the idea of "passivity" itself than of the particular imagination of "politics" that undergirds the term *repression*. His rejoinder, therefore—that under repressive conditions, labor resistance may take the form of absenteeism, sabotage, and poor-quality production—although adequate for his purpose, does nothing to challenge the repression/resistance model for understanding the relationship between the state and the working class, on which rest both his critique and the statement he criticizes.

The second tendency with which I wish to take issue is marked by what, in the context of historians' debates in or about modern India, has been sometimes dubbed *economism*.[3] This is the tendency, first of all, to construct "class consciousness" as a (pre)disposition in favor of economic-secular rationality and then to oppose to it the sentiments and identifications of religion, language, or other markers of what may be called *ethnicity*. The latter are seen as inherently destructive of class solidarity. Without in any way rejecting their overall analyses, I will give examples here of this tendency from the writings of Ahmad and Quataert.

Quataert, we should note, himself offers us a piece of revisionist history writing through his remarks on a favorite theme in Ottoman and Middle East history—the role of religion and ethnicity as destructive elements in the process of working-class formation. Historians, he suggests, may have been "overstating the case" in uncritically adopting the logic and the language of their European-admistrative sources and in thus seeing "Turkish-Armenian or Muslim-Christian hostility behind every olive tree," rather the mobilization and self-interested activites of workers. To explore this problem, he (re?)reads an 1860 report by a British consul at Bursa on the destruction of an Armenian-owned silk factory by a Muslim "mob." Quataert's reading is symptomatic of the ethnicity (religion)/class opposition he employs as his means for scanning the archives. He underlines an "accidental" comment by the consul to dispute the consul's own view that the workers' action was inspired by religious considerations (in this case the factory had been constructed over a former Muslim cemetery). For the consul had also made references to a "short-term downswing in the business cycle" that threatened all the silk mills of Bursa and had recommended immediate decisive action by the authorities. Quataert seizes on this statement to rescue the workers from the consul's charge of "fanaticism." This comment by the consul suggests that it was not the presence of the cemetery but of a downswing, bringing low wages and unemployment, that impelled a riot. Thus the actors here were not fanatics but workers who used the political language of Islam to defend their economic interests.

Quataert's rejection of the label *fanatic* is well taken. But it is not difficult to see how his prose shares with that of the consul the idea of some binary or irreconcilable split between the "secular" (e.g., low wages) and the "religious" (Muslim feelings over the cemetery, for instance). The silk factory affair, it would seem, provides us with an opportunity to engage seriously with the question of "religion" or "ethnicity" as it arises in the history of the working classes in the Middle East. One could ask, for instance, what kind of significance, if any, did the fact that the factory had been constructed over what was a cemetery have for the local Muslim workers' sense of community, place, sacredness, understanding of death, and so on? What were the cultural constructions of wages? What were the different words for it and what were their connotations? I am in no position to suggest any answers to these questions but it does seem to me that by remaining within the discursive-philosophical parameters of official prose—even though he debates some of its specific terms—Quataert's text largely misses the opportunity to investigate some of these questions that could have led to a more thoroughgoing questioning of the secular-religious opposition.

The issue of ethnicity figures in a similar fashion in Ahmad's study of the workers of Turkey. The terms of his discussion are familiar to me from my involvement in writing Indian history: the tendency to see "ethnicity" as something out there to be used by the ruling classes to divide the workers against themselves. In discussing some of the "countermeasures from the Right" that the Turkish state, "alarmed" by a "growing militancy among the workers," adopted in the 1960s, Ahmad approvingly paraphrases a Workers' party sociologist, Behice Boran, who "cautioned" the Diyarbakir Provincial Congress of the party

> that the issue of race and religion was being exploited by the ruling classes; they were trying to manipulate the differences between Turks, Kurds, Circassians, . . . and Abkhazians . . . , as well as Sunnis and Alevis, to divide the working class, to fragment it, and then to continue exploiting it a little longer. (p. 149).

What makes this view distinctive is not hard to see. Boran (and Ahmad) acknowledge the existence of "differences" among workers, but they say in effect that these differences exist in some politically "neutral" or "innocent" state until interested outsiders—such as the ruling classes— "exploit" or "manipulate" them to divide the working people. Again it is not a matter of denying that employers often share this view of the workers and proceed to act on its assumptions. (Often the employers will only reverse the terms of this argument and describe the workers as "manipulated" by their union leaders, the "outsiders" in the bosses' language.) What concerns me, however, are the assumptions behind the idea of "manipulation": workers are "agents," "actors," "subjects," or what have you when they protest against their exploiters, yet the moment they fight among themselves they become, for many Left historians, a collection of immensely gullible people who are no longer "subjects" in their own right but simply passive victims of "manipulation" and "exploitation" from external and interested quarters.[4]

I find both of these positions—one conceptualising the state as something external to the history of class formation and thus primarily as an adversary of the working class, the other opposing religion/ethnicity to class or interest-based solidarities—untenable in terms of both historical evidence and theory. Theoretically speaking, the processes through which modern classes are formed can be logically (and historically) shown to be inseparable from the process of the formation of the modern state (I take the colonial state as a version of it). Acquiring the secular identity of a "worker" is part of the larger politics of modern "citizenship." Needless to say, these politics would differ from country to country but that we have to consider the histories of "class" and "citizenship" together can be easily demonstrated. Consider the standard Marxist argument involving the class-in-itself/class-for-itself distinction that some of the contributors here mention. Surely, the formation of a working-class organization (e.g., a trade union) would be regarded a sign of transition from a class-in-itself to a class-for-itself position. (The same could also said for a business-organized chamber of commerce.) However, can one imagine this union functioning effectively without an adequate "legal" space provided for it by the state; that is, without the "rights of association" that citizenship entails? Which is another way of saying that the struggle to form effective unions must be part of the struggle to forge a "democratic" state. One could therefore say that the shop-floor conditions are not produced in isolation from the larger political history through which the state is formed. The "state" as a category cannot therefore be considered "external" to the category of the proletariat.

The politics of class formation cannot, hence, be separated from the politics of citizenship. "How is it," Marx and Engels asked in the *The German Ideology*, "that personal interests always develop. . .into class interests. . .[which] assume the form of *general* interests?" Their answer hints at the issue of citizenship by invoking the modern split between "private interests" and "public rights":

> Communist theoreticians. . .have discovered that throughout history the "general interest" is created by individuals who are defined as "private persons.". . .what is called the "general interest" is constantly being produced by the other side, private interests, and in relation to the latter it is by no means an independent force. . .—so that this contradiction is in practice constantly destroyed and reproduced.[5]

At the logical end of the question of citizenship—as its horizon, one could say—stands the institution of the modern state. Indeed, as Philippe Ariès has recently reminded us, the public/private opposition takes meaning only in the context of a particular way of positioning the individual with regard to the state.[6] Working-*class* histories, therefore—to the extent, that is, they purport to be accounts of the becoming of a working class—can be written only as a part of the relevant history of "citizenship" and hence as a part of the biography of the state.

My reservations with histories that oppose "class" to "ethnicity" follow from this, for the processes of state formation always involve the fashioning—this is primarily the work of nationalism and its ideological clones—of new ethnicities by the realignment (and often freezing) of identities that may have once been more fluid. The (nation-)state—and the argument would apply with modifications to cases of colonial industrialization—within the embrace of which the working class is born and developed invites us to belong to two (apparently) contradictory constructions of identity. One is formed through the universal-sounding discourse of "rights" of the citizen, the discourse that informs and shapes the life of civil society. This is where the secular interest-based affiliations of class are often thought to belong. The other identity is that of the "people" whose "essential" cultural unity the state claims to represent. This is fundamentally a construction of ethnicity. It is the more "particularistic," but no less intrinsic, side of the cultural project of citizenship. This seeming contradiction of "rights" and "ethnicity" is what constitutes the practice of citizenship. To become modern under the aegis of the modern state is to have to live out this contradiction.

Here, I will leave to one side the interesting question of what role modern civil society—by definition organized, as the science of civil society, the discipline of economics, would tell us, on the twin principles of "scarcity" of resources and the consequent "competition" for them—could itself play in the construction of "ethnicity" in "public life." Let me try to prevent a possible misreading of my critique so far. It is not my point that governments never act as adversaries of labor movements, nor could one deny the massive evidence of "state repression" assembled here by the various contributors. It is also, of course, true that the bosses try to take advantage of "ethnic" divisions within the work force whenever they think it is in their interest to do so. My questions arise at a more abstract level. How do we conceptualize the relationship between the modern state and the formation of the modern working classes? How do civil society and the public sphere relate, within our theory, to issues of class and ethnicity? I have suggested that the contradictions between the state and the working class, or between ethnicity and classness, are better seen as belonging to the same series of processes and policies of citizenship and state formation.

I would therefore suggest that much of the history discussed in this volume may be read as accounts of the multifarious struggles, the various historical contingencies and uncertainties, that mark the process of universalization over the last two centuries of certain critical institutions that have their roots in European histories and philosophies (themselves the sites of many a struggle and act of contestation) but that have now, thanks to the violence of imperialism and modernizing nationalisms, become the defining characteristics of modernity itself—I mean the modern state and its attendant politics of citizenship, public sphere, and civil society. It is therefore no accident that the struggle for a legal space within which the working class could operate as a class occupies a major part of the labor historian's attention in the Middle East. Quataert documents the importance of the press (i.e., the public sphere) to the Ottoman workers after 1908, struggles over the Ottoman constitution, legality of trade unions and so forth. Ahmad records a telling—but not surprising—instance of the merging of the worker's voice with that of the citizen. He quotes Ahmet Top, a worker from Anatolia, saying in 1963: "those who sit in parliament are not on the side of labor and the laws they pass do not benefit the worker. If we can put representatives of peasants and workers in parliament then this situation would change and laws to our benefit would be passed" (p. 145). How does one separate here the history of the Turkish working class from the history of citizenship in modern Turkey? I could go on multiplying evidence: at the workshop Salim Nasr provided us with some illustrations from the Lebanese context. But Nasr's discussion was also helpful in another way. It reminded us of an important point that historians, working within a tradition where "histories" are usually organized as national histories, are wont to overlook: that the process of the formation of a modern state is seldom confined to the boundaries with which the state and the nation eventually identify themselves. Modernity—and hence the working class as well—always happens within an international frame.

II

This brings me to the question of "difference" with which I began this chapter, and I want to return in this concluding section to the question of writing "open-ended" histories. Labor histories, as a genre, are incredibly susceptible to sociological-sounding generalizations that make all working classes look the same. Bayat gives us an example of the habit, noting that under repressive conditions, labor resistance may take the form of absenteeism, sabotage, disturbances, theft, religious practice, and poor-quality production. Nothing is wrong with this as such; indeed, as Lockman says, "over the past century and a half, workers across the globe have resisted what they have perceived as unjust or arbitrary domination, oppression and exploitation, and they have often done so by engaging in very similar forms of collective action (strikes, trade unions, political activism)." My point until now has been that these observable similarities across cultures and histories do not arise from some transcendental or essential nature of "the working class" but rather from the very historical fact that modern governments and bureaucracies, grounded both in specific histories and in the internationalized discourse of economic development and citizenship (even when only paid lipservice), are an abiding presence in these histories. The language of class, I have argued, is an integral part of the language of citizenship and thus of that of the nation and the state.

The question of "difference" stems precisely from this point. It is obviously true that the idea of citizenship is now part of the political discourse, and of the larger ambient discourse of modernity, in any country. From this, however, it does not by any means follow that the end of citizenship (or that of the modern state) is a given in any particular history, The nation and the state exist by eliding over, and appropriating or assimilating, other, and often contradictory, preexisting visions, categories, and practices of human solidarity. And it is through struggles over these elisions, appropriations, and consequent modifications that different meanings emerge for such familiar and universalized terms as *citizenship, democracy, nation,* and so on.

The problem presents itself, in historical writing, as a problem of translation. Do indigenous categories fit neatly into the schemas that labor historians, as an international scholarly community, use? Most of the scholars represented here are visibly concerned with this problem, particularly given the preponderance of artisanal traditions in the region. Does *ta'ifa* mean "guild" (Lockman)? Or *dawlat* state (Bayat)? And *millet* the nation (Quataert)? Are not there always slippages in translation, excesses of signification that cannot be contained, supplementary meanings that we may acknowledge but are obliged to forget in the interest of a universal language of conversation among (labor) historians?

This problem of translation—I would go further and say that *having* to translate from and into English or French—is part of the phenomenon that Heidegger called "the complete Europeanization of the earth and man." The violence of representation is not unconnected with the violence of European modernity that the whole world has had to embrace. There is an implicit acknowledgment of this element of force in the Turkish intellectual Nejat Ethem's struggle in the early part of this century to explain to his working-class audience the meaning of the word *proletariat*. After trying out several Turkish words, he concluded that the Turks were "obliged" to accept the European category for which, he admitted, there was no Turkish equivalent: "Just as the entire world is using words like *telefon* (telephone), *telegraf* (telegraph), and *sosyalist* for socialist, the proletariat has also been accepted as an international word. We are also *obliged* [emphasis added] to accept it" (p. 139).

Why were the Turks "obliged" to accept the word *proletariat* which did not resonate with anything in their otherwise rich cultural lexicon? Because, clearly, the assumption (and a justifiable one at that) is that one cannot "effectively" deal with the modern/colonial state without embracing this category and the identity-narratives it contains. But this compulsion does not manifest itself as a realization in every person at the same time. And thus a project of pedagogy emerges, for it is not ordained anywhere in nature that a group of people who join factories as industrial workers and have to deal with (quasi-)modern bureaucracies *must*, whatever their cultural and historical pasts, develop the collective identity of the "working class" enshrined and celebrated in modern trade union literature. Admittedly such a compulsion is built into modern institutions but its realization is not a process without contest. Developing the identity of the "modern" worker of trade union narratives entails a battle of sensibilities—often between the workers' own and those of their leaders, be they nationalist or socialist, or often among the workers themselves—and the results of this battle can never be foretold. Ellis Goldberg puts the point well in his perceptive book *Tinker, Tailor, and Textile Worker*: "The basic idea of a trade union appears to flow naturally and historically from that of a guild. In fact, this is not so and the creation of the modern industrial union requires, as many Egyptian workers themselves believed, a wholesale struggle against earlier conceptions of solidarity."[7] The Turkish leader Nejat Ethem, whom we quoted in the previous paragraph, recognized this battle for what it was, a project of pedagogy. His intellectual efforts were aimed at "consciousness raising." "What a pity," he said, "that the proletariat which is growing each day under conditions of exploitation, pressure, poverty, and being pushed down does not recognize itself in so many places."

If we were still writing from a Leninist (by which I mean an avante-gardist) understanding of politics, this would be no problem. But, after Foucault, we should know better. We know that this "consciousness raising" has historically been a part of the effort to make human beings into "citizens," aware of their "rights," which in turn are administered by a (democratic) state, by definition founded on a capacity for coercion, the continual forgetting of which fact constitutes the kernel of the citizen's "everyday life." If this is not a project of power, what is?

Whose project is it? In the widest meaning of the term, it is a project of the nationalist. Lockman's chapter recognizes this clearly, but he appears to restrict the use of the term to the "indigenous bourgeoisie" and people who called them *nationalists* (as against those who called themselves *socialists*). But the project of making people the citizens of a nation-state has been pursued by the Left as well as the Right, sometimes—or perhaps more often than not in the Middle East and other parts of the Third World—against the wishes of the local capitalists.

Writing "open-ended" history is a matter, primarily, of maintaining a critical-theoretical distance from this project. It is to acknowledge in our writings that the universality of the language of "rights," although undeniably useful in many local struggles, is also part of the domination and violence that "modern" arrangements of power are based on, the power-knowledge axis that Foucault so compellingly elaborated in his histories of the prison, the clinic, and the asylum. It is also to admit that this universality is always compromised on the ground; that the very subalterns on whose behalf we produce the liberal-democratic narratives of "labor history" can welcome as well as oppose, embrace as well as discard, the liberal imagination. It is to refuse teleologies and unleash, in the prose of history, narratives of human connections that coexist with, and sometimes challenge, those of the state and citizenship. This history can function only in a mode of irony (because the historian can write only as a modern), and its ethical instinct must be to respect and document scrupulously each and every instance where human beings have been hurt and made to suffer in the name of happiness and prosperity.

We may, then, turning to some concrete examples from Middle Eastern labor history, take issue with Goldberg's assertion that the "craft associations of the twentieth century are best understood as a transitional stage."[8] Goldberg's text illustrates in places problems of historical narratives that are not open ended. He actually documents the liveliness of the craft practices yet refuses to see them as part of Egyptian modernity. He mentions that the unionists in Egypt in the 1930s "found it *difficult if not impossible* [emphasis added] to carry on without some of the practices of craft unions" and yet insists on calling these practices "traditional."[9] To put the point polemically, why could not we think instead of the trade union as a "transitional" form, making its journey (in course of the spread of European modernity) towards the *ta'ifa* structure and finding accomodations in the dispersal of meaning(s) that result from the battle of sensibilities between the avante-gardism of the "modernists" and the multiple narratives, including those of citizenship, that the subaltern classes carry in their own heads?

I will end with this question. For it joins this small effort based on my experience of writing Indian history to the larger critique of Eurocentric thought that has already engaged the attention of many historians of the Middle East.[10]

Notes

Thanks are due to the anonymous reviewers of the SUNY Press and to Gyanendra Pandey for their helpful criticism of an earlier draft of this essay.

1. See Kenneth Ruthven, ed., *Beyond the Disciplines: The New Humanities* (Canberra: Australian Academy of the Humanities, 1992).

2. Martin Heidegger, *On the Way to Language* (New York: Harper and Row, 1982), p. 15.

3. See Ranajit Guha, ed., *Subaltern Studies: Writings on Indian Society and History* (New Delhi: Oxford University Press, 1982–89), vols. 1–6. This use of *economism* is somewhat different from the way Gramsci used it in "The Modern Prince." See Antonio Gramsci, *Selections from the Prison Notebooks*, ed. and trans. Quintin Hoare and Geoffrey Nowell Smith (New York: International Publishers, 1973), pp. 158–168.

4. For a brief discussion of this issue in the Indian context, see Dipesh Chakrabarty, "Of 'Communal' Workers and 'Secular' Historians," *Seminar* [Delhi], no. 374 (October 1990).

5. K. Marx and F. Engels, *The German Ideology* (Moscow: Progress Publishers, 1976), pp. 262, 264.

6. Philippe Ariès, "Introduction," in Roger Chartier, ed., *A History of Private Life: Passions of the Renaissance* (Cambridge, Mass.: Harvard University Press, 1989), p. 9.

7. Ellis Goldberg, *Tinker, Tailor, and Textile Worker: Class and Politics in Egypt, 1930–1952* (Berkeley: University of California Press, 1986), p. 78.

8. Ibid., p. 91.

9. Ibid.

10. See in particular the recent collection *Theory, Politics and the Arab World: Critical Responses*, ed. Hisham Sharabi (New York: Routledge, 1990). I have also benefited from reading Rifa'at A. Abou-El-Haj, "Theorizing Historical Writing Beyond the Nation-State: Ottoman Society of the Middle Period" (manuscript kindly made available by the author). Readers may find my "Postcoloniality and the Artifice of History: Who Speaks for Indian Pasts?" *Representations* 37 (1992), of interest in this connection.

About the Contributors

Feroz Ahmad teaches Middle East history at the University of Massachusetts at Boston. He is the author of *The Turkish Experiment in Democracy, 1950–1975* (Boulder, Colo.: Westview Press, 1977) and *Young Turks: the Committee of Union and Progress in Turkish Politics, 1908–1914* (Oxford: Clarendon Press, 1969).

Assef Bayat was born in a village in Iran, did his undergraduate work in Teheran (in politics), completed his Ph.D. (sociology and political economy) in England, and was a postdoctoral fellow at the University of California at Berkeley. He now teaches sociology at the American University in Cairo. He is the author of *Work, Politics and Power: An International Perspective on Workers' Control and Self -Management* (New York: Monthly Review Press, 1991) and *Workers and Revolution in Iran: A Third World Experience of Workers' Control* (London: Zed Books, 1987). He is currently working on a new book, *The Poverty of Politics*, on the political sociology of urban "marginals" in Iran, 1975–1985.

Joel Beinin teaches Middle East history at Stanford University and is book review editor of *Middle East Report*. During the mid-1970s he lived in Detroit, was employed as a production worker at the Chrysler Warren Stamping Plant, and edited the Arabic section of a monthly workers' newspaper. His concern with the working classes in the Middle East is a product of those experiences, which eventually motivated him to write a Ph.D. thesis on Egyptian workers' history. This thesis was integrated into *Workers on the Nile: Nationalism, Communism, Islam and the Egyptian Working Class, 1882–1954* (Princeton, N.J.: Princeton University Press, 1987), coauthored with Zachary Lockman. An Arabic translation of Part One of *Workers on the Nile* was published in Cairo in 1992 by Markaz al-Buhuth al-'Arabiyya.

Edmund Burke III. is professor of history at the University of California, Santa Cruz. He is the author of the forthcoming *Orientalism Observed: France, Islam and the Colonial Encounter* (Princeton, N.J.: Princeton University Press) and the editor of *Struggle and Survival in the Modern Middle East* (Berkeley: University of California Press, 1993).

Dipesh Chakrabarty. is Ashworth reader in social theory and director of the Ashworth Centre for Social Theory at the University of Melbourne, Australia. He is a member of the editorial collective of *Subaltern Studies* and the author of *Rethinking Working-Class History: Bengal, 1890–1940* (Princeton, N.J.: Princeton University Press, 1989). Shaped in his intellectual history by debates within Indian Marxism, he is interested in the possibilities of interrogating European social theory from postcolonial and postorientalist positions.

Eric Davis teaches political science at Rutgers University, in New Brunswick, New Jersey. He is the author of *Challenging Colonialism: Bank Misr and Egyptian Industrialization, 1920–1941* (Princeton, N.J.: Princeton University Press, 1983; Beirut: Institute for Arab Studies, 1986) and the forthcoming *Memories of State: The Politics of the Past in Modern Iraq*, in which a version of his chapter in this volume will also appear. With Nicolas Gavrielides, he coedited *Statecraft in the Middle East: Oil, Historical Memory,and Popular Culture* (Miami: Florida International University Press, 1991).

Ellis Goldberg is associate professor of political science at the University of Washington and the author of *Tinker, Tailor, and Textile Worker: Class and Politics in Egypt, 1930–1952* (Berkeley: University of California Press, 1986).

Kristin Koptiuch is assistant professor of anthropology at Arizona State University West, in Phoenix. Her work on Egyptian crafts focuses on the interplay of poetics and political economy; she also researches and writes about the process of "third worlding" under way in the postmodern (but very much *not* postcolonial) United States. Her publications include "Informal Sectorization of Egyptian Petty Commodity Production," in *Anthropology and the Global Factory: Studies of the New Industrialization in the Late Twentieth Century*, ed. Frances Abrahamer Rothstein and Michael L. Blim (New York: Bergin and Garvey, 1992) and "Third-Worlding at Home," *Social Text* 28 (1991).

Zachary Lockman teaches modern Middle East history at Harvard University. His Ph.D. dissertation on the emergence of a working class and labor movement in Egypt eventually became Part One of *Workers on the Nile: Nationalism, Communism, Islam and the Egyptian Working Class, 1882–1954* (Princeton, N.J.: Princeton University Press, 1987), coauthored with Joel Beinin. He is currently finishing up a book on the interactions between Arab and Jewish workers in Palestine during the British mandate period and beginning work on a new research project which explores popular culture and social change in Cairo, 1882–1919.

Marsha Pripstein Posusney is assistant professor of political science at Bryant College. She is currently working on a monograph tentatively entitled "Workers With and Against the State: Labor Relations in Egypt, 1952–1987." A seven-year gap between her undergraduate and graduate studies was spent doing political organizing around a variety of domestic and international issues, including workers' rights.

Donald Quataert, professor of history at the State University of New York at Binghamton, began in agrarian history and peasants, moved to transportation and there met the Ottoman railroad workers. The accidental discovery, in 1975, of some materials relating to their strikes encouraged him to continue with these labor history studies. At Binghamton he regularly offers courses on Middle East labor history.

Sherry Vatter has lived in Beirut and Damascus and traveled widely in the Middle East. She has taught classes in Middle East and world history and is now completing her Ph. D. in history at the University of California, Los Angeles, on the social crisis of mid-nineteenth century Syria. Her interest in militant artisans in Damascus reflects her involvement in grassroots politics, including neighborhood organizing and socialist-feminist action, and her concern with the way people outside of the formal political arena can effect social change.

Index

"Arab socialism" (Egypt). *See* Nasserism

Artisans: representations of, xix–xx, 49–62, 94–98; and workers, xix–xx, 1, 8–9, 10, 91–94, 134, 310, 332. *See also* Damascus; Egypt; Guilds; Petty commodity production

Baer, Gabriel, 1, 55, 85, 86

Ba'thism, xi, 271, 287–290. *See also* Iraq

Capitalism: firms and productivity, 111–113; and petty commodity production, 43–46, 62–65; variants of, xxiv

Class: and class analysis, x; and class consciousness, 10–11, 74–77, 185–188, 211, 212–216

Coase, Ronald, 111, 112, 113

Communist activism, parties and movements: in Egypt, 249–250, 253, 254–258; in Iran (Tudeh party), 170, 171, 174, 175, 194–195; in Iraq, 272, 281–282, 285, 286, 287

Craftsmen, crafts workers. *See* Artisans; Guilds; Petty commodity production

Cromer, Earl of, 55, 85

Culture, and working-class history, xxi, 75–76, 185–188, 310–311

Damascus: guilds in, 1, 2, 4, 5, 6, 8; journeymen weavers' strikes in, 1, 3, 7, 9; textile industry in, 2, 3, 4, 5, 6, 7

DISK (Turkish workers' confederation), 152, 153, 155, 156

Egypt: artisans in, 46–48, 49–54, 78–81; communist activism, parties and movements in, 249–250, 253, 254–258; historiography of working class in, 73–74, 249–250, 253, 254–258, 258–266; January 1977 uprising in, 221, 238, 247, 248–254, 258–262; labor activism, unions and movements in, 88–90, 91–94, 113–114, 121–123, 125–126, 223–235, 238–240, 251–252, 255–258; Nasserism and workers in, xi, 213, 247, 255; Nationalist party and workers in, 48, 90, 91, 93, 94, 100–101; peasants in, 81–83; Port Said coalheavers, 83–87; recruitment of factory workers in, 116; representations of workers and artisans in, 41, 49–54, 56–62, 94–101, 254–258, 258–262, 262–266; wages, hours, and working conditions in, 116, 216–223; working-class formation in, 46–49, 73–74

Gender, and working-class history, xxii, 284–285

Gramsci, Antonio, xix, 276–278, 280, 282, 295, 311

Guilds, xx–xxi, 1, 2, 4, 5, 6, 8, 55–56; decline of, 55–56, 85–86; and labor unions, 91–94, 331–332; among Port Said coalheavers, 83–87. *See also* Artisans; Baer; Damascus; Egypt

Handicrafts industries and workers. *See* Artisans; Guilds; Petty commodity production

339